OXFORD STUDIES IN AFRICAN AFFAIRS

General Editors
JOHN D. HARGREAVES *and* GEORGE SHEPPERSON

KINGS AND KINSMEN

KINGS AND KINSMEN

EARLY MBUNDU STATES IN ANGOLA

BY

JOSEPH C. MILLER

CLARENDON PRESS · OXFORD
1976

Oxford University Press, Ely House, London W. 1

GLASGOW NEW YORK TORONTO MELBOURNE WELLINGTON
CAPE TOWN IBADAN NAIROBI DAR ES SALAAM LUSAKA ADDIS ABABA
DELHI BOMBAY CALCUTTA MADRAS KARACHI LAHORE DACCA
KUALA LUMPUR SINGAPORE HONG KONG TOKYO

ISBN 0 19 822704 3

© Oxford University Press 1976

Printed in Great Britain
by Cox & Wyman Ltd
London, Fakenham and Reading

In memory of my father, John W. Miller
1903–1974

Preface

ALTHOUGH historians are accustomed to work with imperfectly recorded information, imperfect at least for their individual purposes, the data which support this study have special qualities which require a preliminary statement of the ways in which they were collected and the techniques used to analyse them. Professor Jan Vansina's pioneering studies of the historical meaning of non-literary evidence necessarily inform any study which purports to combine diverse data drawn from ethnographic, linguistic, documentary, and orally transmitted materials. Since our knowledge of early state-formation among the Mbundu depends on all these types of source, and especially since some of the data were recorded long before any of these disciplines reached their present level of sophistication, the problem of methodology assumes more importance than it ordinarily might.

The data collected during my 1969–70 fieldwork among the Imbangala of Angola require the most extensive discussion. These consist of approximately thirty hours of tape-recorded interviews in Kimbundu and Portuguese; in addition, there is a somewhat smaller amount of written English translation of the Kimbundu texts. A good many more hours of interviews were taken down in rough hand-written notes and expanded in the form of typed working notes. All these materials are in my possession for the present and are, of course, available to anyone wishing to use them for scholarly purposes. I hope that in the near future copies may be deposited in suitable places in Africa and in the oral archives at Indiana University.

I tape-recorded the initial interviews in full with the intent of preparing transcriptions and translations according to the standards outlined by Professor Philip D. Curtin,[1] but local conditions soon made it more useful to abandon the tape recorder and continue with written fieldnotes. No translators capable of producing accurate—or even coherent—Portuguese translations of the Kimbundu texts were available to me. This forced me to interview as much as possible in Portuguese. Although a number of interviews were recorded in Portuguese, the problems of telling Imbangala histories in a foreign

[1] Philip D. Curtin (1968b).

language in a totally artificial context almost eliminated the subtle qualities which the tape recorder is best adapted to capture.

The tape-recorded interview format also became inefficient owing to a shift in the content covered during later conversations with informants. Most later testimony consisted of genealogies and informal discussions of linguistic and ethnographic information which could be preserved as accurately and efficiently through the use of written notes as with a tape recorder. Although a few narrative compositions worth recording appeared in the course of later interviews (attempts to repeat these for taping generally failed), relatively little such material was left unrecorded. The use of written notes, on the other hand, had the advantage of allowing more penetrating investigation than tapes would have permitted of several points felt to be too sensitive for discussion on tape.

Limitations on time and money, as well as certain restrictions on research activities in Portugal and Angola, restricted my opportunity to execute the theoretically optimal research design. It is obvious that historians of Africa will fully utilize available source-materials only when they approach their data with a facile command of both the languages and the cultures involved. At that time it was difficult for a non-resident historian to acquire the necessary sophistication in these fields. The African languages of Angola have not been adequately studied, and although one could gain a working knowledge of a form of Kimbundu in Lisbon, a truly useful familiarity with the language demands study in the field. Angolan ethnography suffers from a similar neglect and imposes similar constraints on the researcher. The historian ideally should precede his historical studies with lengthy language training and ethnographic research, but the unavailability of relevant materials outside of Angola makes this impossible. Conditions in Angola made it impossible to plan an orderly research project extending over several months or years. I therefore found it more efficient to gather as much information as possible in a short time and elected to bypass preliminary rigorous ethnographic and linguistic groundwork in favour of recording the most accessible information as quickly as was feasible. This strategy guided my research over the five months I spent living near the Imbangala in the District of Malanje.

I first located the individuals generally regarded as most likely to provide comprehensive and accurate information on the Imbangala past. It turned out—fortunately under the prevailing limitations on the research design—that most surviving Imbangala historical traditions were known to only a handful of individuals, all of whom spoke some Portuguese. These men, the *ndala kandumbu* (official court historian of the former state of Kasanje) and the *baka a musendo* (unofficial but professional 'historians') became the primary informants for this study. It became clear that most other potential sources of information, who may be termed secondary informants, could add little to the data obtainable from the primary informants. The presence of a secondary informant at an interview, however, often stimulated a primary informant (ostensibly acting as interpreter) to recall information which he did not otherwise bring readily to mind.

Most interviews opened with a voluntary statement by the informant in which he gave his personal version of the history of his title and/or lineage. In the case of secondary informants, these statements, often expressed with no particular skill or artistry, tended to be very brief and incomplete. Some secondary informants chose to omit this phase of the interview. The primary informant, who usually accompanied me to interviews with secondary informants, followed up the initial statement with questions designed to prod the secondary informant to elaborate or to resolve internal contradictions. The accompanying primary informant then offered his own version of the same history under the guise of prompting the secondary informant. Most interviews concluded with my inquiries about confusing points, contradictions which I had noticed, and new concepts and terms that had arisen in the course of the interview.

The initial interviews with primary informants followed approximately the same format, but these led to a series of subsequent meetings which ranged much more widely according to no particular pattern. I generally opened the later sessions with a historical point drawn from a previous interview and asked the informant to repeat or to expand on it. The discussion usually moved quickly through more questions and answers into general ethnographic and linguistic problems as the informant attempted to clarify obscure points. The often repetitive question-and-answer format of these later interviews made the tape recorder superfluous for the most part.

Although ethnographic inquiries might better have been based on the participant-observer method developed by anthropologists, obstacles facing white foreign researchers in Angola made it impossible to live in a village. Some ethnographic information in this study comes from direct questioning on points which seemed relevant in the light of the formal historical material. A second method of investigation was to ask questions based on a list of Kimbundu terms taken from written sources on the Imbangala dating back to the sixteenth century. I merely presented each word to the informants and asked if they knew it and, if so, what it meant. This technique opened up several new and fruitful lines of inquiry, often in quite unexpected places. Other conclusions about Imbangala social structure and cosmology emerged from later analysis of both the formal histories and other data. The historian must beg the patience of his anthropologist colleagues for the lack of systematic ethnographic investigation. The basic linguistic research consisted of an attempt to collect 200 word vocabularies in all eastern Kimbundu dialects based on the list which linguists have used in connection with their studies on glottochronology.[2] Linguistic insights gained from the general ethnographic investigation and the several available dictionaries on the Bantu languages of Angola supplemented these lists.

Written documentation on sixteenth- and seventeenth-century Angola is now scattered over at least three continents. By far the most important collection is housed in the various archives in Lisbon, much of this in the manuscript collections of the Biblioteca Nacional, the Arquivo Nacional da Torre do Tombo, and the Biblioteca da Ajuda. Foreign scholars concerned with African topics have on occasion found access to some of these documents restricted.[3] I requested but never received authorization to consult the collection in the Biblioteca Nacional, while reorganizations reported to be under way in the Biblioteca da Ajuda and the Torre do Tombo prevented me from seeing more than a few of the relevant materials there. I have therefore depended on published versions of most documents in Lisbon except those located in the Arquivo Histórico Ultramarino. Fortunately, all known documents from the sixteenth century and before, as well as a great deal of documentation from the seventeenth century, have been published, the more important ones often in several places. Of the many documents scattered through Italy, Spain, England, France, and Brazil, to name only the most important repositories, it was possible to consult personally only those in the British Museum. The barely explored riches of the Arquivo Histórico de Angola, which were readily accessible, relate entirely to later periods.

Given the limitations created by the conditions just outlined, I

[2] D. H. Hymes (1960), p. 6.
[3] For the experiences of another foreigner, V. Salvadorini (1969), pp. 16–19.

have attempted to steer a course between the Scylla of acknowledging the imperfections of the data to the extent of saying nothing at all and the Charybdis of striving for a coherent reconstruction of events that pushes the data beyond their inherent limitations. This dilemma has a special relevance to the oral materials, since they are less well known than the written ones and since the analysis depends on them at several points. I have therefore devoted a section of Chapter I to a description of the formal and informal histories of the Imbangala and to an analysis of their meaning for Western historians. At this point, I need only explain the considerations which led me to use the traditions as I did. These traditions may be susceptible to study on several other levels—notably, the intriguing possibility of a formal literary criticism now being developed by Professor Harold Scheub of the University of Wisconsin—but the constraints operative in this case made it necessary to work out a relatively low-level 'common denominator' which made the traditions I collected in 1969 comparable to other variants written down in the seventeenth, nineteenth, and early twentieth centuries.

The method chosen, given the atrophying condition of the traditions, could not depend on comparing a great number of variants which no longer exist. Nor could it demand a degree of linguistic facility not obtainable in this case. It was also necessary to recognize that all published traditions exhibited drastic changes from what must have been their original oral form. The versions of these same traditions which I collected suffer from similar (but less extensive) mutilation since I was unable to secure accurate transcriptions or translations of the Kimbundu texts. Even the versions recorded in Portuguese must have undergone considerable modification as the informant translated them for my benefit. As Chapter I, I hope, makes clear, even the condition of reciting these histories for an alien investigator inevitably influenced the way they were told. No analysis dependent on a word-for-word explication of the text could be employed; the words themselves had either not been recorded or could not be understood sufficiently to justify such an approach.

The research which led to the present study began as a rather unfocused inquiry into the history of Kasanje, the Imbangala kingdom founded at the close of the period finally chosen as the subject of this work. The shift in period and subject resulted from the fact that existing studies provided no useful background on which to base a history of Kasanje. The literature generally confused the Imbangala with the so-called 'Jaga', famous and fearsome warriors who probably never existed in the way in which they have been described. Further, no systematic studies on the ethnography of the Mbundu generally, and much less that of the Imbangala, had been published. In short, it was impossible to describe the milieu in which the Imbangala founded Kasanje or even to know who the Imbangala had been in the seventeenth century. Without some understanding of the conditions which the Imbangala encountered when they reached their present home and fairly certain knowledge of the tendencies they brought with them, it seemed to me, one could not expect to write a meaningful history of the kingdom.

The present focus on processes of state-formation emerged from my realization that little of what I had read about the emergence of states spoke to what I felt to be the central issue in the minds of the Imbangala with whom I had spoken: the tension between their loyalties to kin and their respect for kings. An initial survey of the literature on the subject convinced me that the experience of the Mbundu might highlight an aspect of African political and social history which had gone relatively unnoticed. It was with considerable pleasure that I discovered, in the course of writing the study, that historians and anthropologists in Nigeria, such as Abdullahi Smith, Robin Horton, and E. J. Alagoa, had laid out both theory and facts in a manner which at once clarified my own thinking and explained certain lingering uncertainties which obscured my view of the Mbundu past. I hope that they will agree that Mbundu history is susceptible to the sort of analysis which they have pioneered.

In the absence of an officially standardized orthography for Kimbundu, I have attempted to employ a version of the 'practical orthography of African languages' simplified to conform to the capabilities of a standard English alphabet.[4] The major divergence from the system suggested by the International Institute of African Languages and Cultures and the one used here is my substitution of the French 'j' to indicate the sound represented by -s- in the English word pleasure. This should lead to no ambiguity as the English 'j' does not occur in Kimbundu. The spellings are phonemic rather than phonetic and so, for example, the Mbangala/Cokwe/Lunda pronunciation *ci-* appears here in the general Kimbundu form *ki-*.

The references in the footnotes are given in abbreviated form, but the bibliography contains the customary complete citations that will,

[4] International Institute of African Languages and Cultures (1930).

I hope, clarify some of the obscure references found in many older publications on the subject. Many of the documents used have been published in various places by different editors, and I have tried to include all locations known to me in these cases. In alphabetizing Portuguese names, I have followed the U.S. Library of Congress rules, although most readers will be aware that individual libraries (especially those outside the United States) may follow different conventions. Citations of a 'testimony' of an individual refer in every case to interviews conducted during my fieldwork in Angola (see Bibliography for a list of informants).

I have followed the accepted English convention in using no Bantu prefixes before the names of ethno-linguistic groups, with the exception of the name Ovimbundu (properly, the Mbundu) to distinguish the inhabitants of the southern highlands from the Mbundu who live north of the Kwanza. The plural of most Bantu words appears in parentheses following its first occurrence in the text, and a glossary of Bantu terms located at the end of the study should facilitate the identification of terms unfamiliar to the reader.

It is a pleasure to thank, all too briefly, some of the persons and institutions who have contributed to the completion of this study. Dr. David Birmingham and his family made us welcome in London and contributed to both the pleasure and the profit of our stay there. Mme Marie-Louise Bastin Ramos introduced me to some of the materials to be found in the Musée Royal de l'Afrique Centrale in Tervuren, Belgium. In Lisbon, I add my gratitude to the thanks of many others who have benefited from the friendly advice and willing assistance of Professor Doutor António da Silva Rego. I also wish to express my appreciation to Dr. Alberto Iria, director of the Arquivo Histórico Ultramarino, and to the staff of that archive and the Biblioteca da Sociedade de Geografia de Lisboa who assisted me in examining the rich documentary collections in Lisbon. Dr. Dauril Alden more than generously shared the fruits of his explorations in both archives and byways with me and certainly contributed to the education of a novice historian in a new country. Mrs. Asta Rose J. Alcaide, Mr. and Mrs. Robert Bently, and Mr. and Mrs. Grayson Tennison also contributed to the pursuance of my research while in Lisbon.

His Excellency Dr. Carlos Garcia de Azevedo, governor of the District of Malanje in Angola, and Sr. Administrador José Manuel Fernandes de Mota Torres granted the necessary permission to perform fieldwork in the Concelho do Quela. Sr. Engenheiro Agrónimo Manuel António Correia de Pinho, director of the Instituto de Algodão de Angola kindly made available housing facilities owned by the Instituto, without which I could not have worked successfully among the Imbangala. In addition to the professional debt which I owe to the padres and lay brothers of the Missão Católica dos Bângalas for the work completed at the mission, my family and I can never repay the personal kindnesses and cordial hospitality of Padre Alfredo Beltrán de Otalora, Padre José Luis Rodrígues Sáez, Esteban Arribas, Carmelo Ortega, and José Luis Martinez. Others who graciously contributed to the success of my field research include Sr. Adjunto e Sra. Vitor António dos Santos, Sr. Administrador e Sra. Amándio Eduardo Correia Ramos, Sr. Administrador e Sra. Adelino Correia da Silva, Sr. Administrador e Sra. Frederico de Mello Garcés, Sr. Administrador Sigurd von Viller Salazar, Sr. Alberto Manuel Pires, Padre Pedro Uría, Mr. and Mrs. Lloyd Schaad, and many citizens of Quela. Of course, my work owes its greatest debt to the Imbangala whose names appear in footnotes throughout the book and whose expert historical knowledge provides the basis on which every other aspect of this study has been built. A special expression of gratitude goes to Sr. Sousa Calunga and Sr. Apolo de Matos who came, I hope, to accept me as a fellow professional.

In Luanda, the late Sr. Engenheiro Agrónimo Virgílio Cannas Martins graciously put the facilities of the Instituto de Investigação Científica de Angola at my disposal. Dra. Maria Angelina Teixeira Coelho patiently helped me pick my way through the enormous documentation of the Arquivo Histórico de Angola and provided guidance and assistance in many other ways; her generous help and advice opened many new avenues of research. Sr. Arquiteto Fernando Batalha and Dr. José Redinha graciously shared the fruits of their unequalled familiarity with the Angolan past. The late Dr. Mário Milheiros gave freely of his time to help me become acquainted with the archives of Luanda. I wish also to thank Padre António Custódio Gonçalves, director of the Arquivo da Câmara Eclesiástica, and Vice-presidente Ramos do Amaral of the Câmara Municipal for permission to consult the collections of the Biblioteca e Arquivo da Câmara Eclesiástica and the Biblioteca da Câmara Municipal. Coronel Altino A. P. de Magalhães introduced me to the Arquivo Histórico do Quartel Geral. I owe a special debt to the personnel all these archives, too numerous to name here, who willingly and efficiently located the many volumes of documents which I requested. Adjunto Sá Pereira of the Missão de Inquéritos Agricolas de Angola and Eng.ʳᵒ Mendes da Costa of the Serviços Geográficos e Cadastrais permitted me to examine useful documents under their care. Sr. Acácio Videira of the Companhia de Diamantes de Angola introduced me to informants whose knowledge contributed to the completion of my studies. I am also grateful for many reasons to Michael Chapman, Dr. e Sra. Luis Polonah, Mr. and Mrs. Peter de Vos, Mr. Richard Williams, and Mr. and Mrs. Lester Glad.

None who have studied under Professor Jan Vansina can fail to benefit from the example and encouragement he provides his students and colleagues. His vast experience has informed the research and writing of the study from its inception; it is to him that I owe the original choice of subject. Inevitably, one feels that—in the end—the study amounts to little more than elaboration on an idea he once mentioned in the context of something more grand. Professors Philip D. Curtin, John Smail, and Harold Scheub of the University of Wisconsin read earlier drafts and offered invaluable criticism. Throughout my years in Madison, Professor Curtin, especially, exerted a steady and disciplined influence on my thinking and writing. A year's visiting appointment at the University of Wisconsin afforded the opportunity to tap the insight and sharp analytical abilities of Professor Steven Feierman, who guided me toward much of the theoretical material on state-formation. If others find something of themselves in my work, my failure to acknowledge their contribution explicitly does not stem from lack of gratitude. None bears any discredit for whatever weaknesses may remain, and I accept full responsibility for such as there may be.

The research could not have been undertaken at all without a generous grant from the Foreign Area Fellowship Program of New York which enabled me to travel to Europe and Africa and to spend more time in the preparation of the original dissertation (University of Wisconsin, 1972) than would otherwise have been possible. The Program, however, has no connection with the conclusions expressed. I am also grateful to the University of Virginia for a Wilson Gee Institute research grant and additional funds which supported the preparation of the revised manuscript. Glyn Hewson, Beth Roberts, and Paul Zeigler each allowed me the benefit of their special skills.

I have appreciated the sharp eyes and good judgement of the editors of the Clarendon Press in preparing the manuscript for publication. Although the footnotes no longer conform to the style preferred in historical writing, I have accepted the more economical form suggested by the editors in recognition of the present realities of the publishing industry.

My greatest personal gratitude goes, of course, to Janet, my wife, and to my children who gladly followed the sometimes winding paths which led to the present form of this work. Janet has somehow found time to give valuable editorial advice in addition to keeping the family functioning, and she must receive a considerable share of whatever credit the study may merit.

J.C.M.

London, February 1975

Contents

List of Maps

List of Figures

List of Tables

Abbreviations Used in Footnotes
and Bibliography

AA	*Arquivos de Angola* (Luanda)
A.C.E.	Arquivo da Câmara Episcopal (Luanda)
ACU	*Annaes do Concelho Ultramarino* (parte não official)
A.G.S.	Arquivo Geral, Salamancas
A.H.A.	Arquivo Histórico de Angola (Luanda)
A.H.C.M.L.	Arquivo Histórico da Câmara Municipal de Luanda
A.H.U.	Arquivo Histórico Ultramarino (Lisbon)
Ajuda	Biblioteca da Ajuda (Lisbon)
A.N.T.T.	Arquivo Nacional da Torre do Tombo (Lisbon)
AMC	*Annaes Maritimos e Coloniaes* (Lisbon)
ARSOM	*Académie royale des sciences d'outre-mer, Mémoires,* N.S. (Histoire)
A.Q.G.	Arquivo do Quartel Geral (Luanda)
BIICA	*Boletim do Instituto de Investigação Científica de Angola*
B.M.	British Museum (London)
B.N.L.	Biblioteca Nacional de Lisboa
B.N.M.	Biblioteca Nacíonal, Madrid
B.N.R.J.	Biblioteca Nacional do Rio de Janeiro
B.S.G.L.	Biblioteca da Sociedade de Geografia de Lisboa
BSGL	*Boletim da Sociedade de Geografia de Lisboa*
CA	*Current Anthropology*
CEA	*Cahiers d'études africaines*
CSSH	*Comparative Studies in Society and History*
EHA	*Études d'histoire africaine*
IRCB	*Institut royal colonial belge, Mémoires in 8°*
I.S.C.S.P.U.	Instituto Superior das Ciências Sociais e Política Ultramarina (Lisbon)
JAH	*Journal of African History*
JHSN	*Journal of the Historical Society of Nigeria*
MA	*Mensário Administrativo* (Luanda)
MRAC	*Musée royal de l'Afrique centrale* (Tervuren), *Annales,* sér. in 8°
M.R.A.C.	Musée royal de l'Afrique centrale
PA	*Portugal em Africa*
RLJ	*Rhodes-Livingstone Journal*
SWJA	*Southwestern Journal of Anthropology*

CHAPTER I

Introduction

AS MODERN African nations drove toward political independence during the late 1950s and early 1960s, historians did their part by searching the African past for precedents which justified the capacity and right of Africans to enter Kwame Nkrumah's long-awaited 'political kingdom'.[1] They found abundant evidence in the Sudanic empires, Zulu, interlacustrine states, and kingdoms of the savanna which became the benchmarks punctuating the teaching and study of African history up to the present time. All of these stood in apparent stark contrast to vaguely understood 'stateless' areas in the interstices between the states, however, and scholars found themselves asking why and how so-called 'stateless societies' had once made the transition to the various forms of polity which pre-occupied academics and politicians alike. Their efforts, which this introduction summarizes in rather schematic form, drew eclectically on a number of intellectual currents present in Western academic circles but tended to cluster about one of the most hoary myths of the African past—the 'Hamitic' hypothesis—and derived from it a variety of conclusions which this study questions through analysis of the process of state-formation among the Mbundu people of Angola.

The first generation of professional historians concerned with Africa accepted the basically dichotomous concepts of 'states' and 'stateless' societies as their framework for studying African political history.[2] In doing so, they tended to ignore the implications of several anthropological studies which not only de-emphasized the contrast between centralized territorial 'states' and acephalous 'stateless' societies organized in terms of descent groups, age-grades, secret societies, and the like, but also showed that many, if not all, African 'states' incorporated a variety of strong lineages

---

[1] If one may accept textbooks as barometers of the basic outlook of a generation of historians, those of Robert I. Rotberg (1965) and Basil Davidson (e.g. 1959 and 1961, both of which deal with kingdoms in spite of their titles) provide apt examples.

[2] First stated formally in the classic study edited by Meyer Fortes and E. E. Evans-Pritchard (1940), introduction.

and other non-political institutions as basic elements of their
structure.[3]

These historians, more concerned with change than some of their
anthropologist colleagues, found that the available literature offered
little inspiration to help them handle development and process in
the kingdoms they studied. Most contented themselves with accounting for the 'origins' of a state (to use the somewhat oversimplified
terminology which has figured most prominently in the literature)
and then failed to describe any further change in the institutions
thus established. The apparent contrast between the exceedingly
complex states known to historians and the superficial 'simplicity'
of societies lacking political institutions of a type familiar to western-
ers presented analysts with a dilemma in trying to explain how one
form of society changed into the other. Most early explanations fell
back on essentially cataclysmic processes of state-formation in
order to bridge the gap: migrating conquerors, secessions, defensive
reactions, and so on filled the literature as scholar after scholar
joined in the search for a way to link acephalous 'stateless' societies
with the centralized social and political controls observed in the
classic East and West African states known at the time.[4]

A new generation of West African historians has recently directed
the attention of scholars in directions which eliminate the old contrast between 'state' and 'stateless' and correspondingly reduce the
need for cataclysmic theories of state origins. They recognize that
'state-like institutions' (a term I would prefer not to define for the
moment) exist in societies formerly regarded as 'stateless' and that

[3] E. E. Evans-Pritchard (1940, 1949) and A. W. Southall (1953) had earlier
provided monographs demonstrating not only the subtlety of the contrast
between 'state' and 'stateless' but had also described systems in the process of
transition from the latter to the former. Audrey Richards' contribution to
Fortes and Evans-Pritchard (1940) mentioned but did not stress the role of
lineages in the Bemba polity. Peter C. Lloyd (1954) pointed out that 'the position of the lineages in the more highly-developed kingdoms has rarely been
adequately stressed'. Jan Vansina (1962a) showed the great variety of ways in
which already documented political structures related to their component
parts. But explicit anthropological attention turned to the issue of states and
lineages only with Meyer Fortes (1969). Among French anthropologists,
Georges Balandier (1970) was sceptical about the dichotomy prevailing among
his British colleagues, but extended debate on the issue appeared in France
only in 1973 when Claude Tardits (1973) and Jean-Claude Galey (1973)
challenged the prevailing Lévi-Straussian association of 'elementary structures'
(roughly equivalent to lineages) with 'stateless societies' and the identification
of 'complex structures' with states.

[4] A representative summary of theories current in the early 1960s appears
in Herbert Lewis (1966).

the process of state-formation often consists simply in bringing one of these indigenous institutions to a position of overriding influence in the society. The 'stateless' society may thus be converted to a 'state' through a series of nearly imperceptible steps which cumulatively alter the relative significance of the great many structures, centralized and decentralized, territorial and kinship, social and political, found in most African cultures.[5]

The present study extends their ideas, which I see as a major new emphasis in the study of state-formation in Africa, by reviewing the data on the Mbundu of north-western Angola, people who lived in a part of the continent as yet hardly touched by these stirrings of innovation. It indicates the ways in which some of the Mbundu built varying political structures during the centuries up to and including the establishment of the small Portuguese state of Angola after the turn of the seventeenth century. As a historical study, it demonstrates, or suggests, how people organized states in a particular social and intellectual framework, but it has little to do with devising taxonomies of political structure or constructing generalized rules about 'process'. The latter tasks more properly belong in the capable hands of anthropologists. As a historical study of non-literate Africans, however, it necessarily borrows eclectically, and hopefully wisely as well, from the ethnographer's conceptual tool-kit in order to explain the thought and behaviour of Mbundu state-builders. If it is successful, it may describe some of the diverse forms of 'state-like institutions' of the sixteenth and seventeenth centuries in terms which make the Mbundu experience comparable to that of others elsewhere in Africa. It may also suggest ways in which each institution changed, and simultaneously was changed by, the political and social environment in which it flourished. The basic question, for comparative purposes, might be phrased: how have institutions resembling the conventional notion of a 'state' been formed in the context of strongly autonomous descent groups in the case of the Mbundu of Angola? This formulation of the problem is intended to postpone the need for a precise *a priori* definition of 'state' since the entire study represents in one sense a search for an empirical identification of Mbundu 'political structures' based on their historical experience. Perhaps the Mbundu states will ultimately contribute

[5] I refer particularly to recent work by E. J. Alagoa (1970, 1971a, 1971b), Abdullahi Smith (1970), and Robin Horton (1969, 1971). Steven Feierman (1974) has introduced different but equally important approaches to the early history of eastern African states.

to someone else's universal definition of the 'state', but the considerable extent to which the Mbundu states were conditioned by the
society in which they existed stands as a warning against comprehensive definitions which fail to consider the so-called 'non-political'
aspects of society.

The 'Hamitic Myth' and its Legacy

The first analysts of state-formation in Africa relied excessively on
theoretical constructs drawn from simplistic European assumptions
about what was then regarded as 'traditional Africa'. Whatever the
practical difficulties of recovering comprehensive historical data on
the remote periods when the most familiar African states had
coalesced, most early historians allowed the European intellectual
background to dominate both known fact and sometimes common
sense as they substituted often grotesque 'elephants for want of
towns'[6] at the basis of the early kingdoms. Since anthropologists of
various persuasions had been among the first European scholars to
take the civilizations of sub-Saharan Africa at all seriously, their
underlying premises had the greatest initial influence on the question
of how states had begun in Africa. The basic assumptions of two
major schools of inter-war European ethnography,[7] the culture-
historical or diffusionist Kulturkreise school represented in Africa
by Seligman and Baumann and Westermann,[8] and British functionalist social anthropology descended from Malinowski and Rad-
cliffe-Brown,[9] had the greatest effect. The diffusionists' search for
the external origins of elements in societies all over the world,
coupled with their predilection for migrations to account for the
spread of these elements, led historians to accept cataclysmic theories
of state origins, usually in the form of a 'conquest theory'. The
functionalists' emphasis on the integration and harmonious operation of societies left little room for change and prompted historians
to assume that an essentially ahistorical period of stability succeeded

---

[6] Jonathan Swift, On Poetry: A Rhapsody (London, 1733), line 177.

[7] American cultural evolutionists have affected African historical writing
only very recently. Robert F. Stevenson (1968) explicitly rejected the static
assumptions of early functionalism and Conrad P. Kottak (1972) and T. N.
Huffman (1972) have dealt in this vein with the problem of state origins in
regard to two classic African cases. Some indirect influence (e.g. R. L. Carneiro's on the relation between population pressure and state-formation (1968))
may be detected in Horton (1971).

[8] Charles G. Seligman (1957), Hermann Baumann and D. Westermann
(1962). For the Mbundu, see most notably H. C. de Decker (1939).

[9] Most pre-1970 studies in English, including Fortes and Evans-Pritchard
(1940), represent variations on the basic theories of this school.

the foundation of most states and lasted until change ('decline') resumed during the European conquests at the end of the nineteenth century.[10]

The general image of African state-formation thus came to depend on the arrival of skilled outsiders who imposed fully-developed state institutions on less skilled peasants with little subsequent alteration in the basic political structures established at the 'conquest'. Such a theory received no small reinforcement from the superficial content of many African oral traditions which held that 'the world as it was first created is the same as the world as it is now'.[11] As a result, few early historians sought more complex theories of state-formation or looked in any systematic way for evolution of state structures through time.[12]

The now infamous 'Hamitic myth' both anticipated and epitomized these trains of thought and in a certain sense provided the basis on which most early histories of African states were constructed.[13] It is certainly no longer necessary to refute the racist overtones of this theory, which have been exposed from a variety of angles,[14] but it may still be useful to consider the 'Hamitic myth' as the proto-type of several later and more subtle versions of the same logic of state-formation. In its original form, the 'Hamitic myth' tended to equate all 'civilizations' in Africa with large centralized states and argue that

[a]part from relatively late Semitic influences ... the civilization of Africa are the civilizations of the Hamites, its history the record of these

---

[10] Neo-Marxist evolutionists have had relatively little to say about state-formation in Africa owing to the obvious inapplicability of the 'Asiatic mode of production' to conditions in Africa; see, for example, Jean Suret-Canale (1964). Recent revisions suggested by Catherine Coquery-Vidrovitch (1969) to reduce the dichotomy between 'states' and 'stateless societies' seek local pressures that might cause state structures to coalesce. Emmanuel Terray (1974), though still tending to underrate the political and economic potential of lineage-based societies, has begun to integrate descent groups into the Marxist understanding of African states.

[11] Jan Vansina (1965), p. 105.

[12] Lloyd A. Fallers (1965) nicely illustrates the prevailing assumption that 'change', or at least discernible change, began when European influence penetrated.

[13] Seligman (1957) gave the classic formulation to the idea, of long standing in the cultural tradition of Europe, that a vaguely racial/cultural/linguistic group known as 'Hamites' spread themselves and much of their culture over sub-saharan Africa.

[14] J. Greenberg (1949), St. Clair Drake (1959), R. G. Armstrong (1960), B. A. Ogot (1964), and Edith Sanders (1969), to name only some of the most systematic critiques.

peoples and of their interaction with the two other African stocks, the Negro and the Bushman, whether this influence was exerted by highly civilized Egyptians or by such wider pastoralists as are represented at the present day by the Beja and the Somali. . . . the incoming Hamites were pastoral 'Europeans'—arriving wave after wave— better armed as well as quicker witted than the dark agricultural Negroes. . . .[15]

For the history of state origins, Seligman's vivid image of spear-brandishing 'Hamitic' herdsmen descending upon placid and dull farming populations encouraged historians to accept the 'conquest state' hypothesis that most African states had resulted from the imposition of alien institutions over indigenous agriculturalists. The search for non-African origins for the states of the western Sudan had already led to the purported discovery of European-like Jews in the ancestry of the kings of Ghana; the derivation of all later western Sudanic states (Mali, Songhai, etc.) from Ghanaian precedents spread the original alien inspiration widely throughout West Africa.[16] Historians of the East African lake regions, with only marginally greater justification based on the clear association of nineteenth-century rulers there with cattle, ascribed 'Hamitic' origins to Bunyoro and all the other states allegedly derived from it.[17] 'Hamites' have popped up in the history of other kingdoms as far south as Rhodesia, but it is sufficient to mention here only a single example to demonstrate their influence on Mbundu historiography. A leading ethnographer and student of the Mbundu as recently as 1962 connected the origins of the most powerful sixteenth-century Mbundu state with the south-westerly sweep of conquering invaders whose 'civilizing' influence, even without the cattle of the classic 'Hamites', strongly resembled that of Seligman's prototypes.[18] All of these invading state-founders, whether 'Hamitic', 'Semitic', or 'Cushitic',[19] played the essentially identical roles of bringing fully-formed political institutions to establish the African states which emerged as those best known to nineteenth- and twentieth-century European observers. The accuracy of this image was limited to the

[15] Seligman (1957), pp. 85, 140–1.
[16] Maurice Delafosse (1912), ii, 22–5, 38; E. W. Bovill (1968), p. 50; early editions of John D. Fage (1961), p. 18, repeated this notion. Similarly alien founders were given credit for founding the Hausa city-states; Smith (1970), pp. 329ff.
[17] See authorities cited in Ogot (1964), pp. 284–5.
[18] José Redinha (1962) and Antonio Miranda Magalhães (1934), pp. 540–1. The so-called 'Jaga' in Angola have also been identified explicitly as 'Hamites'; see Conde de Ficalho (1947), pp. 49–51, and my critique (1973a).
[19] A modification introduced by George P. Murdock (1959), p. 44.

extent to which it reflected turn-of-the-century European myths about the African past.

Shorn of its most objectionable racist qualities, the old 'Hamitic myth' achieved renewed respectability at the end of the 1950s in the form of a revamped 'Sudanic state hypothesis' propounded in the first modern synthetic history of Africa.[20] According to this argument, a 'civilization' of vaguely Egypto-south-west Asian provenance overspread much of sub-Saharan Africa at an early date and brought with it the first large-scale centralized kingdoms to appear in that region:

Essentially the 'Sudanic' state was a parasitic growth, fastening itself upon the economic base of pre-existing agricultural societies. To these societies it contributed certain new ideas of political organization, and certain new techniques, notably in the field of mining, metallurgy, and trade. Its earliest propagators seem to have moved south-west from the Nile Valley, and to have established themselves, probably with the aid of the horse and of cavalry warfare, among the agricultural peoples immediately to the south of the Sahara. . . . [later] the first miners and ivory-traders reached the Lake regions, the Katanga and Rhodesia, using their superior techniques to establish political power according to their own traditional patterns. . . .[21]

This hypothesis retained the central premise of the old 'Hamitic myth'—that outsiders had brought statecraft to sub-Saharan Africa —but substituted 'Sudanic' for 'Hamitic' in conformity with the evident effect of the new hypothesis, that of shifting the value judgement implicit in the contrast between mounted foreigners and local farmers. The 'Sudanic state' theory clearly favoured the indigenous agriculturalists who, it could now be seen, had had to suffer the 'parasitic growth' of an essentially alien form of political structure, imposed *in toto* through the more complex technology of the invaders, rather than their racial superiority. The old 'Hamitic myth' of the late 1800s had achieved mid-twentieth-century respectability clothed in the less pejorative terminology of technology rather than race.[22]

The first generation of historical monographs devoted to African states quickly demonstrated the inadequacy of the assumptions

[20] Roland Oliver and J. D. Fage (1962), pp. 44–52.
[21] Oliver and Fage 1962, pp. 51–2.
[22] An observation also made by Robin Horton (1971), p. 110, n. 47. The parallels between the 'Sudanic hypothesis' and once-current theories about the imposition of European colonial rule in Africa are too obvious to require extensive comment.

underlying both the 'Hamitic myth' and the 'Sudanic state' hypothesis. To name all the studies which refuted the ideas that a single 'origin' accounted for all or most African states or that a single political structure lay beneath the variegated detail would require a list of most state histories written since the early 1960s. In general, they first attacked the notion of a single origin by identifying 'clusters' of states, each group of kingdoms presumably with an independent source of innovation and a subsequent outward diffusion of institutions within a restricted radius. Emphasis then turned to the uniqueness of each individual state and tended to discount the importance of any external influence.[23] But most of these studies still retained the basic diffusionist idea in the guise of local outsiders who founded most African states and the functionalist notion that fully-developed and integrated political institutions survived more or less unchanged from the time of the state's foundation until 'decline' set in during the nineteenth century. The 'conquest theory' thus remained fundamentally intact, since revisionists had really changed little other than to substitute local African conquerors for the 'Hamites' and 'Sudanic states' of their predecessors.

The next major innovation in historians' approaches to African state-formation explored the possibility of showing structural change in pre-colonial political institutions. These studies began to cast doubt on the lingering idea that 'state-formation' occurred in a single cataclysmic revolution. It became evident that the mature institutions of the late nineteenth century, which most historians had projected back into the past in largely unchanged form, represented the end result of a lengthy process of gradual accretion, and that states known only in their latest phases might have had entirely different shapes in less familiar times. M. G. Smith's study on the Zazzau state of northern Nigeria made the crucial breakthrough for West Africa.[24] Almost simultaneously, Vansina produced histories of the Kuba and Rwanda kingdoms in Central Africa which convincingly demonstrated the fundamental changes which had occurred before these states attained their late-nineteenth-century form. Another study, based less on ethnographic data than the previous

---

[23] Jan Vansina (1966a) was the most advanced of these studies and introduced the notion of at least three separate origins for the clusters of states that he identified in the southern savanna. The volume of studies edited by Daryll Forde and P. M. Kaberry (1967) brought home the point of unique origins for parts of West Africa. A good statement of these, and other, issues appears in Peter C. Lloyd's review article (1968).

[24] M. G. Smith (1960).

two, proved with documentary sources that the Kongo kingdom had undergone revolutionary changes during the sixteenth and seventeenth centuries.[25] In East Africa, it became apparent that Buganda had altered the balance between two types of office-holders in the course of the nineteenth century, ending the period in a much more centralized and bureaucratic form than it had begun.[26] With the appearance of these books, the historian's concern with change had begun to overcome the static tendencies inherent in earlier studies based on the functionalist school of anthropology.

The last assumption of the 'Hamitic myth' to fall by the wayside was the reliance on outsiders to explain state-formation. Anthropologists, inspired by the power of structural analysis to reveal unsuspected dimensions of oral traditions, began the assault against the predominant tendency to interpret traditional materials literally by showing that primarily ideological reasons might motivate African rulers and subjects alike to ascribe foreign origins to founding kings whatever the real circumstances.[27] The alien origins of the ubiquitous *heros civilisateur*, they argued, gave him and his successors a legitimacy denied to simple residents of the country, who seemed doomed to remain prophets without honour among their own kind. Further, identification of the king as an outsider divorced him from any connection with local interest groups and rendered him theoretically impartial in dispensing justice to the people of his kingdom. Historians have apparently hesitated to recognize the doubt which this hypothesis casts on explanations of state-formation which depend on outside conquerors, perhaps because of the ahistorical implications of some structural anthropology; as a result, invading foreigners continue to perform their customary function in some of the most recent studies dealing with state-formation in Africa.[28]

Even so schematic a review of state-formation theories as this[29] indicates the continuing pervasive influence of the 'Hamitic myth'

[25] Jan Vansina (1964a, 1964b) made available in French conclusions first reached in (1963). See also Vanisina (1962b and, for Kongo, 1966, pp. 130–4, 138–42, 147–52).

[26] An argument first advanced in Martin Southwold (1961).

[27] As examples of structualist studies in Africa one may cite J. S. Boston (1964), T. O. Beidelman (1970), and Luc de Heusch (1972).

[28] Citing only a few recent examples from East, West, and Equatorial Africa: I. A. Akinjogbin (1971), pp. 307–11; Israel K. Katoke (1971), pp. 512–14; Jean-Luc Vellut (1972), pp. 62–3. B. Crine-Mavar (1973) preserves 'massive migrations' in his peculiarly Lunda-centric view of the early history of southern Zaïre.

[29] I have been influenced in my interpretation by Jack Goody (1968), John D. Fage (1965), Daryll Forde (1967), and Roland Oliver (1968).

after more than a decade of modern historical studies on Africa. First propounded in overtly racist terms during the late nineteenth century, it was dismissed on principle after the Second World War but retained its influence in the form of its underlying assumptions. Of the four major elements of the 'Hamitic myth' present to varying degrees in most later approaches—state-formation by conquest, identification of the conquerors as outsiders, attribution of some type of superiority to the conquerors, and total and instantaneous state-formation with little later modification of political structures—all survived in only slightly modified form in the 'Sudanic state hypothesis'. Despite the attempts of critics to arrive at a more sophisticated understanding of 'migrations', 'conquest', and 'origins',[30] versions of the same ideas continued to influence historians even after they had abandoned the idea of a single outside source for all African kingdoms. Historians are now extending their quest for evidence of change in African states as they develop more refined techniques for the recovery and analysis of data. Most recently, they have begun to examine more carefully the historical significance of the omnipresent migrating outsiders who appear to have founded many African kindoms.[31]

The history of early states among the Mbundu provides an opportunity to test further the applicability of new approaches currently under development by historians of other parts of Africa. The Mbundu clearly had large and sophisticated political structures at the time the Portuguese arrived, but had these in fact been founded by the classic sort of migrating conquerors from the interior which literal interpretations of some of the traditions seemed to indicate?[32] Did Mbundu political history amount to no more than the establishment of an already fully developed state which expanded geographically but showed no internal evolution? Is there evidence of technological superiority associated with state founders among the

[30] Notably, Vansina (1966a), pp. 14–18, and Lewis (1966). The warnings expressed in these studies do not appear to have been universally heeded. Also see 'Introduction' in Vansina, Mauny, and Thomas (1964), pp. 86–90.

[31] Feierman (1974); Jan Vansina (1971b); John D. Fage (1974); and Rex S. O'Fahey (1970) call attention to other dimensions of growth and change in African state-formation and development.

[32] The standard Portuguese accounts, which focus on the activities of Europeans among the Mbundu are: Alfredo de Albuquerque Felner (1933) and Ralph Delgado (1948–55). David Birmingham (1966), esp. pp. 17–20, 26–41, has given a sound critical treatment on the written sources but in integrating published traditional materials has retained the migration hypothesis, based largely on G. L. Haveaux (1954). Vansina (1966a) does not deal with the question.

Mbundu? The data will show, in conformity with studies proceeding on other fronts, that state-formation in north-western Angola may have been a much more complex process than previous analyses have suggested.

The Methodology[33]

One of the developments which have forced historians to abandon the 'Hamitic myth' has been a shift away from largely 'conjectural history' of the Seligman variety, which was based almost exclusively on European preconceptions rather than data, towards a more truly historical approach founded on more and better factual evidence. In many ways, increasing sophistication in the recovery of information about the African past has provided the catalyst which has forced historians to discard the theories of the 1950s, since these simply did not fit the facts emerging in research published during the 1960s. The historian's reliance on evidence, however, obliges him to exercise careful control over the methods by which he analyses his information, especially if he attempts to develop new ways of elucidating the historical content of oral tradition, linguistic evidence, and ethnographic materials. Since anthropologists, linguists, and historians have by no means reached universal agreement on criteria for interpreting these sources, especially when they deal with the more remote past, the historian ought to set forth the nature of his data as explicitly as possible, specify the means by which he collected them, and outline the logic which supports his interpretation of them. This section deals with the first and last of these responsibilities.

Anyone purporting to write about Mbundu political history before the arrival of the Portuguese in the late sixteenth century incurs a special obligation to explain why such a reconstruction, based preponderantly on non-literary sources, can pretend to any significant degree of accuracy about events which occurred more than four hundred years ago.[34] One way to justify the approach is to spell out unambiguously the inherent limitations of the study, since the familiar rule that no historian can hope to write the entire history of an era applies with special emphasis in this case. It is the nature of the evidence which limits knowledge of early Mbundu history to a

[33] I use the term 'methodology' to refer to the logic governing my interpretation of the sources for Mbundu history; the Preface contains a brief review of the *techniques* used to collect the data.

[34] Other recent studies which explore the technical limits on data on the distant African past include Christopher Ehret (1971) and David W. Cohen (1972).

rather small fraction of the obviously much more complex totality of Mbundu life in the sixteenth and seventeenth centuries. Although the traditions provide a fairly coherent picture of the development of Mbundu political *institutions*, they have almost nothing to say about individuals at this period. This point may bear some additional emphasis, since most previous writing on the area has tended to interpret the traditions literally as dealing with individual human protagonists; in fact, the recoverable history of the Mbundu (before Portuguese documents highlight a few individuals) deals almost exclusively with dynasties (rather than kings), offices (not officials), and emblems of authority (rather than the holders of authority).[35]

Except as contemporary documents yield a modest amount of information on actual patterns of human behaviour, moreover, the knowable history of the Mbundu deals only with idealized versions of reality instead of with the presumably less regular vagaries of actual historical events. This distinction—between normative and statistical perceptions of reality, which has long been a basic concept to anthropoligists, who distinguish between what is, what is believed to be (or reported to be), and what ought to be—affects all history, documentary[36] or otherwise. But the gap between the idealized past and actual behaviour becomes somewhat wider than usual in this case owing to the highly normative quality of the traditions. What may be known about the early political history of the Mbundu, therefore, is limited to a rather idealized perspective on selected aspects of the institutional development of early states.

Mbundu oral traditions are histories of groups (general, local, and familial, to employ the terminology proposed by Vansina[37]) and strongly reflect the state of Mbundu social and political structures at the time they are recited.[38] The traditions therefore never deal with individuals. They further refer selectively to only certain parts of the past, those which have evident analogues in the present.[39] Imbangala

---

[35] Cf. Jack Goody and Ian Watt (1963), p. 308, where the authors point out that the characters in the genealogies in Genesis refer to groups rather than to individuals. I do not cite the growing volume of recent work in this field.

[36] Cf. this argument applied to statistics dealing with the Atlantic slave trade; Philip D. Curtin (1969) suggests that slavers regularly reported as fact what they felt exports *ought* to be rather than what they actually were. Such estimates greatly exceeded figures verifiable from statistical sources.

[37] Vansina (1971b), p. 451.

[38] Aspects of the Malinowskian concept of a 'mythical charter' have obvious relevance to the way in which the Imbangala use information about the past.

[39] In addition to the sort of histories discussed here, the Imbangala tell a wealth of personal recollections which cover the period back to about 1870.

historians,[40] from whose testimonies come most of the traditions used here, view past centuries through the prism of social and political conditions of their own time, seeking the origins of descent groups, political titles, and structural relationships which have importance in the present.[41] This means that the Imbangala tend to preserve as 'history' (i.e. that which occurred in the period before living memory) only those events which established social or political precedents influencing contemporary behaviour patterns (e.g. lineages A and B regard each other as enemies; the modern holder of an ancient political title plays a specified role at the king's court; lineage C occupies the lands of lineage D subject to specified conditions, and so on). Since the Imbangala explicitly view their history as concerned with the present, their versions of the ancient past acquire a synchronic timeless quality in the eyes of literate historians trained to view the world in a sharply diachronic perspective. The Imbangala word which most closely approximates to the English word 'history', *musendo*,[42] has the predominantly synchronic sense of 'connection' rather than 'origin'.[43] The Imbangala in many ways see their past as little more than a slightly refracted mirage of the present and envisage the past as events removed somewhat from the perceptions of living people but still present in the form of their consquences. They draw an analogy between the near-congruence of past (history) and present and the resemblance of potsherds to the formerly whole pot; alternatively, they sometimes point out that history is like an ancestor spirit (*nzumbi*, plural *jinzumbi*) in relation to the ancestor when he was alive.[44] In so far as the Imbangala visualize the past

[40] The Imbangala are a subgroup of the Mbundu who lived on the eastern edge of the Kimbundu-speaking area; they are generally acknowledged to have the most vital traditions still to be found in northern Angola.

[41] Cf. Goody and Watt (1963) who note (p. 310) that the non-literate individual typically 'has little perception of the past except in terms of the present'.

[42] The term *musendo* may assume a plural form, *misendo*, in other contexts, but the Imbangala seem to use only the singular to approximate to 'history' in the literate sense; see Chatelain (1894), p. 21.

[43] The simultaneously diachronic and synchronic character of Imbangala thought about the past finds parallels generally in non-literate African societies; Horton (1967), esp. pp. 176–8. Also E. E. Evans-Pritchard (1939), esp. pp. 212–14. The crucial influence of the absence of writing, as recognized by Horton, receives extensive treatment in Goody and Watt (1963). See also Vansina (1965), pp. 104–5.

[44] Testimony of Kiluanje kya Ngonga.

Since these have entirely different characteristics from the historical traditions, and since they do not concern the period under study, I exclude them from my analysis.

as little more than an aspect of the present, their outlook on the past does not depart significantly from that of many non-literate societies.

The intimate association which the Mbundu see between history and modern society and politics obviously affects the way in which literate historians may interpret these traditions. Since the modern traditions tend to include only those past events which have visible manifestations in the present, they do not provide a coherent or integrated series of past events related to one another in any causal or chronological sense. They instead refer to a set of unrelated past happenings which modern Imbangala historians embed in an artificially contrived narrative framework if they wish to make intuitive sense of their materials for their audience.[45] Therefore, implied narrative connections between the episodes of an Imbangala historical performance, apparently antecedent and consequent, rarely correspond to historical cause and effect, since decades may have separated the events that the historian links for dramatic or didactic effect.[46] Interpretations of these traditions cannot depend on the literal content of the narrative to supply information about the motivations of actors or the conditions determining a given action. Two events may appear in sequence in a tradition not because one followed the other chronologically in the past but because some other logic (geographical, structural, etc.) causes the modern Imbangala historian to relate them in that order. The Imbangala view of their past, as expressed in the traditions, consists of a series of historically unrelated points drawn from the past; there is no developmental chain of related events set on a time-based continuum.[47] This

[45] The recitation of history is very much a public performance among the Imbangala, and historians obviously try to tailor their performances to the tastes of their listeners. I owe my sensitivity to this dimension of Imbangala history to Professor Harold Scheub of the University of Wisconsin; cf. reference by Vansina (1971b), p. 446 and n. 8.

[46] See, for example, the reigns of three early Imbangala kings whose reigns were said to have spanned only a few days but who in fact ruled for nearly fifty years according to documentary sources; Joseph C. Miller (1972a, and forthcoming(c)).

[47] The analogous structure of the Imbangala view of the past with notions of time-reckoning observed in other societies is apparent; cf. Evans-Pritchard's point that the Nuer rely on reference points rather than an abstract continuum to express time (1939). The same notion has been phrased as 'eventual time' by D. F. Pocock (1964). The Imbangala, of course, have a variety of other time-reckoning systems conforming to the purposes at hand. I am specifically concerned here with perceptions of time and not with time in the philosophical sense.

precludes any absolute chronological calculations based exclusively on the content of the traditions.[48]

The influence of contemporary social and political conditions on the Imbangala historical traditions compensates for the loss of exact chronology by causing them to retain records of some very ancient events. Wherever institutions have survived for a long time, they have tended to preserve the concomitant oral evidence of these very early (though of indeterminable calendrical date) social and political forms. Some officials now found in Mbundu lineages, as well as many of the descent groups themselves, have clearly existed for hundreds of years.[49] Traditions accounting for the origin of these titles and groups may be assumed to have come from similarly remote periods in so far as the institutions have not undergone substantial structural modification in the intervening years. Many Mbundu institutions have, of course, suffered substantial changes in the past, and their accompanying traditions will have shifted correspondingly from their original form, but in general enough elements appear to have survived for the modern traditions to provide a partial but reliable picture of Mbundu social and political structures dating back to well before the sixteenth century. Documentary sources show that the dominant institutions of the late nineteenth century (states, lineages, etc.) had become established at least by the mid-1500s. The correspondingly complete modern traditions therefore afford a relatively good guide to events since that time.

The close association between the historical traditions and the institutional structure of Mbundu society further introduces great stability in the traditions which survive. Since social and political changes tend to cause old versions of traditions to disappear, those remaining would seem to describe historical events connected with the establishment of their affiliated structure with a high degree of accuracy. Thus, interpretations of traditions describing the origin of kings' titles which still exist today (or existed at the end of the nineteenth century) carry a relatively high probability of veracity. Documentary proof of this stability, deduced up to this point solely from the inherent logic of Imbangala historical traditions, comes

---

[48] I have developed this point at some length with reference to one aspect of Imbangala traditions in (forthcoming(c)).

[49] Based on documentary evidence (see below). Beatrix Heintze (1970) traces a similar stability among distantly related groups south of the Kwanza from before 1600 to around 1900.

from comparing modern traditions with a mid-seventeenth-century tradition[50] which corresponds to them in nearly every significant aspect. Even where major political changes at the centre of a state have modified the main line of transmission, parallel traditions dealing with the same titles may retain their earlier forms outside the area in which modifications have occurred; such archaic traditions often provide good data on early events obscured by later developments in the core area. The inherent stability of the traditions may therefore allow recovery of data bearing on the formative stages even of states with the most turbulent histories.[51]

Two broad categories of Imbangala historical performance comprehend most of the materials used in this study: genealogies, or the *musendo* proper, and narrative episodes called *malunda* (singular, *lunda*).[52] Other forms of Imbangala oral art contain materials useful for historical reconstruction; these include several such genres as proverbs (*jisabu*, singular *sabu*), praise names (*kumbu*, singular and plural), songs, and other more purely aesthetic and didactic performances. The time available for field research did not allow me to collect sufficient material to permit the sort of sophisticated criticism necessary to make historical sense out of such sources. In partial justification of my decision to limit analysis to the two primary modes of historical performance, I conform to a firm distinction which the Imbangala draw between the *musendo* and the *malunda* on one hand and all other categories of oral performance on the other.[53] The following brief descriptions of the Imbangala genealogies and historical narratives illustrate how they embody aspects of Imbangala historical thought as outlined above.

The historical genealogies, or *musendo*, consist of sets of personal names linked to each other by the conventional relationships of descent and affinity: fathers have sons, husbands have wives, brothers, daughters, nephews, and so on, and all figure in the genealogical trees which Imbangala historians recite in classic Biblical form.

---

[50] Pe João António Cavazzi de Montecúccolo (1965). Detailed analysis follows in Chapter VI.

[51] The argument that significant historical evidence may be preserved in the form of archaisms outside the central area of development is analogous to that used to reconstruct early Rwanda history in Vansina (1962b), or to the tendency of archaic linguistic forms to appear in peripheral regions. On the latter tendency, see Joseph Greenberg (1972), pp. 193–4.

[52] The term is verified in Chatelain (1894), p. 21; also Sigurd von Willer Salazar (n.d., *c.* 1965?), ii. 160.

[53] Testimony of Domingos Vaz.

Ngola a Kiluanje [a male political title] came from Kongo dya Mbulu [an ethnic group shown here as a female] and begot Ndambi a Ngola and Mwiji mwa Ngola, Kangunzu ka Ngola (who is of Negage [a locality in north-western Angola]), and Mbande a Ngola [all subordinate male political titles]. Mbande a Ngola, now king in Marimba [Portuguese administrative post near the Kambo river], begot Kambala ka Mbande and Kingongo kya Mbande. Kingongo kya Mbande begot Mbande a Kingongo. Mbande a Kingongo went to *ngana* Kabari ka Nzungani [i.e. took a wife from this descent group] and begot Ngonga a Mbande, Fula dya Mbande, Kamana ka Mbande, Ngola a Mbande, and Njinje a Mbande. Ngola a Mbande married Mbombo ya Ndumbu [a woman of an unidentified descent group]. . . . Kabila ka Ngola begot Kakunga ka Kabila, Muhi wa Kabila, Nzungi ya Kabila, Ngola a Kabila . . . the ones I have just named are the present *sobas* [Mbundu political-title-holders recognized by the Portuguese government] near Mucari [former administrative post east of Malanje].[54]

The testimony quoted, which is typical of the form of the Imbangala *musendo*, may be represented as a genealogical tree shown in Fig. I. Although such 'family trees' appear to portray a process of biological generation, with marriages and descendants, etc., they in fact refer exclusively to political titles (the male figures) and to descent

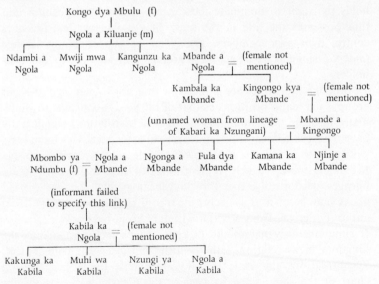

FIG. I. Representative Musendo Genealogy

[54] Testimony of Domingos Vaz.

groups (the females), all of them institutions which survive into the present. This lends a synchronic quality to the genealogy, which may be confirmed, as the historian did at the end of this passage, by referring to living individuals who hold the titles mentioned.

The genealogy does have significant historical content, of however specific and limited a sort. Relationships between political titles linked as 'father' and 'son' in the genealogy indicate in the contemporary sphere that the holder of the 'son'-title must treat the incumbent in the 'father'-title (e.g. Ndambi a Ngola to Ngola a Kiluanje, with respect analogous to that owed by human offspring to their biological/social father. The holder of the junior title is politically subordinate to the holder of the senior title in this sense. Historically, these relationships also mean that an occupant of the 'father'-title created the 'son'-title, awarding it at some time in the past to an unmentioned member of a descent group (possibly but not necessarily also a biological son of the senior title-holder at the time). The genealogy identifies the descent group either by its own name (e.g. Kabari ka Nzungani) or by the name of a historical woman of that lineage (e.g. Mbombo ya Ndumbu). The 'marriages' shown in the genealogy thus link (mostly) 'male' political titles as 'sons' to the 'female' lineages as 'mothers'; the maternal lineage holds the right to nominate incumbents to the 'son' position and thus possesses the title in the sense that Imbangala matrilineages control their own members. The elders or 'uncles' of the lineage (*makota*, singular *kota*) act as guardians and advisers to the title-holder.

Although most titles are affiliated with a single 'maternal' descent group, such major positions as that of the *ngola a kiluanje*, to which many lineages may nominate occupants in rotation, significantly have no specific lineage (or female name) associated with them (as a 'wife'). In this case, the *ngola a kiluanje* descends from Kongo dya Mbulu, a name vaguely representing all the northern Mbundu lineages. Historically, therefore, a genealogy like the one quoted above may be read as a diachronic record of the spread of political authority derived from a major Mbundu king, the *ngola a kiluanje*. It simultaneously names the descent groups incorporated into the kingdom in association with the titles entrusted to their control. Synchronically, the same genealogy amounts to an organization chart of the state, since it specifies the hierarchical relationships between titles and, by extension, between the affiliated lineages.

A genealogy composed of titles reveals nothing about the absolute chronology of the state-building process. One cannot calculate on the basis of assumed human life spans, for example, the minimum or maximum time elapsed between the creation of the *ngola a kiluanje* title and the *muhi wa kabila* position. An unknown number of human incumbents could have occupied both of these positions, as well as all the intervening titles, and any one of the occupants, first, third, or tenth, could have awarded the subordinate position listed as a 'son' in the genealogy. It is permissible to draw only the limited conclusion that the creation of a 'son' title necessarily succeeds the origin of its 'father' title chronologically, but theoretically this interval may vary from a year or less to several centuries. Nor does it follow that 'sibling' titles (e.g. Ndambi a Ngola, Mwiji mwa Ngola, Kangunzu ka Ngola, and Mbande a Ngola) must have been created more or less contemporaneously, since succeeding occupants of the 'father'-title may grant subordinate positions of equal genealogical rank. In general, positions in the senior levels of the genealogy tend to be older than those near the bottom, for historical reasons, but enough exceptions are known to make historical inferences on this basis highly untrustworthy.

Presenting all these names as a single complex genealogy distorts slightly the Imbangala conception of their *musendo*, since they recognize a number of distinct genealogical trees, each corresponding to a major social or political institution such as a state or an ethnic group. The genealogy reproduced above begins with a name taken from a distinct semi-mythical aetiological genealogy (Kongo dya Mbulu)[55] and then traces the development of a portion of the sixteenth-century *ngola a kiluanje* state through the main line of 'male' (i.e. political) descent. The female figures in the genealogy all come from other independent genealogies describing structural relationships of the descent groups ruled by the *ngola a kiluanje* and its associated subordinate titles. Because my data come primarily from the eastern fringe of the Mbundu ethno-linguistic area, I

[55] I use the term 'mythical' in its technical sense of referring to events believed to lie in a period outside of history, timeless, composed of unconnected episodes, the period of 'God on earth', as described, for example, by M. I. Finley (1965). Although all Imbangala 'history' exhibits certain 'mythical' characteristics by literate standards (magic, and so forth), the Mbundu clearly distinguish between their aetiological tradition and the historical *musendo* genealogies. The names in the latter 'exist' in the sense that they have living incumbents; those of the former do not and never have. If the Imbangala have an elaborate cosmology phrased in mythological terms, it did not come up in the context of discussions of history; for the Mbundu generally, see Chatelain (1894).

cannot give an exhaustive list of all Mbundu lineage genealogies, but the regular structure of these traditions suggests that there must be a six or seven sets of names in all, one for each of the names in the aetiological genealogy (of which Kongo dya Mbulu is only one).

The internal shape of these lineage genealogies may vary considerably. Of the three for which I have adequate information, one exhibits certain features of a classic segmentary genealogy in which the component descent groups are articulated into a single comprehensive genealogical tree, very deep (twelve or more 'generations') and pyramidal in shape. The other two show explicit links only between closely related lineages, rarely exceed two or three generations in depth, and jump directly from these levels to an apical putative ancestor; this structure resembles that of a clan, with many lineages of approximately equal rank, none of which can trace its exact descent from the common founder.[56] The variation in the internal structures of these lineage genealogies makes no difference for their historical interpretation, however, since the same sort of 'marriage' relates them all to the political genealogies.[57]

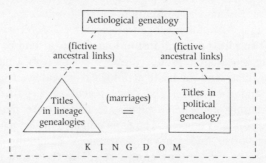

FIG. II. Diagram of how Genealogies Combine to Describe a Kingdom

Separate political genealogies composed of titles rather than lineages exist for each political entity recognized by the Mbundu, one for the *ngola a kiluanje*, another for the Mbondo state of the *ndala kisua*, another for the Lunda empire, yet another for the Kasanje

[56] These groupings of lineages are only incipiently clans, however, since they do not descend from discrete eponymous ancestors (several groupings with different names claim to come from the same ancestor). They lack 'totems' and impose no significant political obligations on their members.

[57] Fig. II shows the links in diagrammatic form. Boston (1964), p. 112, describes a parallel symbolic 'marriage' among the Igala.

state of the Imbangala, and so on.[58] A few isolated titles not connected with any of these coherent genealogies survive as remnants from ancient states no longer in existence. Their separation from the fixed genealogical structures of the main *musendo* frees them to move about in the other genealogical fields according to the whim or design of individual historians; some of these may be dated to before the middle of the sixteenth century by documentary sources. The Mbundu *musendo* may therefore be thought of as a number of distinct genealogical sets which fall into two basic types: lineage genealogies, which show structural relationships between existing lineages and at the same time reveal aspects of the historical processes of lineage fission which have led to the present distribution of descent groups, and political genealogies simultaneously showing the composition of Mbundu states and giving part of the historical development of these kingdoms. The individual historian, like Lévi-Strauss's *bricoleur*,[59] constructs composite genealogies, like that reproduced in Fig. I, to link individual descent groups to one or another of the state structures, portraying these links as 'marriages' between male political titles and female descent groups. An overriding aetiological genealogy ties recognized Mbundu subgroups to each other and relates the Mbundu as a whole to some of their neighbours (see Fig. III).

The *malunda* narrative episodes, the second form in which the Imbangala recite their history, are appendages to the names of both the political titles and the descent groups given in the genealogies.[60] The oral historian may, after reciting a genealogy, tell in his own words as few or as many as he chooses of a fairly standardized set of narrative episodes connected with each name in the *musendo*. He draws on a relatively small set of prose expositions to make a defined number of points about the origins, rights, or responsibilities of the titles or lineages involved. Each *lunda* accounts for a recognized duty or privilege, and the finiteness and standardization of the set of *malunda* associated with each title derive from the limited number of formal relationships which most positions maintain with lineages or with other titles.

[58] Fig. III shows the main political structures recognized by the Mbundu as circles in the lower half of the diagram.

[59] Claude Lévi-Strauss (1966), pp. 16–36.

[60] The historical *malunda* constitute a subset of a much larger body of non-historical but similarly structured prose compositions (animal tales, stories dealing with domestic themes, etc.). Chatelain (1894) has published a number of the Mbundu *malunda* in Kimbundu with English translations.

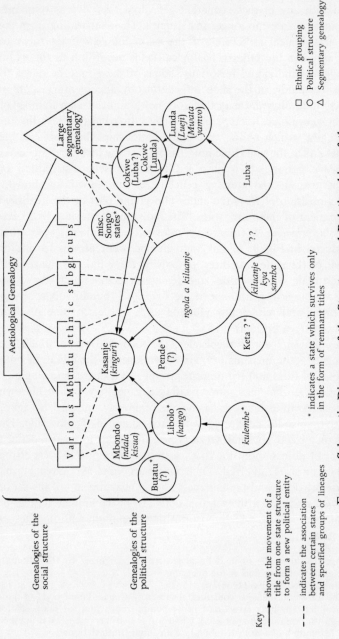

FIG. III. Schematic Diagram of the Structure and Relationships of the Mbundu Historical Genealogies

Historians apparently use similar narrative episodes consistently to make the same points about titles and descent groups over long periods of time. This conclusion stems from comparing variants collected from the seventeenth to the twentieth centuries of some of the best-known *malunda*. Individual historians may, however, employ strikingly diverse images, metaphors, clichés, or plots as they apply their creative skills to make their performances works of aesthetic as well as historical value. The resulting flexibility of detail in variant *malunda* contrasts markedly with the apparent stability of the central point of each episode which, in cases which can be verified, has remained constant through decades and, in some cases, centuries. In all known cases where documentary or eye-witness recollections of an event may be compared with later narrative episodes dealing with the same occurrence, the *malunda* accurately preserve a nucleus of historical fact even while the historians who recite the episode surround it with fictional artistic elaboration.[61] Since the context of an authentic historical performance[62] usually establishes the historian's purpose in selecting given episodes to include in his narrative (e.g. to vindicate lineage rights to a title, to establish a precedent, to instruct, to honour a title-holder present, and so on), and since the historical nucleus of the chosen narrative episode usually pertains directly to the historian's aims, analysis of the performance allows the determination (at least at the level of a workable first approximation) of the historical significance of most narrative episodes. The probabilities of accuracy become fairly high when a number of variants of the same *lunda* may be compared to identify the stable part which recurs in all instances.

The metaphors, the symbols, even the plot which historians choose to illuminate the significance of each *lunda* to their listeners belong

---

[61] I refer here to the seventeenth-century near-eye-witness account recorded in Cavazzi (1965) and to nineteenth- and twentieth-century *malunda* describing the same events; additional confirmation comes from an analysis of personal recollections and written eyewitness accounts of mid-nineteenth-century wars which were beginning to be recounted in the form of *malunda* in the 1960s. The stable nucleus of historical fact in an Mbundu *lunda* may be compared to the 'core clichés' of Xhosa *intsomi* analysed by Harold Scheub (1975). The origin of the idea of a stable nucleus goes back to Lévi-Strauss; cf. J. S. Boston (1969), p. 36.

[62] An 'authentic historical performance' by definition arises only from the normal activities of people in the society, usually in connection with legal disputes or other occasions calling into question the formal relationships between titles and/or descent groups. Such circumstances occur with sharply diminished frequency in modern Angola, and this circumstance accounts for the atrophied condition of the modern traditions.

to the rich and complex fund of Mbundu artistic and intellectual themes rather than to history.[63] The artistic and intellectual level of the *malunda* may provide a fertile field for the sort of structuralist analysis which has proved valuable in penetrating the intellectual processes and cosmologies of non-literate peoples the world over, but the fact that Imbangala historical narratives exhibit this dimension at one level does not eliminate their value as historical sources at another.[64] Comparison of the *malunda* with documentary sources demonstrates empirically that historical content is present, and the internal logic of a historical performance, which relates *malunda* to specific titles and lineages and to a resticted range of historical points, makes it possible to distinguish the less obviously historical content, which the individual historian may add on his own initiative, from the stable historical skeleton of the narrative episode.[65] The Western critic, by distinguishing carefully between the historical nucleus and the artistic embroidery, may confidently use the *malunda* as sources for the limited range of topics with which this study deals.[66]

The *malunda* may be further sub-divided into political or lineage episodes according to the type of name or title with which they are associated. Those attached to the political genealogies generally describe circumstances surrounding the creation of the titles and establish the right of their descent group 'owners' to control them. Other *malunda* connected with the same title may relate events believed to account for its formal relationships to other political positions. They may also deal with the origin of authority emblems connected with the title, spell out its magical powers, or explain ritual proscriptions affecting its occupants. Narrative episodes appended to

[63] For an analysis of similarly complex symbolic systems of the related Ndembu of north-western Zambia, see Victor Turner (1967).

[64] I concur with the analogy offered by Vansina (1971b), p. 455, where he argues that the highly symbolic overtones of conventional American school-text versions of the story of the *Mayflower* do not destroy its historical content; the symbolism merely disguises the history. But for more sceptical opinions, see Beidelman (1970) and Wyatt McGaffey (1970); both of the latter, it seems to me, demand that 'history' should attain a higher degree of probability (approaching virtual certainty) about the past than many modern historians would consider necessary.

[65] The relatively limited fieldwork on which this study is based did not permit me to study systematically the important subject of Mbundu symbolism. Analysis of the historical significance of the artistic dimension of the *malunda* remains a unexplored field of great potential importance, hence my qualification on the meaning of the artistic aspects of the *malunda* as 'less obviously' historical.

[66] Feierman (1974) contains the most sophisticated attempt to elaborate the historical content of similar materials known to me.

lineage genealogies almost always justify the fission of a new lineage from its parent descent group, trace the route which members of the 'nephew' lineage followed to reach their current home, and relate the conditions under which the group received rights to occupy its present lands.[67] Other *malunda* spell out the descent group's relations with its neighbours, defend its claim to control political titles and so on. The obvious functional importance of the narrative episodes in legitimizing present lineage or title rights does not obviate the fact that most, if not all, current relationships rest on historical precedents which may—with care—be identified through analysis of the *malunda*. The present, as the Imbangala say, is like the bones of an ancestor, and the analogy between historical reconstruction based on Imbangala narrative episodes and palaeo-zoologists' techniques of physiological reconstruction may be apt.

It is important to recognize that each narrative episode may be told entirely independently of all others. All properly performed *malunda* have their own complete plot, a beginning and an ending, and do not depend on other episodes for their meaning or their artistic integrity. The Imbangala historian may recite in sequence any number of *malunda* bearing on a given title, however, and if he is skilful he may succeed in weaving together plots, themes, and imagery which transcend the individual episodes and link the discrete elements of his performance into a much longer, integrated historical and aesthetic composition. But the Western historian would be ill-advised to mistake the plot line constructed by the performer for evidence of consistent historical development running through the entire string of narrative episodes. The *malunda* selected for any performance depend in part on its context rather than on the logic of the historical events, and no two performances are likely to include the same set of narrative episodes. It follows that these longer performances are not subject to analysis which depends in any way on connecting the implications of one *lunda* to those of another in any direct sense; rather, the historical content of each episode must derive from its own internal logic. Clearly, there can be no chronology, even relative, based on the order in which episodes may be told. It is often possible, on the other hand, to find indirect

---

[67] The structure of these traditions resembles that of lineage traditions discussed—and dismissed as history—by McGaffey (1970), *passim* but esp. pp. 18ff. The stability of Mbundu lineage genealogies and the greater coherence of Mbundu descent groups render Imbangala *malunda* less stereotyped and give them considerably greater value as history than the Kongo traditions described by McGaffey.

indications of ths historical sequences of the events described by the episodes. If, for example, the *malunda* detail the stages in a physical movement from one geographical location to another, placing the episodes along a straight line connecting the two points may approximate fairly well the order in which the actual events occurred.

The interpretation of Imbangala historical *malunda* obviously requires that the historian should use all available external sources which may help him to distinguish fact from fiction. Such sources include words, especially proper names and toponyms, terms for authority symbols connected with the titles and lineages of the genealogies, and other technical terms which may indicate historical processes of diffusion or population movements across known language or dialect barriers. Analysis of ethnographic evidence, especially authority symbols or practices closely identified with distinct groups of people, can provide similar assistance. Since both these types of evidence exist only in the present and are often difficult to establish directly for the past (except for archaeological recovery of material objects), their application to the traditions dealing with the sixteenth or seventeenth century imposes an obligation to determine that language boundaries have not shifted in the mean time or that social and belief systems have not changed significantly.[68] The usual rule that 'the absence of evidence of change allows the historian to assume past stability' seems less and less acceptable in the light of growing evidence, to which the Mbundu contribute, that major shifts can and do take place even in those aspects of African life once thought to be most resistant to change. I have tried to rest my analysis on such stability of social structure and language only when positive evidence indicates the probability of no significant change.

Under the circumstances, documentary sources become crucial adjuncts to the use of the non-written sources described in the preceding paragraphs. It is the availability of sufficient written material for sixteenth- and seventeenth-century Angola which, in the final analysis, makes it possible to attempt to reconstruct Mbundu political history for the period. I have already justified use of Imbangala *musendo* and *malunda* on the grounds that early documentary materials confirm both the absence of significant change in their content over three centuries or more and the close correspondence of the traditions to events described by eye-witnesses. I have made the use of ethnographic and linguistic evidence dependent on the

[68] Useful introductions include Daniel F. McCall (1964) and Vansina (1968 and 1970).

possibility of establishing, largely by documentary methods, that the necessary condition of stability holds. Written records for the Mbundu are relatively abundant and accessible owing to the six-teenth- and seventeenth-century activities of the Portuguese govern-ment, Dutch trading companies, and missionaries from several European countries (primarily Italy) in the area.[69] Fortunately for modern knowledge about Mbundu history, a few of these Europeans took an active interest in things African and wrote accounts giving their impressions of Mbundu traditions as they existed in the seventeenth century. It is important to emphasize the distinction between Mbundu histories as they were then told and seventeenth-century European perceptions of them, since few writers understood much of what they heard. Comparison of the written records with modern oral and ethnographic evidence shows that the documentary sources are only slightly less encrusted with the personality of their authors than are the *malunda* with the artistry of individual Mbundu historians. The documents are also comparable to the oral traditions in that they provide nearly as selective a view of seventeenth-century reality as do the genealogies.[70] Written and unwritten sources over-lap often enough to establish a complementary basis for mutual criticism, but they also treat completely different aspects of events sufficiently frequently to illuminate a relatively broad range of Mbundu political history. The documents, for example, typically describe battles against Mbundu title-holders whose origins and significance in African terms may be deduced from the traditions.

This outline of the forms and characteristics of the sources for early Mbundu political history provides the background necessary for an explicit statement of the methodology which lies behind the following historical reconstruction. The major technical difficulties hinge on finding a rationale for (a) projecting facts observed in the nineteenth and twentieth centuries (word lists, ethnographic data, but also oral traditions) back over three centuries in time, (b) projecting eastward in space the seventeenth-century documentary evidence which deals primarily with the westernmost parts of the

---

[69] In addition to Cavazzi (1965), the account of António de Oliveira de Cadornega (1940–2) provides valuable information. Nearly all known docu-ments for the years before 1600 and many of those between 1600 and 1655 are published in António Brásio (1952–71).

[70] Cf. G. I. Jones (1963), p. 391, who states that European documents for the Niger Delta region 'may be more legendary in character than the African and subject to just the same processes of compression and the same dependence on "structural time"'.

Mbundu region, and (c) generalizing to the entire Mbundu area from field data collected mainly among the Imbangala subgroup of the Mbundu. Recognizing that all history is a matter of probabilities rather than of certainty and acknowledging that the probabilities in this case may not approach the level attainable in other times and places, the qualities of the available data seem to vindicate drawing conclusions about the institutional history of the Mbundu since (a) the major Mbundu social, political, and intellectual systems cover the entire region, (b) like all such structures, they are tightly integrated with one another so that knowledge of the existence of one aspect of the culture in one place allows us to infer a great deal about other related aspects of the culture in other places, and (c) changes in one part of the culture may be expected to induce changes in others. If, therefore, an institution is known in some detail for the nineteenth or twentieth century and parts of it are visible near the coast in the seventeenth-century documents, the historian may proceed as if the entire structure existed elsewhere during the earlier period.[71] I should not exceed the limitations of this method if I deal only with the history of political and social institutions based on oral traditions, incorporating other aspects of Mbundu history, the behaviour of individuals, and the like, when documentary sources make them accessible.

The Perspective

An initial statement of the perspective adopted for this study may make its argument more readily intelligible. I am attempting to assume the point of view of a literate outside observer standing somewhere near the centre of Mbundu territory, watching on the one hand political developments which occur without visible external influence among the people living nearby, and observing on the other a series of changes stimulated by contacts between the Mbundu and other people who live around them. The study thus describes changes through time in a single relatively small region and shows its political contacts with neighbouring areas in order to assess how external influences affect and are in turn affected by a basically continuous process of local historical evolution. It rejects, therefore, the approach of following migrating conquerors across the landscape and holds that relatively little large-scale demographic change has taken place within the discernible past, that the Mbundu of today

---

[71] Arguments referred to as those of 'inference' and 'extrapolation' in Vansina (1968), pp. 106–8.

are for the most part biological descendants of sixteenth-century Mbundu, and that this sort of demographic continuity extends back to the time of the introduction of agriculture and perhaps before. State-formation seems to result more from the diffusion of ideas, institutions, authority symbols, and the like than from mass movements of people. This approach certainly conforms to our present understanding of more recent periods in African history where the examples of long-distance movements of large numbers of people are well known only because of their rarity.[72] No obvious reasons suggest that such migrations should have been less rare in the nineteenth century than in the sixteenth or the fourteenth centuries.

The evidence for the Mbundu shows an institutional history of the origin and diffusion not of 'states' but of principles of political organization. These may be traced via the genealogies describing the relationships between titles based on them and through surviving distributions of the emblems connected with each form of authority. The formation of an Mbundu state thus represents less a movement of people than the reorganization of an existing population into new groupings, established according to new sets of symbols of group unity, and related to one another on the basis of the pattern followed by the new authority emblem as it diffuses. The major historical problem involves the construction of a reliable sequence for the multiplicity of authority symbols now present among the Mbundu as evidence of their highly complex political history. Diffusion processes are handled as individual items moving over a limited area and thus avoid the worst pitfalls of the *Kulturkreise* school and its world-wide diffusions of 'complexes' of culture traits. My handling of the ethnographic evidence tries to avoid immutable 'survivals'

---

[72] Only the *mfecane* comes to mind as a documented example of the kind of mass migration customarily posited for early African state-formation; more subtle and gradual population movements have occurred among such groups as the West African Jula, the Fang of Gabon, the Cokwe in Angola, and others, all without the formation of strong centralized states. Jan Vansina (1969), pp. 20–44, outlines such a diffusion of an authority symbol (the *nkobi*), again without attendant large-scale migration. More extensive population movements can and do take place where technology allows people to fill an empty ecological niche; the movement of herders into areas occupied only by agriculturalists constitutes the most important instance of this phenomenon in Africa. One documented migration explicable in these terms is that of the Cokwe; Joseph C. Miller (1970). Clearly, the relative permanence of population stocks and the relative ease with which ideas and institutions spread has been more common. The Alur and Anuak examples (p. 2, n. 3 above) may be typical, allowing for minor movements of individuals (not groups) in all times and places.

in favour of 'retentions'[73] which may have undergone considerable modification in the course of the centuries. Modern Mbundu culture may, in short, be read as a congeries of independent (though integrated) symbols, words, traditions, institutions, and practices which come from varying times in the past. In so far as documents and logic can reveal the sequence of their appearance as parts of an evolving Mbundu culture, the historian may suggest hypotheses which explain how and why people adopted them. Such must pass for the early political history of the Mbundu.

[73] A term suggested by Jan Vansina; personal communication.

CHAPTER II

The Setting

HISTORIANS HAVE recently begun to recognize the importance of the environment—in both the geographical and social senses—for understanding the process of state-formation in Africa. The early political history of the Mbundu becomes fully understandable only in terms of its geographical setting of mountains, rivers, economic resources, crops, and climate, and in terms of the general social and intellectual background of their culture. Since few aspects of the physical geography of Mbundu territory have changed since the sixteenth century, no significant technical problems cloud the following outline of the main ecological influences on Mbundu political history. The human geography of the sixteenth-century Mbundu is somewhat less certain, not only because the boundaries of the main Mbundu ethno-linguistic subgroupings have changed since then but also because even modern ethnic distinctions within the Mbundu region are not well understood. Rather less probabilistic, for reasons of documentation discussed in Chapter I, is the review of selected aspects of early Mbundu social structure which concludes this chapter and completes the review of background materials necessary to evaluate the earliest known Mbundu states.

Physical Environment

The general contours of Angolan geography conform to the broad pattern of the southern half of the African continent which geographers liken to a great inverted saucer: a low and narrow strip of sandy land separates the Atlantic in the west from ranges of hills which rise in terraces towards a high interior plateau in the east. This basic relief pattern is less distinct in the north near the mouth of the Congo (or Zaïre) river, where the interior elevations are lower but it becomes very well marked towards the south where the highlands attain altitudes well in excess of 6,000 feet, sometimes rising in abrupt escarpments above the coastal plains. Numerous rivers run generally from east to west, draining the mountain slopes in shallow, rocky beds which do not widen to navigable dimensions until they approach very near the coast. Even the largest rivers—the

Congo, the Kwanza, and the Kunene—allow ocean navigation to penetrate for only 100 miles or less, and all but the Congo have only short reaches of open water in the interior. The rivers of the northern interior tend to flow east and north towards the main tributaries of the Congo, while those in the south feed the upper Kwanza, the Kubango–Okavango, and the Zambezi systems. The Kwango is the main northward-flowing tributary of the Congo in Mbundu territory.

Rainfall decreases from north to south, ranging from generally reliable, though seasonal, rains near the Congo river to desert conditions as one approaches the lower Kunene. It also moderates from east to west owing to the prevailing easterly wind patterns. Most precipitation in the interior comes from the east during the summer months, from September to April in the north but with a markedly shorter rainy period towards the south. The entire coastal lowland is significantly drier than the highlands behind since prevailing onshore winds blow cool air from the cold Benguela current from southern Africa almost as far north as the mouth of the Congo. This air warms and dries as it passes over the land and drops almost no precipitation except where the windward slopes of the mountains force these winds aloft. A generally cloudless and pleasant dry season in the interior highlands contrasts with a cool, humid, and cloudy (but rainless) winter known as *cacimbo* along most of the coast.[1]

Sixteenth-century Mbundu demography corresponded roughly to the hydrography of north-western Angola. Ethno-linguistic boundaries tended to follow major watersheds except in the west where the mountains east of Luanda island provided a natural boundary separating the Mbundu in the highlands from Kongo in the meteorologically and geographically distinct lowlands.[2] Otherwise, the Mbundu were generally confined to the region drained by the Kwanza river. The most important northern tributary of the Kwanza, the Lukala, flows down through a plateau sloping upward from elevations of around 3,000 feet on its western tongue along the middle reaches of the river to over 4,000 feet in what was in 1969 eastern Malanje district. The northern boundaries of the Mbundu, which divide them from the Kongo, follow the hilly highlands which

[1] See F. Mouta and H. O'Donnell (1933), D. S. Whittlesley (1924), and Domingos H. G. Gouveia (1956).
[2] This corrects the general but apparently erroneous impression that Mbundu territories extended to the ocean; Joseph C. Miller (1972b) and remarks following.

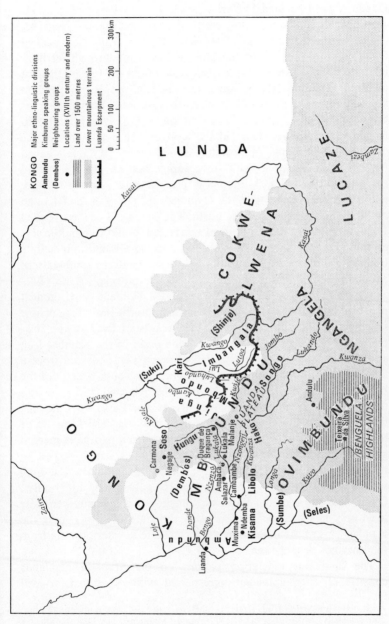

MAP I. Geography of the Mbundu and their Neighbors (Modern)

rim this plateau around the headwaters of the Nzenza (Bengo) and Dande rivers (the area known later as the 'Dembos') up to their crest near the modern Portuguese towns of Carmona and Negage.

The southern tributaries of the Kwanza flow from the so-called Ovimbundu highlands, or the Benguela plateau, through territory inhabited by the Mbundu at least as far south as the Longa, the first major river south of the Kwanza. The highland people who lived on the watershed to the south and south-west were known later as Ovimbundu[3] and differed somewhat more from the Mbundu in language and culture than did the Kongo. The inhabitants of the dry coastal lowlands immediately south of the Kwanza—called Kisama as far as the lower Longa, Sumbe between the Longa and the Kuvo, and Seles, Mundombe, etc., beyond—appear to have had more in common with the Ovimbundu than with their Kongo or Mbundu neighbours to the north. The occupants of the so-called Luanda Plateau, the area drained by the Kwije and Luhando rivers east of the upper Kwanza, also belonged to the Mbundu; no definite boundary demarcated their south-eastern limit and the south-eastern Mbundu shaded gradually into Cokwe and Ngangela.

The major exception to the generally highland environment occupied by the Mbundu occurred in the far north-east where people sharing the same ethno-linguistic characteristics lived in the relatively low (1,200 to 2,000 feet) and wide basin of the Kambo, Lui, and Kwango rivers. A nearly vertical escarpment, varying from a few hundred to over 2,000 feet in height, runs south-west from the headwaters of the Kwale to beyond the Kwango and separates these lowlands, known more recently as the Baixa de Cassanje, from the much higher elevations just to the west. The Mbundu of the northern parts of the Baixa de Cassanje seem to have merged gradually into Kongo, while those along the Kwango tended to resemble the Cokwe/Lwena and Lunda who inhabited the high savannas which extend east from that river for nearly 1,000 miles. Other than those of the Baixa de Cassanje, the Mbundu generally lived only in the higher elevations of the plateaus surrounding the Kwanza east of the mountains which separate its interior basin from the lowlands near the sea.

The dominant vegetation pattern on the Mbundu highlands consists of open grassland interspersed with occasional wooded

---

[3] For the purposes of this study, the Mbundu are the people under examination generally, and they speak the Kimbundu language. The Ovimbundu live on the Benguela plateau and speak the Umbundu language.

savanna, now restricted to a few areas but probably more extensive in the sixteenth century before increased hunting with fire in recent years destroyed many trees. Other exceptions to the prevalent grassland environment include rain and cloud condensation forests covering the mountains along the western edge of the Luanda plateau, patches of gallery forests (*mishito*, singular *mushito*) along the lower courses of the larger rivers, and patches of forest on the escarpment of the Baixa de Cassanje.[4] Generally moderate amounts of rain, varying from 36 inches per year in the west up to 55 inches annually near the Kwango, prevent the growth of heavier vegetation elsewhere. The rains come in an extremely uneven seasonal pattern— light and irregular from September or October to December, then a short and highly variable dry spell, with the heaviest precipitation following in February and March—and consequently had an important influence on human economic activity.[5]

Although little research has illuminated sixteenth-century Mbundu agricultural techniques, it is clear that most people farmed and it is probable that they mainly grew varieties of millets and sorghum. In the absence of a drought-resistant staple crop, such as manioc,[6] successful agriculture depended on taking maximum advantage of the rainy portion of the year to grow sufficient food to last through the dry months from May to September, when no rain falls in most years (although one or two storms occasionally punctuate the dry season), and the first part of the ensuing growing season. The Mbundu supplemented these dietary staples with wild vegetables and fruits, and they valued especially the plants found in the *mushito* forests along the rivers. For these reasons, and because the unavailability of a dry land crop such as manioc restricted the amount of land suitable for growing food to somewhat less than the Mbundu farm today, they tended to settle in the lower and moister areas, especially river bottoms and mountain valleys where ground moisture evaporated less quickly than it did along the ridges.[7] To these

---

[4] John Gossweiler (1939); E. K. Airy Shaw (1947) has summarized Gossweiler in English.

[5] Angola, Serviços Meteorológicos (1955) contains maps showing recent rainfall and temperature patterns for the region; paleoclimatological studies do not exist.

[6] The Mbundu north of the Kwanza today depend on manioc as their main agricultural ataple, but all varieties descend from plants (mainly *manihot utilissima*) imported from Brazil in the seventeenth century; José Redinha (1968), pp. 96–7.

[7] Even with manioc, farming techniques still are based on a strategy of maximal use of ground moisture; reports in the archive of the Missão de

vegetable foods, the Mbundu added wild game, which individuals pursued with bows, arrows, and traps throughout the year and which large groups of men hunted with fire towards the end of each dry season. The dry months also provided opportunities for fishing while lowered water levels in the rivers confined fish to a few accessible pools. There is no reason not to assume that most Mbundu tended chickens, goats, and pehaps some sheep; cattle probably grazed only in the high elevations south of the Kwanza since tsetse fly made herding unreliable elsewhere.

The Mbundu had a form of iron-age technology based mainly on local supplies of ore. Ore deposits were found both north of the Kwanza in the Nzongeji river valley and south of the river in the hills which ascended toward the Benguela plateau. Some iron may have reached the eastern Mbundu from the Cokwe/Lwena east of the Kwango,[8] and the southern Mbundu doubtless had access to supplies of iron lying in Ovimbundu territory near Andulo and the modern town of Teixeira da Silva.[9] Salt, which seems to have been second only to iron in its importance for iron-age African societies,[10] came both from the sea and from saline marshes scattered through the interior. One source of maritime salt, the Kakwako lagoons just north-east of Luanda island, was well developed by the sixteenth century, but it lay within the area of Kongo suzerainty and available evidence does not show whether its production went north to Kongo or east up the Bengo/Nzenza to the Mbundu.[11] The Mbundu had a more likely supply of salt south of the Kwanza in Kisama; the first Portuguese to travel there reported that the Mbundu traded this salt throughout much of the interior.[12] Salt also came from marshes

[8] Testimony of Mwa Ndonje.

[9] Near the sources of the Kuvo river (the modern town of Teixeira da Silva) and along the left-bank tributaries of the upper Kwanza near Andulo; David M. Abshire and Michael A. Samuels (1969), p. 300.

[10] Brian M. Fagan (1969) emphasizes the early importance of salt and iron in Rhodesia. It seems fair to generalize his hypothesis to the Mbundu in the light of the data presented in the succeeding chapters of this study.

[11] The appearance of a trade route running up the Bengo based on slave exports by the second half of the sixteenth century suggests that the Kongo on the coast may have had earlier contacts with the Mbundu who lived up-river; Miller (1971).

[12] Antonio Mendes to Padre Geral, 9 May 1563 (B.N.R.J., 1–5, 2, 38); Brásio (1952–71), ii, 495–512; also AA, sér. 2, xvii, nos. 67–70 (1960),

Inquéritos Agricolas de Angola in Luanda. Testimony of Sousa Calunga, 27 July 1969, for the Baixa de Cassange area. José Redinha (1958), p. 228, confirms that early villages in Angola had been concentrated along the river valleys since neolithic times.

located somewhat farther east in Libolo, and the Mbundu were using this salt as a medium of exchange on both sides of the Kwanza as late as the end of the eighteenth century.[13] The Baixa de Cassanje contained two important centres of salt production. The Lutoa, a tributary of the middle Lui, supplied salt to many of the eastern Mbundu and to the Cokwe/Lwena to the south-east; the Kihongwa river, an affluent of the Luhanda, fed extensive salt marshes along its lower course, and residents of that area exported their production to the northern Mbundu and even to the eastern Kongo in the sixteenth century.[14] These sources of salt and iron probably formed the nodes of a complex set of regional trading networks which brought the Mbundu into contact with one another and with their neighbours on a regular basis. Certainly by the seventeenth century, copper from Katanga and palm cloth from the forested regions to the north were reaching the Mbundu, and there is no reason to doubt that other similarly wide-ranging economic contacts had developed long before the arrival of European traders on the coast.[15]

Ethno-linguistic Subdivisions in the Sixteenth Century
The outlines of sixteenth-century Mbundu ethno-linguistic sub-groupings are even less distinct than the nature of early economic activities in the Kwanza valley. Murdock's judgement, delivered in the late 1950s, that the Mbundu were 'among the least adequately described [people] in the entire African continent'[16] remains true today for the present characteristics of the people but applies with special force to earlier centuries as well, since the intimate contacts of some Mbundu with literate observers since before 1600 generally failed to provide meaningful ethnographic data. Linguistic studies on their language, Kimbundu, research on Mbundu material culture, and information on their social and political institutions remains at a lamentably low level despite the intermittent efforts of amateur and professional Portuguese ethnographers over the last three centuries.[17] As a result, neither the external boundaries of the

[13] R. J. da Cunha Mattos (1963), p. 317.
[14] Miller (1973a) provides evidence for this trade route.
[15] In general, see David Birmingham (1970) and Jan Vansina (1962c).
[16] Murdock (1959), p. 292.
[17] The first recorded ethnographic data on the Mbundu appeared in the correspondence of the Jesuit missionaries who went to Angola in the 1560s;

14–27. António Leite de Magalhães (1924), map and p. 5, gave the exact location as near Ndemba, some 40 kilometres south-west of Muxima by road.

Mbundu nor variations within the Mbundu area are well known. My field research has clarified some aspects of Mbundu ethnography, especially that of the people living in the southern Baixa de Cassanje, and has suggested the need for major revisions in conventional attitudes toward much of the remainder.

Most ethnographic classification schemes distinguish the entire Mbundu group of peoples only from such equally gross categories as the Kongo to the north, the Cokwe/Lwena in the east, and various Ovimbundu groups to the south. These distinctions rest primarily on linguistic differences since linguists have been able to identify Kikongo, Kicokwe, and Umbundu as separate languages from Kimbundu, although Kikongo and Kimbundu seem more closely related than any of the others.[18] Languages exhibiting features of both Kikongo and Kimbundu (such as Hungu, Ndembu, and Soso) blur the hypothetical dividing line between these two groups.[19] Kimbundu dialects of a similarly transitional nature (Shinje and Minungo) may bridge the gap between the eastern Mbundu and the neighbouring Cokwe/Lwena in the same way.[20] An almost total absence of precise information on the Kimbundu dialects spoken south of the Kwanza obscures the nature of the linguistic border there, but there are some indications that it lies near the Longa river since the Libolo variety of Kimbundu becomes unintelligible south of that line.[21] According to modern linguistic evidence, then, the western Kimbundu-speakers live roughly between the Longa

[18] Malcolm Guthrie (1967); Kikongo is his Zone H, Group 1; Kimbundu is Zone H, Group 2. The Umbundu languages are in Zone R, Group 1; Cokwe/Lwena falls in Zone L. In his later *Comparative Bantu* (1967-72), iii, Guthrie indicates his uncertainties about the classification he has adopted for the subgroups of the Kimbundu language group. His caution appears well-advised in the light of my data.

[19] Guy Atkins (1954, 1955).

[20] Based on comparison of 200-word basic vocabularies (D. H. Hymes (1960)) of Mbangala, Shinje, Minungo, Cokwe (western), Songo, and Mbondo.

[21] I know of no Kisama word-list recorded before the twentieth century; see Mattenklodt (1944), pp. 106-7, for the 1920s. A short 32-word vocabulary (including 10 numbers) is the only known information on the Libolo languages ('Libolo, Seles, Novo Redondo, Benguela Velha, Amboim, Quibala, and Gango'); Leite de Magalhães (1924), pp. 55-7 (reprinted in José Ribeiro da Cruz (1940), pp. 166-7). For the linguistic boundary along the upper Longa, Paes Brandão (1904), p. 226, and António Miranda Magalhães (1922), p. 11. Redinha did not specify the sources on which he based his conclusions.

see Gastão Sousa Dias (1934). Modern ethnographic descriptions still rely basically on such nineteenth-century compilations as José Joaquim Lopes de Lima (1846) and José de Oliveira Ferreira Diniz (1918).

river in the south and the Bengo/Nzenza in the north; to the east, their limits run from approximately the Luhando river in the south to the lower Kambo in the north.

These external boundaries appear to have changed significantly since the sixteenth century only in the west, where the Kimbundu language area now extends to the Atlantic ocean south of the Bengo near the city of Luanda and to the region of Kisama beyond the Kwanza river.[22] A variety of evidence suggests that this was a relatively recent development since speakers of Kikongo lived near Luanda during the sixteenth century; the language of the region would have changed after Europeans brought large numbers of Kimbundu-speaking slaves to the coastal plain during the seventeenth century and after.[23] The inhabitants of Kisama still spoke a variety of Umbundu as recently as the latter part of the eighteenth century[24] before epidemics of sleeping sickness at the beginning of the present century sharply reduced the original Kisama population[25] and probably contributed to linguistic change through repopulation by speakers of Kimbundu. The southern boundaries of the Mbundu, although greatly disturbed by political upheavals during the seventeenth century, do not seem to have moved. Changes in the north brought by southward expansion of the Kongo kingdom seem to have been largely complete by the sixteenth century and probably contributed to the formation of such currently transitional groups as the Ndembu and the Hungu.[26]

More extensive changes seem to have affected the internal subdivisions of the Mbundu, since their aetiological tradition, which may be presumed to reflect historic rather than modern divisions within the group, does not correspond well to the present distribution of dialects and lineages.[27] In general, wider gulfs divided Mbundu from one another than is the case today. In terms of language, for example, two dialects of recent origin, an eastern and a western one, have incorporated a number of Portuguese words and are tending

[22] See José Redinha (1961).
[23] Miller (1972b).
[24] Bernardo Maria de Cannecattim (1854), p. xv.
[25] Heintze (1970), p. 170. Birmingham (1966), p. 145, implicitly confirms that this linguistic change probably began somewhat earlier, since he notes that Kisama had become a refuge for (presumably Kimbundu-speaking) slaves escaping from Luanda by the late eighteenth century.
[26] For the Kongo kingdom, with which I do not intend to deal here, see Vansina (1966a), pp. 38–40, and Georges Balandier (1969), chapter I.
[27] Analysed in my unpublished dissertation 'Kings and Kinsmen' (1972), chapter III.

to replace some of the older dialects. The western variant, centered in Luanda, has resulted from the modern congregation of Mbundu and other Africans from all parts of Angola in the city. They have begun to identify themselves as 'Akwaluanda' or 'Ambundu' to distinguish themselves and their language from their rural relatives.[28] The eastern pan-Kimbundu dialect, known as Ambakista, originated in the growth of a Luso–Mbundu community of traders near the Portuguese *presídio* of Ambaca on the middle Lukala during the seventeenth and eighteenth centuries; their Portuguese-influenced dialect spread as a trade language throughout much of the eastern Mbundu area during the nineteenth century. Both these dialects now serve as Kimbundu *linguae francae* and a pan-Mbundu life-style with a pseudo-Portuguese component had in 1969–70 begun to emerge as a result of shared experiences in the cities of Luanda and Malanje, the conscription of young men from every corner of the Mbundu region into the armed forces, and the spread of literate education. The sense of a common 'Mbundu' identity, publicized by the writings of a small community of Luso-Mbundu intellectuals in Luanda,[29] is of relatively recent provenance and should not be allowed to contribute to the false assumption that a similar unity prevailed in the past.[30]

Even the recent strong influences working towards the creation of a single homogenized Mbundu language and culture have not erased the local diversity surviving as evidence of earlier distinctions which the Mbundu observed among themselves. Outlying Mbundu groups have at least as much in common with their nearest non-Mbundu neighbours as they share with distant Kimbundu-speakers.[31] Despite the paucity of solid ethnographic data, available evidence shows that some of the most basic features of Mbundu culture and society have always occurred in non-congruent distributions which overlap with other people on all sides. These facts make it difficult to identify any deep-running ethnic divisions in western Angola.

[28] By far the most thorough sociological study of the African population of Luanda is Ramiro Ladeiro Monteiro (1973).

[29] Douglas Wheeler, in Wheeler and René Pélissier (1971), chapter IV, has described the intellectual aspect of this development.

[30] It is well known that the first documentary mentions of the Mbundu as a named group come from the Kongo. This suggests that the term originated as a collective referent used by outsiders.

[31] I have been unable to locate, for example, western Kimbundu-speakers who can understand the Mbundu dialect of eastern Kimbundu; Cokwe-speakers find Mbangala almosts as easy to discern as Mbundu born and raised in Luanda.

The Mbundu aetiological tradition outlines the historic distinctions which sixteenth-century Mbundu drew among themselves. The major groups included the Lenge, the Ndongo (a subgrouping and not simply an alternative collective name for all Mbundu as most authorities have claimed), the Songo, the Mbondo, the Pende, the Hungu, and the Libolo. According to the professional Imbangala historians, the westernmost Mbundu, the Lenge, lived in the mountains between the Nzenza (or Bengo) and Kwanza rivers. Their lands included the iron-workings located in the Nzongeji river valley. The Ndongo seem originally to have occupied only the highlands which form the upper drainage basin of the Lukala river and the Wamba. The northernmost Mbundu, the Hungu, lived on the south bank of the Kwale river as far east as the Kwango. The so-called Pende had one of the largest territorial distributions of any of the ancient Mbundu subgroups, extending all over the northern Luanda plateau east from the Lenge to the entire Baixa de Cassanje. The Songo lived beyond the Kwije river on the southern part of the plateau, reaching from the rim of the Baixa de Cassanje to the sources of the Luhando. The Libolo included a variety of little-known people on the south side of the Kwanza and may perhaps have been divided into the Libolo proper (west of the Luhinga river) and the Hako (east of the Luhinga).

Without anticipating the political history to follow, it may be worth while briefly to trace subsequent changes in this very early ethno-linguistic pattern, probably dating to some time before the fifteenth century. The Hungu absorbed infusions of Kongo culture as the Kongo kingdom expanded east and south and as such Kongo-related groups as the Suku formed east across the Kwango.[32] Influences from Libolo penetrated north across the Kwanza and helped to create a new Mbondo ethno-linguistic subgroup from Pende who lived on the high plateau just west of the Baixa de Cassanje. Then a series of Ndongo ideas and institutions from the north moved toward the Kwanza, absorbing some of the original Pende population along the lower Lukala, causing the Lenge to lose their distinctive identity almost completely, and overspreading some

[32] For the Suku, etc., see Vansina (1966a), pp. 203–4. This would have taken place before the sixteenth century, since the *mani* Kongo was already distinguishing himself as 'lord' of the Suku (among others) by the 1530s. This title made an implicit contrast with the position of 'king' which he claimed within the integral Kongo provinces that he ruled directly. See Letter from Rei do Congo, 12 February 1539 (A.N.T.T., Corpo Cronológico, I–64–25); Brásio (1952–71), ii. 70–2.

northern Libolo areas as well. All these changes occurred before the arrival of Europeans.

The seventeenth and eighteenth centuries witnessed further shifts in the identity and location of Mbundu ethnic subgroupings. These may be mentioned here briefly only to connect the earlier patterns to the present distribution of the Mbundu peoples. The western Lenge/Ndongo came under direct Portuguese administration during the 1620s, thus beginning the process of homogenization and assimilation which culminated in the emergence of the Ambakistas in the nineteenth century. The remaining Ndongo, who lived mainly beyond the upper Lukala, had achieved a degree of political unity centred on the successor state to the Matamba kingdom ruled by the famous seventeenth-century Queen Nzinga (by then located in the Kambo river valley). They acquired the name of 'Jingas' from the Portuguese, who tended to call many Africans after the titles of their rulers (in this case, Nzinga). The Hungu broke out of their original homeland during the later years of the eighteenth century and, thoroughly Kongo in language and culture by that time, expanded westward as far as the headwaters of the Dande river.[33] The eastern Pende fragmented into several new groupings, mainly Holo and Imbangala gathered into a pair of strong kingdoms in the Baixa de Cassanje, and a variety of small populations living along the lower Lui in the interstices between the states. The latter acquired such ethnonyms as Kari and Paka. Some of the original Pende may have abandoned the Kwango area and moved to their present homes in the Bandundu province of Zaïre.[34] The incipient split between Libolo and Hako became more pronounced, and only the Songo remained relatively unaffected by change. Great numbers of people from all parts of the Mbundu territories were taken to Luanda where they became slaves and employees of a growing Portuguese community; there they coalesced into the group now known as 'Ambundu' or 'Luandas'.[35]

Selective Review of Mbundu Social Structure

One useful way to describe Mbundu society is in terms of the many and diverse institutions which it contained. Since nearly every Mbundu took care to participate in the activities of as many of

---

[33] This movement began in the 1760s and continued into the nineteenth century; Birmingham (1966), pp. 150–2.

[34] For the Pende, Vansina (1966a), pp. 95–7, and sources cited.

[35] These names appear in Redinha (1961).

these institutions as possible, and since people sometimes found that their functions overlapped and conflicted with one another, the plurality of organizations afforded most people an opportunity to play one institution against another in order to advance their own interests. Although nothing about this aspect of Mbundu society distinguished it from any other social system in the world, I want to introduce the concept explicitly at the outset because the potential for conflict inherent in the presence of multiple institutions played a key role in Mbundu political history. Understanding the pattern of Mbundu political development in these terms does not require a comprehensive ethnography, which would in any case be impossible to write owing to the insufficiency of data. But it is both possible and necessary to outline enough of Mbundu social structure to indicate the characteristic tension found in many matrilineal societies between the principle of reckoning descent and inheritance through women but leaving most forms of authority in the hands of males and to suggest the importance of 'cross-cutting institutions'[36] which united Mbundu across the social boundaries set up by the dominant matrilineal descent groups.

The Mbundu by the sixteenth century were farmers who had lived in compact village settlements at least since the introduction of agriculture at an unknown time in the dim past. The village geographically expressed the residential dimension of the Mbundu lineage structure since each settlement ideally centred on a group of adult males belonging to a single descent group, or *ngundu* (plural, *jingundu*). Because the Mbundu were matrilineal, the adult male core of a mature village tended to be composed of a senior group of full brothers and a middle generation of their nephews, that is, children of their sisters. Adult females belonging to other lineages lived as wives with the nephews of the village, and the youngest generation usually included the children of these marriages, who were all members of their alien mothers' *jingundu* and therefore not part of the village lineage core. Widowed or divorced sisters of the men in the oldest generation often returned to reside with their brothers. This residence pattern had the effect of reinforcing the lineage identity of the village by gathering its most senior living members together in a single place. The junior members of the Mbundu lineages, young married women and their children, lived dispersed in neighbouring villages with the kinsmen of their husbands and

---

[36] The idea and the term have both received systematic treatment in the stimulating chapter by Horton (1971).

fathers. Since they rarely held positions of lineage responsibility and did not share directly in inheritance, their absence from the village did not detract from the concentration of lineage activities in the village and the strong solidarity of the lineage group.

The Mbundu lineage-villages each had their own lands (*ishi*) in which the members of the *ngundu* collectively controlled access to the soil for farming, to the streams for fishing, and to the meadows and woods for hunting and for gathering fruits, berries, and nuts which grew wild there. As crops exhausted the fertility of the soil and it became necessary to open new fields elsewhere, individual farmers moved their plots every few years from one part of the lineage lands to another in a system of shifting cultivation. A lineage might invite outsiders to live with them and to share their resources, but such men always remained guests and could not pass on their personal privileges to their nephews. The lineage authorized and directed the communal fire hunts which took place at the end of each dry season. The major units of economic co-operation therefore tended to coincide with the Mbundu descent groups, just as did the residential units. The collective *jingundu* remained stable through time, each associated with its own fixed *ishi*.

Individual Mbundu moved from place to place, however, in a pattern common to matrilineal societies where the nieces of a lineage spent their child-bearing years away from their own kinsmen, residing in the lineage-villages of their husbands and raising the lineage's children there. Girls were usually born in their father's lineage village, remained there until marriage, and then went to live with the kinsmen of their husband. Frequent visits to the village of their mother's brother kept up their contacts with their own *ngundu* and prepared the way for their move 'home' when they ceased to bear children or became divorced or widowed. Most women never lived in their own lineage village until they reached old age. Boys, on the other hand, returned to their own *ngundu*'s village much earlier in life than their sisters. They also grew up among their father's kinsmen but soon after puberty tended to return directly to their own relatives at the village of their mother's brothers, where they remained for the rest of their lives as part of the core of matrilineally related males. Their wives and children, all members of other *jingundu*, lived with them during their mature years but tended to drift away as the women grew old, the daughters married, and the sons moved away to join their own uncles. The constant movement of people in these patterns, from the perspective of the descent groups, meant that each lineage's members were born and grew up away from their own lineage village but returned to it as they grew older, the males somewhat earlier in their lives than the females.

Although the Mbundu descent groups collectively tended towards the sort of structure just outlined, individual *ngundu* moved through a fairly predictable series of stages. A mature lineage typically had a single elderly man in its oldest generation, with a number of fully mature nephews (*behwa*, singular *mwehwa*, 'sister's sons') generally in charge of running lineage affairs. If more than one of these nephews aspired to head his own *ngundu*, the death of the old man caused the descent group to split as each *mwehwa*, or each set of full brothers within the group of nephews, felt himself no longer restrained by the unity imposed by the old man's presence and left with his wives, young children, and sister's sons to establish a new and independent *ngundu*. The new groups might divide the lands formerly held in common, or some of the new *jingundu* might go elsewhere to settle as guests on the lands of related lineages. This sort of lineage fission constantly generated new descent groups but seldom eliminated the old lineages as corporate groups, since one of the nephews customarily took over the position of the dead uncle and preserved the identity of the old *ngundu*. Lineages could thus survive indefinitely, although misfortune might reduce their living membership so drastically that the few remaining survivors would scatter to live with other relatives. In such a case, the formal identity of the *ngundu* might still remain, kept alive by related groups as a memory even though it had no living members.

The ability of the Mbundu to preserve this sort of abstract *ngundu* without living members had an explanation in their cosmological system. The Mbundu, in common with the Cokwe, the Lunda, the Ndembu, the Bemba, and others who lived to the east, visualized their society as a set of named roles, personalized social statuses associated with defined rights and obligations which living individuals might temporarily assume to the exclusion of any other person.[37] The Mbundu customarily described the relationship of each such named position to other named positions in the language of kinship, 'father–son', 'uncle–nephew', 'brother–brother', and so on, and regarded all such connections between existing roles as immutable. This aspect of the resulting network of named roles has been termed 'perpetual kinship' in Central Africa, from the kinship idiom used

[37] Ian Cunnison (1956). Although these ideas are known elsewhere primarily as political techniques, they permeate every area of Mbundu social structure.

to describe the social structure and the permanence of the relationships between its elements. Individuals thus might take possession
of one or more of these permanent named roles, or 'enter' (*kuhinga*)
the title, as the Mbundu said, hold it for a time, and then bequeath
it to a successor. Each position had a number of different incumbents
over time, all of whom took the name of the position as their own,
treated the occupants of 'brother' and other related positions as if
they were biological brothers and relatives, and exercised the rights
and duties attendant to the position. Hence, the term 'positional
succession' used to indicate the temporal dimension of the system
in which heirs succeeded to the named roles of their predecessors.

Descent groups in this system of perpetual kinship and positional
succession abstractly consisted not of individuals but of named
positions which existed independently of their living occupants.
Perpetual genealogies described the formal relationships between the
names in the lineages, with a set of closely related positions constitut-
ing an *ngundu*. The matrilineal descendants of the occupants of the
set of names remained responsible for providing living incumbents
in perpetuity. The Mbundu thus distinguished between the formal
structure of an *ngundu*, or the names, and the people who temporarily
filled the positions, and it was in this sense that related descent
groups might retain 'empty' *ngundu* positions when no living kinsmen
were available to occupy them. Lineages often had a few of their
names unfilled at any point in time, or an entire set of *ngundu* names
might become vacant if the descent line responsible for filling them
died out.

Certain names within each *ngundu* endowed their holders with
special responsibilities for the welfare of the group. These duties
attached to the senior positions in the *ngundu* genealogy which the
Mbundu referred to simply as the 'uncles' (*malemba*, singular *lemba*)
of the lineage. Lineage members credited the first holder of one of
these senior titles with having separated the lineage from related
descent groups and usually believed that he had led their ancestors
to their present lands. The *ngundu* took its collective name from this
title, the *lemba dya ngundu*, and looked to its holder to perform many
of the rites which, they believed, assured bounteous harvests, guaranteed the fertility of the lineage women so that they might produce
future occupants for the lineage names, brought copious rains, and
attracted plentiful supplies of game. The *lemba dya ngundu* stood as
an intermediary between the living lineage members and dead occupants of the same positions, the ancestors who collectively repre-

sented the spiritual dimension of each title. He also mediated between the *ngundu* and the spirits of the lands and waters which they owned. His was the position on which the social and ritual life of the lineage turned. The occupants of a varying number of other senior positions acted as councillors to the *lemba dya ngundu* and bore the designation of *makota* (singular, *kota* or *dikota*, literally 'elder'). If their overt responsibilities were somewhat less than those of the *lemba dya ngundu*, their subtle political and social functions as advisers and arbiters were perhaps greater.

This brief description of the structure and officials of the Mbundu lineages leads to a fuller explanation of the lineage genealogies discussed as historical sources in Chapter I. The names in these genealogies were the names of the *malemba* of each *ngundu*. In the context of the genealogies, the *lemba* represented all the subordinate names related to him by separate internal *ngundu* genealogies (which were also different from the relatively unimportant biological genealogies of lineage members which showed only biological, not social, links). The *lemba* and *makota* granted kinsmen the right to leave their ancestral *ngundu* to establish new independent groups; when they did so, they awarded a new name to the relative at its head. This name or title consisted of a distinctive first name followed by the title of the senior *lemba* as a surname, and the new lineage would thus be known through the name of its headman as descended from the old *ngundu*: if, for example, the *ngundu* of Mahashi na Pakasa split, it might lead to the creation of a new descent group called Nzenza ya Mahashi, and each lineage would have headmen of the same names. Lineage fission combined with the preservation of old *lemba*-titles through the mechanism of positional succession to generate Mbundu lineage genealogies relating all existing *jingundu* through ties of perpetual kinship.

These descent groups probably constitute some of the oldest surviving institutions of Mbundu social organization and may date from the introduction of agriculture and the settlement of the ancestors of the Mbundu in permanent lineage-villages. In the absence of thoroughgoing archaeological studies, this hypothesis is subject to verification only through such arguments as the 'age-area hypothesis' which posits that 'wider distribution generally means longer time depth'.[38] The widespread distribution of lineages like those of the Mbundu, and of their associated symbols, would accordingly speak

[38] Vansina (1970); the author adds that 'this is not always the case; thus the test is only partial' (p. 169).

for their great antiquity. The Mbundu traditions emphasize the breadth of the single system of descent groups of which they are a part by including genealogies linking them to people who lived as far away as the Lunda of Katanga. Very similar lineage structures seem to exist south of the equatorial forest as far east as the great African lakes. The Mbundu *lemba dya ngundu*, like his counterparts all over the southern savannas, for example, used a sacred white powder called *pemba* to insure the fertility of the women of his lineage. He dispensed a red powder called *takula*, of similarly widespread occurrence, to the men of the *ngundu*.[39] His authority was closely associated with a *mulemba* tree which the Mbundu always planted in front of his dwelling in the village.[40] The exact symbolic meanings of the *mulemba* in the Mbundu context remain uncertain,[41] but the practical facts that branches from this tree rooted themselves when placed in the ground and grew rapidly (aside from their possible symbolic meanings) assumed some significance for shifting agriculturalists who moved their villages every few years. The *lemba dya ngundu* and the *makota* valued the broad shade which it provided for their deliberations.[42]

The *jingundu* commanded an intense loyalty from most Mbundu. The crucial functions of the lineage in providing access to land, since all arable territories lay in the domain of one lineage or another, in coercing the rains to fall on time and in sufficient quantity, in mediating between the living and the dead, and in defining the individual's place in Mbundu society made it in many ways the fundamental institution in their lives. The Mbundu accepted as fellow human beings only people who had positions in their lineage system, either as holders of one of the *ngundu* names or as formal affiliates ('slaves', pawns, etc.) of some descent group.[43] Not to belong to an *ngundu* in theory excluded a person from the right to call on kinsmen for support, prevented him from marrying or growing food, denied him spiritual solace, and in practice often amounted to a choice between certain death and abject subordination to the will of a patron with a place in the lineage structure. For all these reasons, the Mbundu

[39] Powdered wood of the *pterocarpus tinctorius* according to W. D. Hambly (1934), p. 117.

[40] *Ficus psilopoga*; Chatelain (1894), p. 267, n. 171.

[41] The same tree figures prominently in the complex symbolic system of the Ndembu of Zambia for example; Turner (1967), *passim*.

[42] Testimony of Sousa Calunga, 1 Oct. 1969; cf. Otto Schütt (1881), pp. 84–5. The distribution of the *mulemba* as a symbol of lineage authority is also very broad; José Redinha (1963), p. 72.

[43] Joseph C. Miller (forthcoming(b)).

placed great importance on their lineages and evidently succeeded in preserving their basic structure without great change over several centuries.[44]

If an individual could survive in Mbundu society only within the protective shield afforded by his *ngundu*, the lineage as a group could survive only through close co-operation with its neighbours. The rule of lineage exogamy forced lineage members to marry outside the confines of their descent group, and it may be assumed that a variety of marrige alliances linked particular Mbundu lineages to one another. I have almost no data to suggest the type or scope of these arrangements, certainly not for the sixteenth century, but those I have indicate that preferential marriage rules capable of producing permanent wife-exchanging pairs of *jingundu* tended to occur more commonly among those Mbundu who lacked the deep segmentary-type genealogies of the Songo. The comprehensive Songo lineage genealogy seems to have ordered inter-lineage relations there without necessitating the additional links provided by clearly developed preferred or prescribed marriage rules. It is therefore impossible to say much about affinal alliances as means of structuring inter-descent group relations other than that their importance may have varied inversely with the comprehensiveness of the different sets of lineage genealogies.[45]

From the perspective of an individual Mbundu, the formal relationships between the *jingundu* as collectivities, whether genealogical ties resulting from lineage fission or affinal bonds created by marriage, did not always provide a viable framework through which he could pursue opportunities arising in areas where his network of kinsmen and affines did not extend. The ties of personal kinship derived from his group relationships could be manipulated within limits to produce varying emphases within the structure, but they did not necessarily reflect the personal interests which a man might share with non-kinsmen engaged, for example, in the same economic activities as he. Mbundu society contained several other sorts of institution which responded to such practical needs by uniting people

[44] This is, of course, the crucial assumption for the entire analysis to follow. In the absence of complete data for the seventeenth century, it must rest on the fragmentary data we have to suggest that nothing important has changed and on such arguments as the 'age-area' hypothesis.

[45] Limitations on both time and the scope of my research in Africa prevented the collection of reliable information on Mbundu social practice, as contrasted with Mbundu social theory. These practices, in any case, have clearly altered enormously under the impact of war and urbanization in modern Angola.

across the social boundaries set up by the fierce loyalty of most Mbundu to their descent groups. In structural terms, such institutions cut across the dominant lineage structure of the society. Classed according to duration and specialization of purpose, these cross-cutting institutions ranged from quite informal and *ad hoc* agreements made between strangers thrown together in common pursuit of a limited goal to comprehensive and institutionalized secret societies of several types. It is, of course, impossible to reconstruct any of the more ephemeral institutions of the distant past, but comparisons of modern Mbundu institutions with similar organizations among related peoples give a good idea of the general characteristics of those which must have been present long ago.

Skilled professionals of various sorts—especially the diviners and healers (*nganga*, plural *jinganga*, or *kimbanda*, plural *yimbanda*)—maintained informal but intensive relations with one another regardless of their lineage affiliations. This sort of professional solidarity enabled successful practitioners of these arts to travel far beyond their spheres of kinsmen and to receive a respectful welcome from local colleagues and their relatives wherever they went. Even an informal network of mutual professional interests provided individual Mbundu with a supra-descent group network of contacts and served to transmit skills and knowledge widely throughout the society. Diviners seem to have favoured their sons over their nephews as heirs to their professional status, and to that extent they set themselves apart from the dominant emphasis on matrilineal group membership.[46]

More structured, but also more ephemeral, were curing cults and witchcraft eradication movements.[47] These provided institutional vehicles through which people could temporarily abandon their primary loyalty to their *ngundu* in favour of ties to non-kinsmen based either on common affliction with a given disease or on a common effort to eliminate witches from their midst. Among the Mbundu, these rituals characteristically involved techniques of spirit possession, a notion very closely related to the theory of positional succession, in which the occupant of a name sought ritually to identify himself with the spiritual essence of the position and through it to communicate with some or all of its previous

---

[46] Cavazzi (1965), *passim* but esp. i. 193–200, gives a number of details suggestive of this conclusion for the 1650s.

[47] Here I draw primarily on the terminology and concepts of Victor Turner (1968) and Jan Vansina (1971a).

incumbents. These operated across the lineage boundaries and had quite different consequences for Mbundu social structure from other spirit mediumship techniques (the *kushingilisa*, see below) which worked exclusively within the lineages and tended to reinforce the solidarity of the individual descent groups.

Mbundu neighbourhoods held regular circumcision camps in which the young men of a locality joined together regardless of their positions in the descent group genealogies. They formed a kind of incipient age-set, united temporarily by their shared experiences in the circumcision camp, and retained limited ties throughout their lives. Aside from the educational function of the ceremony, and its certification of Mbundu boys as young Mbundu men, it also provided cross-cutting ties among the young males residing locally with their fathers. When these men dispersed after the initiation ceremonies to join their mothers' brothers in other, perhaps distant, villages, they created a web of association which ultimately stretched over a wide area. The graduates of the circumcision camp carried special circumcision names which indicated their ties to each other in a manner analogous to the permanent names and genealogies of the *jingundu*.

An association of master hunters (*yibinda*, singular *kibinda*) provided a good example of how these associations created personal ties which united people outside the structures of kinship. The permanence and close connection of the *kibinda* society with some later forms of Mbundu political authority make it worthy of more extensive description than some of the others. The *kibinda* was a hunter skilled not only in the use of bow, arrow, and spear, which he used to kill hippopotamus, lion, leopard, wild boar, large antelope, red buffalo, and crocodile, but also a specialist believed to know the magical arts of making himself invisible to his prey, flying through the air, or wielding charmed weapons which never missed their mark. Whatever the methods by which the *kibinda* stalked and killed his quarry, he performed several functions essential to the welfare of the *ngundu*. His was the responsibility of entering the forest in search of certain animals believed necessary to divine the intentions of lineage spirits or to augur the success of some contemplated enterprise. If the *kibinda* hunted well, lineage members could rest assured that their relations with the spiritual world were harmonious, but if no game appeared they took his bad luck as a sign that they should discover the source of the apparent supernatural displeasure. In this and other ways, the activities of the *yibinda* master hunters reinforced the integrity of the Mbundu descent groups.

A different aspect of the *kibinda* association, however, united all Mbundu professional hunters to one another regardless of their lineage status. An aspirant hunter (*mona a yanga*, or 'child of the *kibinda*', who was also known as a *yanga*) could apprentice himself to any master for training in the professional hunter's arts. The relationship between *mona* and master was regarded as analogous to that of son to father, that is, cutting across the matrilateral ties of uncle to *mwehwa*. On the occasion of the death of a famous *kibinda*, *yibinda* and *bana a yanga* from far and near assembled to participate in ceremonies which culminated in the extraction of a tooth from the dead hunter's jaw and a communal hunt. The bonds uniting *yibinda*, who recognized each other by secret signs, extended far beyond the limits of kin and even ethnicity to include Songo, Pende, Imbangala, Cokwe, and Lunda alike. To meet anothe *kibinda* in the forest was said to be like encountering a kinsman, and the status of master hunter obliged a *kibinda* to extend to his colleagues all the benefits he derived from his own *ngundu*.[48] These strong ties facilitated the movements of hunters who often penetrated unknown regions in pursuit of large game and provided a potent mechanism for integrating Mbundu society beyond the framework afforded by the lineage structure.

Finally, some indication of Mbundu ideas about the nature of authority may help to prepare the ground for the following examination of early Mbundu political history. The Mbundu distinguished clearly between the locus of authority and the wielder of authority, much as they made a distinction between the abstract named roles of the social structure and the living incumbents. Authority rested on the ability to invoke supernatural sanctions and inhered not in human beings but in the authority emblems associated with the titles. Sometimes the Mbundu expressed this idea by emphasizing the intimate connection between a living incumbent, powerless in himself, and the dead predecessors in his title who collectively 'were' the authority of his position. Names carried varying measures of authority of this sort, and the most influential names in the lives of most people before the appearance of states were the titles charged with responsibility for the welfare of the descent groups, the *malemba dya ngundu* and the *makota*. Renowned professional hunters, diviners,

[48] Testimonies of Alexandre Vaz and Ngonga a Mbande, 23 Sept. 1969; Sousa Calunga, 2 Oct. 1969.

mediums, and the like primarily exercised their authority not over people but over animals, oracles, or spiritual forces.

The holder of a powerful name usually gained access to the spiritual forces behind it through possession of some object believed to mediate between the visible world of the living and the invisible world of the supernatural. The *lemba dya ngundu*, for example, was helpless without the *mulemba* tree or his *pemba*, just as diviners worked through a variety of physical objects which they endowed with special powers, and the *kibinda* master hunter achieved his success through possession of his master's tooth or through the manipulation of carved figures, animal horns, or plants. All of these mediatory objects also served as visible badges of office, emblems of the special status accorded to the possessor of the name or title to which they belonged.

The notion of authority as access to spiritual forces obtained through possession of special objects meant that any Mbundu in control of an authority emblem could delegate a portion of his power simply by awarding a part of his object to another. This kind of logic lay behind the ceremonies which marked the fission of the lineages; the founder of the new *ngundu* usually took a branch from the *mulemba* tree of the parent lineage and planted it, along with the spiritual essence of the descent group as well as the authority of the *lemba*, wherever he settled in his new village. Hunters initiated aspirants into *kibinda* status by giving them charms which presumably gave them access to the same magical powers which had given the master his own success. Diviners transferred their skills not only through instruction but also through the presentation or sale of objects which gave their heirs and customers more or less limited access to the same secrets as they possessed. On a more ephemeral level, the *lemba dya ngundu* could appoint agents empowered to act in his stead simply by giving them a material symbol of his authority.

The formation of the first Mbundu states occurred in a social context not unlike the one just described: strong and independent matrilineal descent groups which tended to monopolize the loyalties of most individuals. The cohesiveness and autonomy of the lineages diminished the importance of institutions which cut across the social boundaries set up by the rule of unilineal descent, but a number of such institutions blurred the lines separating kinsmen from non-kinsmen. Of these, the most durable and extensive seems to have been the association of *kibinda* hunters. To the extent that these institutions allowed men to circumvent the rigidity of descent groups based on positional succession and perpetual kinship, they broadened the scale of interaction among the Mbundu and afforded opportunities for people to co-operate towards ends not met by the lineage structure. In so far as some of these institutions tended to endure through time, they resembled 'state-like institutions' which performed 'political' functions. The remainder of the book examines the ways in which the Mbundu developed such incipiently political institutions as these through the distribution of authority symbols and delegation of authority into several political structures which closely resembled 'states' by the beginning of the seventeenth century.

CHAPTER III

Indigenous Beginnings

THE WORLD, according to the Mbundu, began when Ngola Inene arrived from lands far to the north-east and settled where the Mbundu live today. Ngola sired a daughter, Samba, and Samba in turn gave birth to Kurinje kwa Samba and Kiluanje kya Samba. Kurinje kwa Samba (leaving aside momentarily the descendants of Kiluanje kya Samba) was the parent of Mbulu wa Kurinje and Mbulu wa Kurinje produced Zundu dya Mbulu, Kongo dya Mbulu, Mumbanda a Mbulu, Matamba a Mbulu, Kajinga ka Mbulu, Mbumba a Mbulu, and perhaps Kavunje ka Mbulu, the founders of the Ndongo, Hungu, Pende, Lenge, Mbondo and Imbangala, the Songo, and the Libolo. The world, also according to the Mbundu, began when the ancestors of the same present-day ethno-linguistic subgroups came with *malunga* from the sea and stopped when they reached the hills and valleys where their descendants are now to be found. Others add that the world may have begun with Adam and Eve, two people who lived very far away and who had many descendants. Among them was Cain, father of all the black people.

For most Europeans, on the other hand, the origins of the world are too remote to consider in connection with the formation of the Mbundu, and it is easier to believe that several local stone- and iron-working populations, known only from the artifacts they left behind in long-abandoned campsites, have occupied north-western Angola for many centuries. No less contradictorily than the conflicting stories of Ngola Inene and the *malunga* from the sea, the Bantu language the Mbundu speak today links them to people who now live far to the north-west in modern Nigeria. In the face of the archaeological and linguistic facts, what, if anything, do the traditions about Ngola Inene and the *malunga* reveal about Mbundu *history*, as opposed to mere legend? The most plausible answer is that the traditions refer not to the origins of the people but, like the Mbundu adaptation of the story of Cain and Abel, indicate the appearance of new modes of political organization and are therefore germane to the question of how Mbundu descent groups first organized themselves according to standards other than those of lineage fission.

The traditions of Ngola Inene and the *malunga* clearly belong to 'historical time' for the Mbundu rather than to the preceding 'mythical' and 'proto-historical' periods found in the oral art of many African peoples.[1] Many non-literate societies envisage their remote past as falling into three stages, moving from a mythical epoch when inverted monsters roamed the world through a transitional age of supermen into a fully historical period populated by humans not unlike modern men.[2] The Mbundu make no attempt to link whatever philosophical beliefs they may hold about the creation of the world to the relatively straightforward accounts of how their social and political structures took form. They clearly regard both Ngola Inene and his progeny and the people who brought the *malunga* from the sea as very much like themselves. Even though some of these proto-typical humans knew how to make strong magic, none of them walked on their heads, as more mythical ancestors in other societies are said to have done, or otherwise signalled their non-humanity by grotesque or shocking behaviour. Their essentially human qualities suggest that they represent authentic historical events and stand for more than a statement of present Mbundu cosmology in a mythical idiom. The mythical and heroic ages of the past usually purport to describe the formation of present social structures through presenting a contrast between a former period of chaos and the emergence of orderly modern social arrangements.[3] The essential humanity of Ngola Inene and the *malunga*-bringers, if this is so for the Mbundu, thus signifies that the Mbundu believe that the outlines of their present social institutions were already present at the time their historical traditions begin.

Even though the shortage of information on the earliest phases of Mbundu political history leaves an element of conjecture in any interpretation of this period, certain continuities in the structure of their society enable the historian at least to delineate the areas where reliable reconstructions are possible and to acknowledge those parts of the Mbundu past which remain shadowy or entirely unknown. Using ethnographic data collected from the Mbundu and

[1] I employ the terminology of E. V. Thomas and D. Sapir (1967).

[2] Frank E. and Fritzie P. Manuel (1972), pp. 84–90, illustrate this sequence in Greek mythology.

[3] One can appreciate such analyses as John Middleton (1965), pp. 18–24, or Beidelman (1970) without condemning all historical traditions to the never-never land of 'ideological data' (Beidelman, p. 96).

their neighbours during the last century, one can say with fair certainty that one form of change in their society before 1600 consisted of frequent and small-scale innovations in social organization, ideas constantly appearing and flickering briefly within the limits of a single descent group or confined to a few lineages before they died out and left the aggregate pan-Mbundu social institutions largely unaffected. New religious beliefs, for example, spread in this manner and then vanished; lineage headmen invented and tested new magical techniques which they hoped might bring them copious rains or numerous nephews. Men everywhere made formal but temporary arrangements with their neighbours or acquaintances by fabricating and displaying visible tokens of their intentions: an amulet, hats, skins, bracelets, pieces of iron, carved wooden figures, staffs, bells, gongs, and a variety of other emblems.

Since most such innovations failed, as the disparity between the high hopes they raised and the inadequacy of their means bound them to fail,[4] the great majority had no lasting effect on Mbundu society except for a minor residue in the form of an obscure charm in the magical armoury of a lineage official or a new feather in the cap of a title-holder. These remain lost to history forever. Yet some innovations remained and became fixtures of Mbundu social structure, providing new links between people where none had existed before, reinforcing the authority of certain officials at the expense of others, and cumulatively propelling the Mbundu through a sequence of historical developments which in retrospect seems to possess an identifiable structure, to define a recurrent pattern. The beginnings of Mbundu political history therefore consist of identifying and placing in the proper chronological order the most important innovative techniques of social organization, the ones which permanently affected Mbundu social structure and have thus encouraged the conservation of the corresponding physical symbols as bits of evidence from the past. All else must remain unknowable.

The multiplicity of symbols now in use among the Mbundu shows that successive generations of officials have eclectically incorporated new emblems without abandoning the older authority symbols of their ancestors even after their faith in the power of the antique relics had begun to wane. The precise meaning and use of each emblem undoubtedly has varied through time. Many of the present minor symbols of authority, for example, linger as faded remnants of objects whose reputations once inspired awe in the hearts of all

[4] A point mentioned by Jack Goody (1971).

Mbundu. Title-holders accumulated whole sets of such symbols, adding to their collections as they claimed new powers for themselves in response to changing times much as Western law rests on a thick sediment of statutes reflecting the circumstances of times past. The outsider may thus read the panoply of objects associated with present Mbundu title-holders as a record of techniques of governance tried in the past.

The Mbundu oral traditions describing their 'origins' in terms of Ngola Inene and the *malunga* explain the provenance and meaning of two important symbols of this type. They are thus the conscious record of political development, couched in the personalized idiom of human founders but meant to account for two of the numerous authority emblems in the hands of present lineage headmen and holders of political titles. It is because of this that lineages whose headmen today care for an authority emblem called a *lunga* (plural, *malunga*) recount the traditions about ancestors who came from the sea. Histories of Ngola Inene explain the central sacred relic of descent groups which attribute their headman's powers to a small piece of iron called an *ngola* (plural, *jingola*). And, true to the pattern of explaining 'origins' in terms of whatever protective devices the lineage may regard as most fundamental, Mbundu adaptations of Biblical origin myths tend to appear in villages situated on mission property or those counting a substantial proportion of Christians among their members.

The superficial contradictions found in multiple myths about Adam and Eve, *malunga*, Ngola Inene, and others are not to be resolved by selecting a single Mbundu 'origin' as definitive. They result from a long and complicated history in which a number of different principles of social and political organization have had different effects on the present Mbundu lineages. The available data, complex as they are, still consist only of a small part of the total history: those authority emblems and associated traditions which have survived the passage of the years to remain as respected symbols at present. Presumably, these are the ones which achieved the widest diffusion and provided sufficient advantages for the people who adopted them to integrate these emblems at the heart of their lineage structure. Although such symbols may have been the 'most important' in this sense, a great many other paired symbols and organizational techniques failed to spread or achieved only temporary significance before they were abandoned in favour of newer, more satisfying, or more timely ideas. The process of continual invention, diffusion, alteration, and disappearance of religious movements among a twentieth-century people with similar social institutions, described for the Kuba of the Kasai province of Zaïre in fascinating detail,[5] cannot differ significantly from the attitude of social and religious experimentation which must have animated the Mbundu many hundreds of years ago and which still motivates them today despite the stultifying effects of colonial rule on fluid African social institutions. Movements of this type may hold the key to the appearance of states among the Mbundu.

Since the available records show only a fraction of the social and political institutions which the Mbundu have tried, the present discussion is limited to two developments which the Mbundu remember as the most fundamental since the coalescence of the basic *jingundu* matrilineages and their acceptance of the *mulemba* trees and the lineage headmen (the *malemba dya ngundu*) associated with them. Both these emblems, the *lunga* and the *ngola*, at different times seem to have supported two contrasting movements which underlie Mbundu political history: tendencies toward particularism and localism centred in the lineages, and opposing attempts to transcend the level of lineage organization through the development of larger-scale centralized political structures.

The Coming of the Lunga

The Mbundu lineages living on the middle and northern reaches of the Lui river revere a kind of lineage emblem called a *lunga*, a sacred relic which assumes various physical shapes but usually has taken the form of a human figure carved from wood. These *malunga*, the Mbundu explain, came originally from 'Kalunga' which they identify as the 'great water', without any clear notion of where this aquatic source may lie. Because almost all European observers have interpreted the word as referring to the Atlantic Ocean, or to the African 'great lakes', the Mbundu today also give this meaning to the name 'Kalunga' and believe that their ancestors who long ago brought the first *malunga* set out from the island of Luanda where the Portuguese have had an administrative centre for nearly 400 years.[6] There is obviously no basis in fact for this assertion. *Malunga* today have a close association with rain and with water, 'dwelling' in rivers and lakes and helping their guardians call the rains. They are linked also with the success of agriculture and hence with life

---

[5] Vansina (1971a).
[6] A published example of this sort of tradition appears in Haveaux (1954).

itself in the Mbundu farmer's view of the world. The ancestors who first came with the *malunga* were Kajinga ka Mbulu, who founded the Mbondo, Matamba a Mbulu, ancestress of the Lenge, Mumbanda a Mbulu, mother of all the Pende, Kongo dya Mbulu who gave birth to the Hungu, and Zundu dya Mbulu, great ancestress of the Ndongo, and perhaps others now forgotten. An outsider might also observe that the *malunga* had something to do with an early organization of the Mbundu lineages into the ethno-linguistic subgroups recognized today.

Several characteristics of the *malunga* suggest that they spread among the Mbundu lineages at a very early period. Their close association with water and with the land, since lineages with *malunga* are also the land-owning descent groups, points to their connection with the oldest significant stratum in the present Mbundu social and political structure. The broad grouping of the Mbundu into Ndongo, Lenge, Pende, and so on was already present at least as early as the late sixteenth century when the first documentary sources picked up some of these names. The Mbundu expressly concur in the opinion that the landowners are the most ancient kin groups in their territories. The *lunga*-holding lineages, where they survive, govern the use of the land, authorizing changes in residence, selecting the sites for new villages, locating water by divining techniques based on manipulation of the physical *lunga*-object, as well as summoning the rains at the end of each dry season.[7] The *lunga* has in some cases become assimilated to the complex of symbols centred on the *mulemba* tree and the *lemba dya ngundu*, since the human guardian of the *lunga* distributes the lineage *pemba* to his kinswomen and performs other duties normally associated with these officials. The female identity of the ancestors who brought the *malunga* reinforces their connection with the lineages since the Mbundu perceive their descent groups as feminine in contradistinction to most extra-lineage institutions which they see as 'masculine'.

The extensive modern distribution of ancestors and state-founders with names based on the root -*lunga* also gives the impression of great antiquity. These figures appear in a wide band through the southern savannas in association with very ancient forms of authority, from the Kuba where 'Keloong' (Kalunga) is said to come from very ancient times,[8] through the Luba where traditions portray Kalala Ilunga as the founding ancestor who brought a new political

---

[7] Testimony of Kimbwete.

[8] Jan Vansina, personal communication.

order in the form of the 'second Luba empire',[9] to the southern end
of Lake Malawi where traditions have 'Kalonga' arriving near the
beginning of political history with new institutions brought from
Katanga.[10] Closer to the Mbundu, the Yaka peoples, who live just
down the Kwango from the eastern Mbundu, include certain very
old Kalunga 'clans', and the Cokwe to the east of the Kwango
recognize a Kalunga as one of the founding 'parents' of their lineages.[11] The *malunga* survive as dominant lineage emblems within
Mbundu territory primarily among the remnant Pende populations,
the Hari and the Paka of the lower Lui who seem to have escaped
incorporation in any of the kingdoms which supplanted the *lunga* in
most other regions. This sort of evidence is too fragmentary to
suggest a point of origin for the *lunga*,[12] but the very vagueness of the
data testifies to its great age since subsequent political developments
have intervened to obscure its history in most areas.[13]

The modern characteristics of the *lunga*, where it has survived
without significant change, suggest something about the way ancient
Mbundu lineage headmen assimilated the *lunga* to their descent
group positions and modified their lineage alliances in terms of these
emblems of authority. In contrast to the Mbundu *mulemba* tree,
which represented a purely kinship-based lineage structure not unlike
the classic segmentary lineage system,[14] the *lunga* brought a form of
territorially based authority into the lives of the Mbundu, since the
holder of the *lunga* claimed authority over anyone who lived in a
territorially defined domain regardless of their relationship to him
or his lineage. According to Horton's analysis of the ecological and
demographic conditions which favour specified types of social and

---

[9] E. Verhulpen (1936), pp. 90ff.

[10] Harry W. Langworthy (1971).

[11] M. Plancquaert (1971). For the Cokwe, Redinha (1958).

[12] Wauters (?) (n.d.), p. 1, found that the modern Pende remembered a
'kingdom' named Kalunga based on the *lunga*-emblem in their original home
among the Mbundu.

[13] Confusion reigns in most secondary authorities over the meaning of the
root -*lunga* and the so-called 'high god' Kalunga. Future research could
reinterpret this vague figure as an archaic form of political authority and re-
evaluate his alleged 'origins' in the ocean as a simple association of this form
of authority with water. 'Ka-' occurs commonly as a Bantu prefix (class 12)
denoting unusual size, either large or small, and turns up specifically as a
prefix on words for authority symbols which both personalizes them as
'founding ancestors' and stands for the abstract principles of the authority
itself (e.g. Kalunga, Kanuma, and Kajinga are founding ancestors of states
with the *lunga*, the *numa*, and the *kijinga* as central authority emblems).

[14] The *mulemba* tree may be taken as the symbol of Horton's 'Type 1 segmentary lineage system' among the Mbundu (1971, pp. 84–93).

political organization, this sort of territoriality[15] tends to appear when alien groups block the path of the kin groups on the edges of an expanding segmentary lineage system.[16] It would be excessively speculative to account for the appearance of *lunga*-based authority in the basin of the Kwango by applying this hypothesis to vague notions of population movements at so early a period of Mbundu history,[17] but the nature of the structure associated with the *lunga* seems clear. Each *lunga* 'lived' in a specified river or lake under the care of an official who alone knew the secret of communicating with the spiritual forces believed to inhere in it. This guardian of the *lunga* exercised powers of granting access to land to stranger lineages who could find no unoccupied territory to settle. He controlled the fertility of the fields and the rains which fell over the drainage basin of whatever stream or river his *lunga* occupied, with the *lunga*-guardians of major watercourses claiming a vague superiority over the *malunga* and people living on tributary streams. The control of the *lunga*-guardians over land and rain gave them an obvious lever with which to demand the respect, and perhaps the tribute, of local farmers who depended on them to ensure adequate harvests. They could command outright subservience from outsiders who owed them their right to occupy land.

Aside from pointing out the potential of the *lunga* for establishing an incipient hierarchy of lineages within a given territory, nothing indicates how politics may actually have functioned under these emblems. Presumably, control of the *malunga* passed matrilineally within descent groups then as it does now. To that extent the *malunga* reinforced the solidarity of the *ngundu* as the basic social institution in Mbundu life. Initially, at least, the *malunga* need not have introduced a significant degree of centralization beyond the formal restructuring of parts of the lineage hierarchy on the basis of hydro-graphy. They may thus have linked for the first time lineages not connected by descent group genealogies generated by lineage fission. But the essentially static qualities of the *malunga*, fixed in place by their connections to specific bodies of water, gave the hierarchy a rigidity and artificiality which prevented lineages from forming new alliances in response to changes in economic conditions or the rise

[15] Horton's 'Type 2 dispersed territorially defined community' (1971, pp. 93–7).

[16] Marshall D. Sahlins (1961).

[17] Possibilities might include the interaction of Kongo lineages expanding to the south and Mbundu lineages moving northward from the centre of the Songo segmentary lineage system.

of an unusually able leader or confrontation with an external military threat requiring reorganization and centralization for defence. The *malunga* provided a partial answer to Mbundu needs for institutions which cut across the basic lineage genealogies of their society, but it did not satisfy the need for flexibility which ultimately led many Mbundu to replace them with another method of linking descent groups into new and larger aggregates.

The Ngola *as a Lineage Symbol*

The authority principle which provided for greater flexibility for most Mbundu came with the spread of small pieces of iron known as *jingola*. This emblem reached the Mbundu much more recently than the *lunga* and is still revered by most lineages as their fundamental symbol. As a result, many more details have survived about its origin and function in Mbundu political history. It was originally an iron object of defined shape, a hammer, a bell, a hoe, or a knife. Its significance has declined along with that of the *malunga* in recent years as more recent states, including the present Portuguese administration, have made its reputed powers seem less effective; lineages now accept almost any misshapen or rusty piece of metal as their *ngola*. Like the *malunga*, it was incorporated by the descent groups at first and tended to reinforce their independence without significant centralization of authority above the lineage level. Essentially, the *ngola* provided yet another way of building non-hierarchical links between Mbundu descent groups.

When an Mbundu lineage received an *ngola*, it appointed a guardian for it in the belief that it, like their other symbols of authority, gave him access to special spiritual forces useful for regulating the affairs of men. They ascribed to the *ngola* some of the same functions that obsolescent relics and emblems had once performed and eventually adopted it as their most important lineage emblem. It mediated between the living and dead members of the descent group, as had other objects associated with the *mulemba* tree. It helped its guardian to resolve disputes by divining the justice of each party's cause and assisted him in making decisions affecting the welfare of his kinsmen. The Mbundu lineages raised these guardians of the *ngola* to the status of important lineage officials called *malemba dya ngola* (the 'uncles' of the *ngola*) and gave them many of the duties formerly performed by the *lemba* of the lineage. This left some *malemba dya ngundu* with only the less worldly concerns of distributing *pemba* to the women of the kin group while the *malemba dya ngola* became the effective lineage headmen and the predominant political officials of the group.

The *ngola* solved the problems of structural rigidity and inflexibility, which had remained even after the spread of the *lunga*, by increasing the physical and social mobility of the Mbundu lineages. It freed them from their ties to a single plot of ground and provided a symbol which allowed lineages to move as a group without disbanding. Just as the *mulemba* tree had symbolized the integrity of the kin group, its roots had represented the attachment of each *ngundu* to the ground in which the tree grew. The association of *malunga* with specific rivers and lakes had also tied the spiritual well-being of each *ngundu* to the lands it occupied under the guidance of the *lunga*-guardian. These features of earlier political systems had tended to restrict the mobility of the Mbundu lineages as groups. The *ngola*, however, was portable, both physically and symbolically, as the *malunga* and *mulemba* were not. Lineages with *jingola* could move freely in pursuit of opportunities arising from trade, warfare, or other circumstances. The *ngola* thus brought the potential for revolutionizing the relatively static Mbundu world of *lunga*-kings and *mulemba* trees by introducing the element of mobility which previous structures had lacked.

Increased rates of lineage fission probably attended the increase in physical mobility, since the techniques of dividing the *jingola* provided easy ways of legitimizing the creation of new groups. In accordance with established patterns of division of authority, younger men who wished to escape domination by their elder kinsmen simply requested a new *ngola* from any lineage willing to sponsor them in exchange for their agreement to assist the sponsor in war or some other enterprise. Nephews could thus leave their uncles' villages and establish new lineage segments under their own control on the basis of the power of *jingola* derived from unrelated descent groups. Lineages could break existing alliances based exclusively on geographical contiguity to form new bonds reflecting economic or other ties which did not find formal expression under the old systems. Wealthy or influential lineages could offer subordinate *jingola* as means of building lineage coalitions in which they held the central position. The *ngola* thus brought a potential for the rearrangement of lineages in more complex hierarchies than before.

All evidence points to the highland regions near the headwaters of the Lukala river as the proximate source of the *ngola* which produced these changes in the nature of Mbundu social structure. The people who brought the *jingola* to the Mbundu are remembered as 'Samba', obviously the 'Samba a Ngola' of the *ngola* aetiological legend.[18] Although the original Samba have now disappeared as an identifiable ethnic group, their heirs still act as guardians of these symbols in most Mbundu lineages. Matamba, the sixteenth-century Kikongo name for the ancient province lying in these same highlands identifies the source of both the Samba and the *ngola* since the Portuguese form of the name, 'Matamba', was the same word as the Kimbundu term 'Samba'. Sound shifts which distinguish Kimbundu from Kikongo show that the original form of the name had *ts-* as its initial consonant.[19] Since Kimbundu had no initial *ts-*,[20] the Mbundu evidently dropped the *t-* from their pronunciation of the word and say 'Samba' instead of 'Tsamba'. The Portuguese rendition of the same word dropped the *-s-* from the original Kikongo, since Portuguese also lacked an initial *ts-*, and *-tamba* became the standard designation for this region in all written sources. Addition of the Bantu plural prefix *ma-*, which commonly designates ethic groups,[21] completed the transformation from Tsamba to Matamba and now establishes the identity of the two words.

The location of the chiefs holding the oldest Samba titles in the Mbundu historical genealogies confirms their origin in the area now known as Matamba. The oldest remembered Mbundu Samba position, the one called Kiluanje kya Samba, belonged to lineages living on the middle Lukala river just south of ancient Matamba.[22] A number of other political titles, less important in later periods but of equal antiquity, preserved the name of Samba in the area of the

---

[18] Although other authorities have not emphasized the role of the Samba in the history of the Mbundu, the name has appeared in published accounts of other Mbundu traditions. See Wauters (?) (n.d.), pp. 4–5, for a note that the Pende lineages (he called them 'clans') claimed descent from a 'Gangila Samba' (Kanjila (ka) Samba?, the 'great bird of the Samba'). Atkins (1955), p. 344, found that the Holo (formerly Pende near the middle Kwango) remembered an ancient female known as Samba.

[19] Current pronunciation in parts of Zaïre has preserved the original form of the word; Plancquaert (1971), p. 13, where he gives the names Tsaam and Tsamba.

[20] See Atkins (1955), p. 328, who gave Tsotso as the Matamba form of the name that Kimbundu-speakers pronounce 'Soso'.

[21] e.g. Masongo, Maholo, Mahungu. These sound shifts explain why the Kimbundu personal name 'Matamba', as in Matamba a Mbulu, has no connection with the kingdom of Matamba; the Kimbundu form of the name of the kingdom would be Masamba.

[22] Lopes de Lima (1846), iii. 131–2.

upper Lukala as late as the nineteenth century.[23] One of the important early divisions in the political genealogies of the Samba titles divided them into two major groups at a place near Matamba called Kambo ka Mana on the middle Kambo river.[24] Traditions of the Nkanu and Soso, neighbours of Samba lineages now living in Zaïre, attribute the origin of these Samba to the sources of the Kwilu, a river which flows north from the ancient province of Matamba towards the Kwango.[25]

Documentary evidence from both Kongo and the Mbundu further confirms the origins of the Samba in Matamba. Seventeenth-century Mbundu descendants of the Samba called their original rulers by the title of *musuri*, the Kimbundu word for blacksmith.[26] Somewhat earlier, in 1535, the king of Kongo, Afonso I, had identified himself in his official correspondence as 'Senhor dos Ambudos, d'Amgolla, da Quisyma, e Musuru, de Matamba, e Muyllu, de Musucu, e does Amzicos e da conquista de Pamzualubu . . .'[27] Although the stylistic irregularities of sixteenth-century written Portuguese would allow this sequence of proper nouns to be combined in various ways without violating the loose grammatical rules of the time, most scholars have translated the elements in the series as parallel and independent terms: 'Lord of the Mbundu, of the Ngola (i.e. a king of the Mbundu), of Kisama (the region south of the Kwanza), of Musuru (not identified), of Matamba (the province), of Mwilu (not identified), of Musuku (a region east of Kongo) . . .' and so on.

A different and more accurate interpretation of this title emerges by regrouping its elements on the basis of the distinction implied by the use of both 'de' (of) and 'e' (and) as connecting particles. With modernized spellings, the passage would then read: 'Lord of the Mbundu of the *ngola* of the Samba,[28] of Musuri (the king) of Matamba, of Mwilu (king?) of the Suku, the Tyo . . .' The Kongo king in fact had given both the names of the neighbouring peoples

[23] See, for example, the map of Chatelain (1894). The use of Samba as a surname indicated direct descent from the Samba people. These Samba titles occupied subordinate positions in the (probably later) Ndembu states; see Mattos (1963), p. 321.

[24] Testimony of Sousa Calunga, 29 September 1969.

[25] Plancquaert (1971). This river should not be confused with another (and better known) Kwilu which flows east of the Kwango.

[26] Cavazzi (1965), i. 253; cf. J. Pereira do Nascimento (1903), p. 51.

[27] Letter from el-Rei do Congo to Paulo III, 21 Feb. 1535 (A.N.T.T., C.C., I–3–6 and I–48–45); published in Brásio (1952–71), ii. 38–40.

[28] This interpretation assumes that 'Quisyma' embodies an orthographic eccentricity also found a century later in Cavazzi (1965), i. 253.

and the titles of their rulers in the order of their location along the frontiers of their kingdom, beginning with the Mbundu on his southern border and moving through the Suku in the east to the Tyo in the north-east. A scribe at the Kongo court evidently attempted to distinguish peoples from rulers through careful use of 'de' and 'e' but failed to convey the significance of the distinction to most European readers. 'Musuru' of Matamba appears to be the same *musuri* (or 'Ngola-Musuri') mentioned over 100 years later in seventeenth-century Mbundu oral traditions as the idealized founding smith-king of the *ngola*. The coincidence provides a strong case for identifying Matamba as the home of the Samba.

Seventeenth-century Mbundu traditions associated the Samba with sophisticated iron technology and may thereby suggest one reason why the *ngola* spread rapidly among their lineages. The legendary founding Samba king, 'Ngola-Musuri', brought iron-working skills which enabled the Mbundu to make axes, hatchets, knives, and arrowheads for the first time.[29] The traditions of modern groups living in Zaïre agree in portraying the Samba as excellent blacksmiths who long ago introduced new methods of working iron east of the Kwango river.[30] In confirmation of the connection between the Samba and new iron-working techniques, the *jingola* which they spread among the Mbundu always took the form of objects fabricated from iron. This contrasted strikingly with earlier authority emblems which included a variety of non-metallic objects: carved wooden figures, head-dresses, feathers, mats, and so on. The emblems brought by the Samba appropriately symbolized the skills which made them welcome among the Mbundu.

The *jingola* probably arrived as a new form of lineage symbol diffused peacefully from lineage to lineage without the waves of migrating conquerors brandishing axes, knives, and arrowheads who have dominated some European descriptions of these events. A variety of local conditions could have predisposed many *jingundu* to adopt it voluntarily. They could use the *ngola* to reassert their autonomy in opposition to constraints imposed by such outsiders as the *lunga*-kings of the major rivers. The powers attributed to the *ngola* permitted each *ngundu* to disregard existing outside rulers by substituting it for whatever subordinate authority emblem they had at the time. The lineages preferred the *ngola* to other symbols because their elders, rather than outsiders, nominated the incumbents who

[29] Ibid.
[30] Plancquaert (1971).

filled the office of *lemba dya ngola*. These incumbents, by their initiation into the position, theoretically acquired the status of a 'Samba' outsider, even though they might have been born locally, and thus had prestige and neutrality in lineage affairs which enabled them to act as arbiters in disputes between lineages; by assuming this function, they replaced lineage councils, *lunga*-kings, headmen of descent groups with senior positions in the perpetual genealogies, and others. The powerful supernatural sanctions attributed to the *ngola* allowed a lineage with this emblem to ignore, if they wished, other descent groups and officials on whom they had previously depended. The receptiveness of the lineages meant that the *ngola* probably brought relatively few alien people with it. Instead, it travelled by borrowing, converting local Mbundu who adopted it and its associated technological benefits into 'Samba' by initiation.

Although the *ngola*, originally no more demanding of exclusive lineage loyalties than any other authority symbol, may have co-existed for a time with older emblems, its advantages gradually made it the predominant form of political power among the Mbundu. In the end, it produced a revolution in inter-lineage relations which reached far beyond the internal changes it worked in the structure of individual descent groups. As the *ngola* grew in prestige, it regrouped Mbundu lineages into completely new units based on the distribution of *jingola* rather than the old ties of lineage fission or geographical contiguity. Each *ngola* carried a perpetual name which simultaneously denoted the object itself, the spiritual forces it represented, and its *lemba* or guardian. Senior *malemba dya ngola* could grant similar but subordinate titles to other lineages by awarding them portions of their own *jingola*. A new permanent relationship, expressed in kinship terms like all the others, linked the resulting titles and united the lineages which held them in a new perpetual genealogy. The lineages thus adapted the ancient institutions of perpetual kinship and positional succession to build new title and lineage groupings based on the *ngola*.

Certain other customs and beliefs may have reached the Mbundu from the Samba along with this political symbol. One such custom forbade any contact with the chameleon. The same avoidance distinguishes the Zaïre Samba groups now living on the right bank of the Kwango from their non-Samba neighbours.[31] Even though the Mbundu still hestitate to touch a chameleon, they no longer

[31] Ibid. The fact that the Kongo have this prohibition as well may confirm the link between the Samba and the Kongo border region of Matamba.

associate this prohibition explicitly with Samba descent. They seem to have lost sight of the origins of the idea, since it originally served to distinguish lineages possessing the *ngola* from those without one. Once Mbundu lineages uniformly adopted the *ngola*, avoidance of the chameleon lost its distinguishing function and the Mbundu forgot its association with the Samba. All full members of the Mbundu descent groups now consider themselves 'Samba', and the avoidance persists only as a vestige which now differentiates locally born people from slaves of non-Mbundu origin.[32]

No person eligible to hold an office connected with an *ngola*-owning lineage could eat the flesh of a bushbuck.[33] The *ngola* eventually exerted so fundamental an influence on Mbundu beliefs that they extended this prohibition to any titled position whatsoever and made it a mark of full lineage membership. The Mbundu explain this custom by noting a fancied resemblance of white spots on this antelope's back to leprosy sores and arguing that they may contract leprosy from eating its flesh. Since they know that slaves and other non-Mbundu, who do not claim Samba ancestry, eat bushbuck without fear of infection, the prohibition evidently has a primarily symbolic value in connecting them with the *ngola* and the Samba.

This description of how the *ngola* solved problems at a period when Mbundu social organization depended mainly on the lineages and on the *malunga* does not exhaust the ways in which other symbols still in use among various groupings of Mbundu lineages also affected the patterns of authority and alliance. But these two illustrate some of the principles which governed the origin and spread of such symbols. Each came associated with certain powers, expressed in terms of supernatural forces lurking somewhere behind the physical object itself, and gave its possessors a form of authority which the lineages assimilated without altering the basically descent-oriented structure of their society. They assigned the care of these symbols to permanent named roles, just as they had always given the *malemba* similarly specialized power, and often simply collapsed the powers of the *lunga*-guardian and sometimes even the *malemba dya ngola* into a single lineage position. The spread of *malunga* and *jingola*

[32] Fear of the chameleon is not uncommon elsewhere in Central Africa; the Luba, among others, avoid it carefully. See, for example, Verhulpen (1936), p. 70.

[33] An antelope with white spots on its back called *ngulungu* in Kimbundu; John Charles Baron Statham (1922), p. 281, and Gladwyn M. Childs (1949), p. 43, gave the species as *tragelaphus scriptus*.

therefore did little to diminish the dominance of the lineages as the basic institutions of Mbundu society. Although the *lunga* contained an element of territoriality, it initially involved no significant central-ization of power or increase in the scale of social organization. The *ngola* represented a return from territorially defined authority to links uniting descent groups regardless of the physical distance which separated them. Both symbols stand as examples of cross-cutting institutions adopted by a lineage-structured society to elaborate the simple links provided by lineage fission. But neither in itself marked more than a hesitant development in the direction of incipient states.

Incipient States based on the Lunga

Although the adoption of the *lunga* at first led to no more than a partial and non-hierarchical realignment of Mbundu lineage relation-ships, certain *lunga*-holders built their positions into something which the Mbundu remember as very akin to 'states'. The available data indicate that these achieved their highest development among lineages considered to have been Pende inhabiting the Luanda plateau from the present town of Lucala eastwards to the escarp-ment of the Baixa de Cassanje. They also occupied the lowlands of the Baixa east of the Kambo river.[34] The descendants of these lineages have preserved a few *malunga* which once belonged to kings of considerable note.

One of the most powerful of the Pende *lunga*-kings was Butatu a Kuhongo kwa Wutu wa Nyama. The traditions now recall only the title of this king, probably because his authority declined long before the formation of the present perpetual genealogies in the seventeenth century. At the height of the influence of the kings who held this title, 'Butatu' ruled all the lands beyond the Kambo, probably on the basis of a *lunga* living in the Luhanda or Lui river. A more concrete source of power may have come from their control over salt pans along the lower Luhanda. Ownership of these valuable economic resources enabled the kings who bore this title to extend their authority down the trade routes which channelled salt from the Luhanda to much of the northern Baixa de Cassanje. These kings went into decline as a result of reverses suffered during the early 1500s at the hands of

[34] Various testimonies of Sousa Calunga. The Pende testimony reproduced in Haveaux (1954) has usually been interpreted to indicate that the Pende lived near Luanda Bay in the late sixteenth century. Sufficient evidence to the contrary has already been presented to obviate the need to offer a formal refutation of the point.

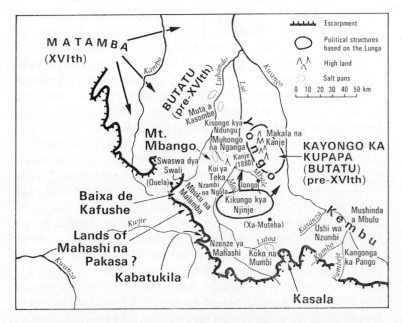

MAP II. Lunga-Authorities in the Baixa de Cassanje (Sixteenth Century and Earlier)

rulers from the expanding state of Matamba.[35] Although Butatu's title dwindled in influence after his kingdom had crumbled, it did not disappear. The position passed into the lineage of a Pende title-holder called Kanje who lived far to the south-east, and this lineage preserved Butatu's name as a subsidiary title of their own chief down to the present day.[36] The case of Butatu provides a good example of how ancient titles and symbols survived in altered form to provide evidence of the past in the present.

The figure of another early *lunga*-king, Kayongo ka Kupapa, emerges from the mists of remnant Pende traditions as the ancient ruler of Yongo, the region between the Lui and Kwango rivers north of the present government post at Iongo. Since subordinate Mbundu

[35] Cavazzi (1965), i. 22, mentioned that a 'Batuta' was the victim of the expansion of the Matamba kingdom. Printed versions of manuscripts from this period commonly confused the closed letters 'a' and 'o' with the open 'u'.

[36] Testimonies of Sokola; Kasanje ka Nzaje; Domingos Vaz; Sousa Calunga, 16 June 1969; maps of Schütt (1881) and H. Capello and R. Ivens (1882), ii. All agree that Kanje in the late nineteenth century lived on the west bank of the Lui river near Mt. Mbango (see Map II).

political titles often took the proper name of their overlord as their own surname, the alternative title of these kings, Kayongo ka Butatu,[37] indicates that the men who held this position once paid tribute to the Butatu a Kuhongo kwa Wutu wa Nyama. Kayongo ka Butatu (or Kupapa) apparently broke away from Butatu a Kuhongo kwa Wutu wa Nyama when the senior title's kingdom went into decline. The surname Kupapa could have been acquired from unknown sources at that time, or it might have been a title belonging to these rulers before they became subject to the great Butatu.[38]

Other Pende *lunga*-kings ruled the southern Baixa de Cassanje under titles of a type known as *yilamba* (singular, *kilamba*).[39] Title-holders called Mahashi na Pakasa controlled the portion of the Lui which turns eastward below the valley called the Baixa de Kafushi. Their influence extended as far north as the salt marshes of the Luhanda.[40] The holders of Mahashi na Pakasa granted at least one subordinate *lunga*-title to their southern neighbours, where Nzenze ya Mahashi became the ruler of the flatlands along the upper Lui river.[41] Another title, Swaswa dya Swali, owned the heavily wooded hills between the Lui and Mount Mbango.[42] A *lunga*-king known as Kikungo kya Njinje dominated the Pende of the Moa river basin on the south side of the Lui. At an unknown time, probably after the decline of Butatu, Kikungo kya Njinje briefly expanded his authority north into Yongo.[43]

---

[37] The modern form of the name occurs as Kayongo ka Kutatu; the surname 'Kutatu' probably represents a distortion of the archaic title Butatu.

[38] Kupapa and the titles of most other Pende *lunga*-kings seem to have been praise names. The term *kupapa*, for example, may be an archaic Kimbundu word having to do with making a crackling noise, as a fire crackles. António de Assis Júnior (n.d.), p. 221, gives related verbal extensions, *kupapajana*, *kupapana*, and *kupapanesa*, all having to do with crackling.

[39] Imbangala informants described them as *yilamba* in the 1850s; Francisco de Salles Ferreira (1854–8), p. 26. Dias de Carvalho (1898), p. 15, paraphrased Salles Ferreira. The antiquity of these titles was evident from the fact that seventeenth-century Portuguese knew the Baixa de Cassanje as the 'Kina kya Kilamba'; *kina* designated any depression in the ground, as a cave or a grave; see Assis Jr. (n.d.), p. 131. Later authorities attributed one or another extended sense to the term: Chatelain (1894), p. 8, Leite de Magalhães (1924), p. 73. The term is adopted here for convenience in order to distinguish these rulers from other sorts of chiefs. For the seventeenth century usage, p. 218, n. 120 below.

[40] Testimony of Sousa Calunga, 22 July 1969.

[41] Testimony of Alexandre Vaz, 31 July 1969; *mahashi* are spurts of blood and, by extension, various serius illnesses believed to be caused by excess blood; Assis Jr (n.d.), p. 271.

[42] The *swaswa* is an unidentified species of tree; Assis Jr. (n.d.), p. 358.

[43] Testimonies of Sousa Calunga, 24 July and 29 Sept. 1969. This title, unlike the others, is composed of personal names. The *njinje* is a small wild cat.

The continual rise and fall of rulers which marked the history of Yongo, the middle Lui, and the Luhanda river valleys did not occur in the southern corner of the Baixa de Cassanje.[44] There a static array of *lunga*-kings ruled relatively unchanging territories. Kangongo ka Pango controlled the higher elevations of the Kembo region in the southern corner of the Baixa near the entry of the Kwango river into the valley.[45] Another, Ushi wa Nzumbi, ruled the rolling woodlands which slope eastward from the Xá-Muteba region towards the valley of the Kwango.[46] Koko na Mumbi had control over the flat plains of the Lutoa river basin and exploited the valuable salt pans which were located there.[47]

Kingdoms based on the Ngola

Some Mbundu lineages turned the *ngola* from a lineage emblem into the basis of a new type of political structure, just as others had earlier performed the same transformation on the *lunga*. Since the most powerful of the kings who based their authority on the *ngola* still ruled the western Mbundu at the time the first Portuguese reached Angola during the sixteenth century, more information illuminates the history of these states than of those based on the *lunga*. The most successful of the *ngola*-kingdoms attained a degree of centralization, had a hierarchy of several levels, and expanded to greater size than any of its predecessors. Armies capable of defeating European military forces backed the will of its kings and enabled them to establish effective control over the affairs of many lineages, perhaps for the first time. By creating hierarchical centralized political institutions on the basis of the *ngola*, they had reversed the structural significance of an emblem which had first come to the Mbundu as no more than another in the long series of symbols and ideas absorbed by the Mbundu lineage system.

[44] The surviving fragmentary traditions describe only the political situation at the moment of the Imbangala conquest of Kasanje. They may therefore give a false picture of stability in this part of the Baixa de Cassanje.

[45] The name of this *lunga*-king apparently refers to an official staff given to an emissary of a chief; *kangongo* is a stick with designs carved on it, while *pango* (or *pangu*) means 'news' according to Assis Jr. (n.d.), pp. 96, 332.

[46] According to Assis Jr. (n.d.), p. 374, *ushi* refers to a seller of honey; the significance in this context is unclear. An *nzumbi* is an ancestral spirit.

[47] Koko na Mumbi's titles referred to his reputation as the only person who knew the secret of climbing to the top of Kasala, a thousand-foot-high vertical cliff which lay above his lands and provided roosts for numerous storks. The word *koko* refers to a species of climbing vine (*dervis nobilis*) and a *mumbi* is a stork in Kimbundu; Assis Jr. (n.d.), p. 154; Rodrigues Neves (1854), p. 35; testimony of Sousa Calunga 10 Sept. 1969.

The evidence on how the earliest *ngola*-kings transformed their authority from essentially egalitarian lineage alliances to something which was clearly a kingdom remains speculative, unless seventeenth-century Mbundu oral traditions provided meaningful information when they described the first great 'Ngola' as the bringer of 'axes, hatchets, knives, and arrows, the things which help the Black man in hunting and in war'.[48] The prevalence of founding smith-kings in the oral traditions of states all over Africa makes highly suspect the image of iron-wielding conquerors who create states by virtue of their superior armament and skill. Scepticism seems especially appropriate in view of the services which such iron-bearing conquerors have performed in the 'Hamitic myth' and other dubious conquest theories of state-formation. In the case of the *ngola*-kings, no known ethnographic data suggest a massive influx of conquering foreigners either during the preliminary diffusion of the *ngola* as a lineage symbol or during the later expansion of *ngola*-states. Rather, one or another of the *ngola*-holding officials of the local Mbundu descent groups must have extended his authority to neighbouring lineages by virtue of subordinated new *ngola*-titles rather than through the co-ordinate relationship of allied lineages.

The basic Mbundu aetiological genealogy of 'Ngola Inene' traces the main lines of these new rulers' development. The 'Ngola Inene', or the 'great *ngola*', represents the abstract principle of political organization based on the *ngola* and may be equated with the period before the *ngola* became an important political symbol among the Mbundu. 'Samba a Ngola', whom the genealogy depicts as the 'daughter' of 'Ngola Inene', stands for the Samba people of Matamba whom the Mbundu associate with the *ngola* at that period. The rest of this genealogy, like most Mbundu political genealogies, describes the genesis of a hierarchy of political titles composed of successive generations of 'son' titles created by incumbents in immediately superior or 'father' positions. Thus, the first remembered *ngola* political title among the Mbundu was the *kiluanje kya samba* held by lineages who lived not far from the source of the *ngola* in Matamba. The meaning of the title *kiluanje*, 'conqueror',[49] seems to indicate that the Mbundu regard this title as the spearhead of the advance of Samba political institutions into Mbundu territory.

The *ngola* came into its own among the Mbundu with the rise of

48 Cavazzi (1965), i. 253.
49 Assis Jr. (n.d.).

a second position called the *ngola a kiluanje*. Its status in the genealogy as a 'son' of Kiluanje kya Samba implies that it originated
as a subordinate position in the original state of the *kiluanje kya
samba*. Kings in the *ngola a kiluanje* title then eclipsed the holders
of the senior title during the early sixteenth century, thus continuing
the southward movement which had begun in the shift from Matamba to *kiluanje kya samba*. The *ngola a kiluanje* made their capitals
between the lower Lukala and the Kwanza near the mountains which
bounded the Luanda plateau on the west.

A seventeenth-century narrative tradition described the rise of the
ngola a kiluanje in terms which parallel the sequence evident from
the modern genealogies. Despite some confusion on the part of the
missionary who recorded this tradition, it made clear that the great
'Ngola Musuri' (equivalent to Ngola Inene) in Matamba had yielded
to lineages belonging to the Mbundu subgroup which lived on the
upper Lukala. According to the narrative, Musuri, the king in
Matamba, married an unnamed woman known only by a title,
ngana inene or great lord. This 'wife', evidently no more than a
distorted reference to some other honorific title belonging to Musuri,
bore three daughters, 'Zunda dya Ngola', 'Tumba dya Ngola', and
a third whose name the missionary neglected to record. A slave of
the great smith-king contrived his master's death, and the royal title
fell to the daughter 'Zunda dya Ngola'. The other daughter, 'Tumba
dya Ngola', married a man called Ngola a Kiluanje kya Samba
('Angola Chiluuangi Quiasamba') and eventually came into conflict
with her sister. After an appropriate series of treacherous deeds,
'Tumba' and her husband defeated 'Zunda' on the strength of
superior armed might, and Ngola a Kiluanje went on to become the
first great conquering king of the Mbundu. He had 'a great, great
number of descendants through his various concubines, who were
the chiefs of the most important families of the realm'.[50]

In conformity with the canons of modern Mbundu perpetual
genealogies, this tradition showed the pairs of linked lineages and
titles which dominated the *ngola*-kingdoms of the fifteenth and sixteenth centuries. 'Ngola Musuri' represented the *ngola*-kings in
Matamba. The name of 'Zunda dya Ngola' has been altered from
its proper form, which appears in the modern aetiological genealogies
as *zundu dya mbulu*, to make it conform to the rule that 'daughter'
titles take the first name of the 'father' position (in this case, Ngola)
as their surname. Zundu dya Mbulu (Ngola) was the legendary

[50] Cavazzi (1965), i. 253–5.

ancestress of the Ndongo subgroup of the Mbundu, precisely the lineages which lived on the middle Lukala where the *kiluanje kya samba* (mentioned in the tradition only by implication through the appearance of his title as a surname for Ngola a Kiluanje kya Samba). The tradition thus stated that the lineages of the upper Lukala (read 'the *kiluanje kya samba*') built a kingdom on the powers they derived from the great *ngola* in Matamba.

Since the missionary who recorded the tradition confessed his confusion about the correct names of the three 'daughters' of 'Ngola-Musuri', there is no reason to suppose that he recorded 'Tumba dya Ngola' correctly. The name 'Tumba' occurs in no modern variant of the Mbundu traditions and in this case was probably introduced from the histories of peoples who lived east of the Kwango where the name now figures as an ancestress of the Cokwe. 'Tumba' very likely took the place of Matamba a Mbulu, the aetiological ancestor of the Lenge people of the lower Lukala. By the rule that marriages in these genealogies signify the claiming of a title by a lineage or group of lineages, the marriage of 'Tumba a Ngola' (read 'Matamba a Mbulu', or the Lenge people) to Ngola a Kiluanje and their eventual victory over the Ndongo of the northern Lukala describes the battles in which the southern Mbundu wrested leadership from the *kiluanje kya samba* and built a new centre of *ngola*-based political power on the lower Lukala.

The capitals of the *ngola a kiluanje* state lay in the Lenge province, as the tradition suggested, and economic factors probably contributed to the expansion of these kings' power, just as the salt pans of the Lui had formed one basis for some of the *lunga*-kingdoms in the Baixa de Cassanje. The Lenge region included the iron-workings of the Nzongeji river valley, and the superior metallurgical techniques known to the Samba apparently made these ore supplies a valuable strategic prize. Not only did the *ngola a kiluanje* locate their capitals very near the mines, but they later tenaciously resisted all Portuguese advances towards this area while showing relatively little concern about Portuguese penetration elsewhere in their domains. The kings' sensitivity to threatened loss of this region may have come from their desire to protect their capital towns, as the Portuguese attackers assumed, but their dependence on control of the ore deposits could also have influenced their tactics. A secondary economic axis of the kingdom turned on possession of the Ndemba salt mines south of the Kwanza in Kisama. The *ngola a kiluanje* seem to have established their hegemony over the local political authorities near these mines early in the history of their kingdom since by the 1560s they had imposed a tax on salt which the Kisama title-holders sent to the court near the Nzongeji. Blocks of this salt circulated as a kind of 'currency' in the prestige sphere of exchange in the kingdom.[51] As late as 1798, successors of the Kisama rulers still sent tribute to the heirs of the ancient *ngola a kiluanje* who by the latter date had moved to the Wamba river and bore the Portuguese titles of the 'reis jingas'.[52]

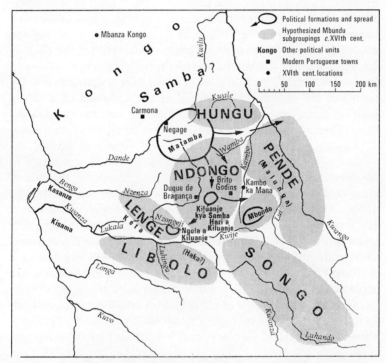

MAP III. Pre-Seventeenth Century Mbundu Subroups and Political Institutions

Once firmly in command of the economic resources of the kingdom, the kings who held the title of the *ngola a kiluanje* extended their influence into the lineages living far away through the distribution of subordinate noble titles derived from their *ngola*. In an elaboration

[51] Antonio Mendes to Padre Geral, Lisboa, 9 May 1563; Brásio (1952–71), ii. 495–512.
[52] 'Notícias do paiz . . .' (1844), pp. 123–4.

of the classic Mbundu technique of linking lineages by the award of a new perpetual named position, they awarded 'son' titles surnamed -*a ngola* to many descent groups. If possible, they took a wife from the lineage and awarded the original title to a biological son born of this marriage; they trusted him, and later his successors, to represent royal interests to their kinsmen and related lineages. One of the missionaries who visited the court of the *ngola a kiluanje* in the 1560s provided eye-witness confirmation for the seventeenth-century tradition which stated that the king had 'a great number of descendants through his various concubines, who were the chiefs of the most important families of the realm'; he reported that the ruler of the 1560s kept over 400 wives at his court.[53] Allowing for the obvious mistranslations of the Mbundu terms for 'wife' (as 'concubine') and lineage (as 'family') in the written version of the seventeenth-century tradition, the original tradition had clearly consisted of a classic political genealogy showing the ties between subordinate political titles ('descendants') and the lineages ('concubines') which held them.

Drawing on these economic bases and structural devices, the *ngola a kiluanje* kings began about 1510 to extend their influence in all directions from the lower Lukala. The evidence for the date of these developments comes from Jesuits who visited them during the 1560s and calculated that an 'Ngola Inene' had begun to overwhelm the many small states which had preceded the kingdom some fifty years earlier.[54] There is no reason not to equate the 'Ngola Inene' they mentioned with the first of the *ngola a kiluanje* kings rather than with the *kiluanje kya samba* or the 'Ngola-Musuri' in Matamba. The missionaries confused the political principle of the *ngola* ('Ngola Inene' in the usual phrase of the Mbundu) with the first incumbents in the *ngola a kiluanje* position. The Mbundu custom of referring to the major political title-holder of each Mbundu subgroup by the name

[53] Antonio Mendes to Padre Geral, Lisboa, 9 May 1563; Brásio, (1952–71), ii. 495–512.

[54] Pe Pero Rodrigues *et al.*, 'Historia da residencia dos Padres da Companhia de Jesus em Angola e cousas tocantes ao reino e conquista', 1 May 1594, Asquivo Romano da Companhia de Jesus, Lus., 106, fols. 29–39; published by Pe Francisco Rodrigues (1936), and Brásio (1952–71), iv. 546–81. Also Antonio Mendes to Padre Geral, Lisboa, 9 May 1563; Brásio (1952–71), ii, 512. Documentary allusions from the Kongo seem to support this date. As late as 1512, the Kongo king (Afonso I) claimed authority over the 'Ambudos' to the south, but by 1520 the Portuguese were preparing an expedition to visit the 'rey d'Amgola', obviously the *ngola a kiluanje*. The Portuguese emissary who eventually reached the Mbundu king's capital found a monarch powerful and arrogant enough to keep him prisoner until 1526. See Birmingham (1966), pp. 28–30, and documents cited.

of its symbolic ancestress explains the mistake. Kilamba kya Ndungu, for example, one of the most powerful Pende title-holders, is often called 'Mumbanda a Mbulu', the legendary founder of the Pende people. In the case of the *ngola a kiluanje* in the sixteenth century, the Mbundu would have praised the king to European visitors as 'Ngola Inene', founder of the Samba people. Such a convention would merely have reflected the political dominance of the *ngola a kiluanje* at the time the Jesuits collected the information.

Recognition that 'Ngola Inene' was an idea rather than a person and that the names of his 'descendants', Kiluanje kya Samba and Ngola a Kiluanje, represented perpetual titles rather than individual rulers pushes the dates for the early history of the Samba states back at least to the fifteenth century. The early sixteenth-century date for the emergence of the *ngola a kiluanje* remains acceptable on the basis of the near-contemporary record provided by the Jesuits in the 1560s. The *kiluanje kya samba* probably preceded the *ngola a kiluanje* by much more than the single biological generation implied by an interpretation of the genealogy as a human lineage; no data known to me suggest a more definite date for the rise of this position. Since the *ngola* first spread as a lineage emblem at an even more remote period, it could have reached the Mbundu as part of the general southward spread of Kongo influence and political structures as early as the thirteenth or fourteenth century.

Modern political genealogies preserve enough of the network of titles created by the sixteenth-century *ngola a kiluanje* to outline the expansion which extended their influence to all the Mbundu regions and beyond. An Ndambi a Ngola and a Kangunzu ka Ngola, from the appearance of 'ngola' as the second term in their names both evidently titles awarded directly by incumbents in the *ngola a kiluanje*, became important positions in the Matamba highlands north of the kingdom's centre. The establishment of these titles, and doubtless others as well, may have followed the defeat of the Matamba people in the wars between the northern Mbundu ('Zundu dya Ngola') and the central lineages ('Tumba dya Ngola') described in the seventeenth-century Mbundu traditions. Other titles, Kalunga ka Ngola, Muhi wa Ngola, and Nzungi a Ngola among others, brought the lineages of the central Mbundu plateau near the Mukari, Lushimbi and Tumba rivers under the sway of the *ngola a kiluanje*.[55] The award of still other *ngola*-titles west of the upper Lui extended

[55] Testimonies of Sousa Calunga, 21 Aug. 1969 and 30 Sept. 1969; also Domingos Vaz.

the central kings' influence eastward among the Pende lineages
living in the Baixa de Cassanje. The northern and eastern expansion
depended, for the most part, on the incorporation of unrelated
political titles, perhaps those of independent political structures
which had preceded the appearance of the *ngola* in those areas. A
marriage between the *ngola a kiluanje* and a lineage known as
Mbekesa a Lukunga extended these kings' authority to the north
bank of the middle Kwanza.[56] Farther to the west, the *ngola a kiluanje*
absorbed a cluster of titles in the Lenge region surnamed -*a keta*.

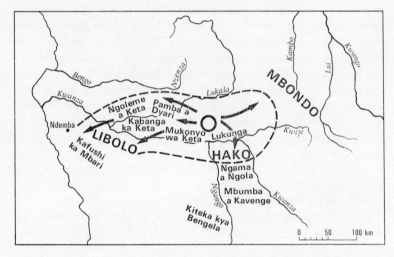

MAP IV. Expansion of the Ngola a Kiluanje (Before 1560)

The existence of several positions with the same surname indicates
that a little-known but ancient kingdom had grown up in that area
before the expansion of the *ngola a kiluanje*. By the early seventeenth
century, all of these positions had become local representatives of
the *ngola*-kings, including the most powerful of them, holders of the
ngoleme a keta in the Ilamba area west of the Lukala river.[57] The

[56] Testimony of Sousa Calunga, 21 Aug. 1969.

[57] Ngoleme a Keta later became an important enemy of the Portuguese. He
was prominent when Paulo Dias de Novaes first arrived in the 1560s and was
still a major power when the second Portuguese expedition to Angola came in
1575. See letter from Paulo Dias de Novaes to el-Rei, 3 July 1582 (B.M., Add.
MSS. 20, 786, fols. 182–183ᵛ; Brásio (1952–71), iv. 341–5. A later Ngoleme
still possessed sufficient strength in 1644 to defeat a Portuguese army, but he
finally succumbed in the late 1650s as the Europeans took reprisals for his
1644 victory; Cadornega (1940–2), i. 349–55 and ii. 141–9.

original *keta* had probably based their state on control of the iron-ore deposits located in the mountains there.[58] These *keta*-kings apparently never developed the ore deposits to their full potential, perhaps because their limited iron-working technology prevented them from making as effective military use of the ore as did the Samba under the *ngola a kiluanje*. Their inability to fabricate weapons would have left them vulnerable to the better-armed outsiders.

A variety of titles carried the authority of the *ngola a kiluanje* south of the Kwanza at an early stage in the history of the kingdom, but these nobles tended to break away from the control of the central kings as soon as they penetrated beyond the Mbundu culture area. According to the modern elders of the Kibala kingdom in the Ovimbundu highlands beyond the Longa river, descendants of some of the most far-flung *ngola* title-holders in this diaspora, several titles had crossed the Kwanza at about the same time; these included such non-*ngola* positions as Kiteke kya Bengela, Kafushi ka Mbari, Mbumba a Mbundo, and Mbumba a Kavenge, in addition to the more standard position of Ngama a Ngola. The holders of the *kafushi ka mbari* moved south-west until the title eventually came to rest among the non-Mbundu people at the Kisama salt deposits. The others settled on both banks of the Ngango river, with Ngama a Ngola and Mbumba a Kavenge moving along the left bank in Hako and Kiteke kya Bengela going farthest south into the highlands where they established themselves as rulers of the 'Marimba' people south of the Longa.[59] A few isolated titles descended from the *ngola a kiluanje* may have penetrated as far south as the Hanya who lived in the mountains above the later Portuguese town of Benguela; their modern descendants still ascribe their origins to the 'great Ngola of the north'.[60] All of these southern title-holders broke

---

[58] Seventeenth-century documents usually spelt the name 'Caita' or 'Gaeta'. G. Weeckx (1937), p. 151, equated Keta with Musuri and Mbumba a Mbulu, implicitly confirming the antiquity of the title. Sousa Calunga, testimonies of 11 and 30 Sept. 1969 gave genealogies for the titles of this state and added that *ngola a kiluanje* later took wives from those lineages (i.e. incorporated them).

[59] Brandão (1904), pp. 77, 407–8. Brandão's note that the Kisama recognized the *kiluanje kya samba* as their overlord rather than the *ngola a kiluanje* suggests that this phase of the expansion may have preceded the rise of the latter *ngola*-title. Although it is probably impossible to arrive at an exact date for these events, it is quite possible that these titles spread south long before the arrival of the Portuguese, contrary to the naïve chronological calculations of Brandão, who argued that the positions were those of *ngola*-officials fleeing before Portuguese military forces in 1582. Ngama a Ngola's presence in Libolo was documented during the 1650s; Cavazzi (1965), i. 28.

[60] Alfred Hauenstein (1967b), pp. 229ff, and (1960), p. 222. Hauenstein's

away from the *ngola a kiluanje* and became politically independent as the people who controlled the positions adapted them to local cultures which lacked the Mbundu sense for the subtleties of perpetual kinship and positional succession.

A brief seventeeenth-century history listing the early holders of the *ngola a kiluanje* title provides tantalizing glimpses of the internal political history of the kingdom. Its basic structure, an alliance of lineages linked by fictitious 'marriages' to a single dominant title, meant that the descent groups in control of the most powerful subordinate positions of the state fought among themselves for control of the royal title. The written versions of this tradition, distorted as usual, took the form of a kinglist:[61]

1. Ngola a Kiluanje;
2. Ndambi a Ngola;
3. Ngola a Kiluanje;
4. Jinga a Ngola a Kilombo kya Kasenda (a usurper);
5. Mbande a Ngola.

The missionary who recorded these 'names' confused the title of the position, *ngola a kiluanje* (numbers 1 and 3), with the names of the subordinate titles which rotated in control of the kingship (numbers 2, 4, and 5). Comparison of this kinglist with the modern political genealogies of the *ngola a kiluanje* state shows that the succession from (presumably) the original *ngola a kiluanje* to the *ndambi a ngola* marked the passage of power from lineages in control of the senior title to those holding the subordinate *ndambi a ngola* position. Geographically, there was a movement from the founding lineages on the lower Lukala back to northern lineages living not far from the Matamba area where the Samba had originated. Their accession marked a resurgence of the northern Samba over their southern relatives who had broken away to build the *ngola a kiluanje* into its independent status. The takeover by the *ndambi a ngola* may have occurred during the 1540s when the occupant of the southern *ngola a kiluanje* position tried to contact the Portuguese king.[62] His desire

[61] Cavazzi (1965), i. 256–7. Contemporary sources customarily confused titles of rulers with the names of the incumbents.

[62] Antonio Mendes to Padre Geral, Lisboa, 9 May 1563; Brásio (1952–71), ii. 497. I concur in the analysis presented by Birmingham (1966), p. 34.

speculation that these *ngola*-chiefs moved south after the 1671 defeat of the puppet *ngola a kiluanje* in Pungo Andongo is not based on any evidence. It seems much more likely that this title represents part of the expansionary period of the state rather than its dying gasp.

to contact the Europeans could have arisen from pressures which the southern Samba king was feeling from his northern relatives in Matamba.

The hypothesis that this diplomatic initiative of the 1540s came from a king who felt himself on the defensive against holders of a subordinate 'son' position, the *ndambi a ngola*, explains the behaviour of the succeeding northern king. He received in a hostile fashion the missionaries whom the Portuguese crown finally dispatched to the Mbundu twenty years later in the 1560s. The king whom these Jesuits met presented himself as 'Ndambi a Ngola', a 'son' of the *ngola a kiluanje* who had requested them two decades before, and made it clear that he, unlike his 'father', regarded the Europeans as a threat. His hostility to the foreigner could have stemmed from fears that they might discover the change in the descent groups in control of the title; the location of the capital among the southern lineages far from his own kinsmen would have made him vulnerable to an attempt at restoration of the former regime.[63] At the same time, the *ndambi a ngola* obviously hesitated to treat his guests too roughly. His consequent inability to reconcile conflicting opinions at his court as to the best way to handle their presence led to the vacillating policies which kept the leader of the expedition, Paulo Dias de Novaes, and his Jesuit companions captives at the capital for most of the decade.[64]

During the 1570s, 1580s, or 1590s, power seems to have passed from the lineages behind the *ndambi a ngola* to other descent groups in control of another political title remembered in the traditions as a 'usurper'. Since this was a period when the Portuguese were largely confined to a beach-head they had established at Luanda in 1575 and to the lower Kwanza valley, written sources add almost nothing to the internal history of the *ngola a kiluanje* kingdom. The intruder, called 'Jinga a Ngola a Kilombo kya Kasenda', may probably be identified through the modern Mbundu genealogies. Pende lineages of the Lui valley in one of the old *lunga-kingdoms*, that of Swaswa

[63] Alternatively, of course, Mbundu attitudes towards the Europeans might have changed as a result of stories reaching them from Kongo where the Portuguese residing at the *mani* Kongo's court were falling from the favour they had enjoyed during previous years. Their ability to disrupt the internal politics of that state was becoming increasingly apparent.

[64] The documentation on the visit of Dias de Novaes and the Jesuits to the court of the *ngola a kiluanje* during the 1560s has been published in the *AA*, sér. 2, xvii, nos. 67–70 (1960), 8–32; these letters also appear in Brásio (1952–71), ii and iv, and in Sousa Dias (1934).

dya Swali, had created a small subsidiary state in which the central title bore the name Kasenda ka Swaswa (dya Swali). 'Jinga a Ngola a Kilombo kya Kasenda' may thus have been an *ngola-title*, the *jinga a ngola*, which belonged to the Pende lineage of Kilombo kya Kasenda (ka Swaswa dya Swali). Perpetual genealogies from the middle Lui suggest that lineages related to Swaswa dya Swali were among the most powerful descent groups in the Baixa only a few years later during the 1620s to 1640s. Their prominence at the later period may well have derived from a period of control over the *ngola a kiluanje* during the late sixteenth century. They could have originally won the *ngola*-title as a result of their proximity to the Luhanda salt pans once dominated by the *lunga*-king Butatu. The shift in the internal political balance of the *ngola a kiluanje* state to the Baixa de Cassanje may have coincided with the spread of *ngola*-titles to the Pende of the middle Lui.[65]

The accession of 'Mbande a Ngola', the next title named in the seventeenth-century kinglist, represented the transfer of effective political power to a third lineage or group of lineages. These descent groups also lived in the Baixa de Cassanje, somewhat west of Swaswa dya Swali in the basin of the Kambo. The later *ngola a kiluanje* looked back on the *mbande a ngola* as a legitimate king in contrast to the usurper 'Jinga a Ngola a Kilombo kya Kasenda', but the apparent discontinuity in terms of legitimacy concealed an underlying continuity in terms of the lineages who controlled the position, as indicated by the fact that power remained in the east, in the Baixa de Cassanje. The holder of the *mbande a ngola* title who claimed the *ngola a kiluanje* had been a 'son' of the usurper 'Jinga a Ngola a Kilombo kya Kasenda'. Since the sources for this tradition (recorded in the 1650s) could have recalled these events from living memory (not more than sixty to eighty years earlier), they probably referred to a biological son, not a derivative title, of the intruding holder of the *jinga a ngola*. This *jinga a ngola* had evidently married a woman from a lineage in possession of the legitimate *ngola-position* of the *mbande a ngola* and had then manoeuvred his real son into the title to which he would have been fully entitled under the rules of matrilineal succession. The entry of the son, whose personal name was evidently not recorded, kept the lineage of the father (Kilombo kya Kasenda) in position to exercise a strong voice in the affairs of the realm. Although no evidence dates the accession of the first *mbande a ngola*, the *ngola a kiluanje* who died in 1617 was probably from

65 Cf. Muhi wa Ngola, etc., p. 79.

this lineage, and the king who died in 1624 certainly bore this title.[66]

Defeats by Portuguese armies interrupted the autonomous political processes of the *ngola a kiluanje* state during the 1620s. The victorious Portuguese transferred the central title to another group of lineages, holders of the *hari a kiluanje*, a senior *ngola* position in a collateral line, a 'brother' position to the *ngola a kiluanje* and a direct descendant of the old *kiluanje kya samba*. Although the *hari a kiluanje* had legitimacy or even seniority in a technical sense, holders of that position had apparently never exercised much influence in the affairs of the kindom, and the Mbundu never acknowledged them as heirs to the *mbande a ngola*. The title does not appear at all in the modern political genealogies, and the *hari a kiluanje* kingdom belongs to the history of the Portuguese conquest rather than to the study of state-formation in the context of the Mbundu lineages.

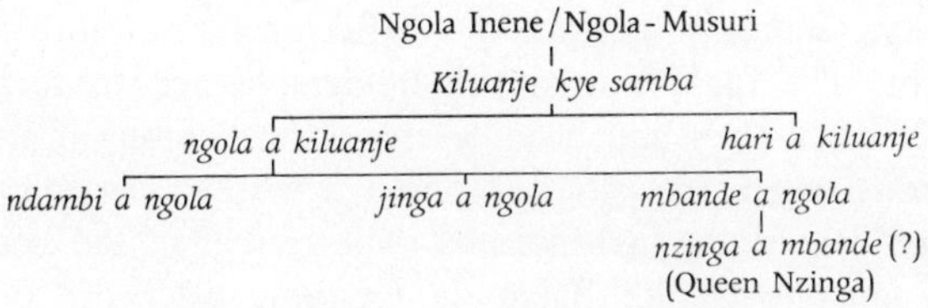

Ngola Inene / Ngola - Musuri
|
Kiluanje kye samba
|
ngola a kiluanje   hari a kiluanje
| |
ndambi a ngola   jinga a ngola   mbande a ngola
|
nzinga a mbande (?)
(Queen Nzinga)

FIG. IV. Relationship of *Ngola*-Titles.

TABLE 1

Chronology of the Ngola a Kiluanje

Ruler(s)	Location	Dates
'Ngola Inene'/'Ngola-Musuri'	Matamba	?
kiluanje kya samba	Upper Lukala	(fifteenth century)
ngola a kiluanje	Middle Lukala	*c.* 1510–1540s
ndambi a ngola	Matamba	*c.* 1550s–1560s
jinga a ngola (usurper)	Baixa de Cassanje	*c.* 1570s–1590s?
mbande a ngola	Baixa de Cassanje	*c.* 1600s?–1624
* { *hari a kiluanje* (puppet)	Pungo Andongo	1624–1671
{ Nzinga	Baixa de Cassanje	1620s–present

* rulers of the separate successor states ('Hari' and 'Matamba').

Up to that point, politics in the *ngola a kiluanje* kingdom had revolved around competition between lineages or coalitions of

---

[66] Bishop D. Simão Mascarenhas to el-Rei, 2 Mar. 1624 (A.H.U., Angola, cx. 1); Brásio (1952–71), vii, 199–203.

lineages based on the pre-*ngola* lineage groupings. Each had tried to place their own kinsmen, holders of the senior state titles, in the central position of the *ngola a kiluanje*. The central kings presumably tried to break down the solidarity of these lineage groupings through the placement of subordinate *ngola*-positions in the lineages most likely to give their loyalty to the central kingship. Although the holders of the *ngola a kiluanje* grew powerful through their control of the iron-rich country near the Nzongeji river and seem to have maintained their capitals in that region, the men who exercised this authority came from a variety of lineages located elsewhere in the kingdom. Generally, the lineages to the north and east seemed to dominate through their possession of such senior state titles as the *ndambi a ngola* and the *mbande a ngola*.

The holders of the pre-*ngola* titles in the south and west never acquired much influence at the centre of the kingdom, although some of them—notably Ngoleme a Keta, Kafushi ka Mbari, and Kiteke kya Bengela—became powerful provincial lords in their own right. The far southern title-holders tended to break away, especially when they had become established among non-Mbundu populations where the *ngola* exercised a weaker attraction than it did nearer its origins in Matamba. The retreat of the heirs of the *ngola a kiluanje* to the Baixa de Cassanje after the Portuguese defeated the main kingdom in the 1620s therefore represented a withdrawal of the capital toward the lineages which had held effective authority since the 1560s. This hypothesis accounts for the survival of the successor 'Jinga' state in the Baixa de Cassanje during the eighteenth and nineteenth centuries. The puppet *hari a kiluanje* who remained on the plateau represented an entirely different set of lineages and were regarded by the Mbundu as a separate state which existed only at the pleasure of the Portuguese and had no legitimacy in traditional terms.

Conclusions

The *lunga*-kings of the Baixa de Cassanje and the kingdom of the *ngola a kiluanje* were only the two best-known examples of a much larger class of early Mbundu states which sprang from entirely local roots. Although many of the other early state-like structures which appeared among the Mbundu have, like the *keta*-kings of the Lenge, almost entirely dropped from the historical record, all may be analysed entirely in terms of indigenous Mbundu beliefs about authority, the distribution of symbolic objects to confer authority over men, and beliefs in positional succession and perpetual kinship. Mutually corroborative evidence from documentary sources and oral traditions suggests that Mbundu state-building techniques were a product of a fundamentally inflexible lineage structure, made unusually rigid by the ability of perpetual kinship and positional succession to preserve historic ties between kin groups. Since the Mbundu did not have the freedom to alter their lineage genealogies to reflect changing social and political conditions as did similarly structured societies elsewhere,[67] they had to provide other social channels through which men might pursue personal ambition or respond to circumstances not comprehended by the patterns of kinship. Although the traditions do not indicate the exact conditions which prompted certain lineages to adopt new symbols and to restructure their relationships to other descent groups, numerous descent groups clearly made such adjustments repeatedly throughout their history. The early *malunga* and *jingola* provide examples of non-centralized and basically non-hierarchical reorganizations of this type.

Once a new symbol of authority had spread among the Mbundu lineages, however, individual holders of certain titles were repeatedly able to expand their personal spheres of influence beyond the confines of their lineage to claim a measure of authority over persons not related to them. In the case of the *malunga*-kings of the Baixa de Cassanje, control over an extensive salt trade radiating from salt pans located within their territories seems to explain the rise of the Butatu and later the Swaswa dya Swali dynasties. Factors of a similarly economic nature seem to underlie the growth of the *ngola a kiluanje*, since those rulers derived some of their strength from their domination of the iron mines of the Nzongeji River. The expansion of this kingdom clearly pointed toward the salt pans of Kisama, and later internal political developments revealed the strength of the north-eastern lineages nearest the Luhanda river salt deposits. However important the economic causes of the growth and expansion of the early Mbundu kingdoms may have been, these elements inevitably attract the attention of historians since the evidence of their presence survives for all to see in the form of salt pans and abandoned iron tailings. What history has lost, in all these cases, is the role of individual human genius, the play of chance, and most of the intricacies of political manoeuvring which must also have contributed to the development of these states.

[67] A classic case is the Tiv of Nigeria; Paul and Laura Bohannon (1953).

The generalized model of indigenous Mbundu state-formation takes as its starting-point the assumption that new cross-cutting institutions continually appeared among the Mbundu descent groups. The strength of the kin groups was sufficient in many cases to convert the symbols of these movements into emblems of the lineage structure, as it did initially with both the *malunga* and the *jingola*. Among the countless anonymous holders of titles associated with these symbols, a few talented or fortunate individuals managed from time to time to convert their control of a valuable economic resource into effective political power. Their states took the form of more or less extensive lineage coalitions based on awards to other descent groups of political titles subordinate to their own. Some of these states were growing even as others were declining throughout the entire period before 1600. The *lunga*-kings were well into their history before the holders of *ngola* reached their peak towards the middle of the sixteenth century. The *ngola a kiluanje* state eclipsed all but the most remote of the *lunga*-kings before it, too, bowed to outsiders, the Imbangala and the Portuguese, who introduced new political structures of a fundamentally different type in the opening decades of the seventeenth century.

CHAPTER IV

New Ideas from the South

THE FOCUS of the preceding chapter on indigenous Mbundu methods of building states leading up to the sixteenth-century expansion of the *ngola a kiluanje* excluded any mention of an important contemporaneous kingdom called Libolo. Libolo, which was centred among the Mbundu south of the Kwanza river, requires separate treatment because its kings used political institutions entirely different from the perpetual titles and linked descent groups of the northern Mbundu state to restruct the Mbundu lineages into a kingdom. Although the origins of Libolo as yet remain even more obscure than those of the *lunga* and the *ngola*, its major organizing technique, a title called a *vunga*, has left clear evidence that it came from regions outside the Mbundu area where positional succession and perpetual kinship reigned supreme. The *vunga* embodied a conception of authority which was structurally the opposite of the hereditary titles awarded to the lineages by the *lunga*-kings and the *ngola a kiluanje* since it introduced for the first time a type of position which lay outside the control of the descent groups.

The Kulembe

Although the *vunga* reached the Mbundu through the intermediary of the Libolo political system, these titles had originated in an earlier state known only by the title, *kulembe*, of a shadowy line of kings who claimed authority over portions of the Benguela plateau several centuries before the present Ovimbundu kingdoms in that region were formed. The capital of these rulers lay somewhere near the sources of the three major rivers draining the north-western part of these highlands, the Longa, the Kuvo, and the Ngango.[1] Documentary and oral sources concur in dating the rise of the

---

[1] Kings bearing the title of Kulembe kwa Mbandi still preserved this name in the 1850s when they lived in 'Selles', roughly the highland area just west of the sources of the Kuvo river. See László Magyar (1859), p. 379. An area known as 'Lulembe' still existed somewhere on the highlands south of the Kwanza in the late seventeenth century; Cadornega (1940–2), iii. 249. The prefix to the -*lembe* root varied considerably in written sources of this period.

kulembe to long before the mid-sixteenth century.[2] It was thus one of the earliest Benguela Plateau kingdoms now visible in the surviving evidence. None the less, the significance of the *kulembe* state has eluded most historians, who have described the area south of the Kwanza almost exclusively in terms of the later Ovimbundu states. Neglect of the *kulembe* has probably resulted from the fact that the traditions of the later Ovimbundu kingdoms, like those of the Mbundu, date from the formation of these political entities (roughly the late seventeenth century) and have eliminated all but the faintest traces of earlier historical periods.[3] Outside the Ovimbundu area, however, Mbundu perpetual genealogies have preserved memory of the *kulembe* title as the progenitor of a series of derivative political titles which ultimately led to the later dynasty of Mbondo kings.[4] The social and political structures of these pre-Ovimbundu states remain too poorly known to justify speculation beyond the fact that the *kulembe* apparently ranked among the most important early states in the Benguela highlands.[5]

Expansion of Libolo

The distinctive political institutions which originally emanated from the *kulembe* reached the Mbundu indirectly through an intermediary dynasty of kings who bore the title of *hango*. These rulers built another kingdom, now known as Libolo,[6] located somewhat north of the *kulembe* among Mbundu who lived on the Ngango affluent south

[2] Testimony of Alexandre Vaz, 31 July 1969; the date is deduced from the position of the *kulembe* title in a genealogy including later perpetual names known through documents to have become powerful well before 1600. E. G. Ravenstein (1901), p. 85 (where the spelling of the name was 'Elembe'), and Cavazzi (1965), i. 188–90.

[3] The best summary of the history of the later Ovimbundu states is Childs (1949), pp. 164–90. New fieldwork on these kingdoms, and their successors, is urgently needed. One obvious direction in which such studies might look is towards the builders of the numerous stone ruins which now dot the Benguela highlands.

[4] This instance of remnant traditions surviving outside the area of their origin parallels other examples of traditions no longer extant among the Imbangala but still alive among the Cokwe, Songo, and Ovimbundu; the following chapters provide examples.

[5] Beyond the position of the *kulembe* in the perpetual genealogies, most documentary sources from the seventeenth century contain references to the *kulembe* as a 'great and powerful king'. The vague quality of these references confirms the impression that the kingdom had declined by that time.

[6] The ancient Mbundu probably used the name Libolo only for the regions south of the Kwanza where the *hango* kings had their capitals. Mbundu kingdoms usually took their names from the title of their kings, in this case the *hango*. Libolo, is however, the name used today by Mbundu historians.

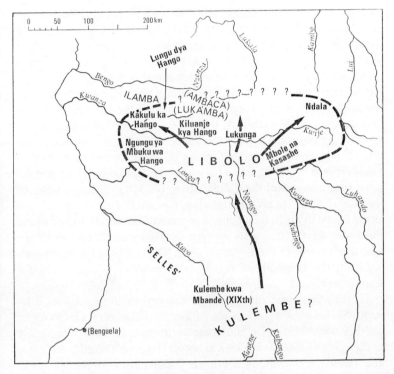

MAP V. Kulembe and Libolo (c. XVth–XVIth?)

of the Kwanza. The *hango* expanded their control in part by granting perpetual subordinate titles to the lineages as the *ngola a kiluanje* had done, but they also relied on a type of temporary position which retained a greater concentration of power in the hands of the central kings. Although, once again, a nearly complete lack of historical data on Libolo precludes detailed reconstruction of the rise of the kingdom, it was one of the earliest large states to appear among Kimbundu-speakers, probably contemporary with the Pende *lunga*-kings and certainly older than the *ngola a kiluanje*. It evidently flourished well before the mid-sixteenth century, when documents implicitly showed that it had already fallen into decline and had been replaced by the *ngola a kiluanje* everywhere north of the Kwanza.

Mbondo perpetual genealogies identify Hango dya Kulembe, the Libolo king, as a 'son' of the *kulembe*. While these traditions accurately trace the derivation of the authority claimed by the *hango*, they do not describe the historical process by which Libolo kings grew powerful and eventually asserted their independence from the older state to the south. The predecessors of the *hango*-kings might have existed among the southern Mbundu for some time, probably under another name, before they obtained a 'son' title from the *kulembe* at whatever time the influence of the older kingdom penetrated the upper Ngango region. Alternatively, the *kulembe* may have first asserted their authority over the southern Mbundu lineages together by imposing a provincial governor to rule them under the title of *hango*. Whatever the origins of these kings, the history of Libolo comes into clear focus only after the *hango* had prospered for some time and spread their authority to the Mbundu living north of the Kwanza. At its height, the kingdom reached as far north-east as the Pende living in the highland sources of the Kambo river above the Baixa de Cassanje. Its eastern provinces included the Songo who dwelt north of the Luhando river. The southern Libolo boundary with the kingdom of the *kulembe* remains undetermined for want of evidence.

The locations of a number of seventeenth-century political titles surnamed 'Hango' establish the former boundaries of Libolo along and beyond the lower Lukala in the north-west. Officials subordinate to the *ngola a kiluanje* entitled Kakulu ka Hango governed the Museke and Ilamba region along the lower Lukala river as late as 1592.[7] Even though they had by that time become provincial governors of the *ngola*-kingdom, their titles revealed that they had originated as outposts of Libolo and had survived the decline of Libolo to be incorporated in typical Mbundu pattern as elements in later political structures. Other *hango*-positions dotting this area provided evidence of former Libolo control: Kiluanje kya Hango lived in the Lukamba area of the middle Lukala, and Ngungu ya Mbuku wa Hango held the north bank of the Kwanza just below the falls at Kambambe.[8]

[7] Cadornega (1940–2), iii. 235, 240, placed Kakulu ka Hango on the southern bank of the Kwanza near Mushima in the late seventeenth century, where he had probably fled from the advancing Portuguese; Sala a Hango remained in Ilamba at that time.

[8] Domingos de Abreu e Brito, 'Rellação breve das cousas, que se contem neste tratado dangola e Brazil' (B.N.L., MS. 294); published in Alfredo de Albuquerque Felner (1931), and *AA*, iii, nos 25–7 (1937), 249–90; also excerpted in Brásio (1952–71), iv. 533–45. The Portuguese spellings were quaquluquiambo Quiloange quiambo, and Gungu ambo cambo; comparison with Cadornega (1940–2) leaves no doubt that these spellings all represented 'Hango'.

Elsewhere, only a few hereditary named titles of Libolo origin appear in written sources or oral traditions. Lukunga, a position identified as subordinate to the *hango*, ruled the area north of the confluence of the Kwije and the Kwanza.[9] Lungu dya Hango lived in Ambaca during the latter half of the seventeenth century and, although his presence was not recorded earlier, had probably been there for some time.[10] Another title-holder whose capital occupied one of the islands in the upper Kwanza, Mbola na Kasashe, apparently served as guardian of Libolo's south-eastern frontiers.[11] The north-eastern Libolo frontier, to which I shall return, ran along the escarpment above the Baixa de Cassanje.

The central provinces of the Libolo kingdom during its most prosperous periods lay in the valley of the Ngango river. The later Portuguese name for this area, 'Hako', identifies it as the seat of the *hango*-kings since the European toponym probably represented a European corruption of the Kimbundu title.[12] The perpetual genealogies show a concentration of *hango*-derived titles in the Hako region, including the *kaza ka hango*, a position whose incumbents became famous in the 1620s as allies of the Mbundu queen Nzinga in her battles against the advance of Portuguese military control. The exact location of these kings' capitals has not been found nor, to my knowledge, systematically sought.

The northern boundaries of Libolo contracted under pressure from the expanding kingdom of the *ngola a kiluanje* during the sixteenth century. Beyond loss of the Lenge titles such as Kakulu ka Hango, which became subordinate officials of the Samba kings, other former Libolo positions like the Lukunga sent women as wives to the *ngola a kiluanje* and received in return subordinate *ngola*-positions as agents of the central rulers. The southward expansion of such *ngola*-title-holders as the Kiteke kya Bengela, the Ngama a Ngola, and others drove the *hango*-kings out of their home provinces in Hako. Only a few *hango*-titles survived there as minor officials at the courts of the new representatives of the great *ngola* in

[9] Testimony of Sousa Calunga, Kambo ka Kikasa; Lukunga was said to have been a '*kota*' of the *hango*, that is a lineage title belonging to a descent group with the right to elect incumbents to the royal *hango*-title.

[10] Cadornega (1940–2), iii. 244.

[11] Various testimonies of Sousa Calunga.

[12] Cf. p. 90, n. 6 above, on the tendency of Mbundu to name regions after political officials, e.g. Hango/Hako. The demonstrated irregularities of seventeenth-century spellings of Kimbundu words ('Hango' in particular) and parallel sound shifts in other words establish the identity of 'Hango' and 'Hako'.

Ndongo.[13] By 1600, only the far south-western province of greater Libolo, the area nearest Kisama, remained as the last refuge for its once-powerful rulers. *Hango*-kings remained as minor local rulers in this remnant state on the southern bank of the Kwanza until at least the end of the seventeenth century.[14]

The *hango* of Libolo managed to dominate a wider area than any previous Mbundu kings (before the *ngola a kiluanje*) by awarding an appointive political title called a *vunga* (plural, *mavunga*). Unlike the perpetual hereditary titles of the Mbundu, the *vunga* carried only temporary authority delegated by the king to his appointed nominee. The Libolo kings seem to have ruled through classic Mbundu perpetual named positions only in their home province of Hako and among the north-western Lenge lineages. Elsewhere, beyond the limits of the relatively easily controlled home territory, the *hango* ruled through provincial governors holding *mavunga*. The *hango*-kings awarded these titles on their own initiative, usually through presentation of some symbol indicating the mandate of the recipient, and these appointments lasted only until revocation or until the death of the individual title-holder. The appointee's emblem then returned to his lord rather than remaining with his heirs.

Since *vunga*-holders could not bequeath their positions to kinsmen, the *mavunga* did not become heritable lineage-controlled titles as did the Mbundu named perpetual positions. The tendency of individual lineages to gain control over the perpetual variety of title had hindered the *lunga*-kings' efforts to build large centralized states, and the kingdom of the *ngola a kiluanje* suffered from continual strife among its component lineages. But, since the *hango*-kings could appoint men who owed their positions solely to the central ruler and would give undivided loyalty to him, no similar instability limited the expansion of a state based on *mavunga*. The *vunga* enabled the *hango* to overcome an additional disadvantage which had beset kings holding *malunga*. The rigid correspondence between the *lunga*-positions and the hydrography of the land made these titles an inflexible means of expansion, while Libolo kings, on the other hand, could appoint as many *vunga*-holders as they found expedient and could locate them wherever and whenever they wished.

The nature of the Mbundu oral traditions filtered out all direct

[13] Brandão (1904), p. 137, noted a *mukila a hango* in such a position at the end of the nineteenth century.
[14] Cadornega (1940–2), iii. 240, recorded the presence of title-holders of this name.

information on how *mavunga* positions functioned in the sixteenth century. The perpetual genealogies preserved a record of only the hereditary lineage titles, and, because the *mavunga* did not fit into any of the limited categories of preserved information, no recollection of these titles could survive. Still, indirect evidence derived from *mavunga* awarded much later by the political heirs of the *hango*, Imbangala and Mbondo kings, allows a sketch of the functions and significance of the ancient Libolo titles.

Mbondo and Imbangala *mavunga* obliged their holders to perform specialized duties in support of the king and his court.[15] Some *vunga*-holders, for example, sent supplies of food to the royal capital; others maintained armed forces ready to defend the king against outside invaders. Still others might keep the roads and paths running through a specific territory in good repair. Each *vunga*-holder discharged his obligation to his king by extracting labour and wealth from the people who lived in the area assigned to him. The demands made by the *vunga*-holders created tensions which divided them from the lineages and placed them in opposition to the lineages' interest in autonomy. They thus depended exclusively on the king for their authority and had little chance of raising the local kinsmen in rebellion against the *hango*. The *mavunga* titles thus produced a relatively centralized state structure, one beyond the reach of the restless Mbundu lineages, which helped the *hango* kings expand north and south of the Kwanza.

The history of the Libolo province (and later the Mbondo kingdom) of the *ndala* (*kisua*) offers the best evidence to date on the nature of *hango* overrule among the northern Mbundu. It provides detail about the names and functions of some *mavunga* and shows how the Libolo governors' titles lost their independence from descent group control and became little more than lineage titles when the power of the central *hango*-kings declined. The lineages of the area which became the *ndala* province of Libolo had once formed part of the relatively undifferentiated Pende population which extended from the Kwango west to the middle Lukala river. The Pende of the highlands east of the Lushindo river and north of the Kwije[16] acquired a distinctive identity as Mbondo when the *hango*-kings brought them into the Libolo kingdom under the immediate authority of a *vunga*-holder called the *ndala*, or mamba, a species of highly poisonous

---

[15] Testimonies of Alexandre Vaz, Domingos Vaz, 26 June 1969; Alexandre Vaz, 30 July 1969; Alexandre Vaz, Domingos Vaz, Ngonga a Mbande.
[16] Testimony of Kasanje ka Nzaje.

snake found throughout southern Angola.[17] The prevalence of similar *ndala* positions south of the Kwanza connects the origin of the Mbondo *ndala* with the Benguela highlands beyond Libolo, perhaps in Kulembe itself. Elsewhere in the highlands, the Ovimbundu, present-day descendants of the ancient people of the *kulembe*, regard the *ndala* snake with great awe, describing it as a magical serpent which dwelt high on the inaccessible slopes of mountains and could fly mysteriously through the air. The modern Ovimbundu imply that the *ndala* is one of the oldest representations of political authority known to them, since they sometimes associate it with the *mulemba* tree and recall that the great *ndala* fled (i.e. declined into insignificance) at the arrival of the present political authorities, whose power rests on other bases.[18]

The location of the Mbondo *ndala*'s capital and the shape of their domain suggest, in the absence of better information, the role they played in the larger Libolo kingdom. The *ndala*'s capital occupied a nearly inaccessible and easily defended location on the crest of the 1,500-foot-high escarpment of Katanya.[19] The eastern and northern limits of the Mbondo *ndala*'s authority lay just beyond the foot of these cliffs and abutted the lands of Pende *lunga*-kings living in the Baixa de Cassanje. The bulk of the Mbondo kingdom extended through thickly wooded grasslands south-west from the capital towards Libolo. From their secure redoubt high above the surrounding lowlands, the *ndala* in effect guarded the north-eastern frontier of Libolo.[20] The identity of the threat which led Libolo kings to place the *ndala* in that location is not known, but Butatu a Kuhonga kwa Wutu wa Nyama, the powerful Pende king of that period, is a likely candidate. A very early trade route running from the Kwanza through Mbondo to the salt marshes of the Luhanda river in the Baixa de Cassanje might have drawn the attention of the *hango*-kings in that direction.

A certain vagueness in the perpetual genealogies surrounds the

[17] See Statham (1922), p. 280, who gave the species as *Dendraspis anguisticep*.

[18] The Mbundu refer explicitly to the alien origins of this title when they say that the words comprising it mean 'different language' (which they do not in any but a symbolic way); testimony of Kingwangwa kya Mbashi. For data on the Ovimbundu *ndala* see A. Hauenstein (1960, pp. 224, 231; 1964, p. 930; 1967a, p. 921).

[19] Testimonies of Sousa Calunga, 21 and 22 July 1969; confirmed for the late nineteenth century by Capello and Ivens (1882), ii. 15.

[20] Both the Mbundu and the Ovimbundu saw the magical variety of the serpent as a supernatural guardian; Pe Albino Alves (1951), i. 812; Cavazzi (1965), i. 210.

origin of the present Mbondo rulers' title, now called the *ndala kisua*. This uncertainty paradoxically identifies it as a *vunga* and simultaneously confirms its great antiquity. Most modern Mbundu genealogies metaphorically describe the foundation of the Mbondo kingdom as the arrival of Kajinga ka Mbulu, a fictional founding ancestress of the Mbondo lineages. Kajinga ka Mbulu, according to the narrative accompanying the genealogies, settled in an area called Lambo in the highlands near the sources of the Kambo river. There she 'married' a male known by a great variety of names: Ndala a Kikasa, Kikasa kya Ndala, Kikasa kya Kikululu kya Hango, Kikasa kya Hango, or Ndala Kisua.[21] The uncertainty about the name of Kajinga ka Mbulu's husband on the part of modern informants indicates that his title originated at a time before the creation of the present Mbondo state and the associated traditions. As a result, Mbondo historians have no means of placing it securely in the framework established by more recent genealogies and consequently disagree about its 'true' position, giving it a variety of names which reflect their feelings about its proper location. Its origin as an appointive *vunga* rather than a perpetual position would have produced the same effect. If such arguments from the nature of the data establish that the *ndala* came to the Mbondo at a very early time, the hypothesis that it originated as a Libolo *vunga* would account for its presence when the Mbondo later adopted Kajinga ka Mbulu as their fictional progenitor.

The occurrence of the name 'Hango' in two variants of the name of Kajinga ka Mbulu's husband almost certainly establishes the connection between the Mbondo *ndala* and the *hango* kings in Libolo. At least four other related positions, whose names identify them as derived from Libolo, have survived among the lineages at the centre of the Mbondo kingdom: Kyango kya Hango, Kongo dya Hango, Kikango kya Hango, and Kabele ka Hango.[22] These titles'

---

[21] Kajinga ka Mbulu should not be confused with the similarly-named Mbundu queen Nzinga, whom the Portuguese usually called 'Jinga'. The name of the later state of 'Jinga' derives from the queen 'Jinga' and likewise has no association with Kajinga. For the names, see testimonies of the Mbondo group; Sokola; Alexandre Vaz, 30 July 1969; Sousa Calunga, 29 and 30 Sept. 1969; Kingwangwa kya Mbashi; Kimbwete; Mahashi; Kabari ka Kajinga; Apolo de Matos, 8 July 1969.

[22] Testimonies of Sousa Calunga, 30 Sept. 1969; Mahashi; Kimbwete; Kingwangwa kya Mbashi. The Mbondo elision of the connecting particle with the surname Kyango Kyango, Kongo Dyango, Kabele Kango, etc. may result from combining a surname which has no meaning in Kimbundu (e.g. *hango*) with familiar Kimbundu first names, leading speakers to combine it

positions in the perpetual genealogies reveal the same ambiguities which surround that of the *ndala*, thus suggesting that Mbondo historians have here, too, faltered on the incompatibility of the *vunga* titles with genealogies based on hereditary Mbundu positions.

One set of Mbondo narrative episodes implicitly emphasizes the connection of the Mbondo state with Libolo by claiming that Kajinga ka Mbulu came from somewhere south of the Kwanza. Her alleged southern origins assume additional significance in this case because this theme contradicts the usual insistence, found everywhere else among the Mbundu, that Kajinga ka Mbulu came 'from the sea' along with the other ancestresses of the major ethno-linguistic subgroups. Interpreted with care, the tradition also accounts for the presence of certain non-lineage Mbondo officials attached to the *ndala kisua*'s court. The titles of these officials may be independently identified as having belonged originally to people living south of the Kwanza. The literal content of the tradition obviously has no historical significance since Kajinga ka Mbulu was a purely metaphorical representation of a group of lineages and could never have 'come' from anywhere in the manner that the tradition describes her journey

Since the tradition requires detailed criticism, I will begin by paraphrasing the recorded version of the narrative.[23] Kajinga ka Mbulu once lived near Luanda[24] with Ngola a Kiluanje. When the Portuguese arrived there, Kajinga ka Mbulu and Ngola a Kiluanje at first fought together against the European invaders but were eventually forced to flee. Ngola a Kiluanje went north-east where he settled on the Wamba river. Kajinga ka Mbulu fled in the opposite direction across the Kwanza river to 'Bailundo'.[25] Although the Kwanza presented a serious obstacle to Kajinga's flight, she managed to cross with the aid of Katumbi ka Ngola a Nzenza, a chief who knew magical charms capable of transporting people across the river. He placed Kajinga in a great trunk or box which floated across the river like a boat. Katumbi ka Ngola a Nzenza, however, had deceived Kajinga, for he intended to capture and kill her when she landed on

[23] Testimony of Fernando Comba, reproduced in Salazar (n.d.), ii. 140–1.

[24] An anachronism: the later Portuguese administrative capital at the coast.

[25] An anachronism: the Mbundu now use this term to denote all the Ovim-bundu kingdoms of the Benguela plateau. No state of Mbailundo existed at the time these events allegedly occurred.

---

with the preceding connective particle. If so, this would provide added evidence in support of the southern, even non-Kimbundu origins of the *hango*-kings' title.

the other side. Once she was safely on the southern bank of the river, he attempted to trap her inside the box by sitting on the lid of the trunk. Kajinga, well equipped with strong magic of her own, managed to escape from the box and slew Katumbi ka Ngola a Nzenza. She cut up the body and made his skin into a rope, a drum, a marimba, and a bowstring which gave her control of her enemy's magical powers.

Kajinga ka Mbulu then resumed her flight from the pursuing Portuguese. Her sorcerer, Muta a Kalombo,[26] flooded each river after they had crossed it to prevent their enemies from capturing them. She eventually fell in love with a man named Kima a Pata. They married, but their marriage produced no children until, after a number of years, Kajinga consulted a diviner about her sterility. He attributed the problem to an unspecified transgression committed during her flight from the Portuguese when she had crossed the river Kazanga without permission.[27] The diviner advised Kajinga to expiate her guilt by throwing a charm made of eggs, palm oil, and *ushila*[28] into the Kori river.[29] Kajinga did this and became pregnant almost immediately; she bore five children in all, Kikato kya Kajinga, Kisua kya Kajinga, Nyange a Kajinga, Yivo ya Kajinga, and Mupolo wa Kajinga. She then travelled north with her husband and children to Kabatukila where they settled near the cliffs surrounding the Baixa de Kafushi, a valley at the edge of the Baixa de Cassanje.

The following interpretation of this narrative elucidates the ways in which it repeatedly indicates southern origins for the modern titles whose names appear as characters in the narrative. The first two episodes, those describing Kajinga ka Mbulu's sojourn with Ngola a Kiluanje at Luanda and the retreat of Ngola a Kiluanje towards the Wamba, are conventional beginnings to most recitations of Mbundu history and have little more historical meaning than the 'Once upon a time . . .' which opens many English stories. Although no queen Kajinga ka Mbulu ever lived in Luanda, modern Mbondo historians customarily place her there in order to establish her as an

---

[26] The meaning of *kalombo* in Kimbundu is 'sterility'; Assis Jr. (n.d.), p. 87.

[27] The name 'Kazanga' almost certainly dates and locates this narrative, since it was an archaic name for the highlands south of Libolo which later became known as Mbailundo; A. V. Rodrigues (1968), p. 183, implied that the name probably predated the sixteenth-century (?) movement of the *kiteke kya bengela* title to Kibala.

[28] Word not identified.

[29] Probably the 'Guri', a minor stream near the mouth of the Luhando river; see Map VI. Anton E. Lux (1880), map, showed it as a 'town'. Cf. *Petermanns Geographische Mittheilungen*, ii (1856), Tafel 17.

equal of Ngola a Kiluanje, the touchstone of historical greatness among the Mbundu. Reference to the arrival of the Portuguese ordinarily explains both the present location of the *ngola a kiluanje* on the Wamba river, clearly an interpolation which falls well beyond the main line of the narrative, and Kajinga's departure from her 'ancestral home'. These episodes have no historical significance whatsoever.

The next episode, detailing Kajinga's encounter with Katumbi ka Ngola a Nzenza, includes the first historical data in the narrative since it serves to account for certain authority symbols held by later Mbondo kings, in particular a drum, a cord, and a bowstring said to have been fashioned from human skin, as well as a marimba. The image of a king facing difficulties in crossing a river is a cliché which recurs throughout Mbundu narrative episodes to explain an innovation in political or social structure. The river presents an obstacle which the ruler must overcome by introducing some drastic change in the rituals and symbols connected with his position. The Kwanza in this case constituted an effective metaphor for specific historical difficulties not recorded in the tradition, since all Mbundu were familiar with the hindrances to travel presented by this large watercourse.

The alleged location of Katumbi ka Ngola a Nzenza on the lower Kwanza near Luanda derives from two sorts of factor, some historical and others non-historical. The standard non-historical setting of the opening narrative in Luanda forces the Mbondo historian to have Kajinga cross that river in order to place her in the southern regions where the rest of the story must take place. In one sense Kajinga's crossing of the Kwanza is no more than a fictional device employed to connect two different parts of the historian's plot, a location determined more by the logic of the narrative than by historical fact. As it happens, however, Katumbi ka Ngola a Nzenza probably did live just south of the Kwanza, since documentary sources locate a so-called 'Jaga' Nzenza a Ngombe in Libolo as late as the early seventeenth century.[30] The authority symbols mentioned at this point in the narrative, the cord, drum, bowstring, and marimba, have elsewhere been associated with 'Jaga' kings in Angola. The presence of the name Nzenza in both titles and the coincidence of the 'Jaga' symbols probably connect the Katumbi ka Ngola a Nzenza

[30] Bishop D. Simão Mascarenhas to el-Rei, 2 Mar. 1624; Brásio (1952–71), vii. 199–203. See also Elias Alexandre da Silva Correa (1937), i. 238, and João Carlos Feo Cardoso de Castello Branco e Torres (1825), p. 164.

of this tradition with Nzenza a Ngombe of the documents. The episode of Katumbi ka Ngola a Nzenza represents the first historical element in Kajinga ka Mbulu's fictitious journey, and accounts for Libolo emblems of power acquired by the *ndala kisua* long before the formation of the present traditions.[31]

The Mbondo historian has introduced Muta a Kalombo into the narrative of Kajinga ka Mbulu's journey because the prototypical *muta a kalombo* title originated as a Libolo *vunga* entrusted with control of certain supernatural powers. Appointive officials holding this title today act as advisers and supernatural specialists at the courts of major Mbondo title-holders.[32] The remainder of this episode consists of a series of images found commonly in Mbundu narrative episodes. The cliché describing charms which cause a river to rise and thus impede the progress of pursuing enemies occurs often in other traditions; such spells formed an essential skill attibuted to some kings and were closely associated with rain-making techniques. The apperance of Muta a Kalombo at this point in the narrative explains how Kajinga might have escaped from the trailing Portuguese army, a feat regarded (for at least the last century in Mbondo) as difficult if not impossible to achieve.

Kima a Pata,[33] Kajinga's 'husband' in the narrative, was a title

[31] It was the location of the episode south of the Kwanza which led the Mbondo historian to include the story of Katumbi ka Ngola a Nzenza in his narrative. The narrative provides a good example of the way in which the Mbondo reorganized much older fragments of traditions to make them conform to the framework of the new *musendo* developed in the seventeenth century. A fictitious journey of the symbolic founder in the new traditions, Kajinga ka Mbulu, leads her in picaresque fashion through all the areas where earlier forms of Mbondo authority originated; it therefore took her south of the Kwanza to Libolo. Owing to the basic structure of the narrative as a journey assumed (falsely) to have begun in Luanda and to have ended in Lambo, geography rather than a sequence of actual events determines the order in which Kajinga is envisaged as having acquired the symbols in question. According to geography, for example, she must have reached Katumbi ka Ngola a Nzenza before she came to the Kuri river. The narrative in fact provides no basis for estimating the order in which the various symbols and titles in fact reached the Mbondo.

[32] Testimony of Sousa Calunga, 16 June 1969. Chatelain (1894), p. 11, had Muta a Kalombo as a 'demon' in Mbundu mythology who was 'king or governor' of the forest, hence in control of hunting and travellers. Mattos (1963), p. 337, said he was the 'god of hunting'. The ability to control rivers was attributed especially to the class of *kibinda* professional hunters. Linguistic analyses presented elsewhere show that the root *-lombo* may be uniquely associated with Umbundu languages, thus reinforcing the hypothesis of southern origins for this title.

[33] Kima appears in the genealogies with various surnames. The *kima* is a species of baboon closely associated with certain political positions.

which belonged to the Swela lineage group which today inhabits both banks of the Kwanza river above its confluence with the Luhando. This area of origin, on the edge of the old Libolo central province of Hako, tallies with the location of the Kori river mentioned in the narrative to identify the *kima* as a Libolo position. Modern Mbondo cite the Swela merely as convenient substitutes for the Libolo, the true originators of the title, since they have forgotten the position's ancient affiliation and invoke the Swela because they are the only modern Mbundu lineages with titles of southern, i.e. 'Bailundo', ancestry. The Swela in fact acquired their present Ovimbundu titles only in the eighteenth century, long after the events described in this tradition. The reference to Kima a Pata therefore comes from a much earlier period, when the Swela had Libolo titles, and thus reiterates Kajinga's connection with Libolo even though modern Mbondo historians no longer recognize the true significance of the title.

The 'marriage' between Kajinga and Kima a Pata described in the following episode is an imaginative description of the union of the *kima a pata* title and the lineages represented by the figure of Kajinga. The image of a 'marriage' accords with the generalized model of title–lineage pairings in the perpetual genealogies. It metaphorically represents the incorporation of a Libolo title by the Mbondo descent groups resident in Lambo.

These events probably took place in Mbondo rather than somewhere to the south, since such political symbols and ideas as the *kima* travelled more easily by diffusion than lineages could move by migration. The title of *kima a pata* still survives in Mbondo as a remnant from the period of Libolo rule when holders of this title, probably subordinate to the *ndala*, lived in the area of Kabatukila. Kajainga's sterility metaphorically represents the fact the Mbundu regarded earlier emblems of authority as somehow inadequate to insure their prosperity. The historical circumstances might have involved almost any misfortune: sickness, lack of rains, or the inability to unite sufficient armed forces to repel an invader, but the tradition typically gives no clues to the nature of the historical difficulties. Kajinga's inability to bear children thus indicates that the Mbondo lineages welcomed the new political system brought by the *ndala* and the *kima a pata*. This idea contrasts with other episodes in this tradition and in other narratives which explain the introduction of new political symbols in terms of conflict and suggests the need to explain why the Mbondo did not resist the imposition of Libolo overrule. No data known to me solve this riddle.

The image of a special charm involving offerings to water spirits[34] alludes metaphorically to the supernatural powers which the Mbondo attributed to their *vunga*-kings. They regarded these powers as crucial to Mbondo prosperity and helpful in spreading Libolo authority symbols to neighbouring descent groups. The union of the *kima* with the Mbondo lineages proved 'fertile' in the sense that it led to the creation of at least five (but probably more) subordinate titles, the 'children' named in the narrative. These new positions almost certainly once used 'Kima' as their surname to indicate the Libolo sources of their legitimacy, but the later decline of the *hango*-kings allowed the Mbondo to change the surnames to indicate a more autonomous association with Kajinga. In a fashion similar to the apparent surname changes which some of the Yongo *lunga*-titles underwent, this tactic provided a local, if falsified, source of legitimacy for title-holders who had lost their foreign sponsor. Although these positions may once have been important elements in the Libolo state structure, they became obsolete when the Mbondo threw off *hango* overrule and survived to the present with sharply diminished functions. The narrative of Kajinga's movement from Luanda to Mbondo, interpreted according to the rules governing Mbundu oral traditions, thus points repeatedly toward the south, that is Libolo, as the source of the most ancient known Mbondo political titles.

The titles of several Mbondo court positions confirm this interpretation of the tradition since they show clear linguistic affinities with titles known elsewhere only south of the Kwanza. The equivalent positions at the capitals of most other Mbundu kings bear different names. The three most important Mbondo court titles, all *mavunga*, bear the names *balanga* (or *palanga*), *kasanje*, and *kitushi*.[35] At least since the sixteenth century the northern Mbundu officials who perform the same functions have been called *tandala*, *ngola a mbole*, and *muzumbo*.[36] Of the uniquely Mbondo terms, *balanga* certainly comes directly from sources in the Benguela plateau region; the term does not exist in Kimbundu but in modern Umbundu

---

[34] *Malunga*? The tradition does not identify them, but new rulers from the south would logically have propitiated the spirits of the former Pende owners of the land.

[35] Testimonies of Sousa Calunga, 16 June 1969; Kasanje ka Nzaje; Kasanje ka Nzaje, Kitubiko, and Nzaje. See also Salazar (n.d.), ii. 102.

[36] For *tandala* and *ngola a mbole*, see Rodrigues (1936).

refers to a court official with the same duties as the Mbondo position.[37]

Despite great confusion in European sources about the significance of the term *kasanje* (it occurs as the name of the later Imbangala kingdom in the Baixa de Cassanje, as the title of its kings, and as the name of the regions where they ruled), it clearly originated as an appointive *vunga* position somewhere south of the Kwanza, probably in the *kulembe* or Libolo kingdoms. Kings all over the Umbundu-speaking area appointed *vunga*-officials with this title, while the Mbundu and their northern neighbours apparently had no such term. The Ovimbundu kingdom of Wambu contained a 'subchief' called *kasanje*.[38] The title turned up again on the south side of the Kwanza when the Portuguese encountered a chief known as Kasanje ka Yela near the Bay of Quicombo during the 1640s; the region was at that time inhabited by speakers of Umbundu.[39] The title usually written as Mbola na Kasashe, the Libolo noble who occupied the islands in the upper Kwanza, may have been *mbole na kasanje* before Portuguese language documents distorted it through inaccurate transcription.[40] The term *kasanje* originally meant any sort of guardian, with the implication that this official had no autonomous powers but merely administered the forces inherent in objects belonging to others. The Imbangala still used the word with this meaning in the nineteenth century as the name of a diviner, the *kasanje ka mbambo*. His name, translated literally, meant the 'guardian of the *mbambo*' basket of divining objects.[41] It also occurred as *kasanje*

[37] Alves (1951), ii. 1045.

[38] Gladwyn M. Childs (1964), p. 376. The reference would be to an appointed official, not a 'subchief' properly speaking, and would represent a title of pre-Ovimbundu origin rather than evidence of the later passage of the Imbangala as Childs suggested.

[39] Letter from Antonio Teixeira de Mendonça, 14 Sept. 1645 (A.H.U., Angola, cx. 3, cap. 8).

[40] The term *mbole* occurs in the context of an Mbundu political official's title, the *ngola a mbole*. The Songo who lived around Mbola na Kasashe spoke Kimbundu and would have used this term for the position. The name *kasanje* came from Umbundu-speakers through Libolo domination of the area. Because the title *kasanje* meant nothing in Kimbundu (in fact, it had a derogative sense), this chief acquired a double title that incorporated one element from each language. Thus he became the Kimbundu (*ngola a*) *mbole* and (*na*) the Umbundu *kasanje*.

[41] Capello and Ivens (1882), i. 384, and picture facing. The Imbangala still use the term to describe one of their divining specialists; testimony of Apolo de Matos, 6 Oct. 1969. The word *kasanje* also occurred in reference to other sorts of guardian. Schütt (1881), map, observed accurately that the exact meaning of the word *kasanje* was 'guardian'; he translated it as *Verwalter*, a

ka ngongo to denote the guardian of the Kasanje king's double gong.[42]

The word *kitushi* does not occur in standard Kimbundu but the root *-tusi* in Umbundu (equivalent to *-tushi* in Kimbundu) means an insult or injury in the specialized sense of an offence permitting the injured party to claim redress through a chief's court.[43] The prefix *ki-* in Kimbundu can indicate the person in charge of the object denoted by the following lexical root.[44] The Mbondo *kitushi*, in fact, hears cases brought before noble title-holders; the Umbundu root *-tusi* and the Kimbundu prefix ki- combine to indicate exactly this function in the Kimbundu-ized form, *kitushi*. The Mbondo also have an official called the *lumbo*, the same title as that of a seventeenth-century *vunga* brought from Libolo or from the *kulembe*.[45] These Mbondo titles possess characteristic features of the original *mavunga* since they are appointed and the men who hold them serve only at the discretion of their king.

Two final details complete the chain of evidence linking the Mbondo *ndala kisua* with the ancient kingdom of Libolo. Mbondo nobles, alone among their Mbundu neighbours, cannot eat the flesh of an ox. Since, in Angola, only people living south of the Kwanza draw this sort of connection between their nobility and cattle, the extension of the custom to the Mbondo points once again to Libolo and to the *kulembe* (whose 'wife', Mbumba a Nyasi, sunned herself on an oxhide, it was said) as the source of their political institutions. Finally, the title *ndala kisua* itself may support the hypothesis through the linguistic evidence it offers. Since the word *ndala* means mamba in both Kimbundu and Umbundu, this term does not help to trace the origin of the title. But the word *kisua* provides a historical etymology in Umbundu, but not in Kimbundu, which seems to identify Libolo as the original overlord of the Mbondo state. The form *kisua* appears in neither modern language, but the

[42] Salles Ferreira (1854–8).
[43] Alves (1951), ii. 1576.
[44] Héli Chatelain (1888–9), pp. 120–1.
[45] Testimony of Kasanje ka Nzaje; cf. Cavazzi (1965), i. 192. Although modern dictionaries provide little aid in locating the sources of other Mbondo titles of this type, those already described adequately demonstrate the connection of Mbondo to the south. Testimony of Kisua kya Njinje; Sousa Calunga, 16 June and 9 July 1969; Sokola; Kasanje ka Nzaje; Kasanje ka Nzaje, Kitubiko, and Nzaje; also Salazar (n.d.), ii. 102, give *tope, kikwiku, kishinga, a mbambi, lwamba*, and *ndala a makita*.

German word used to denote various managers, stewards, trustees, etc., all of whom control property belonging to others.

seventeenth-century reflex of the word took the form *kisuba* or *kisuva*,[46] which turns out to be a western Kimbundu word meaning 'that which remains, or something left over'.[47] The full title of the Mbondo king, *ndala kisua*, therefore designated the 'remaining *ndala*' or the '*ndala* left over' or behind among seventeenth-century Mbundu who remembered the decline of Libolo.

Elsewhere, the *hango* kings' domination of the Songo extended only to the northern lineages of this group but lasted long enough to leave traces which still distinguish these *jingundu*, called Kirima, from their southern relatives, the Songo proper. The Kirima subgroup lives west of the upper Lui and north of the Luhando river as far as the Kwije, roughly within the boundaries of the farthest extension of Libolo rule. The southern and larger group called Songo proper live along the Luhando river and east to the Kwango.[48] The distinction between Songo and Kirima had much greater significance in the seventeenth century than the few refinements in dialect noticeable today. The earliest documentary references to the area consistently differentiated between its two parts as the 'greater' and 'lesser Ganguellas'.[49] The name came from the western Mbundu who used the word *ngangela* to designate all the people living to the east of Ndongo and, although the term indicated no specific geographical region as the Mbundu employed it, the Portuguese generally applied it only to distinguish the two Songo 'Ganguellas'. Lesser Ganguella lay to the north and corresponded to the area now inhabited by the Kirima; Greater Ganguella was Songo proper. Since the *hango* kings had ruled the northern Kirima during the sixteenth century but had not conquered the southern Songo, it was probably the heritage of Libolo overrule which accounted for the distinction made not long after during the seventeenth century between these two groups of Songo lineages.

The Mbondo after the Decline of Libolo

As the *ngola a kiluanje* expanded to the south-east during the sixteenth century, it isolated the Mbondo from Libolo, leaving the *ndala* province free for the first time to develop according to local social and political conditions. The subsequent history of this state

[46] Balthasar Rebello de Aragão, 'Rellação'; Brásio (1952–71), vi. 332–43; also in Luciano Cordeiro (1881), iii. 15. Cumulative errors of scribes and editors caused the word to appear as 'chicova' in this source.

[47] Assis Jr. (1951), p. 143.

[48] Testimony of Sousa Calunga, 21 Aug. 1969.

[49] For example, Cavazzi (1965), i. 214.

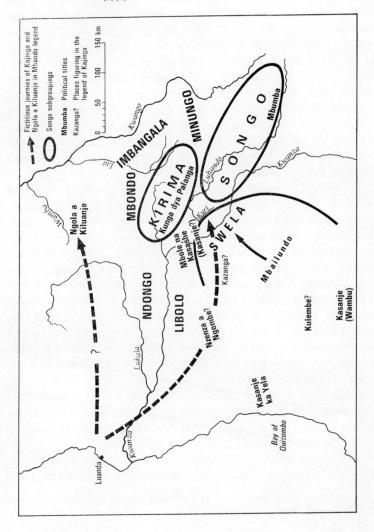

MAP VI. Songo and
Mbondo Early History

illustrates how the Mbundu lineages of the Lambo region, roughly the highland promontory thrusting north-east into the Baixa de Cassanje, took advantage of relaxed *hango* authority to convert Libolo *mavunga* into hereditary lineage titles closely akin to their own perpetual named positions. Since no single lineage managed to claim the central title of the *ndala kisua* for itelf, the Mbondo descent groups ultimately settled on a form of rotating succession in which several groups of *jingundu* shared serially in the exercise of power.

For reasons indicated in connection with my discussion of the Libolo origins of the *ndala* title, the genealogies dealing with the formation of the Mbondo kingdom contain a great many ambiguities, but a few places in the traditions seem to offer the hope of sound historical interpretation. Most of the variation in the titles stems from the fact that they were once *mavunga* and therefore had no 'father' position capable of fixing them securely in relation to other titles in the perpetual genealogies. The first terms of the names, which derive from their original stature as *mavunga*, vary less than the surnames and in fact turn out to hinge on four identifiable positions which mark four phases in the early history of the Mbondo: Kajinga, Kikasa, Kima, and Kingwangwa.

Kajinga, it is clear, represents the local descent groups and stands in implied opposition to the other titles in the genealogy, nearly all of which are political titles, mostly *mavunga* from Libolo. The Mbondo recognized several subdivisions within the large group of *jingundu* allegedly descended from Kajinga: Ndala a Kajinga, Nyange a Kajinga, Mupolo wa Kajinga, Mbamba a Kajinga, Zombo dya Kajinga, Kabari ka Kajinga, and doubtless others as well.[50] The location of the lands of these lineage groupings, which probably represent the earliest remembered subdivisions in the area, are unknown except for those of Kabari ka Kajinga and Zombo dya Kajinga who respectively occupied domains west and east of the middle Lui. The others seem to have lived in the highlands some-where in the vicinity of Lambo. Nor can the historical connections between these groups be traced, since the Mbondo have no coherent and articulated segmentary genealogy like that of the Songo; the attribution to these groups of direct descent from Kajinga undoubt-edly hides a good deal of genealogical telescoping.

The second phase of Mbondo political development came with what the genealogies describe as a 'marriage' between Kajinga and

[50] Compare the lineages named as descendants in the narrative tradition of Kajinga, p. 99 above.

Kikasa.[51] Kikasa, whose title seems to have been associated with lineage titles surnamed *mwinga* or Kyango a Mbashi a Kitata kya Mukombi, may have been an early Pende *lunga*-king before the expansion of Libolo into the Lambo area. The 'marriage' between Kikasa and Kajinga represents an early period when holders of the *kikasa* title held some influence over lineages in the area and does not affect the significance of the later 'marriage' between Kajinga and Kima a Pata.

Kima, in fact, appears next in most Mbondo genealogies and heralds the advent of Libolo overrule. He bears several different surnames, an expectable variability given the probable origin of the title as the *kima a pata* in Libolo. The *vunga* title of the *ndala* does not appear at all in the Mbondo genealogies, but the *kima a pata* stands as a record of Libolo control in its place. The *kima* could have acquired this position in the genealogies if it declined to the status of a hereditary lineage position when the Mbondo escaped from Libolo domination and the lineages which possessed it provided the incumbents for the *ndala kisua* position, apparently through election by a number of Mbondo descent groups who jointly chose incumbents for the central title.[52] The evidence for this assertion comes from the near-unanimous identification of the *kima* as a 'son' either of Kajinga ka Mbulu or, depending on the variant, of the *kikasa*; Mbundu historians evidently vacillate between the two older figures as sires of the Kima *vunga* for want of better knowledge of its true origins. Since the *ndala* (*kisua*) never became the possession of a single lineage, it cannot appear in the genealogies of permanent names except occasionally as an interpolation. The incumbents in the *kima a pata*, apparently in the hands of an unidentified lineage, enjoyed strategic advantages through their occupation of a place called Kabatukila where a mountainous ridge provides the only access to the Baixa de Cassanje from the highlands south of Lambo. They ruled until the 1620s when a 'son' position, the *kingwangwa kya kima*, replaced its 'sire' as the dominant Mbondo title in conjunction with the rise of the new Kasanje kingdom then forming in the Baixa.[53]

Conversion of the *ndala kisua* from a *hango*-appointed *vunga* to a title under the control of a few central Mbondo lineages allowed the old Mbundu tendency towards political fragmentation to

[51] Testimony of Kingwangwa kya Mbashi.
[52] Testimony of Kisua kya Njinje, Kambo ka Kikasa, Sousa Calunga.
[53] Testimonies of Mbondo group; Alexandre Vaz, 30 July 1969; Kimbwete; Kingwangwa kya Mbashi; Sousa Calunga, 22 July, 29 and 30 Sept. 1969; Mahashi; Kabari ka Kajinga; Apolo de Matos, 8 July 1969.

reappear in Mbondo. Some of the eastern Mbondo lineages, known as Zombo dya Kajinga, broke away from the authority of the *ndala kisua* during the period in which the Mbondo kingdom was flourishing independent of Libolo influence. They built a distinct and fairly extensive network of lineage titles in the Yongo region between the Lui and the Kwango. The genealogies show this development as a 'marriage' once again, this time between the lineages of Zombo dya Kajinga and the ancient Pende *lunga*-king in the area, Kayongo ka Kupapa. Holders of lineage titles derived from Zombo dya Kajinga evidently overwhelmed the *lunga*-kings since the title of Kayongo ka Kupapa went into decline and the titles descended from Zombo dya Kajinga ramified through Ndungu ya Zombo in the next descending generation to five or six positions on the succeeding level. Kilamba kya Ndungu became the most important of these in the latter part of the sixteenth century, so that the entire Baixa de Cassanje was known as the *kina* (pit) *kya kilamba* by 1600. The lineages of Zombo dya Kajinga never lost touch completely with the original Mbondo kingdom in the highlands, as indicated in the genealogies by a number of 'marriages' between the old Libolo *mavunga* (such as Kikululu kya Hango and even the *kima a pata*) and the Mbondo lineages beyond the Lui.

The development of the subsidiary Mbondo state of Kilamba kya Ndungu showed most of the classic features of state-formation among the Mbundu. It made use of the usual Mbundu network of perpetual titles rather than developing the potential of the *mavunga* on the Libolo model. It also absorbed older titles present in the region, in this case the Pende *lunga*-kings, by giving the ancient positions new surnames indicative of their incorporation in the new state. In this way, for example, the *lunga*-priest Mahashi na Pakasa, one of the old titles near the Luhanda salt pans, became Mahashi a Mahongi, from Mahongi a Ndungu ya Zombo dya Kajinga, one of the 'sister'-titles to Kilamba a Ndungu. If the incorporation of Mahashi indicated a movement towards the salt pans, the kingdom of Kilamba a Ndungu also conformed to the established pattern of states tending to concentrate near valuable economic resources.

The history of the original Mbondo state of the *ndala kisua* exhibits rather different characteristics from the other early Mbundu kingdoms considered here. It was spawned by the implantation of an alien *vunga* title emanating from south of the Kwanza, unlike the essentially local origins of the *ngola* and *lunga* states. It survived the decline of its original sponsor, the *hango*-kings of Libolo, only to

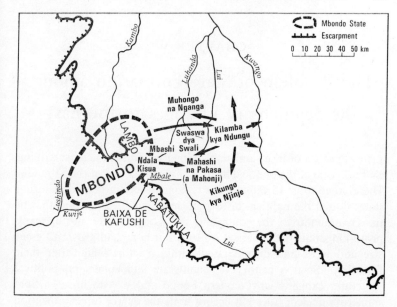

MAP VII. Expansion of the Mbondo Kingdom of the Ndala Kisua and
Subsidiary States (c. Sixteenth Century?)

become a local title claimed by the Pende lineages of the Lambo
region. There it thrived at a time when other Libolo title-holders were
in retreat before the advancing *ngola a kiluanje* or, as in the Lenge
region, becoming subordinate parts of the *ngola* kingdom. The
location of the *ndala kisua* on inaccessible mountain peaks along the
escarpment which rimmed the Baixa de Cassanje may have afforded
these kings a defensive position invulnerable even to the armies of the
ngola a kiluanje. In so far as the Mbondo state expanded, it moved
away from the large western Mbundu kingdom and perhaps only
coincidentally towards the salt pans which had figured so prominently
in the earlier political and economic history of the Baixa de Cassanje.
It suffered its first reverses when the *ngola a kiluanje* spread south of
the *ndala kisua* towards the upper Lui and moved north of the
Mbondo capital into the Kambo river valley. The period of rule by
the lineages of Jinga a Ngola and Mbande a Ngola in the kingdom
of the *ngola a kiluanje* (1570s–1620s?) reduced the Mbondo state to
its core lineages above the escarpment near Lambo.[54]

[54] Current work on this area by Karl Höfer may expand or modify my
reconstruction of early Mbondo history.

CHAPTER V

The Problem of State Formation among the Segmentary Lineages to the East

THE ABSENCE of large and stable kingdoms forms the most striking characteristic of the political history of the areas east of the Mbundu. There, in contrast to the western regions, where large and enduring states dotted the political history of the Mbundu, as well as that of the Ovimbundu to the south and the Kongo to the north, many proto-kingdoms had emerged by 1600 but none had grown to great size and most had disintegrated within a short while after their founding.[1] Such a history of small-scale and ephemeral political structures explains why modern Songo and Cokwe lineages hold numerous ancient titles but accord none the degree of centralization or geographical extent comparable to the *mani* Kongo in Kongo, the *ngola a kiluanje* among the Mbundu, or the *kulembe* in the Benguela highlands. The general failure of title-holders to unite these lineages into viable states forms the main theme of this chapter. The principle line of the narrative follows the two exceptions which prove the rule, the Lunda state of the *mwata yamvo* in Katanga and the band of people ruled by holders of a title called the *kinguri* who began their history in Lunda but ended by assaulting the very existence of Mbundu lineages near the sources of the Kwango. Elsewhere, there was little net increase in political scale in the period before 1600.

Early Political History of the Songo
Of all the Mbundu ethno-linguistic subgroups, the Songo emerge as unique in having had no single strong kingdom.[2] By 1550 or so,

[1] The major apparent exception to this generalization, the so-called Lunda empire, probably did not emerge as a strongly centralized state until the end of the seventeenth century; even then, effective centralization extended to a relatively small area, by no means the entire region usually shown on maps as the 'Lunda empire'. Without anticipating the conclusions of this chapter, my analysis supports the dates for the emergence of the mature state of the *mwata yamvo* suggested in Vellut (1972), pp. 65–7.

[2] The history of the Songo is the least known of any of the northern Mbundu. Beyond a few scattered notes left by nineteenth century travellers, the only

the Ndongo had had their *ngola a kiluanje*, the Pende had seen several *lunga*-states, the Libolo a dynasty of *hango*-kings, the Lenge a shadowy *keta*-state, and the Mbondo their *ndala kisua*. Part of the reason for the anomalous political history of the Songo derives from the fact that their descent groups, alone among those of the Mbundu, belonged to the expanding system of segmentary lineages which, by the sixteenth century, reached from the Kwanza, where the Songo formed its western edge, at least as far east as the northern Lunda in Katanga. Although we can obviously only guess at the extent to which sixteenth-century Songo still approximated the ideal type of segmentary social structure, in which genealogical ties generated by lineage fission coincided with the spatial distribution of the descent groups, the inconspicuousness of political structures in the area suggests that little had yet disturbed the smooth operation of a decentralized system which could still efficiently allocate scarce resources (mainly land) and mobilize sufficient numbers of men for defence.

A comprehensive segmentary genealogy articulated the relationships among the *jingundu* of the Songo and also between the Songo and the Cokwe/Lwena and Lunda. At its summit stood the name Mbumba a Mbulu, a symbolic figure known widely in western Central Africa but of uncertain historical significance. The three major subdivisions in the genealogy appear in its first descending generation, where Tembo a Mbumba appears as the ancestress of the Songo and Cokwe lineages, Tumba a Mbumba as founder of an early set of Cokwe political titles, and Ngamba a Mbumba as the progenitor of the earliest remembered titles in the Lunda heartland near the Kalanyi river in Katanga.[3]

Names in the Songo part of the articulated genealogy refer almost exclusively to relationships between descent groups, but even the

---

[3] All Imbangala testimonies dealing with the aetiological period of Mbundu history concur. Mesquitela Lima (1971), p. 43, has an Ngombe/Ngombo at the head of the Lunda genealogy. Tembo and Tumba appear in various nineteenth-century Cokwe traditions, sometimes 'falling from the sky' as the archetypal human beings in the Cokwe world; in general, the Cokwe appear to claim Tembo as a lineage ancestress, while the Songo attempt to distinguish between themselves and the Cokwe by using Tembo and Tumba. See Hermann Baumann (1935), pp. 139–40; Fonseca Cardoso (1919), pp. 14–16; F. Grevisse (1946–7), pp. 77–8 ('the group [Cokwe] is formed of clans recognizing the woman Tembo as their ancestor . . .'). Crine-Mavar (1973), p. 72, has Tumba, Tembo, and Samba from Lunda sources.

---

source is Afonso Alexandre de Magalhães (1948), p. 38. Hopefully, the recent investigations of Karl Höfer will fill in some of the gaps in our knowledge of this important area.

incomplete versions of the genealogies which I recorded from Songo-descended Imbangala hinted at the presence of a set of extra-lineage names said to be males who 'married' Tembo a Mbumba, the female founding ancestress of the lineages. According to the characteristic idiom of the Mbundu perpetual genealogies, Tembo a Mbumba's 'husbands' stand for the politial authorities which emerged from time to time among various segments of the Songo *jingundu*. Although each of the names (a partial list includes such figures as Kalulu ka Wambwa, Mukoso, Mwili, and Kunga dya Palanga[4]) represent some form of political rule, the limited data on Songo history make it impossible to identify most of these incipient kings, much less determine their exact locations or place them in the correct chronological sequence.

It seems clear, however, that most of these titles originated outside the region occupied by the segmentary lineages and were altered as they were incorporated as permanent named positions connected to lineages, much as the Mbondo converted the Libolo *mavunga*. Modern Songo attribute the sources of these positions to the southwest where the independently documented dynasties of the *kulembe* and the *hango*-kings provide likely backgrounds for political authorities of this type. Of the recorded names, only that of Kunga dya Palanga may be provisionally identified: his title may date back to the sixteenth century or before when one of the major figures in Mbailundo bore the title of 'kungo'.[5] A few of these titles still existed in the late nineteenth century when Songo reported to travellers that a king called Kunga dya Palanga held some form of authority over the people who lived north of the Luhando and east of the Kwanza rivers.[6] In general, however, few of the early Songo kings managed to overcome lineage resistance to centralized political control. The large number of titles remembered as 'husbands' of Tembo a Mbumba and discrepancies in their positions in the genealogy suggest that they did not exercise real power for very long and did not extend their influence very far.

Growth of Centralized Institutions among the Lunda
To find a parallel imposition of alien political titles on the segmentary lineages of Mbumba a Mbulu, it is necessary to wander as

[4] Testimonies of Alexandre Vaz, 30 and 31 July 1969; Sousa Calunga, 29 and 30 Sept. 1969; Domingos Vaz.

[5] A. V. Rodrigues (1968), p. 183. *Palanga* is also a title found most commonly in the Libolo/Mbailundo area.

[6] Lux (1880), p. 96.

far from the Mbundu as the northern Lunda of Katanga where political developments began which later affected the Songo and eventually touched all of the Mbundu. Early Lunda history should be analysed against a background of strongly segmentary matri-lineages and visualized as a gradual movement through several stages of political development characterized by progressively more centralized structures and leading to the emergence of the *mwata yamvo* in the late seventeenth century. Along the way, some Lunda lineages opposed these changes and eventually moved away from the centre of the Lunda state. In the process, they diffused a number of Lunda political titles and authority symbols which became the central positions and emblems of most Mbundu kingdoms after the middle of the seventeenth century.

Since the analysis of Lunda history which leads to these conclusions departs from the conventional interpretation of some fairly well-known traditions, I want to preface my substantive remarks with a review of previously available information on the earliest periods of Lunda political history. The published oral traditions on the most ancient phases of Lunda state-formation come from a wide variety of sources—Lunda, Cokwe, and Pende for the most part—and thus afford the opportunity to make comparisons between them which might indicate the ways in which the milieu in which each tradition has been transmitted has affected its content and structure.[7] They have, however, generally been interpreted without adequate attention to the social and political institutions of the people who told them. Relatively recent (i.e. since 1650) political developments in Lunda have, for example, clearly affected the ways in which the nineteenth- and twentieth-century Lunda recalled very early events which, it would seem, occurred in a setting different in many ways from political and social conditions now.

[7] Still the best record of the northern Lunda traditions is the account of Henrique Augusto Dias de Carvalho (1890a), the earliest recorded and includ-ing the greatest detail on events of the remote period. Victor W. Turner (1955) translated portions of Carvalho's test into English. It is closely paralleled by a Cokwe text (perhaps contaminated with editorial interpolations from Dias de Carvalho) reproduced in Lima (1971), pp. 42–51(?). The uncanny similarities between Lima's text and that of Dias de Carvalho may be explained, however, by the fact that Dias Carvalho's information came largely from Lunda chiefs whose ancestors had long lived among Cokwe, whose descendants later retold the same version of this tradition to Lima. See also the accounts of Léon Duysters (1958), M. van den Byvang (1937), and Daniel Biebuyck (1957) for later and less complete accounts. Crine-Mavar (1973) gives a recent and rela-tively independent version from Lunda sources close to the modern royal court.

Other traditions found outside the central Lunda region, such as those of the Imbangala (whose kings claim descent from predecessors who left Lunda before the changes which later altered the content of the Lunda narratives), may preserve an archaic perspective no longer present in the Lunda homeland. Similarly, modern Cokwe social structures resemble ancient Lunda institutions more closely than do present conditions nearer the Kalanyi; Cokwe traditions may therefore be more informative on the earlier phases of Lunda history than the accounts of the Lunda themselves. I intend to reinterpret early Lunda history by incorporating into the analysis new and probably older traditions found among the Imbangala, by offering some suggestions as to the social system in which early Lunda political development took place, and by applying to the well-known traditions the critical techniques developed to handle the Mbundu narratives and genealogies discussed in preceding chapters. This approach seems justified since the Lunda histories clearly fit the structure of genealogies and narrative episodes found in the Mbundu traditions. Further, since the Lunda are known to have positional succession and perpetual kinship, it seems justifiable to handle their traditions as if they possessed characteristics similar to those of the Mbundu.[8] In particular, I assume that all names in the genealogies refer to perpetual titles and that the narrative portions of the traditions are separable, each from the others, and describe historical events in metaphorical rather than literal terms.

The traditions give every indication that the ancient Lunda had social institutions very much like the present segmentary matrilineages of the Songo and Cokwe.[9] Although the social institutions of the northern Lunda appear to have changed much more in recent centuries than those of the Mbundu,[10] the practices of positional succession and perpetual kinship come from a very early period in

[8] Vellut (1972), pp. 65–6, has noticed this aspect of the traditions but has not worked out the implications for the period before the *mwata yamvo* (c. 1700).

[9] A surprising scarcity of reliable ethnographic data hinders reconstruction of Lunda social history at so great a time depth. The most important published materials on the Lunda appear in Fernand Crine (1963), Crine-Mavar (1963, 1968, 1973), and Biebuyck (1957). Information on related groups and the limited accessible data in travellers' accounts allow the drawing of some fairly firm conclusions.

[10] Crine-Mavar has stated several times that the modern Lunda are bilateral with no strong lineages (1963, pp. 158, 165–6, and 1973, p. 69). But it remains unclear whether all Lunda, or only the holders of political titles, are today 'bilateral', and in which contexts bilateral descent obtains.

their history.[11] Portions of the Mbundu perpetual genealogies dating from the fourteenth or fifteenth centuries, for example, extend to the Lunda, and, since these genealogies include only titles of the permanent type, positional succession and perpetual kinship must have existed in Lunda at that time. The widespread distribution of these practices, in a broad band reaching across Central Africa, but centred on the Lunda area, also suggests that these institutions must have been a part of Lunda life long ago.[12]

Several sorts of evidence suggest that the ancient Lunda had lineages of a segmentary type similar to those of the modern Songo. The Lunda titles appear in the section of the perpetual genealogies headed by Mbumba a Mbulu. Since this genealogy contains only names referring to matrilineages, and/or the perpetual political titles associated with these descent groups, the Mbundu habit of locating the Lunda there indicates that they once had matrilineages organized, at least in part, on the basis of segmentary opposition. Recent research among the Sala Mpasu, northern neighbours of the Lunda in Katanga, suggests that they also once had matrilineages even though they have now abandoned them for other sorts of social institutions.[13] Some Cokwe traditions purport to describe the conditions of life among the ancient Lunda in terms which explicitly mention the essential features of a segmentary lineage system: a number of relatively independent 'chiefs' (i.e. lineage headmen) who occupied distinctive small territories and who banded together under a single 'chief' in case of need.[14] Ancient Lunda political history therefore occurred against a background of lineages and lineage segments occupying a relatively small area on the Kalanyi river, each living on its own small domain (called an *mpat*). The

[11] This interpretation disagrees specifically with that of Duysters (1958), p. 82, who states that the characters in the Lunda traditions were persons and not perpetual titles. Since any Imbangala would state the same opinion if asked directly about the distinction between names and titles in Kasanje, Duysters may have reached his erroneous conclusions through uncritical reliance on his informants' remarks.

[12] Positional succession and perpetual kinship today are found from the Mbundu in the west through the Cokwe and northern Lunda to the Luapula peoples and the Bemba in the east; Cunnison (1956). Crine (1963), pp. 158, 162–3, assumes that perpetual kinship and positional succession are very ancient. See also Biebuyck (1957), p. 794, who confirms that ties of this type link the most ancient surviving Lunda positions (the *tubungu* chiefs).

[13] I am grateful to Professor William Pruitt of Kalamazoo College for generously sharing with me some of the results of his unpublished research on this point.

[14] Lima (1971), p. 43. Crine-Mavar's recent work seems to concur (1973), pp. 66–74.

segmentary aspect of the lineage structure would have restricted the formation of strongly centralized political institutions, much as similar institutions hindered the rise of kings among the Songo. The Lunda 'kingdom' at that time, far from resembling later Central African states or its own subsequent imperial phases, consisted of little more than a collection of lineage villages.

A set of perpetual named positions called *tubungu* (singular, *kabungu*) provided the underlying unity for the Lunda lineages on the Kalanyi. In addition, at the earliest remembered time another set of political titles seems to have been present.[15] Neither the exact relationships between these positions nor their origin is clear, but comparison of the genealogies referring to this period (approximately the fifteenth century or so, but not datable[16]) reveals the existence of a single senior title which the Lunda ranked above several related but subordinate positions. This set of Lunda political titles pivoted on a figure variously called Kunda a Ngamba, Konde a Matita, or sometimes Yala Mwaku; in any case, the position is depicted as the sire of such other positions as the *kinguri*, the *kinyama*, and the *lueji*. Uncertainty over the correct name for the senior position probably indicates that the title had fallen into decline by the time the traditions took their present form so that its exact identity no longer mattered to those who preserved the traditions. As the narrative to follow shows, such seems to have been the case. Most Imbangala historians, who use the name of the senior position only as the patronym (or matronym) of the *kinguri* title held later by kings in Kasanje, agree that it should be Kunda.[17] Other Imbangala have Kunda as 'Konde' and make the position a female, the 'mother' of Kinguri.[18] Those who make the *kinguri* a descendant of a female 'Konde' give his paternal origin as Yala Mwaku, or Mutombo Mukulu.[19] Such references to the latter title, which was an important political position among the Luba Kaniok or Kalundwe, who lived

[15] As in the case of the Mbundu, the earliest *remembered* period of Lunda history picks up the process of state-formation in midstream. We simply have no idea of the phases which may have gone before.

[16] Miller (1972a).

[17] So do the Songo; Magalhães (1948), p. 35. Max Buchner (1883), pp. 57–8, also has the surname Kunda for Kinguri. Schütt's 'Kinguri kya Bangela' (1881, p. 60), or 'Bangala Kinguri' (p. 70), refers to a different title, the *kinguri kya bangela*, a position that appeared in the eighteenth century and had no known connection with the Lunda *kinguri* position.

[18] Testimonies of Mwanya a Shiba, 14 June 1969; Sousa Calunga, 16 June 1969; Apolo de Matos, 18 June 1969.

[19] Testimonies of Apolo de Matos, 18 June and 8 July 1969; also Lima (1971), p. 43.

north-east of Lunda, show the senior Lunda position's connection with the very early states known to have existed among the Luba.

Lunda sources, doing little to clarify the situation, variously portray Konde as the wife of Yala Mwaku, as a child (or grandchild) of Yala Mwaku, and as his sister. The official Lunda court historian in the 1920s gave Mwaku as the senior *tubungu* chief who had a son Yala Mwaku who in turn sired Sakalende (male) and Konde (male). Konde then fathered Kinguri, Kinyama, and Lueji.[20] Nineteenth-century Lunda informants agreed with the Imbangala in identifying Yala Mwaku as the father and Konde as the mother of Kinguri, Lueji, and Kinyama.[21] The Pende portrayed Yala Mwaku and Konde Matita (female) as brother and sister and added an unidentified 'Kavula' as the husband of Konde Matita and father of Kinguri.[22] In general, the Lunda versions giving Konde as a male seem to reflect the modern Lunda preference for patrilineal descent among political titles. The Pende tradition, on the other hand, ignores the Lunda tendency to trace political legitimacy through the male line and evidently attempts to depict Kinguri and Lueji as nephews and hence as legitimate heirs of Yala Mwaku according to their own matrilineal rules of descent. Placing Konde Matita as the female link between Yala Mwaku and Kinguri accomplishes this purpose.[23] If a conclusion may be drawn from such disparate data, the form *yala mwaku* probably represents the Luba (male) political title and the name Kunda (or Konde) the Lunda lineage in possession of the position. A 'marriage' between them, of the sort which appears in several of the traditions, would represent Lunda acceptance of a very early (and otherwise unidentified) form of Luba political authority.

Other details of the traditions reinforce the impression that the *yala mwaku* originated in a set of Luba political institutions which overspread the Lunda and Cokwe some time before the period in which the standard Lunda traditions come into clear focus. Beyond

[20] Duysters (1958), pp. 76, 79, 81.

[21] Dias de Carvalho (1890a), p. 60.

[22] Haveaux (1954), p. 21. Chinyanta Nankula (1961), p. 1, agreed with Pende informants on the place of Matita in the genealogy. Cf. Biebuyck (1957), pp. 801–3, who included the name of a Matita in his highly schematic genealogy.

[23] Another genealogy (Biebuyck (1957), pp. 801–3) shows an extreme example of the way in which the same names shift positions relative to one another to conform to the intent of the person who recites it; in this case four consecutive pairings of brothers and sisters in 'marriages' involving Yala Mwaku, Konde, Matita, etc., are used to dismiss this part of Lunda history as a mythical period before time and lineages became part of the world. Lima's Cokwe tradition exhibits the same feature (1971, p. 43).

120   THE PROBLEM OF STATE-FORMATION

Yala Mwaku's vague association with Mutombo Mukulu, other genealogies show a marriage between Walunda wa Nyama, a female name representing a Cokwe/Lwena linege grouping descended from Tumba a Mbumba, and a male, Manganda a Kambamba a Musopo wa Nyama. The male (presumably political) title was also of Luba origin. A 'child' of this marriage, Kata ka Walunda or Kata ka Manganda, in turn married Kunda to produce Kinguri and Lueji. This marriage thus performs the same function of tracing the main Lunda titles to a Luba (political)–Lunda (lineage) union as the marriage of Yala Mwaku in other genealogies and confirms the Luba antecedents of the Lunda political titles. This interpretation would reconcile all known versions of the genealogy, both Imbangala and Lunda, by hypothesizing a Luba origin for the earliest remembered Lunda senior title.[24]

Although the traditions show that the *yala mwaku* enjoyed a status *formally* senior to the positions held by other Lunda lineages, they reveal little about the historical relationships between these titles. We may surmise that the holders of the *yala mwaku*, in any case, exercised little more than ritual seniority over the other Lunda lineages since it was remembered later as a 'first among equals'. Real political power depended on the lineages' manpower and economic resources, and there is no reason to assume that these corresponded at all times to the formal kinship hierarchy of the genealogy.[25] Since the genealogy could not alter to reflect changes in the historical political balance, it sometimes must have lost its usefulness as a means of structuring relationships between the lineages. In such instances, it became desirable either to adopt a new political system more indicative of political realities or to abolish the senior title which held all other positions in false subordination to it.

Because the traditions have preserved nothing about the historical realities behind the formal genealogies, it is possible only to speculate on what circumstances might have provoked such a restructuring of the relationships among the Lunda political titles. None the less, a

[24] Cokwe traditions also contain hints of an early spread of Luba titles among the matrilineages descended from Mbumba a Mbulu; some nineteenth-century Cokwe attributed the origins of these names directly to Kasongo Nyembo, the most powerful Luba state of that period; Grevisse (1946–7), p. 58. Haveaux (1954), pp. 28–9, notes that the Pende of the Kasai agree that Luba titles played a role in the early history of the Cokwe.

[25] Power and seniority rarely coincided in such later kingdoms as Kasanje or the Bemba where similarly stable systems of titles prevented alteration of the genealogies to reflect changing historical circumstances. See the fully documented argument to this effect in Andrew Roberts (1974).

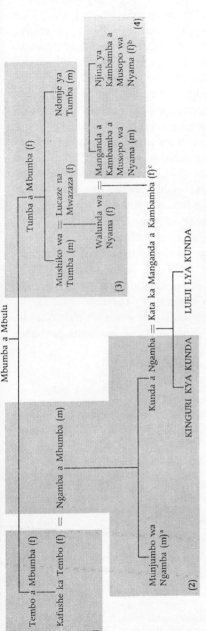

Mbumba a Mbulu

(1) Tembo a Mbumba (f)
Kafushe ka Tembo (f)

Ngamba a Mbumba (m)

Tumba a Mbumba (f)

Mushiko wa Tumba (m) = Lucaze na Mwazaza (f)

Ndonje ya Tumba (m)

Walunda wa Nyama (f)

Manganda a Kambamba a Musopo wa Nyama (m) = Njina ya Kambamba a Musopo wa Nyama (f)[b]

(3)

(4)

(2) Munjumbo wa Ngamba (m)[a]

Kunda a Ngamba = Kata ka Manganda a Kambamba (f)[c]

KINGURI KYA KUNDA   LUEJI LYA KUNDA

(1) Songo Matrilineages; included here to account for the later conversion of the *munjumbo* to a Songo title, as Munjumbo a Kafushe.

(2) The male line of political authority in Lunda, running through Kunda to Kinguri.
The marriage of Ngamba a Mbumba to Kafushe ka Tembo is a recent addition to account for the Songo title of Munjumbo a Kafushe (or Ngamba).

(3) Cokwe/Lwena matrilineages, including an early set of chiefs now attributed to Tumba a Mbumba. Lucaze na Mwazaza is the female ancestress of the Cokwe lineages.

(4) Luba political titles, shown as the male counterparts of the Cokwe lineages they ruled.

Source: Testimonies of Domingos Vaz, Alexandre Vaz, 2 June and 31 July 1969, and Kasanje ka Kanga, 26 June 1975.

[a] Rodrigues Neves (1854), p. 98, confirms this place for Munjumbo, giving him the Songo surname Kafushe.

[b] Dias de Carvalho (1885–6), iv. 121, gives Njina ya Kambamba as an "aunt" of Kinguri. This confirms the Imbangala genealogy if she is a sister of Manganda a Kambamba as her surname suggests. Rodrigues Neves (1854), pp. 96–7, has "Nyama" as the name of Kinguri's homeland, probably in reference to this part of the genealogy. Imbangala informants say that the "Nyama" are Luba.

[c] Testimony of Sousa Calunga, 9 July 1969, calls her Kata ka Walunda wa Nyama.

FIG. V Genealogy Illustrating the Alleged Origins of Ancient Lunda Political Titles.

realignment did occur. The names of many titles which participated in this revolution have probably disappeared owing to the effects of still later changes in Lunda, but those of three positions subordinate to the *yala mwaku* have survived: the *kinguri*,[26] the *lueji*, and the *kinyama*.[27] Their later significance as central positions among the Cokwe, in Lunda, and in Kasanje has caused them to occur in nearly all variants of the list of early Lunda title-holders. Some versions of the genealogy include several other positions classed as siblings of the *kinguri* and subordinates of the *yala mwaku*. An occasional Imbangala history cites vaguely a Maweje who, it is said, left Lunda even before the *kinguri*. The Imbangala know nothing of Maweje's subsequent history except that he allegedly opened the trail which *kinguri* and other Lunda titles later followed towards the west.[28] The Imbangala also remember a 'brother' of Kinguri named Munjumbo who also left Lunda for the west.[29] Others in addition to the standard trio of Kinguri, Lueji (or Naweje, as the Imbangala call her), and Kinyama include a Kayungo or Kalungo, Kasongo, and Iyala.[30] The remainder of the list varies because historians no longer needed to mention all these positions to account for the states familiar to them in the late nineteenth century and after, when all known traditions were recorded. All modern lists of these positions probably include only a fraction of the original titles.

[26] The meaning of this title is not clear.

[27] The word *nyama*, meaning meat or wild game in Kimbundu and in most Bantu languages, occurs with some frequency as a title on the maternal or lineage side of the early Lunda (and Luba?) genealogies, (e.g. Kinyama, Walunda wa Nyama, etc.). Rodrigues Neves (1854), p. 96, gave 'Nyama' as the name of the 'country' where Kinguri had lived in Lunda, mistaking a lineage designation for a 'country' since the Mbundu traditions do not distinguish clearly between lineages and lands which often have the same name.

[28] Testimonies of Sousa Calunga, 16 June, 9 July 1969. The informant may have confused the name of a 'high god' found east of the Lunda (Mawese or Maweje) with one of the *tubungu* titles. For Maweje, see Hermann Baumann (1936), p. 39. The name heads Lunda genealogies recorded among the central and eastern Lunda kingdoms; Chinyanta Nankula (1961), p. 1; also Biebuyck (1957), pp. 801–3. In this case, it may represent a garbled recollection of early Luba influences that spread southwest from Lunda towards the Cokwe.

[29] This title has a very complex history, but its origins clearly lie in Lunda; see testimonies of Sousa Calunga, 29 Sept., 1 Oct. 1969; Domingos Vaz. The Cokwe also recall a title of this name that moved west from Lunda with the *kinguri*; Lima (1971), p. 46.

[30] Testimony of Apolo de Matos, 18 June 1969. Iyala corresponds to the Yala mentioned by Lunda in the late nineteenth century; Dias de Carvalho (1890a), p. 60. The two longest recorded lists of siblings (both Lunda) include Ndonje who turns up as a Lunda title in later Imbangala traditions; Biebuyck (1957), pp. 801–3; Crine-Mavar (1973), p. 71, agrees and adds others.

A set of Lunda narrative episodes reveals a shift from the non-hierarchical political system headed by the *yala mwaku* to a more centralized state headed by incumbents in the *lueji* position. According to the traditions describing this rupture in the perpetual genealogy,[31] Kinguri and Kinyama, the sons of Yala Mwaku, the Lunda king, returned home one evening after an afternoon spent drinking palm wine. They found their father busy weaving a sleeping mat in the courtyard of his compound. A pot of water sat beside him in which he was soaking raffia fibres to make them pliable and suitable for weaving. Kinguri and Kinyama, in part because of their drunkenness, mistook the cloudy water for palm wine and demanded that the old man give them some to drink. When Yala Mwaku denied that the pot contained palm wine, they became angry and beat him very severely. Lueji, their sister, arrived just in time to attend to her father's last wishes before he died. Yala Mwaku willed his title to Lueji as a reward for her faithfulness and punished Kinguri and Kinyama for their disobedience by ignoring their claims to his position.

Although the story as recorded in the nineteenth century continued from this point directly into other events, this much of the tradition originally formed a distinct narrative episode dealing with a single series of historical events. Interpreting the characters in the episode as perpetual titles would mean that incumbent *kinguri* and *kinyama*, or their lineages, became involved in hostilities against the *yala mwaku*, or his lineage, and tried at some point to usurp the authority of the senior position. The palm wine, over which Kinguri, Kinyama, and Yala Mwaku fought, stands as a metaphor for the real, but unstated, historical issues which prompted the junior title-holders to eliminate their senior position. The tradition characteristically reveals nothing about the nature of the historical dispute except to indicate, through the symbolism of the palm wine, which the Lunda associate with males and with political power,[32] that it concerned political authority. The names of Kinguri's companion(s) in this enterprise, which vary in different versions of the narrative, stand for

---

[31] Dias de Carvalho's account is the only published version of the tradition that includes more than a very sketchy presentation of the narrative episodes; the paraphrase given here comes from (1890a), pp. 59–75. Dias de Carvalho wrote his version of the story in a style that obscured the original structure of the Lunda traditions in terms of genealogies and narrative episodes. The following analysis attempts to reintroduce these divisions and to draw out the historical significance of the original structure.

[32] Personal communication from Jan Vansina.

lineages which allied themselves to the *kinguri* in his wars against the *yala mwaku*. The most common variants of the tradition identify the *kinguri*'s main allies as the lineage which controlled the *kinyama*; other versions claim that a title known as the *yala* also supported the *kinguri*'s assault.[33] The variability simply confirms that the traditions have probably preserved an incomplete list of the groups actually involved.

Yala Mwaku's death moved the old Lunda political structures from a period of relative stability into a transitional phase of internecine warfare. It may be assumed that the *kinguri* and his allies eventually eliminated the *yala mwaku* position from the Lunda perpetual genealogy after fighting of undetermined intensity and duration (although the scale of the conflict could not have been large by later standards). The 'death' of the *yala mwaku* title in the language of the narrative episodes does not refer to the assassination of an individual incumbent, although this may have occurred one or more times. The 'death' of a position in a genealogy consisting of permanent named titles signifies that its enemies destroyed its authority emblems and ritually eliminated it from the political structure to which it had belonged. Imbangala traditions mention several later cases in which opponents used such methods to abolish titles among the Mbundu, and traditions of some of the eastern Central African groups with positional succession and perpetual kinship show the same thing.[34]

The 'death' of the *yala mwaku* freed the other Lunda lineages to establish a new political balance unfettered by the hierarchy of perpetual kinship which formerly had bound them in collective subordination. The abolition of a less senior title would have caused relatively minor shifts in the status of a few Lunda lineages. Elimination of the *yala mwaku* meant something quite different, however, since the other titles depended on it for legitimacy and supernatural protection. A period of instability, hidden by the placid style of the narrative episode, must have followed as each Lunda lineage competed with the others for supremacy in the changed political environment.[35] If the *yala mwaku* had had any direct connection with the Luba, as some traditions indicate it did, its overthrow may also have

---

[33] Testimony of Apolo de Matos.

[34] M. G. Marwick (1963), p. 389.

[35] Imbangala traditions obscure all interregna and periods of political instability. The evidence that such a phase occurred here comes from the logical discontinuity in the line of historical development (a challenge initiated by holders of one title, the *kinguri*, and a victory by those of another, the *lueji*).

represented a rebellion by the Lunda lineages against the presence of Luba political titles.

From the traditions, we must assume that lineages led by the *kinguri* struggled for pre-eminence during the period of instability and that the lineage of the *lueji* led the opposition to them. Since, as the narrative stated, Lueji became heiress to Yala Mwaku's royal power, the *lueji* position must finally have built up an alliance strong enough to defeat the *kinguri* and *kinyama* and thus to claim the senior status formerly accorded the *yala mwaku*. Kinguri and Kinyama's mistaken identification of cloudy water as palm wine in the narrative episode metaphorically underlines the irony of their defeat; they had pursued a mirage, eventually losing the battle to the *lueji* despite their original challenge to the *yala mwaku*. The traditions do not, of course, indicate how long these struggles continued. Since the figures in the narrative represent permanent political positions, many years could have elapsed between the assault on the *yala mwaku* by one *kinguri* incumbent and later defeats administered to successors in the same title.

The *kinguri*'s assault on the *yala mwaku* had initiated fundamental changes in Lunda political structures which culminated in a new and more centralized state dominated by the *lueji* position. A separate narrative episode briefly outlines the formation and structure of this successor state. Lueji was still a child when Yala Mwaku died, in the words of the tradition, and could rule only with the counsel of the older and wiser *tubungu* lineage chiefs. They granted her a form of ritual supremacy and allowed her technical ownership of the Lunda lands, but *tubungu* guardians took control of the bracelet which embodied supreme Lunda political authority, the *lukano*. The *tubungu* guardians moved their residences from their own teritories to the *lueji*'s home domain at that time, thus creating the first pan-Lunda capital town. The *tubungu* excluded the lineages of the *kinguri* and the *kinyama* (or the *yala*) from the new confederation, presumably because of their unsuccessful attempt to wrest control of the *lukano* from the *lueji*.[36] The kingdom probably retained this form for some decades, at least, since the traditions stated that various *tubungu* chiefs took turns filling the offices at the court during this period.[37] Thus, although the *lueji* had defeated the

---

[36] Dias de Carvalho (1890a), p. 64.

[37] Haveaux (1954), p. 4; also Dias de Carvalho (1890a), p. 64. Compare this vague reference to the interim rule of Lunda *makota* in the Imbangala *kilombo* (*c*. 1560–1610); the period of interim rule, which received equally summary

kinguri and the *kinyama*, the victorious title-holders had won at the cost of their own independence. The *tubungu* lineage chiefs gained a voice in the affairs of the new kingdom as the price of their assistance during the wars. The threat of the *kinguri* had forced the Lunda to develop a new political structure with a higher degree of centralization than its predecessor(s) but one in which holders of the central political title had to submit to a council of advisors drawn from the Lunda lineages.

Several details mentioned in the first narrative episodes, which stand out as possibly historical because they contrast with conditions when the tradition was recorded, point to the conclusion that Yala Mwaku 'died' much earlier than the late-sixteenth-century date generally assumed for the beginnings of Lunda political history.[38] Hints at the level of technology, for example, repeatedly indicate that these developments took place before the Lunda acquired iron of a quality high enough to manufacture broad-bladed weapons. Lunda culture emphasized fishing rather than hunting at the time, and Lunda hunters captured game only by means of wooden traps rather than with arrows or spears tipped with iron.[39] The title of the *yala mwaku* was said to have meant 'thrower of rocks',[40] a praise name perhaps suggestive of a period before the introduction of iron weaponry. Kinguri and his brother slew their father with a wooden club rather than with the *pokwe* iron knife which later became the characteristic Lunda weapon.[41]

The next episode in the Lunda narrative picks up the theme of renewed Luba influence on the *lueji*'s Lunda state. The tradition relates that Lueji went one day to the river Kalanyi where she found a group of hunters camped in the forest. They had travelled there under the leadership of a Luba noble, later known to the Lunda and Cokwe as Cibinda Ilunga. Noticing that Cibinda Ilunga and his companions lacked salt for the meat from animals they had slain, Lueji offered to provide whatever salt they might need. After a

[38] For the debate on this date, see Jan Vansina (1963a), David Birmingham (1965), Jan Vansina (1966b), and my summary in (1972a), pp. 549–51. Vellut (1972), pp. 65–9, contains new information.

[39] Dias de Carvalho (1890a), pp. 60, 61; also Lima (1971), p. 44.

[40] I have not been able to verify Dias de Carvalho's translation of the name. The significance given to it by the Lunda is more important than a literal translation of the words in any case.

[41] Dias de Carvalho (1890a), p. 67.

treatment in the traditions, lasted at least fifty years; see above, p. 14, n. 46. The Cokwe traditon quoted by Lima (1971), p. 44, explicitly notes that 'some time passed' during this period.

lengthy conversation on the banks of the river, she invited Cibinda Ilunga to remain in her realm. They eventually fell in love and decided to marry, each with the permission of the councillors of their respective kingdoms. After the marriage, Lueji gave her *lukano*, the emblem of Lunda royal authority, to Cibinda Ilunga so that he might rule Lunda in her place.

The 'marriage' of Cibinda Ilunga and Lueji began another new stage in the development of centralized political institutions in Lunda. It united the political authority of the Luba (represented as male) with the lineages in possession of the *lueji* title (represented as female) according to a pattern already familiar from the Mbundu traditions. Transfer of the *lukano* explicitly confirmed that the Lunda adopted some new form of Luba political authority. The meat (male) and salt (female) which Lueji and Cibinda Ilunga exchanged reiterate the complementarity between the hunters and the Lunda and emphasize the naturalness which nineteenth-century Lunda attributed to the partnership of Luba-ized rulers and Lunda lineages.[42]

New Luba ideas and institutions spread among the Lunda at the same time. More advanced iron-working techniques may have arrived in company with the previously unknown *kibinda* hunting society.[43] Cibinda Ilunga clearly stands for the *kibinda* society of professional hunters which the Lunda had lacked up to that time.[44] According to the Cokwe, Cibinda Ilunga's principal authority emblem was a magical dagger, the *kapokolo*; he also came with special bows, *yitumbo*[45] (singular, *kitumbo*), and the *cimbwiya* hatchet which still survives as an important symbol of political power among the Cokwe.[46] The fact that most of these innovations, which were also symbols of the *kibinda* hunting association, involved

[42] On the symbolism of hunters as founding kings, see Boston (1964) and Lucas (1971).

[43] Edouard N'Dua (1971, p. 39), interview (23 January 1971) with Muhunga Ambroise explicitly confirms that Cibinda Ilunga was also a smithy.

[44] The southern Lunda (Ndembu of north-western Zambia) claim that the *kibinda* society (there called the *wubinda* bow-hunter's cult) came from the *mwata yamvo* heirs of Cibinda Ilunga in Lunda; Turner (1967), p. 280. The experience of the Ndembu, who subsequently adopted another (*wunyanga*) hunting cult, suggests that there may have been several of these societies at different periods of the central African past, and so the introduction of this version of the cult to the Lunda need not preclude the possibility that a similar institution was present among the Mbundu from as early or earlier times. Cf. pp. 50-1 above.

[45] *Yitumbo* are a category of charms or medicines made from vegetable substances found in the wilds frequented by *kibinda* master hinters; Lima (1971), pp. 79, 303. Cf. Boston (1964), p. 124.

[46] Lima (1971), p. 45.

sophisticated iron-working techniques suggests, like the *jingola* of the Samba among the Mbundu, that a technological change occurred. Improvements in iron-working need not imply, however, that a massive Luba military conquest took place, since the Lunda had good reasons for voluntarily adopting Luba ideas and institutions.

Strained relations between the Lunda lineages explain why the *lueji*'s people took up these new principles of political organization. The *lueji* had ruled at the head of a loose confederation which had originated as a defensive alliance against the *kinguri* and the *kinyama*. These two had evidently remained not far from the fringes of the Lunda state where they constituted a continuing threat to the lineages which had backed the *lueji*.[47] Unable to destroy the *kinguri* by themselves, they must have sought new and more powerful charms, organizational techniques, and weapons to drive their enemy away. The figure of Cibinda Ilunga symbolizes the arrival of all of these. The danger of the *kinguri* in the end forced the *lueji*'s Lunda confederacy to offer her *lukano* to the holder of the main Luba title in order to consolidate under new leadership the unity which protected them against renewed civil warfare of the type which had occurred during the preceding period of instability. Lunda acceptance of the innovations represented by Cibinda Ilunga, with or without direct military intervention by Luba armies, thus marks a major shift in Lunda attitudes; they began to abandon the fierce independence which had formerly typified relations among the lineages and to move towards the more centralized social and political institutions of the later Lunda empire.

The Spread of Lunda Political Titles to the West

The consequences of this fundamental change in Lunda social and political life affected most of the rest of western Central Africa. Acceptance of Luba centralized political institutions provoked an emigration of Lunda lineages and a diffusion of Lunda titles which, in its earliest phase, extended west to the Cokwe and south to the Lwena and later spread to the Mbundu and Ovimbundu. Related movements still later reached the Ndembu along the headwaters of the Zambezi and the people living east as far as the Lualaba.[48] With the title-holders who moved west, principally the *kinguri*, went the *kibinda* hunting society and several new war charms which Cibinda

[47] For an explicit Cokwe statement to this effect, Lima (1971), p. 46.

[48] For a summary, Vansina (1966a), pp. 84–97. The later phases of this expansion are not discussed here as they had no immediate effect on the Mbundu.

Ilunga had brought to Lunda from the Luba. Given the propensity of the historical traditions to personalize abstract historical processes, it is probable that the movement should be viewed in part as a diffusion of titles and only in part as the migration of individuals which has up to now been assumed.

The historical reasons, as distinct from the non-historical plot of the metaphorical narratives, which provoked the first expansion of Lunda political titles seem connected with the importation of new authority symbols from the Luba. In effect, the new charms and titles replaced the formerly dominant set of positions which had included the *lueji*, the *kinguri*, and the *kinyama*. As the old titles lost their pre-eminence, some remained in the hands of Lunda descent groups but acquired new names in the same way as the arrival of new techniques of political organization had altered the titles of the old Pende *lunga*-kings and some of the *hango*-positions among the Mbondo. Some of the other Lunda titles, having lost their value to the nuclear Lunda lineages, were sold or otherwise disposed of to the segmentary descent groups living in the west where no similarly prestigious type of political authority yet existed. In only one case—that of the *kinguri* —is there clear evidence of a movement of people, and this instance produced major political revolutions which affected all the lineages living along a path leading from Lunda through the Cokwe to the Songo.

The fate of the *lueji* title in Lunda illustrates the process of name-changing and subordination among the older Lunda titles which remained among the lineages on the Kalanyi. The Lunda state changed from the comparatively loose federation of *tubungu* chiefs led by the *lueji* to a much more centralized state under the command of a new Luba title, the *mwata yamvo*. The Lunda genealogies show the *mwata yamvo* position as a descendant of a 'marriage' between a female named Luhasa Kamonga and Cibinda Ilunga.[49] According

---

[49] Luhasa Kamonga is usually described as one of Lueji's 'ladies in waiting'. I cannot interpret in Lunda terms the meaning of this obvious mistranslation. Descriptions of the *mwata yamvo* as a 'son' of Lueji herself come only from non-Lunda sources and are probably not reliable. The distinction between Lunda traditions and those from non-Lunda, mainly Cokwe, better explains the differing descriptions of the origin of the *mwata yamvo* title than does the largely circumstantial distinction between nineteenth- and twentieth-century traditions pointed out by Vellut (1972), p. 66. It happened that most nineteenth-century traditions recorded by Europeans came from Cokwe sources. Abundant comparative data establish the suspect nature of father–son genealogical ties, especially when alien sources attempt to trace internal political changes in other polities; David P. Henige (1971; 1974, pp. 71–94).

to the rules of the perpetual genealogies, this made the *mwata yamvo* originally a Luba position subordinate to one in the possession of a lineage known as Luhasa Kamonga. For unknown historical reasons, this title became the most powerful title among the central Lunda descent groups, and the *tubungu* were reduced to their present status as advisers to the central royal title. The position of the *lueji* retained a status distinct from the *tubungu* but only as a secondary title of a new Luba position, the *swana mulunda*; its new name came with its incorporation into the state of the *mwata yamvo* and reflected its reduced responsibilities in comparison with its earlier primacy. The *yala mwaku* position was also resurrected, again with a new name, the *shakala*. The length of time which elapsed while these changes took place cannot be estimated, although two centuries or more might not fall far short of the true mark.[50]

The circumstances which led the holders of the *kinguri* title to depart from Lunda may be seen in Imbangala narrative episodes which suggest that the lineages behind the title found themselves overwhelmed by Luba magic and remained only until they had borrowed at least some of Cibinda Ilunga's supernatural powers.[51] Naweje, as the Imbangala call Lueji, had taken control of the Lunda kingdom but ruled only as a regent in place of Kinguri who was still a minor and unprepared to assume the royal powers which rightfully belonged to him.[52] One day, as Kinguri and Naweje were walking along the river Lukongolo[53] in Lunda, Kinguri momentarily left his sister alone while he went into the woods in search of some men who were making *maluvo* somewhere nearby.[54] Not long after he left her, a hunter called Lukokesha appeared and spoke to

---

[50] The established time lapse comes from the calculations presented in Miller (1972a) and Vellut (1972), p. 69. The point was also made by Dias de Carvalho's Lunda informants (1890a), pp. 76–7. Some nineteenth-century Lunda informants told Dias de Carvalho specifically that the Luba had arrived long after the first fights between the *lueji* and the *kinguri*. Dias de Carvalho gave this information in a letter (1886, p. 135) that seems to contain a better approximation to the original oral form of the tradition than the reworked version in (1890a).

[51] The following account is based on the testimonies of Sousa Calunga, 21 July, 2 October 1969.

[52] The self-serving intention of this Imbangala emphasis needs no special comment.

[53] River not identified, but possibly an oblique reference to the Luba background of Lunda history, since the names consists of the common *lu-* prefix for river names and the title of the founder of the first Luba empire (see Vansina (1966a), p. 71).

[54] Fermented palm wine, *tombe* in Lunda.

Naweje, offering her as a gift the tail of an elephant he had killed.[55] Naweje accepted it and in return gave the hunter some food, which he gladly accepted since he and his men had spent the previous night in the bush with nothing to eat.

Kinguri, off in the wilderness looking for the men making *maluvo*, suddenly felt his heart begin to pound. Recognizing this as a sign that something had gone amiss at home, he returned at once and found Naweje in her house eating with Lukokesha. The requirements of Naweje's position probibited men from entering her compound, and her *makota* (guardians) usually kept her isolated from all males other than Kinguri. Since Lukokesha's presence in the house violated this law, Kinguri became suspicious of the stranger and inquired about his identity. Naweje explained what had happened and showed Kinguri the elephant tail. Kinguri immediately recognized another transgression of Lunda custom, since only properly installed political chiefs could possess elephant tails which they received as tribute from their subjects. Naweje, as regent, had no right to accept gifts which should have gone to Kinguri.

Kinguri threatened Lukokesha and ordered him to leave at once. When the hunter refused to go, Kinguri attacked him with a magical knife (*mwela*) which he had inherited from his father.[56] The hunter's head spouted fire as Kinguri appoached, and so he turned and fled in fear. He later returned in another attempt to slay the usurper, but this time the hunter's mouth turned into the fangs and jaws of a dangerous jungle cat.[57] Kinguri then realized that his enemy possessed supernatural forces much more powerful than his own. He at first resolved to steal the charms which made Lukokesha so strong but found that he could not and agreed to leave Lunda if the hunter would first teach him his magical secrets.

Lukokesha agreed to the bargain and explained his charms to Kinguri. These included something called *nzungu* made from the *mbamba* tree[58] which grows in the gallery forests along the rivers. The *nzungu* not only enabled Lukokesha to perform the feats which

---

[55] The bristles of an elephant's tail were potent charms.

[56] This is an anachronistic detail of a sort characteristic of the Imbangala traditions; the Lunda did not have the *mwela* at that time.

[57] Either a lion or a leopard; informant was not clear on this point, probably because the detail does not alter the meaning of the metaphor.

[58] An unidentified specific charm. The *mbamba* tree (*imperata cylindrica* Var Thumbergii) is valued for its usefulness in preparing the *yitumbo* medicines of the *kibinda* hunter; Lima (1971), p. 303.

he had used to frighten Kinguri but also parted the waters of rivers and divined the presence of snakes and then killed them. Lukokesha also gave Kinguri a magical bow which allowed its owner to slay even the most dangerous animals of the forest. Armed with these weapons, Kinguri departed from Lunda and began his trip to the west.

This Imbangala tradition may be reconciled with the Lunda and Cokwe narratives of Kinguri's departure from Lunda if we recognize that Lukokesha plays the role named Cibinda Ilunga in the other histories. Both are 'parents' of the *mwata yamvo* and represent the Luba institutions adopted by the *lueji*. The Imbangala use the name Lukokesha instead of Cibinda Ilunga (of whom they have never heard) since their narrative episodes come from a period some time after the original Luba titles had begun to lose their significance relative to the *mwata yamvo*. Just as the old *lueji* position had become the *swana mulunda* as Lunda political structures evolved, the Cibinda Ilunga had lost its original name and had become the *lukonkesha*. The *lukonkesha* came to represent the 'mother' of the *mwata yamvo* title, just as the *swana mulunda* stood as symbolic 'mother' of the Lunda people.[59] The two 'mothers', *swana mulunda* and *lukonkesha*, replaced Lueji and Cibinda Ilunga as metaphoric embodiments of the fundamental paired principles of the later Lunda state, respectively the Lunda lineages and Luba political authorities.[60] The *lukonkesha*, although originally male, became feminine to contrast with the masculine position of the *mwata yamvo*.[61]

Kinguri's fondness for palm wine recurs in this version of the tradition, indicating the essentially political significance of the episode. Lukokesha first appeared when Kinguri left Naweje to search for *maluvo* in the woods. Since the Lunda and Imbangala both associate *maluvo* with males and hence with political authority, this part of the story apparently refers to the period when the *kinguri* abandoned the federation of *tubungu* chiefs headed by the *lueji*, represented here by Naweje, and sought independent political charms

[59] Biebuyck (1957), pp. 791, 802. The spelling *lukonkesha* is Lunda (and used here to refer to the Lunda title) while Lukokesha approximates to Imbangala pronunciation (and is used when the Imbangala metaphor is intended).

[60] This hypothesis explains Schütt's confusion of Lukokesha with Lueji (1881), pp. 82–3; also van den Byvang (1937), p. 43. The confusion reappears in Vellut (1972), p. 66.

[61] The Imbangala have a similarly male position (the *ndala kandumbu*) that they regard as 'mother' of their major political title, the *kinguri* in Kasanje.

elsewhere. This detail from the *kinguri*'s side of the story confirms the Lunda descriptions of events at the court of the *lueji* during the period of hostility between the *kinguri* and the central Lunda federation. Naweje's relationship with Lukokesha resulted directly from Kinguri's search for outside aid (his addiction to palm wine) and confirms suggestions in the Lunda narratives that the *lueji* allied with the Luba in direct response to some threat posed by the *kinguri*.

Lukokesha's present of the elephant tail stands for the *lueji*'s adoption of Luba political institutions in opposition to the *kinguri* within the framework of the existing Lunda state system, since the Lunda believe that the hairs of the elephant's tail possess potent magical forces. Naweje's acceptance of the elephant tail and her reciprocal gift of food to Lukokesha reiterate the union of Luba political power and the Lunda lineages. The Imbangala traditions use the image of a gift of food in place of the corresponding image (salt and meat) in the Lunda traditions since this was a common metaphor in many other contexts in Kasanje traditions.

The symbolic clash between Lukokesha and Kinguri describes the supernatural weapons with which both sides fought during the historical political manoeuvring and armed clashes which must have punctuated the conflict before the *kinguri* finally gave up and left Lunda. The story clearly implies that the *kinguri* departed only after the superiority of Luba institutions had become too obvious to ignore. Lukokesha's magic corresponds to suggestions in Lunda and Cokwe traditions that Cibinda Ilunga introduced new weapons, charms, and organizational techniques superior to the rudimentary equipment of the segmentary Lunda lineages. Kinguri's unsuccessful attacks on Lukokesha dramatize the inadequacy of the Lunda chiefs' powers in comparison to those of the Luba. But the *kinguri*, according to the Imbangala, did not leave before learning some of Lukokesha's secrets. Since it would have taken some time for innovations adopted by the central Lunda to spread to their enemies on the fringes of the kingdom, Kinguri's knowledge of Lukokesha's charms confirms other indications that some time passed between the introduction of Luba techniques and the departure of the *kinguri*.

The secret charms which Kinguri learned from Lukokesha came from the inventory of supernatural skills which the Imbangala attribute to the *kibinda* master hunter. Kinguri's possession of these charms explains to them how he could have left Lunda to wander through the wilderness which lay to the west. Professional hunters, they believed, needed special magical powers which helped them pursue large beasts through unfamiliar territory. Unskilled hunters, who did not enjoy the protection of these special charms, would not undertake such dangerous ventures. In particular, their fear that snakes embodied potentially hostile supernatural beings[62] meant that hunters, who might spend days and weeks walking through thick undergrowth, sought magical protection against them. The Lukokesha's *nzungu* performed this function for the *kinguri*, whose Lunda title included no charms of similar potency.[63] The *nzungu* made it possible for the *kinguri* to undertake his trip through the snake-infested wilderness.

Rivers were also believed to present serious difficulties for anyone who travelled in unfamiliar regions, and the *nzungu*'s ability to dry their waters had obvious advantages for the *kinguri* during his journey.[64] Other magical techniques belonging to the *kibinda* professional hunter guarded against dangers which the *kinguri* might encounter in forests where spiritual beings hidden in the bodies of wild animals lurked in wait of unwary travellers. The Imbangala made a clear distinction between the natural creatures normally encountered there and the supernatural beings in the shape of beasts which sorcerers sent to harm their victims. Normal animals yielded to straightforward pursuit with fire and nets and could be killed with spear, club, or arrows. Supernatural beasts, however, succumbed only to the elaborate precautions and special charms of the professional hunters. Since both kinds of animal looked exactly alike, the *kibinda* could rarely determine beforehand which sort he might confront, and so they always went into the woods prepared to deal with either type. Travellers also had to be wary of supernatural animals, since spirits tended to follow human pathways through the wilderness. Travellers carried various charms for protection while *yibinda* generally used special bows capable of slaying both natural and supernatural enemies. Lukokesha presented such a magical bow

[62] One example is the *kindalandala* snake of the Mbundu mentioned in connection with the early history of the Mbondo state, p. 96 above. The Imbangala, for example, clear the grass from a wide area around their houses to keep snakes (and spirits) away from their dwellings.

[63] The Imbangala all agree that Kinguri was not primarily a 'hunter' (meaning *kibinda*) like Lukokesha.

[64] Compare the story of Kajinga's crossing of the Kwanza and Muta a Kalombo's ability to flood streams to block Kajinga's pursuers. Although the cliché of the parting of the waters is found nearly everywhere in the world, the breadth of its distribution does not detract from its specific function in Mbundu symbolism.

to Kinguri, one which protected its owner both from animals and from hostile human beings.[65] Although the Imbangala acknowledge that modern people have lost the technique of fashioning these bows, they maintain their faith in the possiblity of once again discovering the secret.

Other authority symbols, all of Lunda origin, also spread west from Lunda with the *kinguri*. The later presence of four *tubungu* insignia in Kasanje leaves little doubt that these reached the Mbundu through the movement of the *kinguri* from Lunda. They included the *tuzekele* (singular, *kazekele*) bracelets, small metal rings denoting lineage authority in Lunda but political authority in Kasanje,[66] the *lubembe* double clapperless bell,[67] the *mondo* talking drum, and the *ngoma ya mukamba* drum.[68] Some other symbols found in both Lunda and Kasanje, such as reservation of the leopard skin for political chiefs, occur too widely in Central Africa to permit determination of exact origins when the choice lies between such closely related groups as the Mbundu, Luba, and Lunda.

Although only the *kinguri* left Lunda with the full complement of Luba magical techniques, a number of other titled positions drifted west at the same time. Some attention must be paid to their origins since divisions dating from before their departure later influenced splits within the original group of titles and led to the creation of several Cokwe and Mbundu states. Most of the Lunda title-holders who accompanied the *kinguri* belonged to lineages other than that of their leader. The name of the *kinguri*'s lineage, according to official Imbangala genealogies, was Njimba na Kakundo, a name which also referred to the lands where the *kinguri*'s people had lived (their

[65] This bow reappears (in the hands of Kinguri's successor, Kulashingo) in later Imbangala traditions which come from independent non-Lunda sources; see below, p. 192.

[66] Distinct from the *lukano* bracelet made of human flesh which belonged to the *mwata yamvo* alone.

[67] The *lubembe* is definitely Luba in origin but also associated with the Lunda *tubungu*; personal communication from Jan Vansina. Its appearance in Kasanje lends further support to the argument that some time had elapsed after the arrival of the Luba before the *kinguri departed*.

[68] Duysters (1957), p. 81, gave the list of insignia of the *tubungu* chiefs. For their occurrence among the Imbangala, see testimony of Alexandre Vaz and Ngonga a Mbande on the leopard skin (*ciba ca kulwama*); various testimonies on the *tuzekele*, especially Mwanya a Shiba, 14 June 1969; the *lubembe* no longer occurs in Kasanje, but Cavazzi (1965), i. 162, 201, mentioned it for the seventeenth century (calling it 'longa'); for the *mondo*, testimony of Apolo de Matos, 5 Oct. 1969, and Dias de Carvalho (1890a), p. 501; testimonies of Ngonga a Mbande, 26 June 1969; Sousa Calunga, 11 Sept. 1969, and Mwanya a Shiba, 14 June 1969, for the *ngoma ya mukamba*.

mpat).[69] The positions which accompanied the *kinguri* (and later became the *makota*[70] who acted as guardians of the position in Kasanje) came from two lineages apparently related to each other but not connected to Njimba na Kakundo. Positions called Kinzunzu kya Malemba and two 'nephew' titles, Mbongo wa Imbe and Kalanda ka Imbe, both 'sons' of a sister called Imbe ya Malemba, came from the lineage(s?) of Kandama ka Kikongwa and Kanduma ka Kikongwa.[71] The ancestral home of this group lay near the river Lukongolo, said to be a stream somewhere in Lunda.[72] The other lineage, Kandama ka Hite, contributed the positions of Mwa Cangombe, Kangengo, Ndonga, Kibondo kya Wulu, and Kambwizo.[73]

Imbangala historians who prefer to emphasize the unity of the *makota* with the *kinguri* rather than the lines which divided them declare that all the Lunda titles came from the single 'family' of Lucaze na Mwazaza,[74] a female figure in the segmentary genealogies who symbolizes a large set of Lunda matrilineal descent groups which existed at some time in the past.[75] As the maternal ancestor of the lineages which controlled the Lundu *tubungu*, the Lucaze na Mwazaza group included all of the individual lineages mentioned by other historians as those of the *kinguri* and his companions. Since

[69] Testimonies of Sousa Calunga, 29 Sept., 1 Oct. 1969; compare with the Lunda traditions which specify only that the *kinguri* left with members of his own 'family'; Dias de Carvalho (1890a), p. 76. The *kinguri*'s lineage name apparently no longer matters to the Lunda; this would not be surprising if they left as early as the traditions imply and if the matrilineages later became less important than they were at that time.

[70] The corresponding Lunda term is *karula* (pl. *turula*); Dias de Carvalho (1890a), p. 70.

[71] Alternatively known by the title of the major position in the lineage Kinzunzu kya Malemba a Kawanga.

[72] One variant gives 'Mukongolo' as the name of the lineage of all the Lunda who came with the *kinguri*; testimony of Sousa Calunga, 22 July 1969. This appears to confuse a toponym taken from the name of the river with the title of the lineage. This is a common practice. Neither name has been identified. If, however, they consist of the root -*kongolo* preceded by prefixes *lu-* (given to most rivers in Lunda) or *mu-* (a common Bantu locative prefix), the name could refer once again to the Luba origins of these titles; cf. p. 130, n. 53 above.

[73] Testimony of Sousa Calunga, 9 July, 29 Sept., and 1 Oct. 1969. This list fails to account for one additional *kota*, Kahete, who later turned up in Kasanje and apparently belonged to Kandama ka Hite.

[74] Testimony of Alexandre Vaz, Domingos Vaz.

[75] Cf. Biebuyck (1957), p. 815, who gives Mwazaza Mutombo as one of the three main dispersed Lunda groups. Mwazaza may also occur as 'Mwasanza', a southern Lunda or Cokwe title. The Lucaze people live south of the Lungwebungu river in south-eastern Angola. Both Lucaze and Mwazaza point to the Lwena/Cokwe connections for this group of lineages. See Map I.

the Imbangala often referred to the individual components of a group by its broad collective name, the two versions of the genealogy show no real inconsistency, rather only slightly different emphases.

Modern traditions probably preserve the names of only a modest proportion of all the titles and lineages which left Lunda at the time of the *kinguri*. Further difficulties in identifying the precise composition of the party which left Lunda arise from the operation of the so-called 'lightning rod' effect[76] which has led later traditional historians to enlarge the original group far beyond its historical dimensions by adding titles of entirely different origin. Some recent narratives claim, for example, that most of the senior nineteenth-century political chiefs between the Kasai and the Kwango all left Lunda with the *kinguri*. The Cokwe of south-western Katanga include Katende, Saluseke, Kandala, Kanyika ka Tembo, Cisenge, Ndumba, Mbumba, Kapenda, Kasanje, and Kaita in their list.[77] A few of these names belong to early Cokwe titles but most refer to latecomers who have recently become important in the region where the tradition was told (Katende and Saluseke). The conventional set of the major Cokwe kings (Ndumba, Mbumba, Kanyika, and Kandala) appears along with the title of a nineteenth-century new-comer (Cisenge) and some of the other Lunda titles in the Kwango region (Kapenda ka Mulemba of the Shinje and Kasanje of the Imbangala). A published nineteenth-century Imbangala list of Kinguri's companions shows the same tendency; it adds the names of several later Songo chiefs, various subordinate positions in Kasanje, and some (but not all) of the true Lunda *makota*.[78]

Cokwe States Based on the kinguri

The people who held the *kinguri* position moved westward from Lunda very slowly, apparently settling repeatedly as they sought to avoid the growing area of lineages under the influence of Luba political institutions. The *kinyama* title, which seems to have left at about the same time, moved in a different direction and eventually came to rest among the Lwena of the upper Zambezi. The historical developments behind the movement of the *kinguri*, hidden in the traditions behind the image of a 'journey',[79] were continuations of

[76] The tendency of founding kings to receive credit for the deeds of their successors; Vansina (1965).

[77] Van den Byvang (1937), pp. 426–7, n. 1(h), 432n. and 435. Cf. Lima (1971), p. 46.

[78] Rodrigues Neves (1854), pp. 97–101, has the earliest recorded Imbangala version of the list.

[79] Cf. Kajinga's 'journey' from Luanda to Mbondo, pp. 98–103 above.

whatever forces had initially expelled the title from the *lueji*'s federation of Lunda lineages. The descent groups in possession of the *kinguri* pulled back from contact with the newly centralized Lunda of the Kalanyi, entering areas where lineages organized according to the segmentary institutions of the Cokwe and Songo gladly adopted the *kinguri* and its associated magical powers. It is impossible to say whether the *kinguri* title remained in the hands of the biological descendants of the Lunda who left the Kalanyi or whether enterprising local groups took the title for themselves as it reached new regions. If, as seems probable, the expanding segmentary lineages of Mbumba a Mbulu were reaching the limits of available empty land at that time, the attendant endemic conflict over scarce territories might have led the descent groups to welcome the holders of a prestigious title as arbiters in their continual conflicts.[80]

The *kinguri* title could not remain in a single location, however, because even more effective political techniques based on the Luba titles adopted by the nuclear Lunda were moving outward from the Kalanyi close behind the *kinguri*. As the advancing wave of Luba institutions reached each area where the *kinguri* became established, the title drifted farther to the west and south, became fixed briefly as an ephemeral king among a new group of segmentary lineages, and then moved again as the next surge of Luba political innovations caught up with it. Ultimately these repeated confrontations, perhaps hastened in some places by local reluctance to accept any political authority, led to the creation of a string of *kinguri*-states along a line stretching from the Kalanyi across Cokwe territory towards the headwaters of the Kwango and the borders of the Mbundu.

Despite the general reticence of the traditions on this level of analysis, a number of details in the narrative episodes conform to this interpretation. The Lunda later remembered that the *kinguri*'s band had moved very slowly and that it took many years for them to pass beyond the Cokwe. The magical techniques which they had borrowed from the Luba provided the key to their success in travelling through unfamiliar territory. They hunted in part with traditional Lunda snares and traps but also used the bows and arrows which Kinguri

---

[80] This hypothesis sets a standard explanation (Vansina, 1966a, pp. 85–6) against the background of Cokwe/Lwena social structures. Some evidence suggests that the lineage 'frontier' may have closed around this time. The revolutions taking place in Lunda could have resulted from contact with the Luba states in the north-east, and the Kongo to the south-west had certainly encountered opposition from the *kulembe* and/or Libolo states by this time (*c*. fifteenth century?).

had obtained from Cibinda Ilunga/Lukokesha. A charmed dagger called *mukwale*, in particular, helped them fight their way through anyone who opposed their arrival.[81] The power of the *kinguri*'s new weapons and strong Luba magic made a lasting impression on the people who lived west of the Kasai where late-nineteenth-century Cokwe still remembered the *kinguri* and his terrifying reputation.[82] Such traditions as these would seem to give the viewpoint of essentially stateless people witnessing for the first time the arrival of effective political authority.

Modern traditions unanimously retain this aura through their depictions of the *kinguri* as a fearsome title which demanded the lives of its own people with almost casual abandon. Kinguri, they say, forced two slaves to kneel by his side whenever he wished to rise or sit; he then rested his weight on daggers which plunged into their backs.[83] The image effectively portrays the awe with which the kinsmen of the lineages regarded the *kinguri*. It does not suggest that they viewed individual incumbents in the *kinguri* as cruel or demented but that they feared the spiritual forces of the title and expected them to demand drastic behaviour from their human guardians.[84]

The continuing opposition between the *kinguri* and the trailing advance of Luba institutions is apparent in a Lunda tradition which notes that Kinguri had left the Kalanyi in search of an army strong enough to return and win back the power which he had lost in

---

[81] Dias de Carvalho (1890a), p. 77. Lima (1971), p. 48, also cites Cokwe memories of wars which accompanied the arrival of the *kinguri* in some areas (although three of the four adversaries mentioned, Pende, Holo, and Shinje, refer to the history of the *kinguri* in Kasanje rather than among the Cokwe).

[82] Dias de Carvalho (1890a), pp. 76, 87; also (1898), p. 28.

[83] The image of a ruler raising and lowering himself on daggers plunged into slaves' backs is a widespread cliché in Angola. Testimony of Mwanya a Shiba, 15 June 1969; also various testimonies of Sousa Calunga; Also Alberto Augusto Pires (1952), p. 1; Rodrigues Neves (1854), p. 97; Schütt (1881), p. 79—all for examples attributing the practice to Kinguri. Testimony of Luciano, however, attributed the custom to Nzinga. A. A. de Magalhães (1948), p. 33, recorded from Songo sources that the *mwata yamvo* did it in Lunda. João Vieira Carneiro (1859–61), pp. 172–3, noted that Ngola a Mbande, a seventeenth-century Ndongo king, was said also to have done this. A. Bastian (1874–5), i. 313, attributed the custom to the Duke of Sundi in Kongo. The cliché is common to most of the Mbundu and Kongo areas, at least.

[84] Although Imbangala historians attribute Lunda origins to later and different Kasanje rituals involving human sacrifice, these in fact came from other sources. The idea of Lunda origins probably came from their knowledge that the *mwata yamvo* killed many people to propitiate the spirits behind their own symbols. The Kasanje rituals, in any case, had no connection to the practices described by the cliché.

Lunda.[85] The Cokwe provide a detailed itinerary for Kinguri's 'journey' which shows that he stopped for a 'long time' in at least three places east of the Kwango.[86] The title had crossed the Kasai near the mouth of the Lonyi, a small left-bank tributary of the larger river. It then moved up the Lonyi to higher ground and worked its way west and south across the Luhembe, Kashimo, Lwana, Cihumbo. Sombo, and Lwashimo rivers before making its first prolonged stop among the lineages of an area known as Itengo (in the vicinity of the modern city of Henrique de Carvalho). It then shifted to the region known later as Mona Kimbundu, not far south-west of Itengo, where it also remained for a long time. It finally continued on to the head-waters of the Kwango and Kukumbi rivers and paused again before moving on towards the Songo. Each of these stops represented the establishment of a small state based on the *kinguri* title which the Lunda viewed as a renewed threat to themselves.

A narrative episode which recurs in the traditions of both the Lunda and the Imbangala seems to refer to the hostility which marked relations between the *kinguri* and the Lunda at the time the emigrants stopped near the sources of the Cikapa river.[87] Some time after Kinguri had left the Kalanyi, Lueji sent messengers to make contact with her brother. Kinguri received the emissaries in a camp near a river called the Nangwiji (since renamed the Cikapa). The Lunda begged Kinguri to return home but he refused to heed the entreaties and rejected all further association with his former kinsmen. Before continuing on his way, however, Kinguri renamed the river 'Cikapa' to commemorate his definitive separation. The Imbangala today translate the word *mutswalikapa* as 'we are sep-arated'[88] and allege that this event formally established the bound-aries between the lands ruled by the Lunda and those controlled by the *kinguri*. Since the border between the more recent *kinguri*-state of Kasanje and the Lunda never lay along the Cikapa, this episode must relate to a time before the *kinguri* settled in the Baixa de Cas-sanje.[89] This narrative episode therefore describes the formation of

[85] Dias de Carvalho (1890a), p. 76.
[86] Lima (1971), p. 48.
[87] See Pires (1952), p. 1, for the Imbangala; also testimony of Domingos Vaz. For the Lunda, Dias de Carvalho (1890a), pp. 86–90.
[88] Testimony of Apolo de Matos, 4 Oct. 1969.
[89] This attempted reconciliation could not have taken place after the *kinguri* had reached Kasanje, since the tradition specified that it was the *lueji* who sent out the call to the *kinguri*. Had it occurred later, the *mwata yamvo* rather than the *lueji* would have initiated diplomatic relations between Lunda and Kasanje.

an earlier kingdom near the Cikapa (probably Itengo) where the holders of the *kinguri*-title made a stand against reincorporation into the expanding Lunda state.

The Lunda empire's expansion towards the west corresponds to the wave of Luba political institutions which drove the *kinguri* farther and farther from the Kalanyi. Title-holders spread westward from the centre of the empire to form small states which would act as barriers between the Lunda capital and the *kinguri*. Several of these rulers established themselves among the Cokwe in the movement which would have brought the Luba figure of Cibinda Ilunga to the Cokwe as a culture-hero.[90] One of these rulers drove the *kinguri* away from the second state on the upper Cikapa, and his title, the *mona kimbundu*, has remained the name of the region the *kinguri* vacated.[91] The spread of title-holders from Lunda continued through the seventeenth century as new kings settled among the Shinje lineages living east of the middle Kwango; still others became the western Lunda provincial governors who protected the *mwata yamvo* from the new threat which later Lunda saw in the increasingly powerful *kinguri*-state of Kasanje.[92]

The Decline of Descent Groups among the kinguri's *Lunda*
The years of intermittent movement and constant pressure from advancing Luba produced fundamental changes in the social and political structures associated with the *kinguri* title. The relatively few persons who had originally left Lunda had been organized in terms of a few closely related segmentary lineages (under Lucaze na Mwazaza). But the rigours of repeatedly settling among new lineages had forced the holders of the *kinguri* title to develop ways of quickly integrating large numbers of people with no genealogical connection to themselves. While the cohesiveness of the Lunda lineages had permitted the small group to co-ordinate their activities for purposes of defence, their chances of survival when faced with the mobilizing techniques of the Luba depended on their ability to attract large numbers of new and alien followers. Since social structures based on segmentary descent groups lacked means of integrating quantities of unrelated strangers, the need to build up a

[90] See Marie-Louise Bastin (1966).
[91] The hypothesis of a series of Cokwe/Lwena kingdoms ruled by the *kinguri* both explains interpretive problems posed by otherwise anomalous claims that the Cikapa once divided Kasanje from Lunda and fits with the broader political question of the development of the Lunda empires.
[92] Dias de Carvalho (1890a), p. 91.

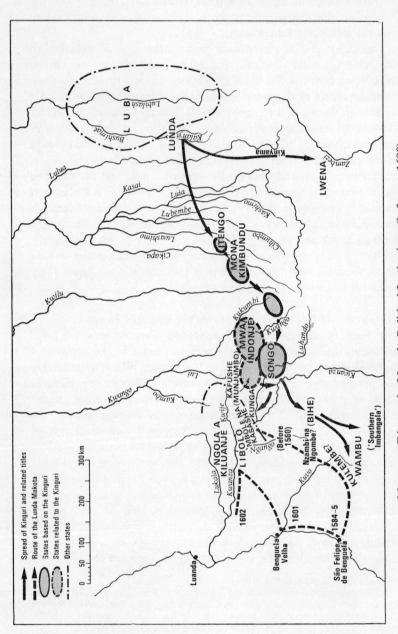

MAP VIII. Dispersal of Lunda Political Institutions (before c. 1600)

large following forced the *kinguri* to suppress cumbersome lineage divisions within their band of followers.

An Imbangala narrative episode relates explicitly how the *kinguri* incorporated groups of local kinsmen wherever it paused on its trip through Cokwe lands. According to the traditional historians, by the time Kinguri reached the area just west of the Cikapa river (now known as Mona Kimbundu), his extreme cruelty had become worrisome even to the Lunda followers who had left the Kalanyi with him. They saw that his practice of killing followers every time he rose or seated himself had greatly reduced their numbers and feared that it might destroy them all if it did not cease.[93] They felt themselves powerless, however, to do anything except continue to furnish the victims Kinguri demanded as long as the spirits behind the title persisted in their need for such sacrifices.

The Lunda recognized an opportunity to replenish their supply of potential victims when they arrived among the Cokwe who lived near the sources of the Cikapa. The senior title-holder in this region, Musumbi wa Mbali, had numerous subjects and was willing to send a number of them to Kinguri where, the Lunda hoped, the Cokwe would replace their own people as human sacrifices to their ravenous central title. Musumbi wa Mbali suspected the real intentions of the Lunda in requesting these people, however, and agreed to send them only under the protection of one of his own subordinate title-holders, Kasanje ka Kibuna (also called Kulashingo).[94] Kasanje ka Kibuna

[93] Perhaps a reference to the decline in numbers of full members of the Lunda lineages relative to the number of outsiders in the band?

[94] Perhaps an appointed emissary of the *vunga* type, judging from the *kasanje* title? The holders of this title later took control of the *kinguri* position and founded the state of Kasanje during the 1620s. The etymology of the name comes from *shingo*, Kimbundu for the back of the neck; see the events surrounding Kulashingo's later accession of power (p. 188, n. 32 below); testimony of Sousa Calunga, 23 Aug. 1969. Although this tradition establishes the origins of Kulashingo in the region of Mona Kimbundu, published Imbangala traditions have wrongly claimed that Kulashingo came from Kisama, near the mouth of the Kwanza river; Oliveira Ferreira Diniz (1918); testimony of Apolo de Matos, 18 June 1969; Pires (1952), p. 1.

The best-known but transparently erroneous etymology for this title has led to major misconceptions about the early history of Kasanje. Salles Ferreira (1854–8) described Kulashingo as a 'vassal' of the 'Mwata Yamvo'. Francisco Travassos Valdez (1861), ii. 155–6, repeated this version almost word for word, but invented the added detail that Kulashingo had been a Lunda noble. Vansina (1963a, p. 363) cited Valdez. Dias de Carvalho, who gained much of his information and most of his errors about Kasanje history from Salles Ferreira, amplified the point by specifying that Kulashingo had been expelled from Lunda and that he was none other than Kinguri himself (1898, pp. 15, 55). None of this finds any confirmation in modern traditions.

would protect the Cokwe from any dangers presented by the Lunda or by Kinguri. To help him, several related groups came as well, led by his mother and her three brothers, Kibuna kya Musumbi, Pande ya Musumbi, and Mbumba a Musumbi.[95] It was in this manner that a Cokwe component, which later became very important in the history of the *kinguri*'s heirs, joined the band. Other Cokwe groups, whose less illustrious subsequent history has erased memory of their incorporation, must have joined as well.

According to the structure of the Mbundu oral histories, a social change of such fundamental importance should have been recorded somewhere in the narrative episodes. Such a narrative appears to have survived among the Cokwe, roughly in the area of the upper Kasai, where the effects of abolishing the *kinguri*'s lineages seem to have left the greatest impression.[96]

As the tradition tells the story, one of the women in Kinguri's group had been about to give birth when they had reached the bank of a river said to be the Kasai. This annoyed Kanyika ka Tembo, a companion of Kinguri who had prohibited all sexual contact, ostensibly in order to avoid the delays caused by births and the presence of small infants. This birth caused unusual difficulties because the party was suffering from hunger at that time and needed to keep moving in search of food. Even Kinguri's magical powers seemed to have failed, since his special bow had not provided enough game to feed them. Although the group postponed their crossing of the river until the woman had given birth, the mother and baby both died. All accepted their deaths as a certain sign of the disfavour of the ancestral spirits.

Kanyika ka Tembo appears to have been a lineage headman, since the tradition portrays him as the uncle of the dead woman and since her husband went to him to report the woman's death.[97] Kanyika ka Tembo berated the husband when he heard the news and beat him severely for having violated his rule against sexual contact with women. He concluded by ordering the man to bury his wife and baby. This order violated all normal procedures in a society based on lineages where the responsibility for burials belonged to the dead persons' kinsmen under the supervision of his lineage head-

[95] Compiled from testimonies of Sousa Calunga, 16 June, 23 Aug., 29 Sept.; Sousa Calunga, Kambo ka Kikasa; Alexandre Vaz, 30, 31 July 1969; Apolos de Matos, 18 June 1969.

[96] Van den Byvang (1937), pp. 433–4.

[97] The surname Tembo confirms the hypothesis; Tembo appears only as a lineage name on the matrilineage side of the Songo and Cokwe genealogies.

man. The husband, who belonged to a different lineage, should have had only secondary duties to perform in connection with the burial of his wife and child.

The point of the tradition is that Kanyika ka Tembo had doubly threatened his kinsman's safety. He had ignored his duties to the spiritual guardians of the lineage by his prohibition of sexual contact. Normally, his responsibilities as *lemba* would have included the distribution of the *pemba* (white clay) intended to safeguard the procreativity of his kinswomen so that they might always bear children and thus guarantee the survival of the group. He had committed a second transgression by shirking his responsibilities in connection with the death of his niece. Failure to perform the proper rituals could cause her spirit to return to plague her living relatives.

The husband finally went to bury his wife at the river bank. There he encountered a large flock of birds flying from the top of a tree.[98] He managed to kill one of the birds, a bit of luck which constituted a sign of supernatural favour, since he could not have felled a bird on the wing without first achieving harmony with the spirits. When he gutted the bird, he found millet and sorghum seeds in its gullet. The seeds of domesticated plants amounted to certain evidence of nearby human habitation and held out the possibility that the hungry band of people might obtain food from these strangers. This discovery revealed the husband as one favoured by the spirits.

The leaders of the group, Kinguri and Kanyika ka Tembo among them, assessed his experience as a sign that they should at once continue to the other side of the river. Since the stream was small enough at that point to cross at a single leap, they began to cross on foot. But each time one of them attempted to jump over the river its waters rose abruptly and engulfed them, causing many people to fall into the torrent and drown. Kinguri's *nzungu*, as well as his magical bow, had apparently lost its power, since one of its most important properties was to facilitate the crossing of rivers. Their difficulties in obtaining food and crossing the river, by implication, stemmed from Kanyika ka Tembo's violation of the ancient lineage customs and rituals which they had known in Lunda.

In spite of the erratic behaviour of the river, they eventually

---

[98] Had the translator of this tradition also recorded the species of bird and tree, the information would have facilitated the interpretation of the tradition.

crossed on a bridge of *muyombo* wood built by one of the other men in the group, Ndonje.[99] The Cokwe, like the Mbundu, regard *muyombo* trees as the resting place of lineage spirits.[100] The specification of the type of wood used in the bridge emphasizes once again that Kinguri's difficulties resulted from the disfavour of the lineage ancestors. The *muyombo*-wood bridge provided a means for the *kinguri*'s people to cross not only the river but also the metaphorical gulf which separated them from harmony with the supernatural world. With good relations re-established, however, they crossed the river and quickly found a village where the people had abundant stores of millet and sorghum. The villages received them hospitably and gave them all they needed to eat. Ndonje and the *kinguri* then left with part of the group to continue westward and left Kanyika ka Tembo and others to settle near the sources of the Kasai.

This episode almost certainly reveals that the *kinguri*'s band had lost its basic organization in terms of matrilineal descent groups through the assimilation of many unrelated foreigners. Kanyika ka Tembo had neglected the most basic rules of the lineages: his prohibition against conceiving and bearing children eliminated the procreative functions of their women and amounted to a crucial step in the abolition of lineages in a matrilineal society. At the moment that a woman bore an infant, the nucleus of a proto-matrilineage took shape in the relationship between the mother and the child. The *kinguri*'s law against child-bearing thus constituted the most direct means of eliminating lineages as the organizational backbone of his following. Henceforth, all children would enter the band through adoption or enslavement and would owe allegiance only to the *kinguri*. Motherhood and therefore kinship would cease to exist.[101]

The tradition comes from descendants of Kanyika ka Tembo, people who had left the *kinguri* rather than lose the security of their

---

[99] 'Ngondji' in the published text, which certainly represents the well-known title of Ndonje, given the numerous irregularities in the author's orthography of other personal names (cf. p. 156, n. 17 below).

[100] Merran McCulloch (1951), pp. 75–6.

[101] The marked hostility to women shown by the *kinguri* has sometimes been assumed to have been a result of military necessity. The argument runs that women encumbered the military campaigns of the band and therefore had to be eliminated. The presence of females did not, in fact, hinder the fighting activities of the males. On the contrary, most African armies could fight only with the logistical support of their wives and children, who operated as a supply train for the men who actually took part in battles.

descent groups. It therefore embodied the pro-lineage biases of those who would not tolerate life without kinship. Their hostility to the *kinguri*'s new way of life appears most clearly in the salvation achieved through reunion with the offended lineage spirits of the *muyombo*-wood bridge. People taught to think in terms of unilineal descent find it difficult to conceive of human society without lineages. To them, any other social system appears chaotic and dangerous. The episode implies that the hunger and other difficulties experienced by the *kinguri*'s group resulted from their neglect of the principle of lineage organization. In their view, reorganization must have afflicted even the *nzungu* and the magic bow obtained from the Luba, since these had failed to save the people from starvation.

The husband who had violated the prohibition against sexual contact, on the other hand, had reaffirmed one of the basic principles of the descent groups and he consequently enjoyed the blessing of the spirit world. The omen sent to him in the form of seeds pointed not just to a nearby source of food but also to a return to a settled agricultural life based on lineages. The seeds symbolized both females and the agricultural economy which the *kinguri* had rejected in favour of wandering and pillaging. The Lunda closely associate women and seed on a mundane level, since their wives customarily plant and harvest most crops. Metaphorically, women and seeds become equivalent since both give birth to a new life. The omen of the seeds therefore indicated to Kanyika ka Tembo (and to the tellers of the tradition) that his future lay in a normal 'civilized' existence rather than in the chaotic wanderings of the *kinguri*.

Other indications that the Lunda abandoned their lineages appear in the consistent opposition of women to the *kinguri* in the traditions, where females repeatedly threaten his emblems of royal authority. The underlying theme that women contaminated Lunda-derived political authority in Kasanje recurs in various traditions to point metaphorically to the elimination of lineages. Only males who had undergone the Lunda circumcision rites could wear the *lukano*. Under certain circumstances the bracelet would not tolerate even the presence of women nearby.[102] The *lukano*'s incompatibility with women is sometimes given as the reason why the *lueji*, a female title, never gained full control of the bracelet while she ruled in Lunda. One variant of the tradition makes the point explicitly, stating that she had to entrust the *lukano* to her *tubungu* guardians during her menstrual periods in order to avoid spoiling it and thus bringing

[102] Testimonies of Domingos Vaz; Sousa Calunga, 21 Aug. 1969.

misfortune to her people. On one such occasion, Lueji gave the *lukano* to Cibinda Ilunga, her husband, instead of to her advisers. This angered Kinguri and led to the dispute which resulted in his leaving Lunda.[103] This narrative episode draws on the omnipresent theme of women's offensiveness to the *kinguri* title in order to explain its departure from Lunda. It explains the origin of prohibitions which forbade any women to touch the *kinguri*'s emblems or to hold that position. Since the Lunda had lost their sacred authority symbol to the Luba while it was in the possession of a female, the *kinguri* would take great care about the presence of women in the future.

Another tradition, perhaps derived from the same historical incident, occurs with a different plot line among the Imbangala. They use the same image of a young woman who died during the crossing of a river to point once again to the decline of lineages in the *kinguri*'s group. According to the Imbangala, when Kinguri reached the Kwango river, at that time called the Moa, its great width presented a serious barrier to his progress. Kinguri himself leapt across the river easily by virtue of his magical powers, but his companions found the leap impossible. Kinguri had a daughter named Kwango who wished to cross the river just as her father had done. The *makota* warned against such a foolhardy attempt, saying that since she was merely a woman she could not manage the feat. She tried, failed, and drowned in the river, which from that time onward became known by her name.[104]

Despite the differences in locale and in the superficial plot, this story is structurally identical to that of Kanyika ka Tembo and the *muyombo*-wood bridge over the Kasai. Both hinge on the relationship between women and the difficulty of crossing rivers. Both contain the theme of women as liabilities to Kinguri, and both use rivers as metaphors for otherwise unexplained obstacles which faced the migrating Lunda.[105]

The different locations ascribed to the event do not affect the equivalence of the episodes, since each informant placed it on the largest river near his own king's lands. The Imbangala chose the Kwango, which flows near Kasanje, while the other version of the story came from peoples living near the Kasai. The identical structure

---

[103] Schütt (1881), pp. 82–3.

[104] Testimony of Domingos Vaz.

[105] Cf., once again, the significance of the river in the story of Kajinga's trip to Mbondo; pp. 97–102 above.

in both cases points out the incompatibility of women and lineages with the survival of the *kinguri*'s people.

Suppression of lineages allowed any outsider to join the *kinguri*'s people with status equal to that of all earlier members. This change overcame the limitations on recruitment imposed by the original kinship structure of the group and permitted unlimited assimilation of new members. It also meant that lineage loyalties no longer diluted the total obedience which the *kinguri* demanded of his people. With lineages, the *kinguri* had been one title-holder in a complex network of lineage headmen, *makota*, and other lineage-controlled positions; abolition of the lineages necessarily weakened the other titles and centralized all authority in the *kinguri*. The new centralized organization brought obvious advantages in terms of group unity and fighting capacity which permitted the *kinguri*'s band to survive as it passed through unfamiliar territories controlled by enemies.

The *kinguri*'s radical solution evidently represented an intolerable sacrifice to the title-holders whose positions lost influence under increased centralization. Various chiefs abandoned the *kinguri* all along their route, where they stopped, adopted a more settled mode of life, and established themselves as new rulers over the local lineages. The prestige of their Lunda emblems of authority made this relatively easy to accomplish among groups without this form of kingship. This fission process accounts for the settlement of several chiefs later identified as Cokwe, such as Mwata Kandala and Ndumba a Tembo.[106]

Through the continual incorporation of aliens, the *kinguri*'s band had evolved by the time it reached the upper Kwango from a small group of related lineages into a larger and more cohesive band lacking the particularistic and potentially divisive presence of segmentary descent groups. This change both contributed to and resulted from the continual movement of the title through a series of Cokwe *kinguri*-states. This type of social and political organization solved the problem of incorporating new recruits into the band, but it simultaneously introduced new difficulties for its leaders as they fought to retain the loyalty of those who resented the loss of lineages. Disaffected headmen, such as Kanyika ka Tembo, had begun to abandon the main group to settle again even before they reached the Kwango. Still, the main band had found a solution to the problem of state-formation among the segmentary lineages to the east of the Mbundu which would have dramatic consequences in the west in

[106] 'Mwandumba' in van den Byvang's text.

the next century. Further, they had the political positions—Kula-shingo who would become the *kinguri* in Kasanje, *mwa* Ndonje, Munjumbo, Kabuku ka Ndonga, and doubtless others—that by 1650 had become royal titles in all the major Mbundu states of Angola.

CHAPTER VI

The Imbangala *Kilombo*—
A Radical Solution

THREE MAJOR lines of early Mbundu political development converged in the upper Songo region during the middle part of the sixteenth century to produce an entirely novel resolution of the tensions which historically had set the particularistic Mbundu lineages against the centralizing tendencies of kings. Facing the *ngola a kiluanje* and Libolo near the upper Kwanza, the *kinguri*'s lineageless band confronted large and centralized kindoms for the first time since it had fled the Luba in Lunda. Also present in the same region was an Ovimbundu male initiation society, called the *kilombo*, one of the numerous social structures described in Chapter II as cross-cutting institutions. The Lunda title-holders who had come with the *kinguri*, under pressure from the large states to the west, fused with the *kilombo* some time in the sixteenth century to form powerful bands of mobile warriors, known as Imbangala, who overspread the Mbundu region after 1610 and ultimately settled down to found a new set of Mbundu states which included all the major powers of the region after 1650—Kalandula, Kabuku ka Ndonga, Matamba, Holo, Kasanje, Mwa Ndonje, and others.

Songo States Based on the Lunda Titles

The dissensions which had caused some followers of the *kinguri* to settle among the Cokwe east of the Kwango finally split the band apart after it had crossed the river into territory occupied by the Songo. When the holders of positions in the once unified set of Lunda titles went their separate ways, spreading as far as the Benguela plateau, a few remained as ephemeral Songo positions, much like the other titles which had preceded them in this area. The result was a reorganization of the segmentary Songo lineages into yet another set of short-lived states not unlike those the *kinguri* had headed among the Cokwe or the coalitions of Songo descent groups established earlier by title-holders from the south-west.

Holders of the *kinguri* title established a fourth small kingdom among the segmentary lineages of Mbumba a Mbulu, this one just south-east of the borders of the powerful Libolo state which, at the height of its power at that time, extended beyond the Kwanza to the upper Lui river. Despite some ambiguity in the traditions, this state probably lay near the Luhando and Jombo rivers in upper Songo. The oldest recorded Imbangala traditions identified the area of this *kinguri* kingdom as near the sources of the 'Pulo' and 'Lukombo' rivers in lands occupied by Cokwe during the 1840s and 1850s.[1] A stream called Lukumbi, probably the 'Lukombo', flows into the upper Jombo at approximately 10° 50′ S.[2] A mid-nineteenth-century Ovimbundu tradition also concurred in identifying the region as near the Luhando river.[3] Modern Songo sources, perhaps because of their more intimate knowledge of the region, refer to the area where the *kinguri* stopped by a praise name not noted on available maps, 'Mutonde a Kalamba Kizembe'.[4] The exact boundaries of the *kinguri*'s Mbundu kingdom thus remain uncertain, but all indications place its centre in the lands of the upper Songo drained by the Luhando and Jombo rivers.

Over a considerable number of years,[5] the *kinguri* applied the tried and true Mbundu technique of awarding subordinate named titles to extend their influence over the southeastern Songo lineages just beyond the Kirima groups controlled by the *hango*-kings of Libolo. The descent groups inhabiting that region claimed a common ancestress called Manyungo wa Mbelenge. Her descent from Tembo a Mbumba through female links in the perpetual genealogies marked her as the symbolic progenitor of a group of Songo lineages. A 'marriage' of the usual type between Manyungo wa Mbelenge and Hango shows that Libolo kings had conquered these Songo lineages before the arrival of the *kinguri*.[6] A second 'marriage', this time with

[1] Rodrigues Neves (1854), pp. 98–9.

[2] The 'Pulo' appears on no map known to me; Imbangala historians do not today locate this state by the names of rivers but do recall another designation, probably a praise name, Kanzulu ka Mbwa. Testimony of Domingos Vaz. Cf. Rodrigues Neves (1854), p. 97, who gave 'Kahunze' as the praise name. The modern Imbangala concur in locating the state vaguely west of the Kwango.

[3] Magyar (1859), p. 286. Childs (1949), p. 173, argued that the Magyar tradition did not come from Bihe, evidently basing his opinion on his inability to obtain confirmation of the story from mid-twentieth-century informants there. Internal evidence presented below, however, definitely identifies the tradition as Bihe in origin.

[4] A. A. de Magalhães (1948), p. 35.

[5] Rodrigues Neves (1854), pp. 98–9.

[6] Genealogies recited in testimonies of Sousa Calunga, 16 June, 9, 21 July 1969; Manuel Vaz; Domingos Vaz; Alexandre Vaz, 31 July 1969; Apolo de

the *kinguri*, represents the settlement of the Lunda title among the lineages of what was then eastern Libolo.[7] Songo genealogies, expectably the most detailed on the expansion of this state, show 'marriages' between the *kinguri* and at least two other female figures representing lineages of the region. One of these, Kahanda, left three descendants, Kakende, Mushinda, and Kunga, as evidence of the former Songo kingdom of the *kinguri*.[8] Kakende and Mushinda have no identifiable modern incumbents, probably as a result of the name changes which generally hinder reconstruction of Songo title histories, but Kunga had apparently been one of the earlier Libolo chiefs settled among the Songo of the lower Luhando where he ruled lineages which traced their matrilineal ancestry to Kavunje ka Tembo, a title connected with the Libolo kingdom.[9] The association of these lineages with Libolo, also supported by Kunga's location near the Libolo outpost on the island of Mbola na Kasashe in the Kwanza river, shows that the *kinguri* replaced overrule by the *hango*-kings when they settled in this region. They incorporated the lineages of the area by absorbing the older title of Kunga according to the name-changing methods employed in the expansion of both the *ngola a kiluanje* and Mbondo states.

The confrontation between the advancing *kinguri* and the kingdom of Libolo seems to have provoked a period of intense civil wars among the Lunda in which several of the secondary Lunda title-holders abandoned the *kinguri* in favour of establishing their own settled states. The Lunda emigrants had met no kingdom strong enough to resist the supernatural powers of their leader between the Lulua and the Kwango. There they had moved through an area of politically unorganized lineages and could penetrate farther each

---

[7] Testimonies of Domingos Vaz; Sousa Calunga, 1 Oct. 1969; Apolo de Matos, 18 June 1969; cf. Rodrigues Neves (1854), p. 97, who mentioned a wife of Kinguri but confused her name/title with that of Lueji.

[8] A. A. de Magalhães (1948), pp. 33–5. The Imbangala genealogies noted in n. 6 above also show a 'Kunga'.

[9] See map in Schütt (1881). Also Lux (1880), p. 96. Testimonies of Sousa Calunga, 29, 30 Sept. 1969; Alexandre Vaz, 31 July 1969.

Matos, 5 Oct. 1969. The calculation of the sequence rests on the fact that titles derived from Manyungo wa Mbelenge, some as far removed as the third descending generation, had already become prominent by the 1620s, notably the Kaza (ka Hango). Kalunga ka Kilombo kya Wabo wa Hango (three generations removed from Manyungo wa Mbelenge) became powerful at about the same time. The imputed chronology does not depend on biological life spans but on the assumption that some time was required for a new and dependent title to gain power in its own right.

time they felt the threat of Luba title-holders behind them. But Libolo for the first time offered serious opposition to their westward progress. The combined pressures from pursuing Luba chiefs in the east and resistance from Libolo in the west squeezed disaffected elements of the *kinguri*'s band outward towards the north and south where no comparably powerful states yet existed, and then, as we shall see, provoked mutiny by the remnants who remained.

Although the historical difficulties encountered by the *kinguri* in Songo probably stemmed from inability to defeat the Libolo rulers beyond the Kwanza, the traditions typically blamed his failure on inadequate magical authority symbols. Kinguri, the traditions relate, attempted to restore the potency of his emblems, already in serious doubt because of the hunger and frustration his followers had experienced in crossing the Kasai (or the Kwango?), by sending back to Lunda for additional magic which might overcome the unexpectedly strong opposition from Libolo. Kinguri requested one of his companions, Ndonje,[10] to go to Lunda and return with one of the emblems of the Lunda *tubungu* chiefs, a drum called the *ngoma ya mukamba*. This drum was a great war charm and later became the most powerful war drum of the Lunda *mwata yamvo*.[11] The *kinguri* apparently delegated this mission to the *ndonje* because his responsibilities included care of the *kinguri*'s authority emblems, an honour given him in return for his help in building the bridge of *muyombo* wood across the Kasai.

This manoeuvre may have indicated the *kinguri*'s growing disillusionment with the Luba symbols of power he had obtained from Cibinda Ilunga, hence his attempt to restore the ancient Lunda authority emblems of his position. The coincidence of the *kinguri*'s request for *tubungu* lineage emblems and the *ndonje*'s association with the *muyombo* wood, also a symbol of lineage solidarity in contrast to the essentially non-lineage Luba magic, probably indicates that the *kinguri* had settled, temporarily at least, as a normal lineage state among the Songo. His award of permanent titles there supports this hypothesis and contrasts with the lack of similar positions east of the Kwango where lineages had disappeared.

The departure of the holder of the *ndonje* title ended not in the intended revitalization of the *kinguri*'s powers but instead led to the creation of a new state among the lineages living along the middle

---

[10] *Ndonje* means teacher or master in Kimbundu; Assis Jr. (n.d.), p. 32.

[11] *Mukamba* in Kimbundu refers both to the dry season of the year and to the manioc plant. *Ngoma* is a widespread Bantu word for drum.

Kwango. The *ndonje* neglected to search for the *ngoma ya mukamba* in Lunda and abandoned the *kinguri* to settle among the Minungu people who seem to have formed a western subgroup of the Cokwe lineages. There his position became the *mwa ndonje* and remained until modern times as the title of an important Minungu king.

Another Lunda title-holder, the *munjumbo*, left to move south while the *kinguri* remained settled in Songo.[12] The full title of this position, Munjumbo wa Ngamba or Munjumbo wa Konde, indicated its origin as a senior Lundu *tubungu* title, either a brother or an uncle to the *kinguri*.[13] The position had left Lunda with the *kinguri* but was separated from it in Songo, and its holders independently founded at least two other major states, first one among the Songo and later another in the Ovimbundu highlands. The first state resulted from the *munjumbo*'s temporary settlement as a permanent named position among the Songo lineages living north of the Luhando along the upper Lui;[14] there its holders granted Lunda titles to the descent groups living around them.

This Songo state then expanded towards the south-west along the borders of Libolo and developed a secondary centre in the Benguela plateau area then dominated by the *kulembe*. Traditions both from the core of the original *munjumbo* kingdom in Songo and from Ovimbundu brought under the control of this title somewhat later confirm the general direction of this movement. The Songo on the Mwiji river, an affluent of the upper Luhando, recalled that Munjumbo came to their area from the north, that is, from the lower Luhando.[15] Northern Songo traditions state that Munjumbo went from there to the mountains called 'Nzambi na Ngombe'.[16] Although this name alone does not identify these mountains, circumstantial evidence suggests that it may refer to the Ovimbundu highlands. 'Nzambi na Ngombe' translates as the mountains of 'the great spirit and of cattle'. The Ovimbundu are not only the nearest mountain dwellers known to the Songo but are also generally associated by the Mbundu with cattle.

[12] Modern pronunciations of the name vary from Munjumbo to Minjumbo and Muzumbo in conformity with sound shifts characterizing these dialects.
[13] Testimonies of Domingos Vaz; Ngandu a Kungu. See p 121, n 29 above.
[14] Testimonies of Sousa Calunga, 29 Sept., 1 Oct. 1969; also Domingos Vaz. Schütt (1881), p 111; Capello and Ivens (1882), i. 191.
[15] Capello and Ivens (1882), i. 158.
[16] A. A. de Magalhães (1948), p. 33. Magyar (1859), p 243, noted that the Bihe dynasty, the best-known heirs of the *munjumbo*, was known as 'kangombe'.

The establishment of the *munjumbo* states provided another instance of Mbundu borrowing *mavunga* titles from beyond the Kwanza. The traditions recall that Munjumbo acquired fearful supernatural weapons, which may be identified as *mavunga*, in order to build these kingdoms. As a Cokwe narrative episode described these events, Munjumbo conquered the Songo of the middle Kwanza with the aid of a magical knife or hatchet (the Cokwe were apparently unclear as to the exact nature of this obviously alien weapon) called *mwela*. The *mwela* had the ability to fly out of its sheath and subdue all who resisted the wishes of its owner, crying with a human voice while it flew about the wilderness in pursuit of its master's enemies. In the end, however, the magical knife turned against Munjumbo and killed him. Munjumbo's descendants in his own lineage inherited the knife and ever afterwards kept it for themselves.[17]

Linguistic evidence identifies the *mwela* as a symbol borrowed from a state in an Umbundu-speaking area. Later kings of Kasanje, whose background included strong Ovimbundu influences, used a sacrificial knife very much like the *munjumbo*'s which they also called *mwela*.[18] The Umbundu generic term for knife is *mwela*, while Kimbundu uses several other dissimilar words, *poko, mbele,* or *mukwale*.[19] An alternative symbol of the same supernatural forces in Kasanje was hatchet called *kimbuya*. The modern Imbangala recognize that the shape and construction of the *kimbuya* differed from the common Mbundu hatchet and suspect that it might have come from non-Mbundu sources. The word *kimbuya* does not exist in Kimbundu but in Umbundu refers to the machete or *catana*.[20] Both words for this weapon clearly owe their origins to the Ovimbundu region. Imbangala historians support the linguistic evidence by citing vaguely known connections between the *munjumbo* and 'Bailundo'.[21]

The very vagueness of these connections supports the hypothesis that the *munjumbo* state expanded through appropriating the *vunga*-titles of its south-western neighbours. The *mwela* or *mukwale* was

[17] Van den Byvang (1937), p. 435. The published form of this tradition distorted this name as well as that of the *ndonje*, in this case giving 'Mung-andja'.

[18] For the *mwela* in Kasanje, testimony of Sousa Calunga, 2 Oct. 1969; Apolo de Matos, 18 June 1969.

[19] Pereira do Nascimento (1903), p. 49. Alves (1951), i. 764. The Lunda word was *mukwale*; see Mattos (1963), pp. 308–9.

[20] A long heavy knife used both for cutting and for chopping. Testimony of Sousa Calunga, 11 Sept.; Alves (1951), i. 706.

[21] Testimony of Sousa Calunga, 1 Oct. 1969.

everywhere used as an emblem of appointive authority and carried
no permanent heritable mandate. The traditions therefore failed
to capture and preserve a clear record of the *munjumbo*'s ties to
the south-west, just as modern Mbondo traditions are unclear on the
links between the *ndala* and the *hango*. The historical fate of the
south-western *vunga*-holders in the *munjumbo* state provides a further
parallel with the history of Mbondo, since, like the Libolo *ndala*
among the Mbondo, the *munjumbo*'s Ovimbundu province survived
as an independent kingdom long after the parent Songo state had
disappeared. The south-western *munjumbo* state covered the northern
slopes of the Benguela plateau, where nineteenth-century Bihe kings
preserved the name Munjumbo wa Tembo as the founder of their
dynasty.[22] The conclusion of the Cokwe narrative episode, in which
the *munjumbo* died when his own magical knife returned to slay him,
metaphorically described the defeat of the Songo *munjumbo* by
mwela-wielding holders of the south-western *vunga*.[23] The passage of
the knife to descendants in the lineage of the *munjumbo*, rather than
to another political title, meant that the Songo lineages formally
reclaimed the position, thus freeing the ancestors of future Bihe kings
to build their state without restrictions from the original sponsor of
their own title. The original *munjumbo* declined to the status of a
local Songo position and changed its name to reflect the loss of its
ties to the other Lunda positions.[24]

The somewhat confused written version of the seventeenth-century
Mbundu traditions on the arrival of the Lunda in Songo substantially
confirms the evidence on the *munjumbo* obtainable from later

[22] A. A. de Magalhães (1948), p. 33, located descendants of the Songo
munjumbo position in the area of Andulo, centre of the old Bihe kingdom For
the Bihe data, see Capello and Ivens (1882), i. 191. The Bihe learned the surname Tembo from the Songo after the Lunda form of the name had moved
south, leaving only the Songo form Munjumbo a Tembo in the north Magyar
(1859), p. 266, linked the Bihe kings with the *kinguri* but did not mention the
munjumbo by name; there is none the less an implied connection.

[23] The Imbangala genealogies add that after the *munjumbo* settled among
the Songo and expanded south to the Kulembe region, holders of this title
eventually moved back towards the north, reasserting their authority over
some of the Songo lineages on the basis of new Ovimbundu political symbols
(the *mwela*).

[24] Ngandu a Kungu confirms that the modern title is basically a Songo
position. Schütt had Munjumbo wa Kafushi as a Songo founding king who
came with Kinguri. A. A. de Magalhães (1948), pp. 33ff., gave Muzumbo as
the son of 'Gambo' (Ngamba?) and Kafuti (the equivalent of Kafushi in the
Songo dialect) ka Mvula. Capello and Ivens had Munjumbo wa Tembo as the
founder of the Songo and companion of the founding kings of the Cokwe
and Imbangala.

genealogies and narratives. According to this tradition, which must be handled with great circumspection,[25] a band of warriors, united under a leader misnamed 'Zimbo' (but probably a distorted derivative of the title of the *munjumbo*[26]) had reached an unspecified part of the interior. Each of the subchiefs who had accompanied 'Zimbo' then went his own way and settled among the various inhabitants of the region. Chiefs called 'Ndumba' and 'Kandonga' settled in unidentified quarters, and the old king 'Zimbo' eventually died, leaving his former vassals in their respective lands where they still ruled as independent kings in the mid-seventeenth century.[27]

All the details of this tradition connect these events with the arrival of the *kinguri* among the Songo and the subsequent dispersal of the original band of migrants. Ndonje, the tradition specified, had come as one of 'Zimbo's' subchiefs but had settled in 'Greater Ganguella', the seventeenth-century name for upper Songo. The name of Ndonje's wife, 'Musasa', provides another clue to the identity of this group, since 'Musasa' probably designated the matrilineages of (Lucaze na) Mwazaza,[28] descent groups still connected by the modern genealogies with the Lunda titles of which the *ndonje* was one. The other two titles named in the 1650s, Ndumba (a Tembo dya Mbumba a Mbulu) and (Kabuku) ka Ndonga ('Kandonga') all appear in other sources as companions of the *kinguri* and the *munjumbo*. Seventeenth-century opinion located 'Zimbo's' (i.e. *munjumbo*'s) original kingdom somewhere in the unknown highlands south of the Kwanza.

A Bihe tradition recorded in the 1840s gave a quite literal description of these events which once again confirms this interpretation of the *munjumbo*'s separation from the *kinguri* and his subsequent expansion towards the south. As the Bihe told the story, Kinguri's band reached the river Luhando after many years of fighting their way through hostile peoples and strange lands in the east. They practiced customs ('*kesila* laws') involving extensive cannibalism and killed many humans as sacrifices to the spirits represented by their chiefs. These spirits required so many victims, in fact, that the band could not settle long in a single spot without driving away or killing most of the neighbouring peoples. This repeatedly forced them to

[25] Joseph C. Miller (forthcoming (a)).
[26] Mbundu informants may have contributed to the error by pronouncing the name 'munjimbo', as a result of the tendency of eastern Kimbundu-speakers to exchange the high front and back vowels (*i* and *u*) of Songo and Libolo names; cf. p. 155, n. 12 above.
[27] Cavazzi (1965), i. 176–7.
[28] See genealogies reproduced in Figure V.

move on in search of new populations to devastate in order to
satisfy their leader's cruel demands.

When the band finally settled on the Luhando, they soon exhausted
the capacity of the Songo to provide sacifices and turned upon each
other to satisfy their need for human flesh. Some leaders foresaw that
internal conflict would weaken them until they would fall prey to the
vengeful enemies who surrounded them. These leaders decided to
abandon their cannibalistic customs and nomadism in favour of a
settled life based on agriculture. They formed a secret society in order
to promote those ends. The leader of the original band, the *kinguri*,
remained devoted to his warlike ways, however, and recognizing that
his opponents threatened to undermine his authority, opposed the
formation of their new society. A series of bloody battles followed
between the *kinguri* and the members of the secret society, but no
clear victor emerged. In the end, the proponents of a settled life
deserted their warlike rivals and migrated south-west across the
Kwanza. They gradually dispersed and settled down to rule the
populations living there and adopted the local sedentary style of
living.[29]

The plot line of this narrative—wars between members of a migrating band over the issue of their leader's cruel domination, movement
south-west by a part of the band, and gradual fragmentation which
resulted in the settlement of kings in Bihe and other parts of the
Ovimbundu highlands—clearly describes the dispersal of Lunda and
related titles in upper Songo. The form in which the story was published reveals its origins among opponents of the *kinguri*, doubtless
the Bihe descendants of the *munjumbo*. The main narrative theme
clearly leads to the foundation of the Bihe kingdom even though the
written version of the tradition did not mention it specifically.[30]
Emphasis on the *kinguri*'s cannibalism and cruelty might be expected
from Bihe descendants of the *munjumbo* who justified their abandonment of the *kinguri* by picturing him as an inhuman monster.[31]

[29] Magyar (1859), pp. 266ff.

[30] Cokwe or Lwena sources, either directly to the European who rendered
the tradition and had travelled east of the Kwango, or indirectly through Bihe
traders in the east, may have contributed details to the published version; for
example, Sha Kambunje, a nineteenth-century Lunda governor of the middle
Kasai, was accorded status equal to that of Kinguri.

[31] The association of the cannibalistic rituals mentioned in the tradition
with '*kesila* laws' probably indicates the writer's familiarity with seventeenth-
century written sources on the so-called 'Jaga' which generally identified
cannibalism with '*kesila*'. *Ocisila* is the Umbundu form of the Kimbundu
word *kijila* used by Cavazzi and presumably by the later Portuguese to refer

The published tradition's term for the secret society founded to oppose the *kinguri*, 'empacasseiros', both identified its leader as the *munjumbo* and suggested one way the *munjumbo*'s kingdom may have been structured. The term 'empacasseiros' may be equated with the *kibinda* version of the professional hunting society brought from Lunda with the *kinguri*. The word *empacasseiros* was a Portuguese term for élite African auxiliary troops attached to European armies in Angola since the early seventeenth century. The Portuguese had formed the word from Kinbundu *mpakasa*, the red buffalo (*bos caffir*), plus the common Portuguese suffix *-eiro* for the person associated with an object,[32] since these mercenaries derived their élite status from their skill in the pursuit of large game like the *mpakasa*. The concept of skilled hunters specializing in dangerous game was, however, purely African. The men who fought as *empacasseiros* for the Portuguese must also have ranked as *yibinda* among their kinsmen in the villages. Since Imbangala historians emphasize that the *munjumbo* held the status of *kibinda* while the *kinguri* did not,[33] identification of the *kinguri*'s opponents as *empacasseiros* marks them as *yibinda* led by the *munjumbo*.[34] A title-holder eager to build new kingdoms would have been looking for an appropriate cross-cutting institution on which he could base his supra-lineage political organization. Since the *kibinda* society cut across existing lineage divisions, it provided a structure that the *munjumbo* evidently converted to political purposes, in conjunction with the *mavunga* appointive titles, for building his new states.[35]

[32] e.g. *cozinha* (kitchen)+ *-eiro* = *cozinheiro* (cook).
[33] Testimonies of Sousa Calunga, 29 Sept., 2 Oct. 1969. Although this narrative episode may appear to describe the formation of the *empacasseiors* or the *kibinda*, it originally dealt with the origins of the Bihe kings. Magyar's synthesis of various traditions, African and European, produced a misleading impression. The Portuguese, not the *kinguri*'s enemies, created the *empacasseiro* in its proper sense of mercenary. The *kibinda* society probably diffused with the Lunda political titles from the east.
[34] The opposition between the *kinguri* and the *munjumbo* also operates at the metaphorical level. The savagery of the *kinguri* made him seem like a ferocious supernatural beast, while the *munjumbo* as *kibinda* had special qualifications for slaying animals of that type.
[35] The Bihe tradition (as well as the Songo versions of these events) implies that the *kinguri* left Songo and eventually settled in Kasanje without further change in the composition of his group. This dates the tradition to the period

to the 'laws' among the Africans in seventeenth-century Angola that they considered cruel and unreasonable; Alves (1951), ii. 1280. Nineteenth-century oral traditions current among the largely illiterate Portuguese population in Angola may have contained these stories even if the writer had not read the seventeenth-century sources.

The Songo states of the *kinguri*, the *mwa ndonje*, and the *munjumbo* illustrate themes already familiar from the earlier history of the Mbundu lineages. Alien Lunda titles entered the region without firm attachment to any specific groups of lineages. The Songo descent groups then appropriated the Lunda positions and made them centres of at least three small kingdoms by procedures which resembled the Mbondo conversion of similarly lineageless *mavunga* from Libolo. At least one of the Lunda positions expanded into a major state, that of Munjumbo (a Kafushi/Tembo/Kalunga, etc.), through awarding *vunga* positions based on the Ovimbundu *mwela* magical knife. Others, such as the *kinguri*, expanded briefly by creating subordinate perpetual titles of the native Songo type. The dispersal and settlement of the Lunda titles as lineage positions, provoked in this case by confrontation with Libolo, merely continued the fission process which had begun while the *kinguri*'s band moved through Cokwe lands far to the east. The propensity of the Lunda titles to revert to a settled existence suggested that the lineageless band did not offer a congenial environment in which they could provide effective rule. Their experience among the Songo thus presaged many of the changes which would affect related positions north of the Kwanza during the seventeenth century.

Origins of the Kilombo

The remaining Lunda title-holders sought a solution to the problems of disunity which they had experienced under the *kinguri* by adopting an Ovimbundu warrior society known as the *kilombo*. The *kilombo* provided two things which the *kinguri*'s original band had lacked: a firm structure capable of uniting large numbers of strangers who had evidently never replaced their lost lineages with comparably viable social or political institutions, and military discipline capable of defeating the large kingdoms which blocked their movement north beyond the Luhando and west of the Kwanza. The mature *kilombo*, which ultimately proved capable of defeating the most successful Mbundu states up to its appearance north of the Kwanza, consisted of a blend of the Lunda perpetual titles, *mavunga* positions originated

---

before the *kinguri* left Songo, since events immediately afterwards resulted in abolition of the position and a long series of wars that fragmented the band. The Bihe tradition is therefore older than most other versions and has not undergone the same distortions as Imbangala and other Mbundu versions of these events. This makes it preferred evidence for determining what transpired in Songo.

among the Ovimbundu, and a warrior cult developed somewhere in the lands of the *kulembe*.

In view of the evident rapidity with which the *kilombo* metamorphosed from decade to decade, and the shortage of data bearing directly on it before the mid-seventeenth century, an attempt to develop too detailed a description of its internal structure at this time would probably be unwise.[36] The available information does show, however, that the *kilombo* first matured as an adjunct to the *kulembe* kings south of the Kwanza and that it represented an evolved form of one of the non-lineage structures of the common type which I have called cross-cutting institutions.[37] The original and primary meaning of the word connoted an association of males, open to anyone without regard to lineage membership, in which members of the society underwent dramatic initiation rituals that simultaneously removed them from the protective pale of their natal descent groups and welded the initiates together as co-warriors in a regiment of supermen made invulnerable to the weapons of their enemies.

The formidable warrior bands of the *kilombo* probably emerged from a combination of Ovimbundu and Cokwe/Lwena institutions forged when the *kinguri*'s band, which had become heavily influenced by Cokwe customs during its passage through Itengo and Mona Kimbundu, met Umbundu-speaking peoples west of the Kwanza. The *kinguri*'s followers had brought a powerful but relatively unstructured cult which, linguistic evidence suggests, they had picked up somewhere among the Cokwe. The Ovimbundu contributed structure in the form of an early version of the circumcision camps now found throughout central and western Angola among the Mbundu and Cokwe as well as some Ovimbundu.

Seventeenth-century Mbundu oral traditions explicitly recorded the creation of the *kilombo* from distinct Cokwe and Ovimbundu institutions in the story of 'Temba Andumba', a legendary queen who

---

[36] Full discussion of the later *kilombo* appears in Chapter VIII.

[37] Seventeenth-century Europeans in Angola, heretofore the only sources on the Imbangala *kilombo*, have misled all subsequent historians through their failure to appreciate the significance of the institution in the eyes of the Mbundu. As a result, the military aspects of the *kilombo* (for obvious reasons the side which mattered most to European soldiers and administrators) have been emphasized to the exclusion of its social and political implications for Mbundu kinsmen. The ensuing discussion of the *kilombo* makes no further reference to the usual but imprecise definitions of the word as (a) a warcamp belonging to the so-called 'Jaga' (Miller, 1973a), (b) a type of fugitive slave settlement found in both Angola and Brazil (cf. Kent, 1965, p. 162), and (c) any temporary camp built by nineteenth-century trading caravans in Angola.

was said to have founded a large kingdom on the basis of a cult, called an 'execrable sect' by offended missionaries, which contemporary Europeans associated with the people whom they erroneously knew as 'Jaga'. The written version of this tradition, though distorted in various ways,[38] accurately specified that the 'laws of the "Jagas"', as the *kilombo* rites were then known, had originated somewhere in the east and appeared with 'Zimbo' (the *munjumbo*), Ndonje, and the others somewhere along the upper Kwanza.[39] The founder of the sect, 'Temba Andumba', was a daughter of Ndonje. She became a brave warrior queen and conquered many lands. She at last grew intoxicated with her military successes, according to the interpretation of the missionary who wrote down the tradition, and introduced laws and rituals (*yijila*, singular *kijila*) intended to preserve her status as the most feared and respected ruler in Angola. 'Temba Andumba' proclaimed her new laws in the most terrifying ceremonies the Mbundu could remember. First, she sent for her own infant daughter, seized the child, and threw her into a large mortar normally used for grinding grain. 'Temba Andumba' then picked up a large pounding stick and mercilessly reduced the baby to a shapeless mass of flesh and blood. She added certain roots, herbs, and powders to the human remains and boiled the entire mixture to obtain an unguent which she called *maji a samba*. Smearing the *maji a samba* on her own body and on the bodies of her closest associates, she called her people to a renewed campaign of terror and destruction. After devastating all the lands within her reach, she commanded her followers to take their own children, cut them to bits, and to eat the remains as a sign of their devotion to the *yijila* laws of her kingdom.

'Temba Andumba', the story continued, later fell in love with a certain Kulembe whose social position made him somewhat inferior to the warrior queen but who equalled her in both bravery and cruelty. Kulembe ambitiously desired to claim 'Temba Andumba's' prestige for himself and so resolved to kill her and to take her kingdom. He concealed his evil intentions for many years while 'Temba Andumba' expanded her kingdom, finally gained her confidence through flattery and feigned affection, and eventually married her. Not long after the wedding he executed the plan he had long hidden, inviting his wife to a ceremonial dinner customary among

[38] Cf. the distortions in the story of 'Zimbo', to which this narrative was joined; Miller (forthcoming (a)).

[39] Cavazzi (1965), i. 177–9. Although Cavazzi did not use the term in this context, his 'execrable sect' and 'savage laws' clearly referred to it.

their people and then murdering her by putting poison into her drink.

Kulembe successfully hid his complicity in 'Temba Andumba's' death from the people of the kingdom and induced them to accept him as her rightful successor and ruler over the adherents of the *yijila*. To consolidate his authority, he sacrificed an untold number of people in memory of the dead 'Temba Andumba' and performed other deeds hypocritically intended to indicate his great piety and grief. He then began a dramatic military campaign in conjunction with several other brave generals (named as 'Calanda, Caete, Cassa, Cabuco, Caoimba, and many others'), and together they soon made themselves masters of an area even larger than that conquered by the famous 'Temba Andumba'.

The significant aspects of these narrative episodes are the statements that certain titles from the east joined with the *kulembe* to form a new and very powerful military organization (the *kilombo*). The analysis first focuses on the position of the *kilombo* chief's first wife, known properly as the *tembanza* but personified in this tradition as 'Temba Andumba'. Titles cognate to that of the *tembanza* appear throughout the Cokwe regions to the south-east, sometimes in association with rituals identical to those called *maji a samba* in the Mbundu narrative, and suggest that this part of the institutions which formed the mature *kilombo* came originally from that direction.

The evidence that the word *tembanza*, meaning the title of the *kilombo* leader's principal wife, came from somewhere in south-eastern Angola comes from an incomplete but suggestive distribution of similar positions with the same name. The husbands of certain Cokwe chiefs' sisters received the title *sambaza*, an evident cognate of *tembanza*.[40] Modern Imbangala have never heard the term *tembanza* in connection with the chief wife of later kings of Kasanje, who also were *kilombo* chiefs, but they none the less feel that the term probably came from the Cokwe.[41] The senior niece of the king of a group of people living now in northern Botswana (the Mbukushu[42]) took the

---

[40] McCulloch (1951), p. 48. The prefixes *sa-* and *ta-* (*te-*) are equivalent in Bantu languages; both mean 'father' of the following word or name. The absence of nasalization in the recorded form of the Cokwe word could result either from an error in transcription or from a sound shift. The Cokwe *sambaza* was the father of the king's heir (his sister's son), which implies that the heir himself was the *mbanza* or *mbaza*.

[41] Testimony of Sousa Calunga, 11 Sept. 1969.

[42] The Mbukushu live on the Okavango river at approximately 18° S. Guthrie does not mention Simbukushu (the language of the Mbukushu) specifically but Murdock groups them with the Ila and Tonga whose languages

title of *mambanje*, also a cognate of *tembanza*.[43] The *mambanje* performed a crucial function in maintaining the well-being of the Mbukushu kingdom since she cohabited for ritual purposes with her uncle, the king, and shared with him the secrets of rain-making. The preparation of these rain-making medicines required the murder of some of the infant children born of the incestuous unions of king and *mambanje*. The Mbukushu electors chose the successors to their kings from the surviving children of this group.[44] The striking resemblance of the Mbukushu rain-making ceremonies to the ritual child-killing necessary in the preparation of the *maji a samba* reinforces the identification of the *tembanza* of the *kilombo* with the *mambanje* title of the Mbukushu.

The migrating lineageless band of the *kinguri* probably adopted the rituals of the *maji a samba*, as well as the central feminine title of the *tembanza*, as they abandoned their lineage rituals among the Cokwe. The lack of lineages deprived the Lunda of an effective means of instilling a strong sense of membership in their band other than through the terror of rule by the *kinguri*.[45] The rituals of the *maji a samba*, on the other hand, conferred a magical invulnerability on the otherwise supernaturally exposed members of the band, thus substituting for the absent descent groups. The attendant rituals explained the significance of the structural change which had occurred in two ways. In a figurative sense, the ruler's preparation of the *maji a samba* through ritual murder of her/his 'child' was a common symbol for the enormity of a ruler's power over his people. 'Children' in the narrative represent the subjects of political chiefs, in contrast to their relatives who are always depicted as 'nephews and nieces'. The ceremony of 'child'-killing symbolized the ruler's absolute power over his subjects just as the image of the *kinguri* murdering slaves every time he rose or sat showed the awe in which his people held him. In a more literal sense, however, child-killing, when practiced by

[43] The prefix *ma-* (or *na-* in some languages) connotes 'mother' of the following name. The Mbukushu *mambanje* was in fact the mother of the king's heir, who would be called *mbanza* there as well as among the Cokwe (the actual reflex being *mbanje*).

[44] Dr. Thomas Tlou of the University of Botswana, Swaziland, and Lesotho kindly provided information on the *mambanje* and the Mbukushu from his unpublished research.

[45] Compare the theory of the uses of terror suggested by E. V. Walter (1969).

fall in Guthrie's Zone M. See Murdock (1959), p. 365, and Guthrie (1967–72), iii. 15. On the Mbukushu, see Thomas J. Larson (1971) and publications cited therein.

an entire population, became a means of abolishing lineages, since the murder (or denial of the social significance of a physical birth) of children had the same structural effect on descent groups as the *kinguri*'s prohibition of their birth; both eliminated the ties of kinship. The story of 'Temba Andumba's' *maji a samba* refers to the developments noted earlier on the basis of independent evidence on the history of the *kinguri*'s band among the Cokwe.

The use of the *maji a samba* may have begun as a ritual practised only by the leaders of the band, as it was later among the Mbukushu, but its structural significance changed completely when it was extended from the king (symbolized in the narrative by 'Temba Andumba') to all the subjects in the kingdom. It then ceased to serve as a means of setting the king apart from his people and instead marked the effective end of lineages. This change, which was noted distinctly in the seventeenth-century Mbundu narrative, illustrates the way in which an extension of an old notion could produce a significant political innovation.

Similar practices, evidently derived from the *maji a samba* of 'Temba Andumba', appeared much later at the courts of kings known to have descended from titles brought across the Kwango with the *kinguri*. Nineteenth-century Bihe kings, heirs of the *munjumbo*, had their magical specialists take the foetus from the womb of a pregnant woman to make an ointment which, they believed, conferred invulnerability.[46] The seventeenth-century Imbangala north of the Kwanza, also descended from the *kinguri*'s original band, had exactly the same practice.[47] The association between Lunda titles and the *maji a samba* provides final confirmation that the origins of the 'execrable sect' lay east of the Kwango in so far as they were associated with the *kilombo* chief's first wife.

The seventeenth-century narrative's detailed description of the courtship and marriage of Kulembe and 'Temba Andumba' describes the union of the idea of the *maji a samba* with an entirely different Ovimbundu institution apparently connected with the *kulembe* state on the Benguela plateau. As in the general model of the Mbundu perpetual genealogies, the 'marriage' of a female (usually signifying a group of lineages, but here a lineageless band) to a male stands for the subjugation of people to a political title. In this case, the 'marriage'

---

[46] Magyar (1859), p. 316. Chiefs' wives elsewhere south of the Kwanza performed similar rituals involving human sacrifices, but their titles distinguished them from the *tembanza*. See, for example, Childs (1949), p. 20.

[47] Cavazzi (1965), i. 126.

represents the union of the adherents of the *maji a samba* cult with the *kulumbe*'s warrior initiation society, the *kilombo*.

Linguistic evidence reveals something about the nature of the ancient *kilombo* even without clear information on the social and political institutions of the Benguela plateau at the time of the *kulembe* state. Several modern Umbundu terms, all related to what appears to be an archaic Umbundu root referring to circumcision or to blood, occur in connection with modern Ovimbundu circumcision rites. The most direct evidence comes from the Umbundu-speaking Mundombe people near Benguela who still called their circumcision camp a *kilombo* in the nineteenth century.[48] *Ocilombo* in standard modern Umbundu refers to the flow of blood from a newly-circumcised penis; a related term, *ulombo*, designates a medicine prepared from the blood and prepuces of initiates in the circumcision camp for use in certain (unspecified) rites.[49] The root -*lombo* which forms the basis for all these words identifies the term *kilombo* as uniquely Ovimbundu since it contrasts with the Mbundu and Cokwe word for circumcision ceremonies, which is *mukanda*.[50] It is also distinct from a similar-appearing root, -*lumbu*, which means 'wall' in all of the major western Angolan languages, Umbundu, Kimbundu, and Kikongo.[51] Despite the possibility that the walls (*lumbu*) surrounding the *kilombo* might have given the site its name because of their military importance in keeping out enemies or because of their symbolic significance in isolating the sanctified inner *kilombo* from the profane outer world, linguistic analysis shows that *lumbo* and -*lombo* were two different words. The word *kilombo* therefore indicated the origin of the *kulembe*'s warrior society as an Ovimbundu circumcision camp rather than referring to the 'walled' aspect of the place.

Formation of the Imbangala

The critical development in the formation of the mature *kilombo* took place when the *kinguri*'s remaining followers, the secondary Lunda titles known as *makota*, rejected the leadership of the oppressive central Lunda position and adopted the *kulembe*'s warrior

[48] Magyar (1859), p. 23.
[49] Alves (1951), i. 547.
[50] Antonio da Silva Maia (n.d. (a)), p. 141; Assis Jr. (n.d.), p. 268; Cordeiro da Matta (1893), p. 87; J. Van Wing and C. Penders (1928), p. 136.
[51] Seventeenth-century Kikongo made a clear distinction between the high vowel (*u*) found in the word for wall in all three languages and the lower vowel (*o*) that occurred only in *kilombo*. In the Kikongo of that time, the word for wall was *lumbu*; Van Wing and Penders (1928), pp. 136–7.

initiation society as the basis of a new political organization, adding a number of *vunga*-positions of demonstrably Umbundu origin. The union of the theoretically centralized *kilombo* with the multitude of Lunda perpetual positions enabled the initiation society to fragment and to spread rapidly throughout the regions south of the Kwanza as many separate warrior bands, now called Imbangala,[52] formed under holders of new subordinate Lunda-type titles. The inherent capacity of the perpetual positions to spawn new named titles provided a legitimate pedigree for any warleader who could gather enough followers to break free of existing political and lineage authorities in the Benguela highlands. An ambitious man could adopt the organization of the *kilombo*, claim charms and a title descended from another *kilombo*-chief, and make his name as an Imbangala king. Even the native Ovimbundu positions, such as that of the *kulembe*, whose reliance on *mavunga* showed that they had not originally exploited the ability to nominate 'son' positions, adopted the Lunda technique and awarded subordinate positions which appear in mid-seventeenth-century documents. The fragmentation which attended the introduction of Lunda titles south of the Kwanza represented the obverse of the centralization which the Ovimbundu *mavunga* had produced among the Mbundu.

The unstable history of the *kinguri*'s band before they reached the Kwanza explains why the *makota* sought new forms of political organization which would free them of their dependence, in terms of Lunda political structure, on the *kinguri*. Defections by some title-holders as far east as the Cokwe, and the recent departures of the *mwa ndonje* and the *munjumbo* confirmed the seriousness of the dissensions which had shattered the band. These were mentioned explicitly in the Bihe tradition which described the formation of the *empacasseiro* society and had been alluded to in metaphoric terms in the story of how Kulembe clandestinely opposed the 'execrable sect' of 'Temba Andumba'. The *kinguri*'s followers no longer accorded their leader the complete loyalty demanded by the supernatural forces behind his title, and—since the performance of Mbundu kings depended on the obedience of their subjects—his charms had ceased to perform as expected. The resulting insecurity drove the *kinguri* to seek new methods of controlling his people; this explains not only his request for the *ngoma ya mukamba* but also his award of new titles,

---

[52] The term Imbangala comes from an Umbundu root, -*vangala*, meaning to be brave and/or to wander widely through the countryside; Joseph C. Miller (forthcoming (d)).

such as the *kunga* and others, to Songo lineages. All these measures represented attempts to find new sources of support among the lineages of Manyungo wa Mbelenge and Kavunje ka Tembo.

If the Lunda *makota* found their association with the *kulembe* advantageous because it helped them to free themselves from the burdensome *kinguri*, the *kulembe* may have found an alliance with the numerous and martial Lunda an attractive means of resisting either Libolo expansion or the southward advance of the *ngola a kiluanje*. In either case, wars followed in which the *kulembe* and the *makota* on one side fought against the *kinguri* and his remaining Songo allies on the other. Seventeenth-century Mbundu traditions referred to these wars in their recollection of the great conquests which followed the *kulembe*'s adoption of the *maji a samba* in conjunction with the 'other brave generals' who were, with a single partial exception, all Lunda titled positions. 'Calanda' was Kalanda ka Imbe ('Caoimba'), 'Caete' was Kahete, and 'Cabuco' was Kabuku ka Ndonga, a title subordinate to the *ndonga* which had come from Lunda with the *kinguri*; only 'Cassa' (the *kaza*) had different origins.[53]

The united forces of the *kilombo* then drove the *kinguri* north and west, as the Bihe tradition later recalled, away from the centres of the *kulembe*'s strength and toward Ndongo. The seventeenth-century traditions confirmed that the last *kinguri* had died in Ndongo,[54] but not fighting against the Portuguese or the *ngola a kiluanje* as most historians have assumed. He in fact 'died' at the hands of the *makota* who had accompanied him from Lunda, and his 'death' meant the abolition of his title rather than the demise of an individual incumbent. These developments culminated on the island of Mbola na Kasashe in the upper Kwanza where the Libolo kings had once stationed one of their *vunga*-chiefs as guardian of the eastern frontiers of their kingdom. By this time,[55] however, the *ngola a kiluanje* had subsequently conquered the area and made it part of 'Ndongo' according to the seventeenth-century usage of the term.

The Lunda *makota* and the *kulembe* owed their victory over the previously unconquerable powers of the *kinguri* to the explosive combination of a mobile band without lineages and the assimilative and structuring potential of the *kilombo* initiation society. Lunda

[53] Cavazzi (1965), i. 189. The *kaza* was originally a Libolo title related to the *hango* but turned up shortly afterwards as a close associate of the Lunda titles; see chapter VII.

[54] Cavazzi (1965), i. 190.

[55] *c.* 1550s–1560s?; Miller (1972a), pp. 560–3.

abolition of lineages had given them the ability to incorporate large numbers of people but this solution had simultaneously eliminated the structural definition provided by descent groups. It thus failed to integrate its members into an effectively unified group, as evidenced by the constant tendencies to fission present through the history of the band. The hostility of Cokwe and Mbundu lineages to the lineageless institutions of the *maji a samba* cult also weakened its effectiveness as a means of forming a large but still cohesive group.

The *kilombo*, on the other hand, possessed well-defined initiation procedures which, together with the centralizing capabilities of the Ovimbundu *mavunga*, compensated for the organizational weaknesses of the Lunda band. These qualities, plus the strong magic associated with the Lunda titles of the *makota*, created the large, unified, and disciplined bands of Imbangala warriors who overran the Mbundu later in the seventeenth century.

The *kulembe*, ironically, seems to have become one of the first major victims of the combined Lunda/Ovimbundu *kilombo*. The seventeenth-century traditions made it clear that the resulting expansion took place primarily under the leadership of the Lunda. The *kulembe*'s once-unified kingdom disintegrated into many small warring chiefdoms led by *kilombo* chiefs, some of which later emerged as Ovimbundu kingdoms of the eighteenth and nineteenth centuries. The chronic instability of the Ovimbundu region not long after these events, approximately the middle of the seventeenth century, suggests that a power vacuum had followed the decline of some formerly centralized state. Warlike chiefs, reported in many documents to have been fighting one another near the headwaters of the Kuvo and Longa rivers during the 1640s, for example, would thus have been former subordinates of the *kulembe*, freed from their overlord to work out a new political balance which later coalesced as the Ovimbundu kingdoms of that region. The title of the *kulembe* survived these changes, but only as one undistinguished position among many more or less equal rulers in the area its holders had once dominated.[56]

Because the *kilombo* structure included no perpetual named positions of the Lunda and Mbundu type, modern Mbundu traditions totally neglect the wars and upheavals visible in documents. They concentrate instead on the formal aspects of struggles which altered the relationships between the *kinguri* title and its *makota*. These traditions tell the story in metaphorical terms reminiscent of early

[56] For example, see Cadornega (1940–2), iii. 249; his spelling of the name was 'Lulenbe'.

Lunda history at the time of the *yala mwaku*, in which the *makota* 'killed' the position of the *kinguri* through application of special magical techniques. Picking up the theme of Kinguri's legendary ferocity, the narratives attribute the mutiny of the *makota* to their reaction against their king's bloodthirsty demands. As Kinguri's incessant oppression bore more and more heavily on his own people, the traditions recall, the *makota* recognized that he posed a threat to them personally and began to devise ways to avoid the growing danger. They finally resolved to take a desperate step: they would attempt to slay Kinguri and take over leadership of the band for themselves. They concentrated on searching for a means to disarm the supernatural forces which protected their king from ordinary sorts of danger. A simple murder of the incumbent would do no good, as this would not affect the spirits to whom all *kinguri* owed their power, and so only magical methods could abolish the problem, and the position, entirely. In particular, they felt they must not allow Kinguri to discover the plot or the aroused and angered forces behind the title would certainly avenge themselves before the *makota* could execute their plan.[57]

The *makota* finally chose a method which operated primarily on the level of the symbolism of their kings' title. The *kinguri* and its attendant spirits were seen as carnivorous animals of the forest. The *kinguri*'s thirst for human blood, for example, reminded them of a lion's roar in the night.[58] Their awe of their leader resembled the fear of men who confront wild beasts in the wilderness.[59] Since the Lunda had always hunted with pits and traps, the *makota* constructed a symbolic trap of this kind, a circular enclosure of heavy stakes situated on the island of Mbola na Kasashe where they had camped at that time.[60] The enclosure had only a single entrance (unlike all

[57] Testimony of Sousa Calunga, 21 July 1969.
[58] Various testimonies of Sousa Calunga; also Mwanya a Shiba, 15 June 1969.
[59] Dias de Carvalho (1890a), pp. 60–1.
[60] Full name: Mbola na Kasashe ka Masongo a Ndembi; testimony of Sousa Calunga, 2 Oct. 1969. Rodrigues Neves (1854), p. 99, gave the area where the *kinguri* died as 'Sunge a Mboluma'. In the nineteenth century, Sunje a Mboluma referred to the general region on the east side of the Kwanza near Mbola na Kasashe; testimony of Sousa Calunga, 1 Oct. 1969; also map of Capello and Ivens (1882). For geographical details on the island, Eugenio Torre do Valle and José Velleso de Castro (1913), esp. pp. 35–41, 98–9. It was one of the very few toponyms known to the earliest Europeans in an otherwise unfamiliar region; 'Carta do Império do Monamotapa' located in the A.H.U., probably a copy of the map of João Teixeira Albernás II, 1665 (Avelino Teixeira da Mota (1964), pp. 32–4). For the nineteenth century, Vincente José Duarte (1859–61).

later royal compounds of the *kinguri* kings in Kasanje which always featured a second entrance as a potential means of escape for a beleaguered ruler). On the pretext that lions roaming in the vicinity endangered them all, the *makota* feigned great concern for Kinguri's safety and persuaded him to enter the enclosure where, they argued, the palisade of thick stakes would protect him from danger.

The *makota* evidently managed to conceal the potential for treachery inherent in the situation, for Kinguri failed to see the ironic reference to himself in the purported dangers from lions.[61] Trusting his advisers and kinsmen, Kinguri did not realize that the palisade of heavy stakes was intended to imprison the one they claimed to protect, rather than to exclude danger. Kinguri entered the enclosure and waited while the *makota* outside looked for a chance to seal the single entrance and leave their king inside to starve to death. Because Kinguri's supernatural powers invariably warned him of dangers before they arose, the *makota* had to wait until he fell asleep and then quickly barred the only exit from the prison.[62] They lingered in the vicinity until Kinguri died from hunger, and then left.

This description of Kinguri's death tells relatively little about the historical wars between Songo adherents of the *kinguri* and the Imbangala warriors of the *kilombo*. But it does reveal a great deal about the significance of these events for later Imbangala history. Several aspects of the narrative express Imbangala beliefs about proper relationships between subjects and their rulers. Supernatural vision, for example, has remained an important ingredient of a chief's powers down to the present time. The tradition takes this into account by having the *kinguri* fall asleep (in the metaphoric sense of negation of his magical powers of perception) in order to explain how so powerful and omniscient a ruler could fall victim to the *makota*'s transparent plot. Starvation was an ideologically suitable means of killing a permanent title because it did not involve bloodshed: only human beings, according to the Mbundu theories of kingship, spill blood when they die and the spirits of a title, the real targets of this attack, do not do so.

Starvation symbolized not just deprivation of food for an incumbent but also abandonment of a title by its followers, since the imagery of food and feeding stood as a metaphor for one of the most basic Mbundu beliefs about their relationship to their chiefs. The

---

[61] *Nguri* means lion in some dialects of Umbundu.

[62] Testimony of Mwanya a Shiba, 15 June 1959, for the best statement of the motivations behind the actions of the *makota*.

archetypal 'marriages' between male political principles and female lineages in Mbundu genealogies establish the responsibilities of rulers and ruled through reference to the analogous duties of a wife to her husband. Wives produced and prepared food for their husbands to eat, and subjects had the same obligation to their rulers. They fed their chiefs in a literal sense by supplying the populations of their capitals with foodstuffs, contributing labour to work the chief's fields, and so on. They also fed their chiefs symbolically, since political titles (as opposed to incumbents) derived their real sustenance from the loyalty of their people. The tradition of Kinguri's 'death' contains two levels of meaning: denial of food may have caused the death of the title-holder from starvation, to be sure, but, more important, abandonment by the people also abolished the title itself.

The most common version of this episode (paraphrased above) makes the essential point of abandonment through the image of a straightforward denial of food to the *kinguri*, but other variants refer more subtly to the same fact either through reiterating the theme of starvation in other terms, or by incorporating the conceptual opposite, surfeit. According to some, the conspirators built a splendid new palace for the *kinguri* and led him into it with great ceremony. The palace, like the palisade in the first variant of the tradition, had only a single entrance. When the *kinguri* had gone inside, the *makota* blocked the door and smothered their king by pouring a great quantity of manioc flour through a hole in the roof.[63] Ironically in this case, not denial of food and loyalty but fulfillment of the *kinguri*'s excessive demands brought surfeit and death by asphyxiation.

Some Imbangala histories use a different but equivalent image based on a cliché which usually occurs elsewhere in the corpus of Mbundu narrative traditions.[64] They explain, just as in the more common version, how the *makota* imprisoned the *kinguri*, but they complete the narrative by arguing that the *makota* continued to provide food for the *kinguri* but gave him only rotten seeds unfit to eat.[65] Given the appearance of loyalty without its substance, the *kinguri* soon expired.

[63] Schütt (1881), pp. 79–80, 100.
[64] See the departure of Kulashingo from Portuguese Angola, below, chapter VII.
[65] Testimony of Mwanya a Shiba, 14 June 1969. Imbangala historians feel free to transpose such clichés under the Mbundu rules of historical composition because the alternative images act as equivalent metaphors for the same historical events.

All variants of this episode agree in emphasizing that the *makota* had to employ supernatural and deceptive means to kill the *kinguri*. The Imbangala sometimes use another image to describe the *kinguri*'s death because it emphasizes the need for deception. The *makota*, according to this variant, dug a deep pit which they carefully disguised with a covering of leaves and grass to give it the appearance of solid ground. They finished their preparation of the trap by adding the ceremonial mat which the *kinguri* occupied on formal occasions. They then invited their king to receive their homage while seated on the mat placed over the pit. The *kinguri* sat down and fell into the hole where the *makota* buried him on the spot.[66] The emphasis on deception, which recurs in almost every variant, also suggests that the *makota* assassinated the *kinguri* by means of certain *kilombo* rituals known as *kiluvia*. In the *kiluvia*, Imbangala honoured and deceived their prisoners of war up to the moment of their death. Like these other captives, the *kinguri* never suspected his fate until it was too late. The apparent reference to the *kiluvia* provides confirmation in the oral narratives that the *makota* had embraced the ceremonies of the *kilombo* as they rebelled against the *kinguri*.

Finally, the *makota* also broke the *kinguri*'s alliance with the Songo lineages of Manyungo wa Mbelenge. As one narrative episode explains the event, the *makota* shut Manyungo wa Mbelenge into the prison with the *kinguri*. She died before the *kinguri* and he, anguished by starvation, ate part of her body before he himself died of hunger. The tradition specifies that the *kinguri* ate only the upper half of the corpse.[68] This episode echoes the imagery of the Bihe traditions which told how the *kinguri*'s cruel demands threatened to consume all his followers.[68] In terms of politics in the later kingdom of Kasanje, the narrative showed that the *kinguri* had left no related titles among the Songo and thus legitimized the authority of later kings who took the *kinguri* title without the usual qualifications of kinship to its ancient holders. Although the narrative indirectly confirms Songo claims that titles derived from the *kinguri* once existed, modern Imbangala

---

[66] Oliveira Ferreira Diniz (1918), p. 93. The same cliché occurs very widely (e.g. Balandier (1968), pp. 38, 271, n. 14, for the Kongo) and often crops up in another context in the Mbundu traditions. This variant echoes the beastly qualities of the *kinguri*, since the pit could also have served to capture large and dangerous wild game.

[67] Testimonies of Kiluanje kya Ngonga; Domingos Vaz. The exact symbolism of the last detail remains obscure except to underscore the savage and bestial nature of the title. It may refer to the impropriety of the male *kinguri* coming into contact with the genitals of the female Manyungo wa Mbelenge.

[68] Magyar (1859), pp. 266ff.

historians always emphasize that, from their point of view, none of these had any claim to succeed the *kinguri*.[69]

The *makota* led their band of Imbangala south-westward somewhere on the southern side of the Kwanza river after their defeat and abolition of the *kinguri*. They no doubt found it expedient to leave the area of their crime for fear of the angered spirit of their former ruler and probably found no further welcome among the Songo lineages who had allied with the *kinguri*. Wars against the *ngola a kiluanje* during the 1560s[70] may have determined the direction in which they moved, since their course led them directly away from the powerful Mbundu king in the north. In their wake, the *makota* left a new set of Lunda political titles in Songo centered around the *munjumbo*, the *ndonje*, and the *kunga*. They also left Libolo much smaller and weaker than they had found it, reduced from a large kingdom to a small state occupying only the westernmost province of its former empire. They had forced the state of Kulembe to disintegrate and had claimed leadership of the *kilombo* for themselves, leaving the bulk of the *kulembe*'s former lands to the *munjumbo*. The arrival of the *kinguri* and the formation of the Imbangala under the leadership of the *makota* had caused a major revolution in the political structure of the peoples who lived on the upper Kwanza.

The Imbangala under the leadership of the Lunda *makota* seem to have travelled towards the coast south of the site of the later Portuguese town of Benguela. From there, they moved northward along the coast through the 1580s and 1590s, arriving in the vicinity of the Kuvo river in or shortly before 1601.[71] There they came into close contact with Europeans for the first time and began yet another phase of the history of the *kilombo*.

[69] Pires (1952), p. 2; testimony of Apolo de Matos, 18 June 1969.
[70] Miller (1972a), pp. 560–3.
[71] Ibid., pp. 563–5; this group of Imbangala probably did not drift as far south as suggested there.

CHAPTER VII

The Imbangala and the Portuguese

THE IMBANGALA led by the former *makota* of the *kinguri* made their way north along the coast towards the Kwanza during the same years that another band of aliens, representatives of the Portuguese crown in Europe, were approaching the Mbundu from the sea. The simultaneous arrival of these two groups of outsiders at the Kwanza set the stage for an Imbangala–Portuguese alliance in the first half of the seventeenth century which revolutionized Mbundu political institutions and geography. Together they reduced the *ngola a kiluanje* from monarchs of a robust and expanding kingdom in 1600 to nearly powerless puppet rulers after 1630 and substituted a completely new set of European and African states founded on the export of slaves from Africa to the Americas. A small Portuguese state of Angola[1] replaced Kongo title-holders on the coastal plain north of the Kwanza[2] and the *ngola a kiluanje* in the old central provinces of Ndongo and Lenge, while Lunda title-holders at the heads of Imbangala *kilombo* bands imposed themselves near Angola where the *hango* of Libolo, the Pende *malunga*-kings, and various subordinates of the *ngola a kiluanje* had ruled before.

The written documentation available for this phase of Mbundu political development permits more detailed reconstruction of Imbangala and Portuguese state-formation than of their predecessors'.[3] Certain structural characteristics of the Imbangala *kilombo* that predisposed holders of the Lunda *makota* titles to join with the Portuguese in the pursuit of slaves seem implicit in the evidence. But these were most compelling for the Imbangala who settled as aliens among the Mbundu north of the Kwanza; the different social environment south of the river allowed the *kilombo* leaders who stayed

---

[1] I refer to the Portuguese-conquered territories in these terms in an attempt to maintain an Mbundu perspective on events. As a result, Portuguese legal distinctions between *donatária*, *reino*, *conquista*, and other forms of European rule have very little significance.

[2] For the details of this part of the Portuguese conquest, see Miller (1972b).

[3] This approach omits the relatively well-known histories of the expansion of Portuguese military and political control in Angola and the defeat of the *ngola a kiluanje*; for these events, readers are referred to Birmingham (1966).

among the non-Mbundu there to remain more independent in their dealings with the Portuguese. The political institutions of the northern Imbangala evolved in the direction of Mbundu cultural norms as the *kilombo* turned into a series of settled states between 1610 and c. 1650.[4]

The primary structural feature of the *kilombo* which influenced the course of Imbangala contacts with the Portuguese was the characteristic instability of relations among the Lunda title-holders, first noted long before the *kinguri*'s band had crossed the Kwango. It affected their relations with the Europeans in two ways. First, rebellious holders of subordinate titles had repeatedly sought outside sources of support as they had broken away from the central position in the band, as the *munjumbo* had adopted *vunga* titles based on the *mwela* magical knife and as the *makota* had originally embraced the *kilombo*.[5] After the Imbangala made contact with the Europeans, the same search for external sources of legitimacy and material aid often brought dissatisfied seventeenth-century title-holders into alliance with Portuguese governors, as ambitious Lunda sought to maintain or expand, their authority over their own people. Second, the tendency of subordinate Lunda title-holders to abandon the parent *kilombo* meant that Portuguese-Imbangala contacts would result in the establishment of multiple Imbangala states rather than a single centralized kingdom. Portuguese governors, then facing heavy odds as they sought to consolidate a very tenuous control between the Bengo and Kwanza rivers, eagerly exploited the fissiparous tendencies of the *kilombo* and ultimately helped to create the ring of Imbangala client kings who surrounded the area of Portuguese control by 1650.

First Contacts—Establishing the Pattern

The crew of a Portuguese trading vessel, which encountered the Imbangala under Kalanda ka Imbe[6] camped on the south bank of the

---

[4] The parallel analysis for the Imbangala south of the Kwanza, while technically falling outside the scope of this study, awaits the collection of much-needed new data.

[5] Cf. the role of outside Luba authority symbols in the early history of the Lunda in Katanga.

[6] A member of this crew, Andrew Battell, later told the story of his experiences in Angola to the British humanist Samuel Purchas. Purchas published Battell's account, interpolating information gleaned from other sources about the coast of Africa. Although it is difficult to distinguish at times between Battell's observations and Purchas's additions, there is no doubt as to the identify of Battell's hosts with the people of the Lunda *makota*. They called

Kuvo in 1601, developed a commercial partnership based on slaving which became the prototype for all later co-operation between the Imbangala and the Europeans. These sailors had gone to the area of the Kuvo as participants in an extension of Portuguese slave-trading activities from the Kongo regions in the north, where they had been active since the early sixteenth century,[7] to the Luanda bay area just north of the Kwanza and to the southern coasts. By the turn of the seventeenth century, the European presence near the Kwanza was divided into two overlapping but distinct spheres of activity: government-appointed officials claimed tenuous control over a military base

[7] See Vansina (1966a), pp. 45–64, or Birmingham (1966), pp. 21–41.

themselves 'Imbangola' (sic) (Ravenstein (1901), p. 84); the name of the ruler of the band was 'Calando' or 'Calandola' (pp. 31, 33, 85–6), obviously Kalanda ka Imbe, the third Lunda *kota* to rule without completing the required initiation ceremonies. (Battell elsewhere, p. 28, called him Imbe ya Kalandula, reversing the first and second elements of the name.) Kalanda ka Imbe claimed to have succeeded a great chief named 'Elembe' (p. 85), almost certainly the Kulembe of the oral traditions. The Imbangala made extensive and prodigious use of palm wine in their rituals, cutting down the trees (*elaeis Guineensis*, or *ndende* in Kimbundu, according to Leite de Magalhães (1924), p. 62) to obtain the fruit, which they ate, and the wine, which they drank. Their requirements were so enormous that they devastated the palm groves wherever they passed, pouring the wine over the graves of their ancestors and using it in attempts to contact the dead through intoxication, trances, and spirit possession. The importance of the palm wine probably derived from the Lunda *tubungu* chief's close association with the drink, already noted in connection with the history of the *kinguri* in Lunda. Their destructive methods of obtaining palm wine distinguished them from local peoples, who tapped the standing trees rather than felling them as did the Imbangala.

Purchas's identification of the Imbangala with the 'Jaga' and even with the Mane of Sierra Leone (pp. 19–20) was erroneous. This passage was probably added on the basis of Battell's statement that the Imbangala had come from the 'Serra de Leão', or Mountains of the Lion. The true identity of Battell's 'Serra de Leão' was not Sierra Leone in upper Guinea; the name probably came from a reference to the *kinguri*, whose name (*nguli* or *nguri*) meant 'lion' in the Wambo dialect of Umbundu (Alves (1959), ii. 959; testimony of Apolo de Matos) spoken in the most mountainous regions of the Ovimbundu highlands. (The Cokwe, Kimbundu, and Kikongo word for lion is *koshi* or *hoje*; the Lunda use *ntambo*; Dias de Carvalho (1890b), p. 347; also Chatelain (1888–9), p. 7, for Kimbundu.) This hypothesis fits other data indicating that the Imbangala at that time used mainly an Umbundu vocabulary. Purchas emphasized elsewhere, contradicting his assertions about the Imbangala origin in Sierra Leone, that only the Portuguese called them 'Jaga' and that no European could have known their origins (pp. 83–4). Other details of Battell's description point to an origin somewhere in the interior and a relatively recent arrival on this part of the coast, since the Imbangala king had never seen white men before. The low prices for which the Imbangala sold their captives also betrayed their unfamiliarity with the coastal region near Luanda since the slave trade had become established many years earlier there and local residents undoubtedly knew the prevailing prices.

on Luanda bay and over a few scattered posts along the banks of the lower Kwanza river, while numbers of private Portuguese merchants traded for slaves in widely scattered interior locations north of the Kwanza and along the coasts on both sides of the river. Actual territorial control by Portuguese government forces consisted of little more than the fortified enclaves near Luanda bay and at Muxima and Massangano on the banks of the Kwanza.[8]

A seemingly insatiable demand for African labour on the sugar plantations in São Tomé and, more recently, north-eastern Brazil, sustained the slave trade in both Kongo and Angola.[9] Given the high demand for slaves, and the efforts of royal slave contractors to tax this trade at Luanda, it is not surprising that these, and doubtless other, Portuguese sailors frequented the unregulated coasts near the Kuvo, nor that the Imbangala camp of Kalanda ka Imbe attracted their attention. From the ocean, they could see the large numbers of people in the group, which they estimated at several thousand.[10] The Portuguese went ashore to determine the identity of the group, probably with the hope of establishing a profitable trade in slaves with them. A week's negotiations convinced the Europeans that these Imbangala would make suitable commercial partners. The Imbangala seem to have accepted the Europeans' overtures in exchange for Portuguese assistance in crossing the Kuvo in order to attack the people who lived on the north bank of the river.

Both partners undoubtedly embarked on this joint enterprise in the expectation that the Imbangala would capture slaves, whom the Portuguese would then buy and ship to the Americas. This was the basic arrangement which formed the keystone of all later Portuguese–Imbangala alliances. The warriors of the *kilombo* would supply captives in exchange for European trade goods. The Imbangala evidently executed a successful attack north of the Kuvo in this case, captured slaves and found the ensuing trade to their advantage, since they continued to raid and trade near the coast for five months.

The Portuguese derived enough profit from this arrangement to send a party of fifty men into the interior in search of more slaves and the Imbangala after their African partners had finally left the coast. There a local ruler forced the European expedition to leave one of

[8] Miller (1971).
[9] Curtin (1969), pp. 110–6.
[10] Battell in Ravenstein (1901), p. 85. Although Battell specified 12,000 Imbangala, the accuracy of the figure is clearly open to question in the light of its correspondence to the twelve 'captains' of the band, each ascribed a symbolic but inexact 1,000 men.

their men as a hostage in his village as a guarantee of their good conduct while they sought the Imbangala in his lands. The Portuguese selected as the hostage the only foreigner among them, an English sailor named Andrew Battell, and evidently gave him up for lost since they never returned to ransom him. Battell realized that he could not expect rescue from his former companions and escaped from captivity to rejoin the Imbangala whom he had known near the coast. Battell's choice of the Imbangala as allies in preference to the local people, and the hostility which the local chiefs showed to the Portuguese, clearly revealed that the Europeans and the Imbangala had established a basis of co-operation which the inhabitants of the region regarded as against their own interests.

The wanderings of the Imbangala during the sixteen months which Battell spent with them in 1601–2 show how completely they dominated the local people. The Imbangala wandered through the lands between the Kuvo river and the southern bank of the Kwanza, attacking the most powerful rulers in the region. Of the places mentioned by Battell, the town of 'Shillambansa' had by far the most significance.[11] This was the capital of an important chief said to be an 'uncle' of the *ngola a kiluanje*. Shila Mbanza's status as 'uncle' meant that he was a *kota* of the Ndongo kingdom, one of the guardians of the royal symbols of authority. Further evidence of his importance comes from the Portuguese plan, developed shortly afterwards, to build a fortified post near his town.[12] The Imbangala attack on the *shila mbanza* showed that they did not hesitate to fight even the most powerful title-holders including close allies of the *ngola a kiluanje* himself.

Such successful harassment of the local residents produced numerous captives and quickly attracted the attention of a generation of Europeans actively in search of slave labour for the burgeoning plantations of the New World. At first the Imbangala showed little respect for the efforts of Portuguese royal officials to regulate the conduct of the slave trade in the interior in favour of the royal contractors and sold slaves to anyone willing to pay for their prisoners. They thus began their participation in the Angolan slave trade as parts of the illegal commerce run by renegade Europeans eager to evade government monopolies and taxes. In at least one instance,

[11] Ravenstein attempted to identify all places mentioned by Battell, but he often forced his analysis beyond the limits of the data (pp. 22–7); 'Shillambansa' is a praise name, not the name of the title itself, since *shila mbanza* in Umbundu means to 'praise the noble'.

[12] Brito, 'Rellação breve', *AA*, iii, nos. 25–7 (1937), pp. 260–1.

they joined a group of mutineers from the Portuguese army in pursuit of captives and booty in the Kisama region just south of the Kwanza. The local chiefs of that region requested protection from the Portuguese governor of the time, João Furtado de Mendonça (1594–1602). Furtado de Mendonça sent an expedition in search of the Imbangala which ultimately forced them to withdraw to a defensive site where they fortified themselves and resisted all Portuguese efforts to dislodge them.[13] The first recorded encounter between Portuguese officials and the Imbangala thus came as the result of problems they caused for the legal slave trade under the care of Portuguese governors at Luanda. This experience gave royal officials first-hand acquaintance with Imbangala fighting skills and confirmed earlier impressions that the Imbangala might become valuable suppliers of slaves to anyone who could win their friendship. Although no records of reactions in Luanda survive to document the case, such experiences must have convinced the Angola governors that the success of the 'official' slave trade depended on the co-operation, or at least on the neutrality, of the Lunda *makota* and their followers.

The Portuguese encountered other difficulties during this period in Angola which must have led governors to seek ways of controlling the Imbangala. Beyond the problems which afflicted all Europeans who attempted to establish land bases in the deadly disease environments of tropical Africa,[14] as well as the opposition of hostile African kings, government representatives in Angola had to contend with a variety of interlopers who were buying slaves along the coasts both north and south of Luanda. These 'smugglers', as they became known in official circles, evaded the Portuguese royal taxes on slave trading just as the Brazilian demand for labour rose to new heights after 1600. At the same time, the obstinate presence of an unfriendly Kongo state called Kasanze immediately inland from Luanda forced Portuguese governors to divert their military campaigns to the distant interior in their search for more captives to ship to America.[15] Their simultaneous need for men and arms near the coast and in the hinterland stretched Portuguese forces dangerously thin on both fronts.

[13] Battell in Ravenstein (1901), pp. 27–8. Cadornega (1940–2), i. 52, cited a campaign under Governor Furtado de Mendonça that fit Battell's description of a battle seen from the other side. The chiefs of Libolo and Kisama evidently called the Imbangala 'Jingas' or 'Guindas' as that time; the former name is unexplained but had no connection with the later queen Nzinga, contrary to Dias de Carvalho's suggestion (1898, p. 30).
[14] Philip D. Curtin (1968a) summarizes theory and documents the resultant death rates for non-immune European populations at other times and places.
[15] Miller (1972b).

Bento Banho Cardoso, governor of Angola from 1611 to 1615, explicitly indicated the strain on his resources when he noted that supplies and men recently sent from Lisbon had not begun to meet his requirements. He complained particularly of the lack of soldiers and horses needed to conduct military forays in the interior.[16]

Trapped between military ambitions in the interior and the need for coastal defence, Cardoso would inevitably have sought the aid of African auxiliary troops to compensate for the lack of men and equipment from Europe. The talents and political position of the Imbangala matched his requirements in almost every respect. They, like the Portuguese, had come to the Kwanza basin as invaders who lived by stealing from the local Mbundu farmers. The Imbangala had a strong incentive to capture slaves for use in connection with rituals involving human sacrifice and to replace warriors who fell in their continual wars, and they had developed specialized military tactics adapted to those purposes. Portuguese interest in these same skills arose from their desire to procure slaves for export to Brazil. It was a natural alliance, and one which the lessons learned from earlier Portuguese–Imbangala contacts must have made obvious to all by Cardoso's time, some ten years or more after the first encounters. Cardoso saw further that use of the Imbangala as mercenaries in wars in the interior would free the slender Portuguese garrison for coastal operations against Kasanze and the illegal slave traders.

A formal alliance between the Imbangala and the Portuguese became effective around 1612.[17] It almost immediately solved Cardoso's problems of insufficient means to attack the African states of the interior, as strident objections from the Kongo king Alvaro II made clear. He complained that the Imbangala (or 'Jaga' as all sources referred to them) were 'eating' many of his subjects, thus making them the first recorded victims of the new Afro-European combination.[18] More successes followed soon after; by 1615, many

[16] Consulta do Concelho Ultramarino sobre as coisas que faltam no governo de Angola para sua governação, c. 1617; A.H.U., Angola, cx. 1.

[17] Miller (1972a), pp. 567–8.

[18] Letter from el-Rei do Congo Alvaro II to the Pope, 27 Feb. 1613; Arch. Vat. Calfalonieri (Rome), t. 34, fols. 301ff.; mentioned in L. Jadin and J. Cuvelier (1954), pp. 329–335. The 'Jaga' were also referred to at pp. 338, 344, 351, and 423, in complaints that continued with some regularity through the decade. The original reference may concern the 1612 campaign against the Dembos; see Delgado (1948–55), ii. 34. Cardoso's first confirmation of his use of the Imbangala (always under the name 'Jaga') came in 1615; see Auto de Banho Cardoso, 17 Aug. 1615; A.H.U., Angola, cx. 1, doc. 46.

Mbundu rulers south of the Bengo, who had previously resisted Portuguese authority, were surrendering as a result of campaigns Cardoso had waged with the aid of Imbangala mercenaries.[19] The new Mbundu vassals included the most powerful title-holders occupying both banks of the Kwanza: Kafushi, owner of the salt pans of Ndemba in Kisama, the *kasanje* of Kakulu ka Hango who lived near Mushima, Kambambe who guarded access to the fabled 'Mountains of Silver' just above the fall line of the Kwanza, and the *ngola a kiluanje* himself.[20] The Mbundu feared the Imbangala far more than they feared the European armies which before that time had not dared venture far beyond the Kwanza river and a very few fortified positions along its banks.[21] From the Mbundu point of view, the Imbangala had helped the Portuguese to establish a new state in the western portions of the *ngola a kiluanje* kingdom. From the Portuguese point of view, Imbangala participation as mercenaries in their 'conquest of Angola' had providentially converted a desperate situation into a period of successful slave raiding and territorial expansion.

The strong pressures which motivated the Portuguese to ally themselves with the Imbangala had their counterparts on the Imbangala side in the amalgam of disparate political institutions which made up the *kilombo* of the Lunda *makota*. Near-total centralization of authority within the Imbangala band made alliance with outsiders an attractive prospect to subordinated Imbangala holders of permanent titles. The limited information available on Imbangala political structure in the first decade of the seventeenth century[22] fits the hypothesis that a single king of the *kulembe* type held the only permanent and autonomous position of power within the band, while all other chiefs held appointive titles of the *vunga* type. The formal structure of the *kilombo* divided the members of each Imbangala band into approximately twelve distinct sections, each under the leadership of its own 'captain'. These regiments lived and fought more or less separately from one another; twelve separate entrances into the joint war camp, one for each regiment, symbolized these

[19] Treslado dũ aviso que mandou fazer o snór. g.[dor] bento banho Cardozo, 21 Aug. 1615; A.H.U., Angola, cx. 1.

[20] Anonymous *relação*, 21 Oct. 161(5?); A.H.U., Angola, cx. 1, doc. 172.

[21] Letter from Andre Velho da Fonseca to el-Rei, 28 Feb. 1612; published in Brásio (1952–71), vi. 64–70; also in *AA*, sér. I, iii, nos. 19–21 (1937), 71–90.

[22] Good data exist only for the 1640s; these receive detailed analysis in the following chapter.

distinctions even though all clustered in the same *kilombo* for purposes of defence.[23]

The 'captains' probably held *vunga* titles appointed by the single Imbangala king. They, and the regiments they commanded, had replaced the lineages, with which the original group of Lunda had begun, as the basic institutions of Imbangala social structure. Since this structure had no place for the numerous Lunda and Cokwe perpetual titles associated with the obsolete descent groups, such as the *kota* positions or the *kulashingo*, the several title-holders in the main Imbangala band had fought continually for control of the kingship which Kalanda ka Imbe held in 1601. As a result, the position had passed frequently from one Lunda *kota* to another during the preceding fifty or so years. According to the traditions, the *kota* Kangengo at first claimed leadership of the *kilombo* but ruled for only three 'days' before he died, allegedly a victim of the curse which Kinguri had uttered just before his death.[24] Mbongo wa Imbe then succeeded Kangengo as ruler of the *kilombo* but he could not withstand Kinguri's enraged spirit and lasted only two days before he died. Kalanda ka Imbe was the third and last of the Lunda *makota* to brave Kinguri's curse; he lived only a single day before he met the same fate as his predecessors.[25]

The increasing tempo of death which haunted the *makota* indicates that their control over the *kilombo* had dissolved into anarchy as the title-holders fought each other for control of the single position of power. The traditions emphasize the supernatural cause of their

[23] Battell in Ravenstein (1901), pp. 28–9; this is implicit in Battell's description of the twelve captains who had come from the earliest origins of the band, each with his own section of the camp.

[24] The three 'days' mentioned in the tradition refer to stages in the initiation ceremonies leading to Kangengo's full installation as ruler. These ceremonies took place in four phases, expressed metaphorically as 'days', and so the traditions may not be interpreted as indicating how long Kangengo actually commanded the band as *de facto* ruler The three 'days' mean only that holders of this title lost control before any of them managed to complete the entire set of prescribed rituals.

[25] Testimonies of Sousa Calunga, 16 June 1969; Domingos Vaz; Apolo de Matos, 18 June 1969. Although the Vaz tradition has reversed the sequence usually given, of these three rulers the certainty of other informants that Kangengo ruled first has led me to accept their version of the events. Except for Rodrigues Neves (1854), p.99, written versions of these traditions do not mention the period of rule by Lunda *makota* Rodrigues Neves said that a 'Kasanje ka Imbe' assumed power directly from the *kinguri*. Although his informant probably meant to refer to Kulashingo, whose original title had been Kasanje ka Musumbi, he erroneously introduced the surname Imbe in a veiled acknowledgement of the missing names of Mbongo wa Imbe and Kalanda ka Imbe.

deaths, allegedly from the curse of the *kinguri*, by noting that all three would-be rulers died at night. The *malunda* thus say nothing direct about the wars which must have occurred during this period, but the shift from Kangengo to Mbongo wa Imbe and Kalanda ka Imbe indicates that the band had separated into two major groups divided along the lines of the lineages to which the Lunda titles had once belonged. Kangengo belonged to the old lineage of Kandama ka Hite, which lost control to Mbongo and Kalanda ka Imbe from Kandama ka Kikongwa and Kanduma ka Kikongwa.[26] The holders of these titles still tended to unite according to the lines of the suppressed kin groups they had known in Lunda.

The holders of non-Lunda titles, who had joined the *kinguri*'s band as it passed through Cokwe and Libolo, had never controlled the most important *kilombo* position and undoubtedly desired to recover the prestige which they had sacrificed to the unity achieved through exclusive use of *mavunga*. Some of these excluded holders of Cokwe and Libolo positions must have recognized the Portuguese as potentially valuable allies if they should attempt to end Lunda domination of the Imbangala. The Portuguese could not have been unaware of the opportunities offered by the presence of title-holders victimized by centralization; they repeatedly exploited similar situations in later African states as they extended their influence in Angola during the nineteenth century. Later, European support for dissatisfied holders of subordinate titles led to the deposition and replacement of strong and independent paramount authorities by weak puppets in more than one African kingdom.[27]

Although no written records confirm the Portuguese part in the formation of the alliance with the Imbangala, the circumstances of other better-known cases suggest a likely sequence of events. Some time after Battell left the Imbangala, then still under the leadership of the Lunda *kota* Kalanda ka Imbe, a holder of the *kulashingo* title led the Cokwe/Lwena component of the group in rebellion against continued rule by the Lunda title-holders. Governor Cardoso supported the *kulashingo*'s drive to control the entire band in return for the *kulashingo*'s agreement to enlist the Imbangala in the service of the governor's military designs. The Imbangala crossed the Kwanza, with the aid of the Portuguese, and entered the fight against the

[26] Testimony of Sousa Calunga, 9 July 1969.

[27] e.g. Kasanje in the 1850s; I have very briefly reviewed my unpublished evidence for this interpretation in (1973b). Portuguese merchants and military men played an identical role in bringing an end to the Mbondo kingdom of the *ndala kisua* in the 1880s and 1890s.

vassals of the *ngola a kiluanje* and the king of Kongo. Carsoso thus acquired not only powerful support for his wars against the Mbundu but also gained an ally who owed his position to the Portuguese and who, therefore, would hopefully prove obedient to Portuguese commands. The Imbangala under the *kulashingo* had become potentially docile allies in the official Portuguese slave trade instead of powerful and troublesome threats to official hegemony.

Imbangala oral traditions support the hypothesis that the *kulashingo* joined the Portuguese at least in part to overthrow the authority of the Lunda *makota*. Since the present narratives represent the official ideology of the *kulashingo* group which later founded the Kasanje kingdom under a restored *kinguri* title, they bear a strong bias in Kulashingo's favour. They thus minimize the documented period of rule by the Lunda and emphasize, perhaps too insistently, the directness of the line of legitimacy from Kinguri to Kulashingo. As the traditions relate these events, Kulashingo received the sacred symbols of power either directly from Kinguri or from the *makota* within a few days of their king's death in the palisade on Mbola na Kasashe. This version of events effectively erases the period of about fifty years (*c.* 1560 to *c.* 1610) when the *makota* ruled in the name of the *kulembe*. Allowing for this alteration (entirely in keeping with the traditions' established tendency to eliminate events which had few effects on later political structures) the traditions accurately preserve the major political developments of this period and show that the *kulashingo* rose to power on the wings of European support.

The relevant thread of the narrative begins during the Kinguri's journey from Mona Kimbundu, where Kulashingo had joined the band, to Mbola na Kasashe. The *makota* had long seen that Kinguri's insatiable demands for human sacrifices threatened the survival of their people, and so they took a number of foreigners, including Kulashingo, from Mona Kimbundu to offer Kinguri in place of their own followers. Kulashingo, however, managed to escape the fate planned for him by catering obsequiously to the demands of the *makota*, especially Mwa Cangombe, Ndonga, and Kangengo, the leaders of the Kandama ka Hite section of the band, who selected the victims who died each day under Kinguri's knives. He had earned the rank of *kibinda*, or master hunter, before he left Mona Kimbundu and consequently spent all his time hunting in the woods where he remained out of Kinguri's sight and beyond the reach of the *makota*. Kulashingo always gave meat to the *makota* when he returned from a successful hunt in order to ensure continued favour. He also conducted a secretive love affair with Imbe ya Malemba, the mother of Mbongo and Kalanda ka Imbe, to gain the confidence of the Kandama and Kanduma ka Kikongwa group of Lunda lineages. Kulashingo's gifts of meat metaphorically portray both his personal loyalty to the *makota* and the special obligations owed by *yibinda* to political chiefs. His marriage to Imbe ya Malemba represented an alliance of the Cokwe/Lwena with at least one segment of the Lunda lineages.

When the *makota* resolved to kill Kinguri at Mbola na Kasashe, Kulashingo feigned support for them but, when he returned home from hunting one evening to discover Kinguri trapped inside the palisade, he secretly heeded the pleas of Imbe ya Malemba, who did not want Kinguri to die of starvation. Each night he would deposit portions of meat from his hunts outside a small hole in the palisade where Kinguri could reach through and take it.[28] Kinguri at first assumed that this food represented tribute from the *makota* and did not immediately realize that he had been abandoned. Since the Mbundu believe that human beings live only five days without food, the *makota* waited unconcernedly for their ruler to die at the end of the prescribed period.

When they found Kinguri still alive on the sixth day, they became suspicious and initiated a search for the person who must have smuggled food to the imprisoned king. The *makota* appointed Kambwizu to stand guard outside the palisade where he could discover the culprit. He ascended a tree overlooking the prison and watched until he saw Kulashingo leave the food that night. Kambwizu reported this news to the other *makota* and they soon discovered Imbe ya Malemba's complicity. They threatened the Cokwe/Lwena and the Lunda of Imbe ya Malemba, with Kangengo in particular berating them for their effort to save Kinguri. When Kinguri overheard this argument going on just outside the walls of his prison, he realized for the first time that his *makota* had imprisoned him and uttered the terrible curse which later killed Kangengo, Mbongo wa Imbe, and Kalanda ka Imbe.

Kinguri died, in spite of the efforts of Kulashingo and Imbe ya Malemba, embittered by his *makota*'s betrayal and grateful to Kulashingo for his aid. These circumstances justified Kulashingo's right to take Kinguri's position as king of the Imbangala. Some variants of this narrative episode state that Kinguri named Kulashingo

---

[28] No variant of this tradition accounts very logically for Kulashingo's sudden sympathy for the *kinguri*.

as his successor before he died, even reaching through the hole in the palisade to place the bracelet symbolizing royal authority (the *lenge* or *lukano*) on Kulashingo's arm.[29] Others claim that the *lukano* miraculously flew off Kinguri's arm at the moment he succumbed and encircled the arm of Kulashingo; various *makota* tried to remove the *lukano*, but none succeeded.[30] Another variant describes how the symbols of power instantly struck down several claimants who attempted to put them on in spite of the Kinguri's curse. Yet, when Kulashingo picked up the bracelet and other regalia, he survived and was at once acclaimed as Kinguri's legitimate heir.[31] The single historical point which links all these variants lies in their emphasis on the supernatural dimension of Kulashingo's accession and the legitimacy of his assumption of Kinguri's power.

Other versions, only superficially contradictory to those which depict Kulashingo as winning over the reluctant *makota*, underscore the legitimacy of his authority by making him the *makota*'s unwilling nominee. These traditions originated in a later period when Kasanje political procedures required the *makota* to elect Kulashingo's successors to the position of the *kinguri*. According to these variants, after Kangengo, Mbongo wa Imbe, and Kalanda ka Imbe had tried to wear the *lukano* but had failed, the remaining *makota* recognized their inability to control the powers of the *kinguri* and implored Kulashingo to take the position to save them all from death. Kulashingo demurred by saying, 'I am not from Lunda. The *misanga* (beads) deserve the neck, not the feet.' This proverb (*sabu*) represented Kulashingo as the feet, lowest and most humble part of the body. The *makota* were the neck of the Imbangala band, the part most closely associated with the head, or the *kinguri*. The *sabu* implied that the honour of leadership (the *misanga*) should devolve upon the *makota* rather than on Kulashingo. The *makota*, according to this variant, insisted that Kulashingo accede to their pleas and he finally and reluctantly agreed, swearing, 'If I do evil, then let me also die.' At this oath, the *nzumbi* (spirit) left Kinguri's corpse and entered the body of Kulashingo.[32] Kulashingo in this case appears as the legiti-

[29] Testimonies of Manuel Vaz; Domingos Vaz; Mwanya a Shiba, 14 June 1969; Apolo de Matos, 18 June 1969.
[30] Testimony of Sousa Calunga, 21 July 1969.
[31] Testimony of Sousa Calunga, 16 June 1969.
[32] Testimony of Sousa Calunga, 23 August 1969. This version primarily accounts for the origin of the name Kulashingo. *Shingo* means neck in Kimbundu, and *kula* is to eat; the name commemorates Kulashingo's defeat of the *makota*; cf. p. 143, n. 94 above.

mate heir of Kinguri through selection by the *makota* rather than by overtly supernatural intervention. The episode, of course, reflects and justifies the electoral procedures in use much later in Kasanje.

Whatever the supernatural sign which legitimized Kulashingo's right to succeed Kinguri, most versions of this episode contend that the *makota* opposed him because they hoped to abolish the position entirely. They recited the genealogies of both Kulashingo and Kinguri to demonstrate that, while the two titles might descend from the same remote matrilineal group (Lucaze na Mwazaza), Kinguri owed his authority symbols to purely Lunda antecedents (Ngamba a Mbumba);[33] Kulashingo, whose title came from different (but not specified) sources, therefore had no right to take Kinguri's *lukano*. The *makota*'s refusal to honour Kinguri's last request sealed the fate which they had prepared for themselves by assassinating him. According to one variant of the tradition, Kulashingo finally yielded the symbols of royal power to the Lunda, and Kangengo, Mbongo wa Imbe, and Kalanda ka Imbe then succeeded one another, each dying from the effects of Kinguri's curse. The *makota* then realized that they could not resist Kinguri's designated heir and in desperation switched their support to Kulashingo.

According to the traditions, the Imbangala first made contact with Europeans while this succession struggle still divided the band. The Portuguese living at Luanda had heard rumours of Kinguri's great powers and wished to meet so famous a king in person. The governor of Angola sent a messenger, called Gaspar Kanzenza, to summon Kinguri to Luanda. Kanzenza found the Imbangala camped on the island of Mbola na Kasashe shortly after the *makota* had imprisoned Kinguri. Because the governor had addressed the message to Kinguri personally, the *makota* felt unqualified to reply in his place and therefore explained, deceitfully, that Kinguri had fallen ill and could not receive visitors at that moment. Since Kinguri had, in fact, died just before Gaspar Kanzenza arrived, the *makota* could not leave for Luanda until someone assumed his position and gained the right to respond to the Portuguese invitation. Only after Kulashingo finally assumed the title did they set out for Luanda where they met the governor and joined the Portuguese in fighting against the *ngola a kiluanje*.[34]

[33] Testimony of Domingos Vaz; also testimonies of Alexandre Vaz, 31 July 1969; and Alexandre vaz. Domingos Vaz.

[34] Testimonies of Sousa Calunga, 16 June, 21 July 1969; Sousa Calunga, Kambo ka Kikasa; Manuel Vaz.

Although the figure of Gaspar Kanzenza is probably a fictional prototype for nineteenth-century Portuguese messengers to Kasanje, the presence of this role in the episode confirms the timing of the Imbangala alliance with the Portuguese, *after* the *makota* had failed to replace the *kinguri*, and shows that Kulashingo (as Kinguri's alleged legitimate heir) rather than the *makota* responded to the Portuguese summons. The otherwise unexplained reluctance of the *makota* to answer the governor's request suggests that the Portuguese would deal only with a holder of the *kinguri* position, and not with the *kilombo* titles controlled by the *makota*. The *makota*'s refusal to acknowledge that the *kinguri* had died probably represents attempts by the historical holders of the Lunda positions to resist Portuguese intervention against their control over the *kilombo*. They might, for example, have spread the false rumour that a *kinguri* still lived, as the traditions say they did, since this would have prevented the holder of the *kulashingo* from resurrecting the *kinguri* title as the basis for his Portuguese-sponsored rule over the Imbangala.[35]

The differing roles of the two major groups of *makota* in these traditions reiterate the divisions noted elsewhere among the Lunda

[35] The published versions of nineteenth-century Imbangala traditions have neglected this event at considerable cost in terms of understanding Imbangala history. Their omission provides an illuminating example of the way in which historians shifted the emphases of the *malunda* to reflect changing political conditions, since circumstances in Kasanje at the time Rodrigues Neves (1854, pp. 99–100) recorded these traditions explain the enigma very nicely. Both Rodrigues Neves and the commander of the 1850 Portuguese military expedition to Kasanje (Salles Ferreira (1854–8)) made a point of recording Imbangala history in their memoirs of the campaign but failed to mention the disqualification of the Lunda *makota* from the Kasanje kingship. The Portuguese commanders had a strong incentive to ignore the Imbangala prohibition, since they hoped to impose illegitimately a member of the *makota* lineages as a puppet Kasanje king responsive to Portuguese pressure. But at the same time they had to avoid offending the sensibilities of governors in Luanda who occasionally tried to respect the oral charters of the African states with which they maintained diplomatic relations. Rodrigues Neves and Salles Ferreira, faithful to the strategy of support for dissatisfied subordinate chiefs against recalcitrant kings that their countrymen had developed in the early seventeenth century, championed the cause of the *makota* lineages against the ruling heirs of Kulashingo. They evidently expected to find grateful allies among lineages that normally had no chance to take power in Kasanje but which possessed ancient titles descended from the 'personal companions' of the founder of the kingdom. If Rodrigues Neves and Salles Ferreira could conceal Imbangala prohibitions against rule by the 'Lunda', their unsuspecting superiors in Luanda might accept a king chosen from the ranks of the *makota*. They could thus install, with the approval of the Angola governor, the docile Kasanje ruler whom they desired. They in fact succeeded in choosing a *kota* (Kalunga ka Kisanga), but the Imbangala never accepted him and he died within a few months under mysterious circumstances.

titles at this period. Not all of them supported the assassination of the *kinguri*, since the leaders of the mutiny all came from the lineage of Kandama ka Hite. Kangengo, Mwa Cangombe, and Ndonga were the *makota* who attempted to substitute the people of Kulashingo for their own followers as sacrifices for Kinguri. Kambwizu, the *kota* who apprehended Kulashingo as he left food for the imprisoned *kinguri*, also came from this group. The *makota* of Kandama ka Kikongwa and Kanduma ka Kikongwa, however, had no connection with the murder. Imbe ya Malemba's encouragement of Kulashingo's aid to the *kinguri* symbolized their opposition to the scheme. Kulashingo had taken care to ally himself to both Lunda factions before the murder, but, if the traditions are read correctly, at the critical moment he threw his support to the party of Kandama ka Kikongwa and Kanduma ka Kikongwa with whom he and his people had a marriage alliance through Imbe ya Malemba.

Although Kangengo and the ringleaders of the plot managed to seize initial control after abolition of the *kinguri*, the political balance soon shifted to Mbongo wa Imbe and Kalanda ka Imbe of the other lineage. Kulashingo and his Cokwe/Lwena probably assisted them in replacing the *makota* from Kandama ka Hite. Kulashingo apparently assumed a subordinate *vunga*-position as the *kasanje* of Mbongo wa Imbe or Kalanda ka Imbe at that time.[36] Since this position made him a close associate of the holders of power, yet still excluded him from access to real authority, Kulashingo was an obvious candidate for Portuguese support to replace the *makota* with more tractable leadership. The duties of the *kasanje* included conduct of relations with outsiders, either through diplomacy or war, and thus provided the occasion for his initial contacts with the Europeans.

Since Kulashingo lacked legitimacy in terms of both prevailing sets of political institutions, the Lunda system of perpetual titles and the rules of the *kilombo*, and since the titles offered by the Portuguese ('Jaga', Kyambole, etc.) had little meaning in terms of Imbangala politics, he resurrected the title of *kinguri* in order to give his *de facto* rule legitimacy in the eyes of his people. Although the *makota* had formally abolished the title, Kulashingo could quite easily have reclaimed it for himself by retrieving the authority symbols abandoned in Mbola na Kasashe, or even by fabricating credible imitations of the originals. Seventeenth-century Mbundu, who would have

---

[36] Kulashingo was also known as Kasanje ka Musumbi, Kasanje ka Kazanza, or Kasanje ka Kibuna. Rodrigues Neves (1854), p. 99, gave the exact title, Kasanje ka Imbe (ya Malemba).

lived through these events, explicitly recalled that Kulashingo abandoned the *kilombo*, describing him as hostile to certain customs of the *makota*, especially those involving the consumption of human flesh.[37] This partial description of the *kulashingo*'s break with the *makota* implied that he had adopted some other basis for his authority.

Armed with the revived symbols of the *kinguri*'s powers and aided by support from the Portuguese, Kulashingo emerged as leader of the Imbangala over the opposition of the *makota* and other officials loyal to the *kilombo*. The Portuguese awarded Kulashingo the title of 'Jaga', an honour of their own invention, and the name 'Cassanje' in acknowledgement of the *kasanje* title he had borne at the time of his first contact with them. The resulting combination, 'Jaga Cassanje', became the official Portuguese designation for all later kings of Kulashingo's Imbangala band, and their followers thems lves became known as 'Cassanjes'.

Kulashingo soon justified his assumption of the *kinguri*'s mantle by winning great military victories which amply demonstrated his firm control over the symbols of authority. Portuguese documentation and Imbangala narratives tell the same story in somewhat different terms. According to the traditions, Kulashingo presented himself before a Portuguese governor in Luanda and offered to fight with him against the *ngola a kiluanje*. The *ngola a kiluanje*, it was said, had built an enchanted fortress which the Portuguese could not penetrate or even locate, and the governor needed Kulashingo's magical weapons in order to defeat him.[38] This story reflects the Imbangala belief that guns and spears alone did not decide battles but merely confirmed a conclusion predetermined by charms possessed by the two sides. It did not surprise the Imbangala, therefore, that Europeans should have found themselves unable to discover the *ngola a kiluanje*'s carefully enchanted refuge. According to these beliefs, the Europeans' disdain for the necessary charms would have made them dependent on the supernatural powers of the *kinguri* to overcome the spells of the *ngola a kiluanje*.

Kulashingo put the magical powers of the *kinguri* to good use. His primary weapon was a bow (*mufula*) called the *kimbundu*. Kulashingo had claimed the ability to vanquish any foe with his special charm, and, since the Portuguese had never before seen such a weapon and doubted its effectiveness, he devised a test to prove its capabilities. He

---

[37] Cavazzi (1965), i. 190.
[38] Testimony of Sousa Calunga, 29 Sept. 1969.

requested nine oxen and fired only a single arrow at the first ox. The arrow killed the ox and then continued on a miraculously curving path until it had killed all nine oxen and felled two thick baobab trees as well. It finally plunged into the sea and disappeared. The Portuguese governor, suitably impressed with this demonstration, agreed to accept Kulashingo's help. The *ngola a kiluanje*, who understood such things even better than the Europeans, became so frightened that he fled at once to Pungo a Ndongo and later moved north to the Wamba river where his descendants still live today.[39]

The modern versions of the tradition allege that these events took place in the square in front of the governor's palace in Luanda. Since no palace existed in Luanda in 1612, such references are anachronisms incorporated into the traditions at a much later date. Even the location of the story in Luanda, while consistent with the Mbundu tendency to place all very early events there,[40] is also false. The capital of the *ngola a kiluanje*, said by the tradition to have been in Luanda, in fact lay well in the interior, probably somewhere between the Lukala and the Kwanza rivers.[41] The historical *kulashingo* almost certainly never saw the coast north of the Kwanza but remained well up in the highlands which begin sixty to eighty miles from the coast. Nineteenth-century traditions noted that he crossed the Kwanza not far from Kambambe,[42] a plausible location not far from the last recorded Portuguese contact with the Imbangala a decade earlier. This was also a logical place to bring a large number of people across the Kwanza, since the river west of the fall line at Kambambe becomes too wide and deep to afford easy passage.[43]

[39] Testimonies of Sousa Calunga, 16 June 1969; Domingos Vaz; Mwanya a Shiba, 14, 15 June 1969. Dias de Carvalho (1898), p. 31, said that the Imbangala received firearms at that time, but this tradition shows no evidence that the Imbangala considered European weapons important. Guns were in very short supply in Angola at that time and, in further refutation of Dias de Carvalho's assumption, the governors used the Imbangala in part to avoid excessive reliance on supplies of firearms and ammunition from Europe.

[40] Cf. the opening episodes of the story of Kajinga, pp. 98–103 above.

[41] Rodrigues, 'História da residência dos padres' (Rodrigues (1936)) gave the distance from Luanda to the capital of the *ngola a kiluanje* as sixty leagues, or about 180 miles; he probably overstated it somewhat. Sr. Fernando Batalha believes that he may have found the general area of this capital along the middle Lukala; personal communication.

[42] Carvalho (1890a), pp. 77–8.

[43] Most other details given in nineteenth century traditions reported by Rodrigues Neves (1854), pp. 100–1) have little relevance to the seventeenth century, as they derive in general from nineteenth century conditions. An unhistorical nineteenth-century equation of 'Jinga', or the queen Nzinga, with the heirs of the *ngola a kiluanje* then living on the Wamba river explains

Kulashingo's Imbangala in Angola

Kulashingo's Imbangala camped for a few years in the territory just outside the small area under Portuguese control in the 1610s in a prototype of all future Portuguese–Imbangala settlement patterns north of the Kwanza. The main title-holder of each Imbangala band settled as an Mbundu king replacing, in most cases north of the river, some form of overrule by the *ngola a kiluanje* with a new state based on conscription of local males into the *kilombo* society. Induction of these men into the *kilombo* simultaneously deprived the most productive part of the local population of their former membership in Mbundu descent groups and subjected it to the direct authority of the Imbangala king and his *vunga*-appointees. The centralized political institutions of the Imbangala created a small but highly centralized state in which the king could mobilize relatively large numbers of men for fighting purposes on very short notice. In a military sense, the Imbangala state of the *kulashingo*, and all the related Imbangala kingdoms among the Mbundu, constituted mercenary camps established on the fringes of Portuguese Angola, dominated by skilled warriors who captured local farmers for sale as slaves in normal times and who readily joined Portuguese expeditions to fight in times of officially-declared wars. Unfortunately, from the perspective of the governors in Luanda, the Imbangala also joined forces with other traders not so closely linked to the policies of the crown's representatives at the capital.

Despite somewhat contradictory traditions,[44] circumstantial evidence points to the middle Lukala as the site of the *kulashingo*'s permanent Imbangala camp since an area there, called Lukamba,

[44] The traditions do not agree on the exact location where the Imbangala lived while settled under Portuguese auspices in Angola but do concur in the essential point that they lived somewhere near the lands then subject to Portuguese control. One nineteenth-century tradition (Rodrigues Neves (1854), pp. 100–1, repeated by Dias de Carvalho (1890a, p. 79, and 1898, pp. 63–4)) stated that the governor gave them lands on the middle Lukala between two nineteenth-century towns, Ambaca and Golungo Alto. Another tradition, dating from the early part of the twentieth century, specified only that the place was somewhere not far from Luanda, probably meaning anywhere west of Kasanje (Oliveira Ferreira Diniz (1918), p. 100). A tradition from the same area as that of Oliveira Ferreira Diniz collected in 1969 (testimony of Mwanya a Shiba, 15 June 1969) made the same point by noting only that the Imbangala had settled somewhere near where the Kwanza meets the sea.

the claim that Kulashingo fought 'Jinga' near Luanda and defeated her before the Portuguese dared to come to the mainland from their based on the islands just off the coast.

became an early and important centre of the slave trade.[45] A slave emporium would necessarily have developed near the main Imbangala settlement as a consequence of their military/economic partnership with the Portuguese. One nineteenth-century tradition underlined the importance of commercial factors by recalling that Kulashingo formally obligated himself to trade with the Portuguese at that time.[46]

Strategic considerations would also have led the Portuguese to settle the *kulashingo*'s Imbangala near Ambaca. The governors of the decade between 1610 and 1620 concentrated their military efforts on penetrating the heartland of the *ngola a kiluanje* state. They first strengthened their position on the lower Lukala by building a new *presídio* at a site called Hango, which would serve as a firm base for launching future operations farther up the river. Lukamba (or Ambaca) would have been the logical position for a mercenary force stationed as a buffer between Ndongo and the weak Portuguese forces farther down the river. The Portuguese then advanced the fortress at Hango to a new site near Ambaca in 1617 as they mounted their drive towards the capital of the *ngola a kiluanje*. The second location of this *presídio* in Ambaca also points to nearby Lukamba as the Imbangala base since the Portuguese would have wanted a fortified post as near as possible to their African allies for purposes of control and co-ordination.[47]

One consequence of the presence of Kulashingo's Imbangala near Angola was that they produced more slaves than official government channels could absorb. Consequently, the second illegal trading system thrived alongside the legal one centred on the customs house in Luanda. Some governors encouraged these illegal ventures and

---

[45] Some traditions (Sousa Calunga, 22 Aug., 2 Oct. 1969) call the lands where the *kulashingo* settled 'Kikanga' (cf. Carvalho (1898), p. 66). *Kikanga* means 'market-place'; Assis Jr. (n.d.), p. 48. The oldest known tradition on this point (1750s), noted by Leitão in Sousa Dias (1938), pp. 16–17), stated that the ancestors of the Kasanje kings had once lived in 'Ambaca'.

[46] Schütt (1881), p. 80. This tradition used the image of an ivory tribute, characteristic of the time at which it was collected, to indicate this.

[47] Nineteenth-century maps of the Ambaca region showed a (perhaps only coincidental) juxtapostion of toponyms that duplicated place names also found in Kasanje. A hill named Kasala lay south of a region called Kasanje in Cazengo between Ambaca and Golungo Alto. The hill had the same geographical relationship to the region as the hill called Kasala in the Baixa de Cassanje had to the capitals of the kings of Kasanje. It is possible, though not proved, that the coincidence of toponyms indicated the exact spot where the Imbangala had camped. See map of 'Loanda and Ambaca and the Course of the River Kwanza', in Capello and Ivens (1882).

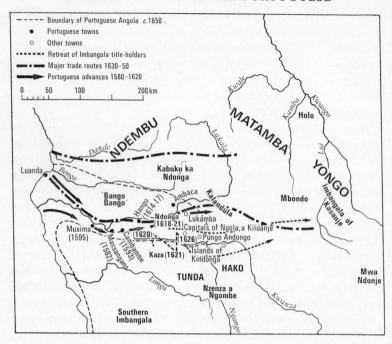

MAP IX. The Imbangala and the Portuguese (c. 1600–1650)

doubtless profited from them. Manuel Cerveira Pereira (governor from 1615 to 1617), for example, encouraged the Imbangala to over-run the local Mbundu without restraint.[48] They caused a great deal of destruction, and local opponents of Cerveira Pereira's policies soon informed Lisbon that his unrestrained use of the Imbangala was harming royal interests in the slave trade more than it was helping. Authorities in Europe replaced Cerveira Pereira as a result of his indiscriminate use of the Imbangala. The next governor, Luis Mendes de Vasconcelos (1617–21), confirmed upon his arrival in 1617 that Cerveira Pereira had left Angola in deplorable condition from the points of view of both the Mbundu and the crown.

Vasconcelos's initial judgement of the status of the Portuguese *conquista* stemmed from revenues lost by the royal treasury. Un-scrupulous traders, he explained, diverted slaves from Luanda to other ports where they could evade royal customs inspectors. Rather

[48] Miller (1972a), p. 569, for the irony implicit in this fact.

credulously, Vasconcelos added (apparently on the basis of reports from traders engaged in the illegal trade) that many other slaves never reached the coast at all since the Imbangala ate them on the spot to satisfy their notorious craving for human flesh. These traders took advantage of the exaggerated reputation of the Imbangala as cannibals to disguise the disappearance of slaves actually smuggled through other ports.[49] With somewhat greater basis in fact, Vasconcelos reported that the allied Portuguese and Imbangala armies had utterly destroyed many *sobas*, or hereditary Mbundu title-holders. Some *sobas* had lost so many of their people that they could no longer provide the direct tribute in slaves demanded by the crown. Vasconcelos pleaded that he could do very little to improve the situation, however, since he found himself opposed unanimously by local traders who argued that the colony would fail without the assistance of the Imbangala warriors.[50] Their argument, at that period in Angola's history, did not greatly exaggerate the facts.

The Spanish king Phillip II, then extending Spanish control into the overseas possessions of Portugal during the period of the Dual Monarchy in Europe (1580–1640), sent an emissary, Rebello de Aragão, at about that time to assess the position of the Portuguese forces in Angola. As a Spaniard, Rebello de Aragão brought a fresh non-Portuguese perspective to the controversy over the role of the Imbangala, and his judgements may therefore be accepted with some confidence. His 1618 report reflected Vasconcelos's initial hostility to the Imbangala and the traders who depended on them for their supply of illegal slave exports. He explained that the Imbangala had served the Portuguese governors well during the early years of the partnership. They had proved such effective and terrifying warriors, in fact, that the local *sobas* had become peaceful and docile purely from fear. But the Imbangala had become haughty and had begun to divert slaves which should have gone to the royal customs house in Luanda. The Spanish inspector thus indicated their involvement in the unofficial and illegal slave trade.

Rebello de Aragão emphasized that responsibility for the sorry state of affairs in 1618 did not lie entirely on the side of the Africans, since the Portuguese engaged in the illegal trade had encouraged their cruelties and the kidnapping of local people.[51] Whenever the

[49] Miller (1973a), pp. 134–5.
[50] Luiz Mendes de Vasconcelos to el-Rei, 28 Aug. 1617; A.H.U., Angola, cx. 1, doc. 129; published in Brásio (1952–71), vi. 283–5.
[51] Rebello de Aragão, 'Relação'; Cordeiro (1881), iii. 12–17.

supply of captives slowed, according to a contemporary account, the captains of the *presídios* sent raiders to harass local chiefs even without the aid of the Imbangala.[52] Portuguese and Imbangala interests in the captives taken in such raids complemented each other perfectly: the Imbangala preferred to keep the youngest boys as recruits for the *kilombo* while the Europeans would buy the females and adult males the Imbangala did not need. The Imbangala could take part in an unofficial raid, give some prisoners to the captain who had permitted the foray, sell part of the remainder to private traders, and keep the rest for their own purposes. Slaves captured and distributed in this manner rarely, if ever, produced the customs duties levied on others taken and sent towards the coast through legal channels.

The Imbangala thus became the ambivalent keystone supporting both arms of the double trading system which matured during the early seventeenth century. One stream of slaves came from legal trading and tribute authorized by the government and taxed accordingly. The effectiveness of this system depended on the formal alliance between the *kulashingo* and the Portuguese governors. The other trade, in which the Imbangala played an increasingly important role during the 1610s, depended on raiding and extortion by officials and traders who smuggled these slaves from Angola under the cover of assertions that the Imbangala had eaten them. By 1617, therefore, the Imbangala had rejected their role as mercenaries employed exclusively by the governor of Angola and returned to their original part as agents of private traders.

Vasconcelos apparently attempted to bring the Imbangala back under government control but failed, instead succeeding only in dispersing the main Imbangala *kilombo* and sending the *kulashingo* in flight far into the interior. He had apparently reached Angola with a sincere desire to collect the export duties imposed by the king and his contractors and to eliminate the illegal trading system. Full implementation of these policies would have placed Portuguese–Imbangala relations on a precarious footing. Vasconcelos succumbed almost at once, however, to the reality which had turned previous governors into enthusiastic supporters of the Imbangala and participants in the unofficial slave trade: low salary, lack of support from superiors in Europe, inadequate control over his own subordinates scattered in inaccessible posts throughout the interior, and a European

[52] Anonymous *relação* (Vasconcelos?), 31 Oct. 161(8?); A.H.U., Angola, cx. 1, doc. 172.

population unanimously opposed to any change in the *status quo*.

Vasconcelos initially attacked the problem of the illegal slave trade head on by raising an army with the expressed intent of driving the Imbangala out of Angola. This was the campaign in which the Portuguese moved the old fortress at Hango to its new site near Ambaca where Portuguese cannon could cover the Imbangala camp.[53] When he reached their encampment, however, he abandoned the expressed purpose of the expedition and joined the Imbangala in a sweeping raid which carried far east into Ndongo and north across the Lukala into Kongo territory. Together they attacked all the most powerful rulers in these regions, including Keta kya 'Labalanga',[54] the *ngola a kiluanje*, and some of the *ndembu* chiefs. This war caused such devastation that trade came to a standstill, roads were closed to travel, and the widespread destruction of crops brought starvation everywhere. The Imbangala, used ruthlessly as in this case, could overwhelm all Mbundu resistance and guarantee that the Portuguese would not lose a major battle.

The Imbangala, who, as Vascencelos's critics later pointed out, had received very lenient treatment from governors up to that point, then began to disagree with their Portuguese sponsors. Vasconcelos may have found that he could not defeat the Imbangala and then embarked on the 1617–18 campaign to demonstrate that their real interests lay with the government rather than with the illegal traders. The spectacular success of this raid, however, could not hide the fact that he also intended to exert closer control over their activities than his predecessors. The Imbangala probably interpreted the new *presídio* at Ambaca correctly as a Portuguese attempt to bring them under tighter reign; a fort and garrison so near their main camp might eventually force them to abandon their participation in the illegal slave trade. As a result of some such consideration, never identified in

[53] Those who have sought 'Manuels' with whom the Imbangala could have dealt at this time should not miss the captain of the new Ambaca *presídio*, one Manuel Castanho; cf. Miller (1972a), pp. 550, 569–70.

[54] Keta kya 'Labalanga' was probably a subordinate chief of the *ngola a kiluanje* who owned his title to the *hango* kings of Libolo that had earlier ruled this region. Modern traditions give a Keta kya Wabo wa Hango ('Labalanga'?) position related to the *hango* kings; testimony of Sousa Calunga, 11 Sept. 1969. This chief definitely was not Kahete as suggested by Delgado in Cadornega (1940–2), i. 89, n. 1. Vasconcelos did not fight against the Imbangala in that war as some authors have assumed; the confusion on this point has arisen due to the similarity of the names of the *mani* Kasanze, a Kongo subchief near Luanda, and the Imbangala ('Cassanges').

the extant documents, *kulashingo*'s Imbangala left Angola in about 1618. Vasconcelos's opponents reported in 1619 that the 'greatest captain among them [the Imbangala], valorous and powerful' had left the Portuguese and departed for the interior. Although this report did not refer to the Imbangala 'captain' by name, the circumstances make it almost certain that he meant the *kulashingo*.[55] The *kulashingo* had left with so many local Mbundu ('slaves and Christian vassals of the Portuguese king'), as well as trade goods, that the Luanda merchants suffered substantial financial losses.[56]

Nineteenth-century Mbundu traditions metaphorically attributed the departure of the Imbangala to failure of the crops they received from the Portuguese and planted when they settled in Lukamba. Kulashingo, they reported, found that the seed had been roasted or had become rotten and would not grow.[57] The Imbangala may in fact have received seeds from the Portuguese, probably as an inducement to settle permanently as farmers, or the image of crop failure may refer to the historical famine conditions mentioned in the documents, but the primary historical content of the episode in Imbangala terms deals with their refusal to abandon the nomadic life of wandering raiders. The planting of seeds represented a temporary conversion to a sedentary farming life, and crop failure constituted an omen warning them against adopting the new style of living. Fear of the spiritual consequences of permanent settlement is thus the remembered cause which drove the Imbangala from Lukamba. The published version of the tradition closest to the original oral testimony draws an explicit

[55] Although the published versions of the Imbangala traditions disagree as to the identity of the king who led the Imbangala to Angola and then on to Kasanje, my informants left no doubt that he held the title of the *kulashingo*. The confusion in earlier accounts comes from the Mbundu habit of referring to a single individual by several different names and titles. Kulashingo was known indifferently by his proper name (Kasanje ka Musumbi, or Kasanje ka Kibuna or Kazanza, etc.), by a praise name or throne name (i.e. Kulashingo), tor by his title (the *kinguri*). Nineteenth-century informants may even have used his (later) Portuguese title (Jaga Cassanje). Only Curt von François (1888), p. 274, accurately identified Kulashingo as the leader who took the Imbangala from Angola to the Lui river.

[56] Copia dos excessos que se cometem no governo de Angolla que o bispo deu a V. Mg.de pedindo remedeo delles de presente e de futuro, 7 Sept. 1619; A.H.U., Angola, cx. 1, doc. 175; published in Brásio (1952–71). vi. 366–74.

[57] Dias de Carvalho (1890a), p. 79. The image of roasted or rotten seeds operates as a cliché that may appear in such other episodes as the story of the *makota*'s murder of the *kinguri* (pp. 173–175 above). One name for the area where the Imbangala stayed in Angola comes from this episode: Lukamba, the name, came from a verb *kukamba* meaning to lack, be scarce, not suffice (Assis Jr. (n.d.), p. 189), since the land would not bear crops.

contrast between a settled, farming life and the Imbangala decision to 'return to hunting'.[58]

Another nineteenth-century tradition used a different image but still depicted a magical sign against settlement and in favour of subsequent return to the wandering life of hunters. The Imbangala had settled in Lukamba, according to this variant, and had planted their seeds when an elephant entered their fields and ruined the crops. Since elephants almost never appeared in that region, the Imbangala interpreted this misfortune as an omen. Kulashingo sent his *yibinda* (specialists in hunting supernatural beasts) in pursuit of the animal and they followed it to the future site of the kingdom of Kasanje.[59] The positive omen of the magical elephant attracted the Imbangala to hunting in this variant, just as the negative portent of ruined seeds discouraged agricultural activities in other versions.[60]

The Mature Portuguese-Imbangala Alliance

The enormous success of Vasconcelos's 1617–18 military campaign and the hardships caused by the defection of the *kulashingo* brought the pattern of European–Imbangala relations north of the Kwanza to maturity. The Portuguese had definitively occupied the territory on the north bank of the Kwanza as far east as their outposts at Ambaca and later, after final defeat of the *hari a kiluanje* in 1671, at Pungo Andongo. Around these lands lay a ring of new Mbundu states founded in the middle of the seventeenth century by Lunda title-holders heading bands of Imbangala. The Portuguese employed these Imbangala as mercenaries in wars and used them as their primary suppliers of slaves in peacetime. As a result, they usually treated the Imbangala kings as generously as possible.[61] This arrangement predominated between the Lukala, the Kwango, and the Kwanza from the 1620s until after 1850.

Much of this history centres on holders of Lunda *makota* titles who

[58] Dias de Carvalho (1885–6), p. 136. Later Imbangala historians may have blamed crop failure on Portuguese treachery because of the hostility with which late nineteenth-century Imbangala regarded the government in Luanda.

[59] Rodrigues Neves (1854), p. 102.

[60] Modern Imbangala traditions, in acknowledgement of colonial political realities, emphasized that Kulashingo left Luanda with the governor's blessing and that he settled in the interior as an emissary of the Portuguese government.

[61] See the *relação* of Garcia Mendes Castelo Branco, 16 Jan. 1620; Ajuda, 51–VIII–25, fols. 93–95v; published in Brásio (1952–71), vi. 446–52; also in Cordeiro (1881), ii. Castelo Branco argued that the Portuguese king should assist the merchants of Luanda with three casks of wine each year which would be given to the Imbangala to maintain their loyalty and the profitable slave trade that sprang from it.

remained in Portuguese Angola after the *kulashingo* had departed for the interior. All of them clearly depended on Portuguese support for their positions of dominance over the local Mbundu lineages. The *kulashingo*'s alliance with the Portuguese between 1612 and 1619 had exacerbated the deep rivalries which divided the title-holders in his group of Imbangala. Few of the Lunda *makota* would have willingly accepted co-operation with the Europeans on a basis which supported the *kulashingo* at their expense. As claimants to independent sources of legitimacy through the *kilombo*, and unwilling to reconize the *kinguri* title which they had abolished once before, they dispersed about the time the *kulashingo* left for the interior to found as many as thirty separate bands near Angola. Although a few of these *makota* initially reverted to open hostility against Portuguese official forces, they achieved very little success with this policy. Ndonga, one of the *kinguri's* original *makota*, lingered briefly after 1618 in the devastated parts of Ndongo but suffered defeat by a 1620–1 expedition which followed up on the great campaigns of 1617–19; in this instance, the Portuguese captured the chief and completely destroyed his army.[62] This defeat effectively ended Ndonga's contact with the Europeans and caused some remnants of the band to flee with the title to the Baixa de Cassanje where they rejoined the *kulashingo*'s Imbangala in the nascent state of Kasanje.[63]

Kabuku ka Ndonga, a title-holder subordinate to the *ndonga*, assumed control of other parts of the *ndonga*'s band and reversed the policies of his predecessor, joining with the governor of Angola in a 1621–2 campaign against the *mani* Kasanze near Luanda.[64] Kabuku ka Ndonga continued north after winning a victory against Kasanze and invaded the southern Kongo provinces of Mbamba and Mpemba where he defeated the Mbamba army and killed both the duke of Mbamba and the marquis of Mpemba. Kabuku ka Ndonga and the Portuguese returned to Kongo on the side of the *mani* Kongo in 1623, defeating two *ndembu* chiefs who had revolted against their Kongo overlords.[65] The rise of the junior position to replace the

[62] Cadornega (1940–2), i. 90–4.
[63] All Imbangala testimonies.
[64] Miller (1972b), pp. 51–3.
[65] The extent of Imbangala involvement in this campaign and the nature of their conduct may have been exaggerated by the Kongo kings. Most descriptions of these wars come from São Salvador, where the Kongo traditionally used the Imbangala as whipping boys when complaining to Europe against the alleged injustices of the governors of Angola. In this case, the Kongo kings succeeded in obtaining the intervention of the Pope against Vasconcelos, resulting in his recall that same year; Jadin and Cuvelier (1954), pp. 456, 458,

ndonga and his support of the Portuguese paralleled the pattern established when the *kulashingo* had eclipsed the *makota* and joined Bento Banho Cardoso in 1612, but this partnership proved somewhat more enduring than that of the *kulashingo*.

Kabuku ka Ndonga settled down to build a semi-independent kingdom on the southern border of the *ndembu* region where he stayed on the Portuguese northern frontier as a buffer against the hostile *ndembu* rulers across the Nzenza river. His strategic position between the Portuguese and their enemies recalled the location of the *kulashingo*'s Imbangala settled near Ambaca as advance guards against the *ngola a kiluanje*.

A Dutch invasion of Angola during the 1640s, part of the Thirty Years War in Europe, brought one of the few notable—but temporary—defections of a *kabuku ka ndonga* in a 200-year-long alliance. The holder of the title wavered briefly in his loyalty to the Portuguese at the outset of the Dutch invasion,[66] but he soon returned to the side of his old allies and in 1643 launched an expedition from his base in Wumba north of the Lukala to harass *ndembu* chiefs who had helped the Dutch during their occupation of Luanda.[67]

A succession crisis in the *kabuku ka ndonga*'s kingdom later allowed the Portuguese to repeat their tactic of replacing legitimate Imbangala kings with puppet successors who depended on European support to maintain their positions. The kingdom of Matamba, centred on the Wamba river, had by the 1640s become one of the most powerful eastern Mbundu states under the rule of the justly famous queen Nzinga. She had attempted to re-establish the *ngola a kiluanje* title there after the Portuguese had put puppets in the place

[66] During the tenure of Governor Pedro Cesar de Meneses, 1639–43; on the Dutch conquest of the coastal portions of Angola, see Charles R. Boxer (1952).

[67] Cadornega (1940–2), i. 278–9, 286–7. Consulta do Conselho Ultramarino, 17 Aug. 1644; A.H.U., Códice 13, fols. 108–108ᵛ (Brásio (1952–71), ix. 153), contains a commendation to the 'Jaga' Kabuku for his assistance. Another *consulta* of the Conselho Ultramarino, 23 July 1644 (A.H.U., Angola, cx. 3, published in Brásio (1952–61), ix. 28–38) shows that Governor Antonio Abreu de Miranda (1643–4) befriended an unnamed 'Jaga', very likely Kabuku ka Ndongo, in the area of Ambaca and tried to get him to harass the Dutch. The expedition was described in a letter from the Goverador to el-Rei, 9 Mar. 1643; A.H.U., Angola, cx. 2.

etc. Rei do Congo to Mons. Vives, 26 Feb. 1622; Biblioteca Vaticana, Cod. Vat. Lat. 12516, fols. 81–81ᵛ; Brás Correia to Dom João Baptista Viues, 10 Dec. 1623; ibid., fols 95–96ᵛ; Conego da Sé do Congo to Pe Manuel Rodrigues, S.J. (1624); Biblioteca e Arquivo Districtal—Evora, MS. CXVI/2–15, no. 7; all published in Brásio (1952–71), vii. 3–4, 166–70, 291–7.

of the original Ndongo kings during the 1620s.[68] As part of her policy of harassing Portuguese official interests, she co-operated with the Dutch while they held Luanda from 1641 to 1648. Kabuku ka Ndonga was still fighting on the Portuguese side against the Dutch in 1645 or 1646 when Nzinga's army captured the ruling Imbangala king somewhere east of Ambaca. Nzinga, who also claimed allegiance to the laws of the *kilombo*, spared his life out of respect for his close relationship to the *ndonga* position whose occupants she regarded as allies. This entitled the imprisoned *kabuku ka ndonga* to the rights of blood-brotherhood which united all adherents of the *kilombo*. She would not, however, release him to the Portuguese.[69]

Kabuku ka Ndonga's people, deprived of their legitimate leader, chose as their new ruler his brother-in-law who had held the appointive *vunga*-position of *funji a musungo*,[70] one of the war leaders of the band. Since his predecessor was known to be alive, he could not claim full rights to the position and ruled as a regent through the support of his wife, a daughter of the original Ndonga named Kwanza, whom the Imbangala regarded as the rightful guardian of the position.[71] The Portuguese probably encouraged the choice of the *funji a musungo*, since it gave them the opportunity to install a title-holder only remotely qualified for his position and thus dependent on them for support.

The new *kabuku ka ndonga*, like the *kulashingo*, acknowledged his debt to the Portuguese by enlisting his people in another military campaign. Despite his lack of royal qualifications, he proved himself an effective military commander in this attack, probably in part because the assault on Nzinga gave his people hope of rescuing their lost chief, then still alive but captive in Nzinga's lands. The rescue attempt failed and the old king eventually died in Matamba. The new *kabuku ka ndonga* then remained very close to his European sponsors, fighting in battles against the Dutch and their African auxiliaries during the late 1640s,[72] against the *ndembu* chiefs in 1648,[73] and finally in 1648–9 against Panji a Ndona, the successor of the *mani* Kasanze

[68] The move of the *ngola a kiluanje* to the Wamba was that mentioned in all Imbangala traditions as taking place immediately after the arrival of Kulashingo in Angola. On Nzinga, Joseph C. Miller (1975).

[69] Cadornega (1940–2), i. 349–54.

[70] The title translates roughly as 'sustenance of the army'; *funji* is manioc porridge and *musungo* is an appointive war leader of the type used by the Imbangala.

[71] Cadornega (1940–2), i. 240.

[72] Ibid., i. 463–4, 490–1.

[73] Ibid., ii. 66–7.

near Luanda.[74] The Portuguese honoured his fidelity by awarding him the title of 'Jaga' and by condescendingly referring to him by the possessive form, 'our Jaga'.

The death in 1652 or 1653 of the *kabuku ka ndonga* who had fought so loyally for the Portuguese ended for a short while the period of close co-operation with the Europeans. His successor, who probably had a better claim to legitimacy in the eyes of his own people, soon abandoned the Portuguese to join Nzinga under the banner of the *kilombo*. The Portuguese retaliated with a military expedition in 1655, captured the chief, his wife (still with the name Kwanza), and all of the major officials of the *kilombo*.[75] Although later chroniclers claimed that the governor forgave this *kabuku ka ndonga* for his wayward behaviour, contemporary documents show that the governor sent him and his followers to Brazil as slaves, in keeping with the custom of many seventeenth-century officials. The *kabuku ka ndonga* who received a pardon was a later incumbent, evidently another Portuguese puppet in the position.[76]

What had by that time become a standard Portuguese strategy of installing pliable incumbents in sensitive positions again produced the desired results. The new *kabuku ka ndonga* fought loyally against several Ndongo chiefs led by Ngoleme a Keta during the rule of governor João Fernandes Vieira (1658–61).[77] The dependence of later holders of the *kabuku ka ndonga* title on the Portuguese gradually increased and they simultaneously abandoned the laws of the *kilombo* entirely. One incumbent finally admitted a pair of Carmelite missionaries to his kingdom and accepted Christian baptism in the 1670s.[78]

By the 1680s, the *kabuku ka ndonga* had become a model of the kind of alliance which Portuguese governors from the time of the *kulashingo* onward tried to establish with neighbouring Imbangala rulers. They favoured incumbents with an authentic Imbangala title who owed their position to the Europeans rather than to the support

[74] Ibid., ii. 25–6. See also Miller (1972b), pp. 53–5.
[75] Consulta do Conselho Ultramarino, 13 September 1677 (A.H.U., Angola, cx. 2) refers back to these events but gives no date.
[76] Compare Cadornega (1940–2), ii. 75–9, 498, with Consulta do Conselho Ultramarino, 13 July 1655; A.H.U., Livro 1 de Consultas Mixtas, fol. 187 (Códice 13). The defeated Kasanze of 1622 had suffered the same fate.
[77] Cadornega (1940–2), ii. 164–5. Cadornega also had him fighting on the Portuguese side against the count of Sonyo in Kongo during the early 1670s; see ibid., ii. 278–80.
[78] Ibid., ii. 426.

of their own people.[79] Such kings enlisted their subjects as mercenaries in Portuguese armies whenever officials in Luanda requested their aid. The value of their titles necessarily declined under such circumstances so that the *kabuku ka ndonga*, for example, completely abandoned their Imbangala position in the course of the eighteenth century. In an echo of the familiar Mbundu pattern of changes in titles to reflect new sources of legitimacy, the title then acquired a new patronym, becoming Kabuku ka Mbwila, known thereafter to the Portuguese as the *ndembu* Kabuku.[80] The change indicated that the *kabuku* had transferred their allegiance to the most powerful local system of political titles, the neighbouring *ndembu* positions of southern Kongo.[81]

The history of the Lunda *kota* position, Kalanda ka Imbe, or Kalandula as he became known, paralleled that of the *kabuku ka ndonga* in providing another example of how much Imbangala kings north of the Kwanza depended on the Portuguese for the security of their positions. The occupants of the *kalanda ka imbe* had abandoned the *kulashingo* when he left for the interior and, like the *kabuku ka ndonga*, had settled near Portuguese Angola. According to tradition, an incumbent named Kashita (not otherwise identified) swore allegiance as a Portuguese vassal, the 'Jaga' Kalandula, during the conquest of Lukamba.[82] The *kalanda ka imbe* could have provoked the *kulashingo*'s departure for the interior by convincing the Portuguese that he, as a legitimate leader of the *kilombo* and successor to the *kalanda ka imbe* in charge of the band as late as 1601, might lead the Imbangala in the service of Portugal more effectively than the *kulashingo*. A Portuguese switch to co-operation with the *kalanda ka imbe* might explain the documentary reference to Vasconcelos's 'abuse' of the Imbangala, that is, abuse of the followers of the *kulashingo*. It would also explain the *kulashingo*'s decision to take the *kinguri* title and seek his fortune in the far interior, leaving control over the *kilombo* to the *kalanda ka imbe* and others who had gained the favour of the Portuguese from which the *kulashingo* had tried to exclude them.

[79] Ibid., *passim*.

[80] 'Noticias do paiz de Quissama . . .' (1844), p. 124.

[81] A.H.A., Códice 240, *passim*. The Mbwila was the most powerful of the numerous *ndembu* chiefs north of Ambaca.

[82] José Maria Mergú (Capitão-chefe of Ambaca) to Gov. Geral José Rodrigues Coelho do Amaral, 1 Dec. 1856; *Boletim Oficial de Angola*, no. 585 (13 December 1856). This independent tradition agrees with other sources in placing the Imbangala near Lukamba in 1617–18.

The *kalanda ka imbe*, in any case, settled as the 'Jaga' Kalandula on the frontiers of Ambaca where he guarded against the *ndembu* chiefs to the north-west and against Nzinga's Matamba to the east. His position there made him another in the line of Imbangala client states which ringed Portuguese territory to the north. During the 1640s, Kalandula faithfully fought the Dutch in the company of the Portuguese and Kabuku ka Ndonga.[83] Much of this warfare centred on control of a major trade route which ran from Nzinga's kingdom of Matamba through the *ndembu* region to the Dutch traders active on the coast north of Luanda. Most of the slaves who left Angola during the Dutch occupation came down this trail, and the Portuguese, Dutch, and their respective African allies fought continuously to control it.

The *kalandula* abandoned the Portuguese only once, when he went over to Nzinga with the *kabuku ka ndonga* in 1653.[84] Since the *kalandula* occupied an important position along the Portuguese northern defences, the governor in Luanda immediately tried to win him back.[85] The Portuguese could not defeat him as they had crushed the *kabuku ka ndonga*, nor did an opportunity arise to manipulate the succession to his title, but they eventually employed diplomatic methods to regain his services. The terms of a 1656 treaty, in which Nzinga formally renounced her thirty-year enmity against the Portuguese, required that she return the *kalandula* to Portuguese vassalage.[86] The later *kalandula*, often in association with the *kabuku ka ndonga*, repeatedly sent their army to fight in Portuguese wars.

The location of the two former Imbangala chiefs' lands on the north side of the Lukala above Ambaca[87] kept them dependent on Portuguese support since it left them in an exposed position near the powerful *ndembu* and Kongo chiefs to the north. The kings of Kongo

[83] Gov. Sousa Chichorro to el-Rei, 8 Dec. 1656; A.H.U., Angola, cx. 4.
[84] Cadornega (1940–2), ii. 75–9; Cavazzi (1965), ii. 33–4, said that Nzinga defeated Kalandula . He gave the date, wrongly, as 1657.
[85] Luis de Sousa Chichorro to el-Rei; 29 July 1656; A.H.U., Angola, cx. 4.
[86] Capitulos e Pazes que fas a capitão manoel frois peixoto Como embaixador nesta corte da Rainha Donna Anna de Souza por mandado do senhor governador e capitão geral destes Reinos Luis Martins de souza chichorro Retificados pelo capitão Joseph Carrasco; A.H.U., Angola, cx. 4; published in *AA*, sér I, ii, nos. 7–8 (1936), 9–14; Cavazzi (1965), ii. 332–3 (doc. 46). See also letters from Luis de Sousa Chichorro, 14 Oct. and 8 Dec. 1656; A.H.U., Angola, cx. 4.
[87] Cadornega (1940–2), iii. 244–5. The exact location of the *kalandula*'s lands probably changed from time to time. The territory was known as Kitukila in 1656 and lay on the boundary of the lands of Nzinga to the north and of Ndongo to the south.

killed at least one *kalandula* in 1658 as part of a general harassment of chiefs loyal to the Portuguese.[88] Other *kalandula* fought against the *ndembu* Nambo a Ngongo in the 1660s,[89] accompanied the Portuguese expedition to Sonyo (in Kongo) under João Soares de Almeida in 1670,[90] and again against the *ndembu* Mbwila in 1693.[91] The Portuguese granted the title of 'Ngola a Mbole' or 'Kyambole of the Portuguese king' to the *kalandula* and provided them with arms and supplies in return for their participation in many military expeditions throughout the eighteenth and even into the nineteenth century.[92]

Nzinga, ruler of Matamba and pretender to the title of *ngola a kiluanje* after the defeat of the Ndongo kingdom of the same name, adopted the rites of the *kilombo* in the 1620s and considered herself Imbangala. But her kingdom developed in ways quite atypical of the other Imbangala states elsewhere in northern Angola since she was able to maintain a much more consistent opposition to Portuguese activities in Angola, a record equalled only by such southern Imbangala kings as the *kulembe* and Kakonda.[93] Matamba turns out to be the exception which illuminates the fundamental reason why most Imbangala kings maintained such close relations with the Portuguese. Nzinga, alone among the Imbangala rulers of the north, claimed political authority (i.e. certain local titles in Matamba) derived from the indigenous Mbundu system of titles. Her local sources of legitimacy, although never secure, allowed her to command her own people with marginally more security than the alien Imbangala bands and thus to behave more independently than the holders of exotic Lunda titles who never gained the confidence of the lineages they claimed to rule.

The economics of the slave trade also contributed to Nzinga's independence of Portuguese control before 1656. The trade route which developed during the 1630s from Matamba through the

---

[88] Gastão Sousa Dias (1942), pp. 39, 103, 105.

[89] Cadornega (1940–2), ii. 191–6; Kalandula was not mentioned by name, but there is little doubt that he was the 'Jaga' referred to.

[90] Feo Cardoso de Castello Branco e Torres (1825), pp. 202–3; also Levy Maria Jordão, visconde de Paiva Manso (1877), p. 254.

[91] Gonçalo da Costa de Meneses to el-Rei, 25 Apr. 1693; A.H.U., Angola, cx. 11. Again, the *kalandula* was not mentioned by name but the identification is quite certain.

[92] Numerous references in A.H.A.; e.g. Gov. D. Antonio de Lancastre to D. Francisco Agostinho Rebelo, Jaga Callandulla, 14 Aug. 1775; A.H.A., Códice A–14–4, fols. 89–90ᵛ; also Termo de juramento e vassallagem a Sua Magestade que presta o Jaga Calandulla, D. Manoel Affonso, como abaixa se declara, 20 Oct. 1870 (*Boletim Oficial de Angola*, no. 50 (10 Dec. 1870), 706).

[93] See section following.

ndembu towards the Dutch on the coast ensured her access to European trade goods regardless of her relations with governors in Luanda. She competed for slaves with the *kulashingo*'s neighbouring kingdom in Kasanje, and their rivalry had reached the stage of armed conflict just before the Dutch invaded Luanda in 1641.[94] The Dutch occupation of Angola cleared the way for large-scale exports of slaves from Matamba and fuelled Nzinga's rise to the stature of the most powerful ruler in the interior during the 1640s. She established a virtual monopoly over the slave trade from the interior during that decade.[95] Her ascendency lasted, however, only until the Portuguese expelled her European allies, the Dutch, in 1648 and reopened trading with Kasanje during the 1650s. The shift in the slave trade to Kasanje prompted her to reach a reconciliation with the Portuguese in 1656.

The kingdom of Kasanje under the *kulashingo*, like Matamba under Nzinga, claimed a connection with the Imbangala *kilombo* but found its ultimate sources of legitimacy in the *kinguri* title brought from Lunda. In the case of Kasanje, the successors of the *kulashingo* preserved a degree of independence from Portuguese influence during the 1630s and 1640s through alliances with the *mwa ndonje* and some of the Songo titles of Lunda origin. The slave trade became important to Kasanje only after 1648 when renewed Portuguese hegemony near the coast restored the second major slave trading network in Angola, i.e. the official one. Kasanje controlled the inland terminus of this system, which ran through Portuguese possessions to the south of the parallel illegal trade route from Matamba to the *ndembu* and their allies. The great distance which separated Kasanje from the seat of Portuguese power in Luanda enabled the *kinguri* to pursue relatively independent policies even after the new trading system linked them once again to the Portuguese. In addition, the eastern Mbundu of Kasanje seem to have had greater respect for the Lunda titles than their western fellows, as the proliferation of related titles in Songo had demonstrated. Kasanje also incorporated a variety of native Mbundu positions drawn from the Libolo area.[96] All of these conditions made Kasanje, like Nzinga's Matamba, unrepresentative of

[94] Cadornega (1940–2), i. 205, 207; also Cavazzi (1965), ii. 79.

[95] Report of Pieter Mortamer, 1643; Archief van de Eerste West Indische Compagnie, 46; S. P. Honoré-Naber (1933). The Dutch claimed that they bought 12,000 to 13,000 slaves per year during the early 1640s, nearly all of them from Nzinga. I am indebted to Dr. Phyllis Martin for pointing this reference out to me.

[96] These and other points related to the foundation of the Kasanje kingdom will appear in future studies based on my 1969–70 research in Angola.

the more common case of Imbangala bands closer to the coast who depended heavily on Portuguese assistance for their survival.

The Imbangala South of the Kwanza

The close, almost symbiotic, relationships between the Imbangala and the Portuguese north of the Kwanza river contrast strikingly with the barely broken record of hostility which the warriors of the *kilombo* showed to Europeans south of the river. An explanation for the difference must be sought in terms of the Mbundu and Ovimbundu social backgrounds against which the respective groups operated. In so far as the southern *kilombo* bands have been revealed in the written records, the Imbangala bands on both sides of the river had similar political structures composed primarily of institutions derived from the *kulembe* and the *vunga*-positions, both of which had originated among the Ovimbundu. If, as the histories of several other types of title and symbol among the Mbundu have suggested, the consequences of a political innovation depend on its compatibility with the social institutions in which it takes root, the Ovimbundu-derived *kilombo* should have found a more cordial reception among the peoples living south of the Kwanza than among the alien lineages of the Mbundu. Whereas the hostility of the Mbundu lineages had driven most northern Imbangala into the arms of the Portuguese, the congeniality of the *kilombo* among the Ovimbundu allowed the southern Imbangala to remain fiercely independent of European interference.

Imbangala opposition to Europeans south of the Kwanza did not derive from a want of Portuguese attempts to duplicate their arrangements with the *kulashingo* among the *kilombo* bands who had remained among the Ovimbundu. Manuel Cerveria Pereira, the former governor in Luanda who had made such excessive use of the Imbangala from 1615 to 1617, attempted to extend his alliance with them to the south side of the Kwanza when he left office in 1617. He mounted an expedition which sailed south towards the Kunene in search of Imbangala bands. His venture foundered almost immediately on a decided lack of Imbangala interest, a problem which became a perennial hindrance to nearly all later Portuguese attempts at accommodation south of the Kwanza. Cerveira Pereira intended to use the Imbangala to promote Portuguese penetration of the lands behind a second seaport at Benguela Velha (near the mouth of the Kuvo), just as the *kulashingo* had opened the way to the Mbundu interior. He had good reason to expect to find Imbangala there, since they had been reported in that vicinity at least as recently as 1601.

Cerveira Pereira failed to encounter Imbangala with whom he could initiate a profitable slave trade near Benguela. On account of the absence of African allies, and because of the extreme aridity of the land, he continued southward until he discovered a group of Imbangala camped near a river which he called the 'Murombo'.[97] He convinced these Imbangala that they should raid the local inhabitants for captives which they would exchange for Portuguese trade goods, much as the *kulashingo*'s Imbangala had traded with him near Luanda. This agreement did not work out as well as the Portuguese had hoped, since these Imbangala co-operated only to the point of selling their captives during the day, but then stole them back as soon as night fell. The Imbangala king (whose name was not recorded) also sheltered other slaves who had escaped from the Portuguese and eventually collected about thirty refugees in his camp. When Cerveira Pereira accused the Imbangala chief of duplicity, the *kilombo* leader denied any knowledge of the escaped slaves and threatened to attack the Portuguese if they did not treat him with more respect. His independent attitude so provoked Cerveira Pereira that the Portuguese commander attacked the Imbangala encampment to recover his losses. The European forces twice failed to storm the hill where the Imbangala had built a fortified refuge before some eighty men and two horsemen managed to penetrate the defences. The Portuguese won the ensuing battle, captured the chief, beheaded him, and took back most of the trade goods and slaves which they had lost. They also enslaved as many Imbangala warriors as they could capture.

Cerveira Pereira shortly afterward attempted another slave-trading alliance with a different Imbangala band but experienced no greater success. In this case a chief, 'Ka Ngombe',[98] at first accepted the partnership but broke away as soon as he realized that Cerveira

[97] Probably not the Balombo; see Map X.
[98] Not the same Kangombe given by Capello and Ivens as the fourth chief of Bihe (1882, i. 158); Gladwyn M. Childs (1970), p. 245, placed his reign at *c.* 1780–1805. The form of the name suggests a missing initial element, as in (Kalunga) ka Ngombe, since *ngombe* means ox and occurs as a surname with some frequency south of the Kwanza. Alternatively, 'Kangombe' may have been the *mwa* Cangombe, one of the Lunda *makota* of the Kandama ka Hite lineage who had apparently lost control of the Imbangala to Mbongo wa Imbe and Kalanda ka Imbe somewhere in this part of Angola. The defeat and possible expulsion of the title from the band (not recorded in the traditions) could have caused the name to remain there after the other *makota* continued on their way north.

Pereira intended to make himself the dominant partner. Cerveira Pereira, perhaps wiser from his experience with the Imbangala near the 'Murombo', tried to limit 'Ka Ngombe's' potential for trouble-making by stationing him in an out-of-the-way spot and limiting his forces to only fifty men. 'Ka Ngombe' recognized the danger, how-ever, and fled to the hills under the excuse that he had gone to search for more booty. He stole some of the Portuguese cattle as he departed and took them to his camp on an inaccessible hilltop. The Portuguese managed to storm and sack the camp but then beat a hasty retreat to their main base near the coast under continual harassment from the regrouped Imbangala.[99] 'Ka Ngombe's' Imbangala, like their counter-parts near the 'Murombo', could not have recovered from an initial defeat to mount sustained resistance without the support of local residents. Cerveira Pereira's expectations of a profitable trade had not been fulfilled.

The only southern Imbangala bands who co-operated with the Portuguese on the same basis as those north of the Kwanza were a few who lived near Benguela Nova during the 1620s, notably the *kilombo* of 'Angury'[100] and Kapingena. It was their willingness to provide slaves to the Portuguese that distinguished them (like most Imban-gala) from non-Imbangala chiefs; the Portuguese noted explicitly that they traded with the Ovimbundu primarily for foodstuffs and other supplies but bought only slaves from the Imbangala.[101] Neither 'Angury' nor Kapingena appeared by name in documents again, after the 1620s, although they may have been among the unidentified Imbangala auxiliaries who aided the Portuguese during the wars of the 1650s near Benguela.[102] Another Imbangala king in the same region, Kashana, offered his support when a Portuguese relief expedition stopped in Benguela in 1645 on its way from Brazil to aid the beseiged Portuguese who had fled to Massangano after the Dutch capture of Luanda.[103]

[99] Representação of Manuel Cerveira Pereira, 2 July 1618; A.H.U., Angola, cx. 1, doc. 141; published in Brásio (1952–71), vi. 315–19; also in Cordeiro (1881), iii.

[100] Nguri? There is no probable relation to the *kinguri* except that both names may have come from the Wambo word for lion.

[101] Relação of Fernão de Sousa, 22 Apr. 1626; A.H.U., Angola, cx. 2; published in Brásio (1952–71), vii. 436–8. This distinction lasted until at least the end of the eighteenth century; see J. Pinheiro de Lacerda (1845), p. 488.

[102] Cadornega (1940–2), ii. 43. Cadornega elsewhere (ii. 250) identified the 'Jagas' of Benguela as Kabeto, Kalunga ka Kingwanza, Kasindi, and Ngulu.

[103] Relação da viagem de Sotomaior em socorro de Angola; B.N.M., MS. 8187, fols. 37–60ᵛ; published in Artur Veigas (1923), 18–23; also *AA*, sér II, i, nos. 3–6 (1943–4), 145–53; Brásio (1952–71); ix. 374.

The eagerness of Kashana and the other *kilombo* chiefs in this area to establish friendly relations with the Portuguese offers a glaring exception to the hostility of other Imbangala south of the Kwanza and indicates that some powerful enemy may have driven those who lived near Benguela to seek alliance with the Europeans. The most likely source of their anxiety was another Imbangala king, Kakonda, who lived beyond the mountains east of Benguela. Kakonda consistently fought any European penetration of his lands throughout the seventeenth century and thus fits the normal pattern of Portuguese–Imbangala relations south of the Kwanza. The Portuguese tried repeatedly to penetrate his stronghold but failed except for the construction of a short-lived post there in 1684. Kakonda drove them out the following year, however, and the wars resumed and continued until well into the eighteenth century.[104]

To the north of Benguela, a number of Imbangala bands identifiable as related to the *kulembe* constituted an impenetrable obstacle to Portuguese advances beyond the coastline. The Portuguese fought them intermittently at least from the 1620s, when a report described the region as full of fierce and warlike Imbangala who frustrated the hopes of governors who had tasted the fruits of their alliance with the Imbangala north of the Kwanza and wanted to duplicate their successes in the south. These southern Imbangala refused either to trade with the Portuguese or to pay tribute. They lived in fortified caves where they stored water and food to withstand seiges.[105] The *kulembe* had established a strong kingdom on the upper Longa river after the *munjumbo* had driven him out of the mountains to the south and had become pre-eminent among them. His new domain extended towards the coast where the holder of a subordinate *vunga*-title, the *sungo dya kulembe*, ruled the Sumbi people who lived near the mouth of the Kuvo.[106] The central *kulembe* lands, and those of two subordinates, Nambo a Mbungo and Lunga dya Kafofo, lay beyond the southern borders of Hako and Libolo.

These Imbangala kings regularly made life miserable for any local

---

[104] See, for example, Governador de Angola Dom João de Lancastre, 3 Apr. 1688 (copy of 20 Apr. 1690); A.H.U., Angola, cx. 11; also Cadornega (1940–2), ii. 176–9.

[105] Relação da Costa de Angola e Congo, pelo ex-Governador Fernão de Sousa, 21 Feb. 1632; Ajuda, 51–VIII–3, fols. 11–18ᵛ; published in Brásio (1952–71), viii. 129.

[106] Cadornega (1940–2), iii. 249. The *sungo* was probably a 'war leader' (the *musungo*); cf. the title of the *funji a musungo* among the Imbangala of Kabuku ka Ndonga, pp. 204–6 above.

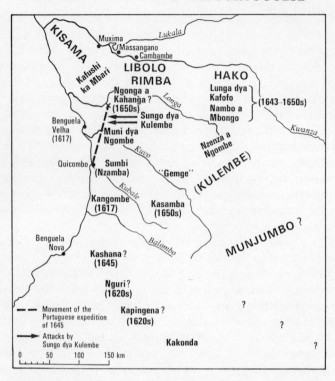

MAP X. Imbangala South of the Kwanza (Seventeenth Century)

chiefs who submitted to European blandishments, and most Portuguese records from this area chronicle little more than their conflicts
with the *kulembe* and his subordinates. The *kulembe*'s Imbangala
raided chiefs loyal to the Portuguese in the early 1640s and fought an
army commanded by Diogo Gomes de Moraes in 1643.[107] These
battles showed that the Portuguese armies could defeat the southern
Imbangala on occasion, but their aftermath emphasized that they
could not exterminate them; in classic guerilla style, the *kulembe*
resumed his raiding of the loyal chiefs as soon as Moraes's army had
left. The next year, another Portuguese expedition went out from
Massangano to fight the *kulembe* once again.[108] His persistent

[107] Cadornega (1470–2), i. 312–13. See also the 'Catalogo dos governadores
do Reino de Angola', published in Feo Cardoso de Castello Branco e Torres
(1825), p. 175; and Mattos (1963), p. 275.
[108] Cadornega (1940–2), i. 344–6, 354.

resistance to the Portuguese had by that time given him a reputation as the most powerful Imbangala chief south of the Kwanza. One governor referred to him, with some exaggeration, as 'that great Jaga Lulembe [sic] who has conquered from here to Mozambique',[109] and Mbundu traditions from that time depicted him in the same glowing terms.[110]

Nambo a Mbungo and Lunga dya Kafofo, the *kulembe*'s provincial governors, continued fighting against Portuguese penetration in later years, turning up on the side of the rebellious Kisama chief Kafushi ka Mbari in the 1650s.[111] Another Imbangala chief in the Rimba province of southern Libolo, Ngonga a Kahanga, opposed the Portuguese at about the same time, but he apparently suffered an unrecorded defeat at some time since he eventually declared himself a vassal of the Portuguese crown.[112] Other hostile Imbangala, unidentified, but very likely connected with the *kulembe*, roamed the province of 'Gemge'[113] which lay east of the Sumbi. The extensive and consistent Imbangala opposition to European activities in this region contrasted dramatically with the relative docility of the Imbangala kings among the Mbundu.

The best-known example of the *kulembe*'s opposition to European penetration of the area south of the Kwanza occurred when the western branch of his Imbangala defeated the 1645 Portuguese expedition sent from Brazil to relieve the Portuguese forces trapped by the Dutch in Massangano. The commanders of the expedition, Teixeira de Mendonça and Lopes Sequeira, landed their forces near the mouth of the Kikombo river. From there, they intended to march overland towards Massangano across territory controlled by the *kulembe*. Their choice of landing site put them at an initial disadvantage, since it forced them to make the same difficult crossing over the Kuvo river which had stopped the *kalanda ka imbe*'s Imbangala nearly a half-century earlier. Nzamba, the ruler of friendly Sumbi living south of the Kuvo, had made an offer of aid which probably influenced the Portuguese strategic planning. The known hostility of the *kulembe*'s subjects farther north and the availability of African allies, still a major concern to the Portuguese everywhere in Angola near the Kikombo may have made this the best of the available alternatives after all.

[109] Relação da viagem de Sotomaior; Brásio (1952–71), ix. 374.
[110] Cavazzi (1965), i. 188–90.
[111] Cadornega (1940–2), ii. 90–1, 103.
[112] Cavazzi (1965), i. 207.
[113] Njenje? Not identified.

Teixeira de Mendonça expected to obtain additional help in this area from an Imbangala chief who had fled from his original lands north of the Kuvo to the southern bank of the river after a dispute with other Imbangala. This chief, Muni dya Ngombe, had good reasons for seeking an alliance with the Portuguese, since he hoped to secure their aid in a planned return across the Kuvo to take revenge on his enemies. Muni dya Ngombe had therefore promised to help the Portuguese cross the river and subdue the lands between there and Massangano, which he accurately pictured as filled with potentially hostile Imbangala. His scheme fit the pattern of friendly Portuguese–Imbangala relations which Cerveira Pereira and others on the Portuguese side had pioneered, and which Teixeira de Mendonça had already witnessed in Benguela. The Portuguese plan to relieve Massangano depended, as had so many others of their designs, on Imbangala co-operation. The co-operation of these mercenaries loomed important enough in the minds of these commanders to out-weigh the other disadvantages of their chosen strategy.

Although this joint Portuguese–Imbangala project began auspici-ously, the enemy Imbangala once again demonstrated their ability to regroup in the friendly territory south of the Kwanza and in the end overwhelmed the united forces of the relief expedition. The men of Muni dya Ngombe and Nzamba constructed a bridge across the Kuvo as agreed and when they completed it the combined Portu-guese, Sumbi, and Imbangala force began the trip northward towards Massangano. They conducted an initial victorious campaign against Imbangala chiefs who opposed, as predicted, their advance to the north bank of the river. Then they marched in the direction of Massangano until they encountered a second group of Imbangala, veterans of the *kulembe*'s battles against Gomes de Moraes in the previous year. These Imbangala, drawing on the experience gained in earlier confrontations with the Portuguese, joined those defeated near the Kuvo, massed their joined forces in a stone fortress facing a river, and administered a crushing defeat to the Portuguese. Muni dya Ngombe's Imbangala deserted at the first sign of the impending loss and left the Portuguese to fight the battle alone; 103 out of 106 Portuguese died.[114]

Only later in the 1670s did the Imbangala of the *kulembe* recognize the advantages to be derived from participation in the European slave trade. They began to seek contact with the Portuguese for purposes of limited commerce during that decade. These arrange-

[114] Relação da viagem de Sotomaior; Brásio (1952–71), ix. 374.

ments began when an Imbangala chief called Kasambe attacked the Sumbi ruler of the Kikombo region.[115] A port had developed near the mouth of the river where Portuguese ships took on ivory and slaves obtained from the peoples who lived upriver. The Sumbi near the coast had established themselves as middlemen in this trade between the *kulembe*'s Imbangala, who up to that time had remained in the interior, and the Portuguese who stayed near the coast. Kasambe's attack indicated that the *kulembe*'s people had ended their aversion to direct commercial contacts with the Portuguese and now desired to capitalize on the opportunities offered by the trade in slaves. They therefore wished to bypass the obstacle represented by the middlemen Sumbi of the Kikombo. The Sumbi chief resisted the Imbangala attempt to eliminate his position in the trade and also defeated a Portuguese expedition commanded by Gaspar de Almeida, thus preserving for the time being the established commercial pattern and his own profits.[116]

Other Imbangala who lived near Libolo, the only Mbundu regions south of the Kwanza, at first fought the Portuguese with a determination equal to that of the others on that side of the river. But they seemed unable to maintain their opposition whenever they entered the regions inhabited by Mbundu. Descending from their homes in the Ovimbundu region known as Tunda,[117] they destroyed crops and raided Hako and Libolo chiefs who had declared their loyalty to the Portuguese at least since the 1620s, perhaps out of fear of their warlike southern neighbours. The Tunda Imbangala apparently gained control of the area shortly after 1620 and seriously damaged Portuguese interests by disrupting the slave trade which ran north through Cambambe to the Portuguese posts just beyond the Kwanza. The bishop Mascarenhas, interim governor of Angola in 1623–4, sent an expedition under Lopo Soares Laço to bring the Libolo border with

[115] His name was spelled 'Cacabe' or 'Caçabe'; Kasambe is the most likely reconstruction. At some earlier date, the Portuguese had come into conflict with Kasambe and had defeated him. Cadornega (1940–2), i. 365, mentioned a German active in Angola who was known as 'Casabe' because he had fought and beaten a 'Jaga' of that name somewhere south of Libolo.

[116] Cadornega (1940–2), ii. 291–4. Although the Imbangala of the *kulembe* influenced the customs and institutions of several of the later Ovimbundu kingdoms, they established permanent dynasties in only one or two instances, probably Ciyaka and Wambo; Childs (1940, p. 188; 1964, p. 374).

[117] For the location of Tunda, see Relação da Costa de Angola e Congo; Brásio (1952–71), viii. 121; and Bispo D. Simão Mascarenhas to el-Rei, 3 Feb. 1624; Brásio (1952–71), vii. 199–203. I have followed Brásio's interpretation of the extremely difficult script of this document (cf. Delgado's reading in Cadornega (1940–2), i. 113, n. 1).

Tunda back under Portuguese authority. Lopo Soares Laço fought against the Imbangala chief, Nzenza a Ngombe, defeated him, and captured others, among them one called 'Bango-bango'.[118]

This victory temporarily brought the Imbangala and Portuguese together in common opposition to the local chiefs, on the model of the Imbangala north of the river at about the same time. The local Hako and Libolo, like the Mbundu on the other side of the Kwanza, but unlike the Ovimbundu to the south, consistently opposed whichever outside invader, Portuguese or Imbangala, posed the greater immediate threat to their autonomy. They had initially allied themselves to the Europeans out of fear of Nzenza a Ngombe, but when Nzenza a Ngombe's defeat tipped the balance of power locally in favour of the Portuguese, the local chiefs immediately switched sides and began to follow the leadership of Kafushi ka Mbari in resistance to the Portuguese. Fernão de Sousa, the next governor in Angola, completed the cycle of political realignments by employing his former enemy, Nzenza a Ngombe, to bring Kafushi ka Mbari and his rebellious allies back to the side of the Portuguese.[119] This strategy enabled de Sousa to control the region without great expense at a time when Dutch threats to Luanda demanded the concentration of all Portuguese forces near the coast. From the Imbangala point of view, alliance with the Portuguese gave them security in the midst of Mbundu lineages hostile to the *kilombo* and protected them from the growing power of the descent groups who had rallied behind Kafushi ka Mbari.

The later history of 'Bango-bango', who had been captured in 1624, underlined the contrast between Imbangala hostility on the south side of the Kwanza and co-operation on the north bank of the river. 'Bango-bango' settled north of the Kwanza in Ilamba and gave up the Imbangala way of life to become a loyal *kilamba*, or captain of the African auxiliaries who fought in Portuguese armies.[120] He, like

[118] Bispo D. Simão Mascarenhas to el-Rei, 3 Feb. 1624; Brásio (1952–71), vii, 199–203. The document does not make it clear whether Laço fought with or against Nzenza a Ngombe. Silva Correa (1937), i. 238, and Feo Cardoso de Castello Branco e Torres (1825), p. 164, specify that he opposed Nzenza a Ngombe and defeated him. Delgado in Cadornega (1940–2), i. 113, n. 1, added an Imbangala chief 'Cazanga' among those defeated; this seems to be an error, as the document reads 'Caça . . .' and probably refers to Kaza, then in disrepute among the Portuguese (p. 219 below).

[119] Fernão de Sousa to el-Rei, 22 Aug. 1625; A.H.U., Angola, cx. 2, and Ajuda, 51–VIII–30, fols, 321–321ᵛ; Brásio (1952–71), vii. 359–68.

[120] Technically, any African authority who received lands within Portuguese territory by grant from the governor rather than by hereditary right (the term contrasted with that of *soba*, which designated indigenous title-holders); most

the *kabuku ka ndonga*, and the *kalandula*, gave loyal service to the governors of Angola for many years, notably against the Dutch in the 1640s. He feigned desertion to the Dutch in 1641 and caused them considerable damage before escaping back to the Portuguese. The king of Portugal later repaid his services with a *mercê* of the Order of Christ; the former Imbangala 'Bangobango' accepted Christian baptism as João Bango on that occasion.[121] His movement to the north side of the Kwanza had deprived him of the local support on which the southern Imbangala depended; this converted him to a supporter of Portuguese advances against the Mbundu.

The movements of the *kaza*, a title originally subordinate to the *hango* of Libolo, illustrate the security which Imbangala chiefs found south of the Kwanza. The *kaza ka hango*, a perpetual title granted to Mbundu lineages near the former centre of Libolo, belonged to people living somewhere opposite the Portuguese post at Cambambe.[122] The holders of this title had adopted the *kilombo* and become quite powerful in their own right before 1620, when the Portuguese respected them as some of the more important Imbangala chiefs of that region. A *kaza ka hango* joined the Portuguese during the period of their military successes in the company of the *kulashingo*, crossing the Kwanza to fight near Massangano on the side of a Portuguese army under captain Luis Gomes Machado. The Imbangala king then refused to co-operate further, or 'rebelled' in Portuguese terms, and settled his people in Ndongo. Another Portuguese military expedition drove the *kaza ka hango* out of Ndongo in 1621, showing that even the most powerful Imbangala bands had difficulty resisting the Portuguese outside their home territory.[123]

---

[121] Cadornega (1940–2), i. 237–8, 247–8, 463, 514. A subordinate position, Malange a Bangobango, also existed; A.H.A., Códice D-20-1, fol. 133ᵛ; published in Dr. Carlos Dias de Coimbra (1953) and in Brásio (1952–71), x. 59–62. Bangobango himself had aided the Portuguese cause in Angola for some thirty years (i.e. since about 1620) and his 'family' tradition of service was said to date from the time of Paulo Dias de Novaes (1575?), long before the other Imbangala had reached the coast. The other data available on Bangobango show that such effusive praise exaggerated the true facts.

[122] Relação da Costa de Angola e Congo; Brásio (1952–71), viii. 121.

[123] Cadornega (1940–2), i. 88–94; also Pᵒ Mateus Cardoso, 16 Mar. 1621; B.N.L., Cx. 29, doc. 26; published in Brásio (1952–71), vi. 566–9. cardosa helps establish the date by mentioning that the governor had been absent in the interior pursuing a long series of wars.

---

yilamba fought with the Portuguese in exchange for their lands. The arrangement amounted to a Portuguese version of the *vunga*.

The *kaza* fled back to the south side of the Kwanza and used the firm basis of support he commanded there to take his revenge throughout the 1620s. He first aided the *ngola a kiluanje* Mbande a Ngola when he opposed Portuguese penetration of Ndongo and then sided with the queen Nzinga in political manoeuvering after his death. As part of his policy of alliance with Ndongo kings, the *kaza* had agreed to protect Mbande a Ngola's 'son' (a title-holder?) and heir to the *njola a kiluanje* title from capture by the Europeans. After Nzinga replaced Mbande a Ngola, however, the *kaza* handed this 'son' over to Nzinga, thus permitting her an opportunity to have him assassinated in a bit of treachery highlighted in most Portuguese accounts of Nzinga's rise to power. From the *kaza*'s point of view, his decision to turn over his hostage to Nzinga maintained a consistent policy of support for whichever incumbent *ngola a kiluanje* seemed likely to use the position to oppose the Portuguese. The *kaza* remained in Ndongo only as long as Nzinga seemed capable of holding off the Europeans, however, for a Portuguese victory in 1626 once again sent him in flight to the other side of the Kwanza. He at first sent word from there that he wished to make his peace with the Europeans, once and for all,[124] but then broke all contact with the Portuguese shortly after 1630. Imbangala traditions show that he moved to the Baixa de Cassanje where he played an important part in founding the state of Kasanje.

Finally, one aspect of Nzinga's behaviour during the 1620s confirms the tendency of Imbangala kings to flee south of the Kwanza in time of distress. She had supplemented her position as *ngola a kiluanje* with a symbolic marriage to the *kaza*[125] which gave her the position of *tembanza* (first wife) of the *kilombo* chief. This crucial Imbangala office, heir to the functions attributed to the 'Temba Andumba' of the traditions, entailed preparation of the *maji a samba* and enabled Nzinga to assert leadership over the remnants of the *kulashingo*'s Imbangala after they dispersed in about 1619. Her claim to this position also explains the strong influence which she seems to have exerted over the *kalandula* and the *kabuku ka ndonga* from time to time during the 1640s and 1650s.

Her alliance with the Imbangala also served a strategic purpose by providing her with a safe refuge near the southern Imbangala on the

---

[124] Cadornega (1940–2), i. 142; also Relação do Governador de Angola, *c.* 1627–8; Ajuda, 51-VIII-30, fols. 247–60ᵛ; published in Brásio (1952–71), vii. 526–7.
[125] Cavazzi (1965), i. 259, and ii. 70–2.

Kwanza river islands of Kindonga whenever Portuguese pressure drove her out of her redoubts north of the river.[126] She retreated to these areas in and beyond the Kwanza several times during the 1620s and also fled at least once (in 1629) towards the Imbangala of *kulashingo*, then already settled in the Baixa de Cassanje.[127] Nzinga moved north to the ancient kingdom of Matamba only after her strategy of taking refuge among various Imbangala groups had failed to protect her position in Ndongo.

Conclusions

The history of the Imbangala contacts with the Portuguese provides by far the best-documented example of state-formation among the Mbundu. Imbangala mercenary armies formed the backbone of the Portuguese expeditions which put Ndongo on the defensive and then replaced Mbande a Ngola with puppet *ngola a kiluanje* in Pungo Andongo, leaving Nzinga free to make a claim to possession of the title from her new base in Matamba. Some of the *makota* who left Kulashingo created new states as a defence line protecting the Portuguese against hostile kingdoms to the north and east. A major Imbangala state arose in Kasanje which, with Matamba, became the major supplier of slaves for the trade which supported the Portuguese state in Angola until the middle of the nineteenth century. All the kingdoms which emerged from the ashes of the Angolan wars, Angola itself, Kalandula, Kabuku, the later kings of Jinga, Kasanje, Holo, and *mwa* Ndonje (as well as several Ovimbundu kingdoms south of the Kwanza) owed their origins to the rulers of the *kilombo*. These became the dominant states of eighteenth-century Angola, completely replacing the earlier kingdoms of Ndongo, Libolo, and Kulembe.

Both Portuguese and Imbangala represented similar challenges of major proportions when viewed from the perspective of the Mbundu kinsmen, whose ancestors had preserved the autonomy of their descent groups against such diverse threats as *mavunga* title-holders

[126] Fernão de Sousa to Francisco de Castro, 8 Apr. 1628; Ajuda, 51-VIII-31, fol. 171ᵛ; published in Brásio (1952–71), vii. 549–50; also Relação do Governador de Angola; Brásio (1952–71), vii. 526–7.
[127] Cadornega (1940–2), i. 165–6. Cadornega's description of the battle between Nzinga and the Portuguese leaves no doubt that it occurred in the region of the Lambo highland. Nzinga retreated down the trade route that led to Yongo, where the *kulashingo* had settled, descended the escarpment of Katanya near the capital of the *ndula kisua*, crossed the Baixa de Kafushi, and ascended the rocky spur of Kabatukila on her way back to the islands of Kindonga.

from Libolo and the centralizing kingdom of the *ngola a kiluanje*. Neither of the new invaders had lineages of the type which the Mbundu regarded as fundamental to human society. Both came as aliens from far outside Mbundu territories. Neither derived their living from agriculture, as did the Mbundu, and both stole or traded for the produce of local farmers.

The Portuguese and Imbangala perceived their common interests, at least in terms of economic and military expediency, if not in full appreciation of their more subtle similarities in the eyes of the Mbundu. They joined forces to establish a new set of slave-trading states which in the most fundamental sense differed relatively little in their impact on the Mbundu, whether they were run by Europeans, as was Angola, or by Africans, as were all the rest. The precarious positions of both parties north of the Kwanza kept them in a firm alliance against the subversive desires of the Mbundu lineages.

The Imbangala south of the river provided the test case which validates this hypothesis, since the *kilombo* there thrived in the more suitable social institutions of the Ovimbundu. Although we cannot yet analyse in detail how Ovimbundu social structures tolerated the *kilombo* in a way that the Mbundu descent groups did not, most Imbangala there found local supporters who enabled them to maintain a stand-offish, if not hostile, attitude to the Portuguese until the end of the seventeenth century and later. These facts suggest that the point would reward further investigation.

Finally, the role of the Imbangala in the Portuguese 'conquest' of Angola helps to explain some of the major features of European history in this part of Africa during the seventeenth century. The strengths and drawbacks of the Imbangala political structures and the relationship of the Imbangala to the Mbundu and Ovimbundu populations on either side of the Kwanza illuminate much of the history of the Angolan wars, both against African kings and against European rivals. The Imbangala gave Portuguese armies their first consistent successes against the Mbundu in the decade after 1610. The warriors of the *kilombo* made possible the increase in the slave trade which converted the colony of Angola from a backwater of the Kongo into an area of major Portuguese economic and political interest. Opportunities to fight at the side of Imbangala armies influenced such specific strategic decisions as the location of the fort at Ambaca and the landing of the 1845 mission sent to relieve Massangano. The Imbangala not only enabled Portuguese officials to initiate large-scale wars designed to capture people for the legal slave trade but also encouraged the development of smuggling which attracted the Dutch and others to the coast north of Luanda. Imbangala mercenary states protected the frontiers which finally emerged from the conflicts of the early decades of that century.

CHAPTER VIII

Institutionalizing Political Innovation

The later history of the Lunda title-holders who headed the *kilombo* war camps brings into clear focus a theme which underlies the entire course of Mbundu political history: the contrast between the evident inventiveness of aspiring political authorities, who created numerous new titles and emblems of power in their search for political hegemony, and the infrequency of successful innovations which spread widely enough and lasted long enough to merit the designation of a 'state'. The Imbangala bands, for example, had stopped and settled briefly in several locations—even from imperfect documents and oral traditions, we know of several places among the Songo, others near the Atlantic coast as Kalanda ka Imbe's *kilombo* worked its way north, and again under the *kulashingo* in conjunction with the Portuguese north of the Kwanza. Yet none of these pauses lasted long enough to fit our largely intuitive definition of a 'kingdom'. On the other hand, several holders of related Lunda positions—the *kabuku ka ndonga*, the *kalandula*, the Kasanje *kinguri*, and others—established permanent political structures on the fringes of Portuguese Angola which have become accepted as important 'states' in the period after 1650. The same contrast between frequent innovation and uncommon permanency recurs in the earlier history of the *kinguri* title, when at least three incipient kingdoms existed briefly among the Cokwe east of the Kwango.

The northern Imbangala kings managed to impose themselves as permanent rulers of the Mbundu lineages in part through their celebrated alliance with the Portuguese, as the differences between their history and that of their counterparts south of the Kwanza demonstrate. But even as northern Imbangala rulers fought for Portuguese governors and traded with European merchants, they also struggled to survive by abandoning the most distinctive aspects of the *kilombo* and adopting local Mbundu ideas and practices. In the end, the Imbangala kings survived as rulers of the Mbundu only by trading the alien political institutions, which had originally enabled them to effect the revolution in Mbundu politics described in the preceding chapter, for local ideas, institutions, and symbols. The history of the Imbangala *kilombo*, therefore, paralleled (in so far as the available evidence allows comparison) the history of the *ngola*, which had originally been integrated into the Mbundu system of descent groups-before it flowered briefly as an instrument of centralization in the *ngola a kiluanje* kingdom and then yielded again to the parochial machinations of lineages within the state. The *mavunga*, which first reached the Mbundu as agents of the distant Libolo kings, had undergone the same transformation as descent groups converted them to little more than local lineage titles by the beginning of the seventeenth century.

The histories of all major Mbundu states in the period before 1650 emphasize that the critical step in the process of state-formation was not the invention of techniques capable of expanding political scale or increasing centralization; it lay instead in the transition from an ephemeral cross-cutting structure to a more permanent political state able to impose some sort of subservience on the Mbundu lineages. In short, the institutionalization of political innovation constituted the key problem for would-be kings who faced a social environment dominated by strong kin groups. Since relatively scanty information on the earlier Mbundu states precludes detailed examination of this problem in connection with the *ngola* and the *vunga*, this point has been left for examination in terms of the Imbangala *kilombo*, for which ample documentation exists.

The major Imbangala political institutions clearly changed rapidly during the first fifty years of their history among the Mbundu, dropping or modifying most of the alien elements in their heterogeneous structure and retaining only the Lunda titles which had come from a background most similar to that of the Mbundu social structures of which they became a part. Many aspects of the original *kilombo* were thus lost. The contrast between the fate of the *kilombo* among the Mbundu and its history in its native area south of the Kwanza, where it underwent far fewer modifications, once again proved that state-formation was to be understood at least as much in terms of the environment in which it occurred as in the nature of the political institutions themselves.

Kin and Non-kin

One of the key innovations which gave the Imbangala *kilombo* its overwhelming military superiority in relation to the Mbundu was the absence of particularizing and divisive lineages of a type which had historically retarded the expansion of political and social scale among

the Mbundu. Evidence from a variety of sources supports the hypothesis that the Imbangala bands reached Angola without descent
groups.[1] Nineteenth- and twentieth-century traditions collected from
descendants of the Imbangala indicate that lineages disappeared
when the *kinguri* abolished kinship among his followers before they
had reached the Kwango river.[2] Seventeenth-century Europeans
repeatedly emphasized such superficially bizarre Imbangala laws as
those prohibiting the birth of children. These laws, clearly among the
most important *yijila* laws of the *kilombo*, effectively denied the
procreative function of women and, because the mother–child
relationship formed the crucial kinship link in the matrilineal social
systems of central Africa, eliminated kinship within the *kilombo*.

It is not necessary to accept the often exaggerated European stories
of sexual abstinence, infanticide, and the abandonment of children in
the bush to understand how these *yijila* produced the intended effect
of suppressing descent as an element of social structure among the
Imbangala. Births continued to occur in practice, and many children
survived the formal proscriptions against their presence, but the
yijila declared all such infants illegitimate in Imbangala terms and
absolutely denied them social status within the *kilombo*. Some infanticide may have taken place as a result of the low prestige of these
children but, contrary to the claims of horrified and often gullible
seventeenth-century missionaries, by no means all Imbangala infants
died from exposure. Illegally pregnant women could circumvent the
letter of the *yijila*, which specified that no children could be born
inside the *kilombo*, by temporarily leaving the confines of the walled
encampment to give birth, thus placing their infants outside the
formal community of the warrior initiation society. Children born
within the sacred enclosure, on the other hand, caused great alarm
among the Imbangala since they violated the ritual purity of the
place, and in such cases the Imbangala killed both mother and child
in order to destroy the incipient matrilineage created by the birth.[3]

[1] All indirect, but conclusive when considered together. The nature of the
available sources readily explains why direct confirmation could not be expected
from them. Seventeenth-century Europeans possessed only the limited ethnographic insights of their time and could not have described the unique characteristics of Imbangala social and political organization in modern technical
terminology. Nor could the Mbundu genealogies preserve a record of this
aspect of Mbundu history since they trace only lineage and political titles of the
sort that the Imbangala abolished.
[2] See Chapter V.
[3] Cavazzi (1965), i. 181. Cavazzi, like most Europeans, mistakenly interpreted
the *yijila* literally to mean that they permitted no births at all.

The Imbangala also refused to acknowledge the significance of birth as a mode of structuring society by denying the fertility of their females. One way in which they expressed this idea was to attempt to banish the fact of menstruation, the most obvious symbol of female fertility. They claimed, for example, that the appearance of a menstruating woman during preparations for important enterprises could doom their prospects for success.[4] Since many central African peoples excluded menstruating women from participation in specifically male activities, this practice alone did not distinguish the Imbangala from other societies with lineages. But the Imbangala developed the general belief to extremes generally not found among their neighbours; according to the seventeenth-century traditions, 'Temba Andumba's' warriors would give up the battle and surrender to their enemies if one of their women began to menstruate during a military campaign. Even the potential kinship represented by a menstruating woman evidently contaminated the lineageless environment of the *kilombo*.

Most Imbangala ceremonies carried out this ideology by prohibiting the attendance of any female whatsoever. The Imbangala allegedly observed this proscription so literally that they refused to eat female flesh in rites involving cannibalism. Later in the seventeenth century, even after the Imbangala had adopted many Mbundu descent group ceremonies unrelated to the original *kilombo*, they still did not use the flesh of women for sacrifices to the lineage ancestors. They had also reintroduced female fertility ceremonies, but never performed them within the walls of the *kilombo*.[5] Among the Ovimbundu, where the practices of the *kilombo* survived somewhat longer than they did among the Mbundu, the Bihe *kilombo* excluded all women from its rituals as late as the 1840s.[6] Imbangala 'adulterers', that is, warriors apprehended in intimate contact with any woman, had to pay much higher fines than such offenders among the neighbouring peoples with lineages; a seventeenth-century Kimbangala suffered death, and Europeans who violated Imbangala females had to pay goods amounting to the value of a slave, a fine equivalent to the life taken from one of their own men.[7] These rules against illicit sexual intercourse enforced the prohibition against procreation on males as well as on women and had the effect of discouraging the development of lineages within an Imbangala band.

Proof that the Imbangala consciously intended their anti-female

<hr>

[4] Ibid., i. 183.
[6] Magyar (1859), pp. 275, 312–13.
[5] Ibid.
[7] Cadornega (1940–2), iii. 269.

prohibitions only to abolish lineages and had no rule against the presence of women generally lies in the fact they excluded only their procreative role and depended on women for certain other purposes. The Imbangala welcomed women as long as they remained outside of the *kilombo* and did not affect the lineageless social structure of the band. They had no recorded objections to the ritual and economic functions of their women, for example, since Imbangala armies always included a great many female camp-followers, wives, and slaves.[8] In their ritual cycle, Imbangala warriors depended on the *tembanza*, wife of the leader of the *kilombo*, for preparation of the *maji a samba* which conferred invulnerability on them. Women performed important duties in ceremonies which Imbangala title-holders and war leaders conducted before every important battle.[9] On these occasions, they had ritual intercourse with their wives, and their ability to consummate the sexual act demonstrated their firm command of the supernatural powers attributed to their office. Ritual intercourse thus acted as an omen which foretold the outcome of the impending battle; successful copulation guaranteed that the Imbangala would win.

The Imbangala king's chief wife participated in a complementary ritual held after the battle which symbolically reaffirmed the people's loyalty to their chief. She accepted the heart or brain of a slain enemy from the leader of the war camp and ate it in a public ceremony. If she became nauseated or could not eat it, the Imbangala assumed that she had been sexually unfaithful during her mate's absence and put her to death.[10]

Ritual intercourse of this type had a primarily symbolic function

---

[8] Cavazzi (1965), i. 219.

[9] Ibid., i. 183, 185. The distinction between the customs of the *kilombo*, which excluded women (except for the *tembanza*) and came from the Ovimbundu, and the Lunda origins of most northern Imbangala kings' titles explains why females had significant ritual roles in association with these rulers. The rituals attached to the Lunda positions symbolized the submissive 'female' role of the people in opposition to the 'male' dominance of the chief and matched the symbolic role of female figures evident in Mbundu *musendo* dating at least from the sixteenth century.

The correspondence of the Imbangala *tembanza* to the Mbukushu *mambanje* (pp. 164–5 above) suggests that the Imbangala probably used the children of these unions in the preparation of the *maji a samba*. This story of 'Temba-Ndumba', who killed her own child to make the first *maji a samba*, makes this point explicitly.

[10] Cavazzi (1965), i. 185. This ceremony recalls the 'ritual meal' of Kulembe and 'Temba Andumba' described in the seventeenth-century narrative on the origins of the *kilombo*.

and did not give rise to lineages. It could thus exist in the *kilombo* despite the ban against kinship in Imbangala society. Despite the superficially exotic appearance of this ritual, its structure conformed closely to oath-taking ceremonies found everywhere in central Africa and the resemblances allow some inferences about the significance of the ceremony. In the analogous Mbundu 'poison oath', a *kimbanda* diviner who specialized in administering the oath gave a drink containing a poisonous substance to a person accused of a crime. The Mbundu believed that spiritual forces under the control of the *kimbanda* revealed the guilt or innocence of the individual through the drink, killing the guilty and sparing the innocent. The Imbangala merely substituted human flesh for the beverage used by others. Since the health of the Imbangala chief's wife symbolized the spiritual health and unity of his people, sexual unfaithfulness revealed faulty loyalty of his people in the political sphere.

The Imbangala extended their efforts to eliminate lineage structures by abolishing circumcision, a genital mutilation which, among other central African groups, functioned as the male equivalent of rites intended to guarantee female procreativity. The Mbundu regarded circumcision as the main prerequisite to the attainment of adult male status in their society.[11] Only adult males, that is, circumcised men, could marry and thus provide legitimate heirs for their wives' lineages. Circumcision guaranteed the fertility of males, just as corresponding lineage ceremonies protected the fecundity of females. Babies born of an uncircumcised male, the Mbundu therefore assumed, could have issued only from witchcraft or from sorcery, and since such children could bring great harm to their lineages, few Mbundu women willingly engaged in sexual intercourse with uncircumcised men. In Mbundu terms the Imbangala abolition of circumcision ceremonies had the same effect as the prevention of their women from bearing children: it eliminated the possibility of legitimate offspring and, hence, of lineages.

Although the amateur ethnographers of the early seventeenth century noted neither the presence nor the absence of circumcision, it almost certainly existed among non-Imbangala at that time. Observers first mentioned it as generally characteristic of the peoples

[11] Although these reconstructed seventeenth-century beliefs are inferences projected back in time from interviews conducted in 1969, the close connection of these customs with the lineage genealogies known to survive from the sixteenth century (and earlier) justify the attribution of these ideas back at least to the period under consideration.

of northern Angola in about 1690.[12] The intimate relationship of circumcision to the basic Mbundu lineage structure, to their marriage customs, and to beliefs about fertility, however, suggests that they practiced it long before the Imbangala arrived shortly after 1600.

The nineteenth-century distribution of western Angola groups without circumcision conformed to the pattern of otherwise unrelated descendants of the seventeenth-century Imbangala and suggested that they had been responsible for elimination of the custom when they overspread the region. Except for the modern inhabitants of Kasanje, the most direct Mbundu heirs of the seventeenth-century Imbangala,[13] the modern distribution of peoples without circumcision centres near the probable home of the *kulembe* kings who had originated the *kilombo*. Nineteenth-century travellers generally did not mention circumcision camps among the Ovimbundu, who still have very few except in the southern and southeastern regions least affected by the sixteenth- and seventeenth-century Imbangala.[14] The people of Wambu, who have preserved several aspects of earlier Imbangala social and political structures, had no circumcision at all as late as the mid-nineteenth century.[15] Peoples on both banks of the Ngango river ('Kibala and Libolo') still did not practice circumcision in the 1920s.[16]

The Imbangala oral narratives and genealogies add circumstantial evidence in support of the hypothesis that the Imbangala had abolished lineages and circumcision in their bands. The chapter on the early history of the *kinguri* showed that descent groups probably disappeared before the Lunda and Cokwe in his band had reached the upper Kwango. This hypothesis would explain why the Lunda

[12] Cadornega (1940–2), ii. 260, specified that Mbundu boys underwent circumcision at the end of the seventeenth century at the ages of about six to nine years. The presence of these rites was confirmed for the late eighteenth century in Mattos (1963), p. 337, and 'Noticias do paiz do Quissama . . .' (1844), p. 212. Lopes de Lima (1846), iii. 200–1, appears to have fabricated his statement that the 'Jaga' (meaning the Imbangala) were the only circumcised peoples in Angola. The allegation came in the context of his argument, equally fallacious, that the 'Jaga' had North African, specifically Muslim, antecedents and had introduced the custom of circumcision (closely connected with Islam in the minds of strongly Roman Catholic nineteenth-century Portuguese) to the Kongo and Mbundu. Carneiro (1859–61), pp. 175–6, emphatically corrected Lopes de Lima on this and a number of other points.

[13] Various testimonies of Sousa Calunga; only the Lunda kings of Kasanje, i.e. the incumbents in the explicitly non-Imbangala *kinguri* title, underwent circumcision, and then only at the time of their installation.

[14] Merran McCulloch (1952), p. 44.

[15] Magyar (1859), pp. 159, 162.

[16] Leite de Magalhães (1924), p. 68.

makota adopted the *kilombo*; its proscription of circumcision confirmed the elimination of kinship from their lineageless band. The
abolition of circumcision in turn forced the *makota* to 'murder' the
kinguri title in Mbola na Kasashe since the Lunda rituals of that
position required that its occupant be circumcised, just as all later
incumbents in Kasanje were also circumcised, uniquely among their
Imbangala fellows. The *yijila* of the *kilombo* had come into direct
conflict with rule by a Lunda *tubungu* position, and the triumph of
the *kilombo* required elimination of the *kinguri* title.

Libolo, the seventeenth-century Mbundu name for the kingdom
ruled by the *hango* and connected indirectly with the *kulembe*,
further associates the abolition of circumcision with the regions
where the *kilombo* began. The word *libolo* means foreskin in Kimbundu[17] and indicates that the northern Mbundu derived their name
for this kingdom from its people's most notable physical characteristic in their eyes; it was the state of 'those with foreskins'. Since the
word occurred in the earliest known documents of the sixteenth
century, the linguistic evidence suggests that the kingdom of Libolo,
probably influenced very early in its history by the *kulembe*, had
abolished circumcision before 1600.[18]

The unsettled Imbangala way of life and their need for constant
military preparedness may have contributed to the original decision
to eliminate circumcision. Imbangala bands moved constantly about
the countryside as they exhausted the food supplies in the regions
where they passed. They could therefore rarely pause long enough in
one place to conduct the lengthy ceremonies connected with the
circumcision camp. Since they maintained the *kilombo* in a state of
permanent readiness for war, they could not exempt young men, the
able-bodied warriors of the band, from active military service for the
time needed to complete the months-long seclusion in the bush.[19]

Imbangala attitudes towards women, which denied their procreative
function even while depending on them for other ceremonial and

---

[17] Kilima or Kirima (the name for the Songo lineages once incorporated in
the Libolo kingdom) means an uncircumcised person in Umbundu; Alves
(1951), i. 525. The word apparently does not exist in Kimbundu.

[18] The hypothesis that the Mbundu of Libolo abolished their lineages under
the influence of the *kilombo* explains why these groups at one time lost their
place in the Mbundu aetiological genealogy. (Miller, 1972 unpub., chapter II,
appendix E, pp. 228–39.) Without circumcision, and therefore lacking lineages,
the Libolo descent groups found no place in a genealogy consisting solely of
names symbolizing kin groups.

[19] Similar conditions seem to have prompted the Zulu kings to eliminate
circumcision in times of extreme duress; Glyn Charles Hewson (1970), p. 64.

practical duties, taken together with their elimination of male circumcision, amount to near-conclusive proof that the Imbangala bands which descended on the Mbundu had abandoned the single most important element of Mbundu society, their descent groups. The Imbangala requirements of mobility and military preparedness provided functional reasons which may have impelled them to take these drastic steps. The absence of descent groups implied, however, the need for some equivalent structure which could regulate and coordinate the activities of the large numbers of people found in a *kilombo* located in regions filled with hostile members of Mbundu lineages.

The Kilombo *as a Military Machine*

The Imbangala *kilombo*, in its true sense of an initiation society or warrior fraternity to which all Imbangala males belonged, replaced descent groups with a strongly centralized political structure and intensive military training. The initiation ceremonies which climaxed the introduction of new members into the Imbangala bands made their camp much more than a walled place used for defence; it became a sacred spot associated with military training and weapons, accessible only to initiated male members of the society. The *yijila* served as rules and regulations designed to develop capable and skilled warriors in place of the songs and chants taught in normal circumcision camps. The *maji a samba*, which the first 'Temba Andumba' had created by killing her own daughter and grinding her remains into a mass of blood and flesh, conferred unity and courage on Imbangala soldiers through the belief that it made the members of the *kilombo* invulnerable to harm.

The conscription of new members into the *kilombo* through initiation ceremonies not connected to kinship gave the Imbangala an unlimited capacity to assimilate large numbers of new warriors. Their ability to expand the size of a band without restriction distinguished them from the lineages of the Mbundu, which could grow through reproduction only at a much more limited rate. In order to ensure that new members of the *kilombo* would be young enough to respond to intensive training and could serve efficiently as soldiers, as well as for ideological reasons connected with their denial of kinship, the Imbangala accepted only uncircumcised young males as initiates. This requirement produced the often cited Imbangala tendency to sell or kill all captives other than boys and very young men who had not yet undergone circumcision in their own lineages and who thus qualified for induction into the *kilombo*.[20]

The initiation ceremonies which converted these uncircumcised youths into Imbangala warriors took place inside the *kilombo* walls in front of reliquaries containing bones preserved from the predecessors of the living Imbangala king.[21] The king and his consort, the *tembanza*, guarded these sacred relics while they supervised the rituals of initiation. The Imbangala troops, all properly initiated warriors, assembled before their leader and began by demonstrating their martial skills in a mock battle. The 'mothers'[22] of the young men then brought the candidates from a place outside the *kilombo* where they had remained hidden up to that point. The Imbangala soldiers confronted the initiates at the gates of the enclosure with drawn bows, as if to defend the *kilombo* from attack. But then, instead of assaulting the boys, they touched them lightly on the chest with arrows to signify a ritual slaying, or capture as prisoners of war. On the following night, the soldiers finally annointed the youths' bodies with *maji a samba*, the ointment which the *tembanza* made from human fat, and brought them inside the *kilombo*.[23]

The leaders of the *kilombo* concluded the initiation by performing rites of an unspecified nature to confirm the validity of the initiation ceremony by recourse to the supernatural forces of the *kilombo*.[24] The *kilombo* initiation clearly fit the classic model of *rites de passage* throughout the world which mark an individual's attainment of a new status within his society. In this case, the youths first suffered a ritual death at the hands of the Imbangala warriors, then spent a

[20] The unusually young age (5–9 years) at which the Mbundu were circumcising youths during the 1680s may have been a response to Imbangala kidnappings; initiation at so early an age would have made their youths ineligible to become Imbangala and might have decreased their attractiveness before they were old enough to serve as warriors.

[21] Battell in Ravenstein (1901), p. 32; Cavazzi (1965), i. 182; Cadornega (1940–2), iii. 223.

[22] This reference to 'mothers' may have been symbolic and, in any case, need not have contradicted other evidence that the Imbangala did not recognize the social relationship of motherhood. On the other hand, it may have reflected an adaptation to the Mbundu lineages already re-emerging among some Imbangala by the 1650s.

[23] This procedure paralleled the course of the circumcision camp in Mbundu culture, where boys spent several months concealed in the bush before formally re-entering Mbundu society under the guidance of their mothers in a two-day ceremony. The role of the Imbangala 'mothers' also followed that of the initiates' mothers in the Mbundu rituals.

[24] Cavazzi (1965), i. 181–2, specified that these rituals involved sexual intercourse between the 'mothers' of the initiates and unidentified partners.

night in an intermediate status unrecognized by the *kilombo*, and finally entered the enclosure and the society as newly adult Imbangala warriors.[25]

The crucial phase of the *kilombo* initiation ceremonies, which was believed to confer invulnerability on the new Imbangala warriors, consisted of rubbing *maji a samba* on their bodies. Seventeenth-century traditions explicitly noted that the *maji a samba* had made the legendary 'Temba Andumba' and all her followers invulnerable to harm.[26] The story of the *maji a samba*, although apocryphal in its details like most Mbundu narratives, accurately connected the Imbangala custom of infanticide and its sociological consequence, the elimination of lineages, to their military strength. By associating the Imbangala warriors' alleged invulnerability with the murder of their own children, the traditions metaphorically attributed their military effectiveness to the tightly integrated lineageless social structure of the *kilombo*.

The metaphorical interpretation of *kilombo* rules makes Imbangala customs appear less grotesque than most writers have portrayed them. The Imbangala did not literally 'kill' their children[27] but 'slew' them only in the sense of abolishing their lineage affiliation during the initiation rituals. This step separated them permanently (i.e. 'killed' them) from their relatives and rendered them eligible for conscription into the *kilombo* without the encumbrance of kinship or kinsmen. In a similarly metaphorical vein, the Imbangala forbade women to enter the *kilombo* only in the sense of excluding them from the initiation rites reserved for young male warriors. There were, in fact,

[25] Battell, in Ravenstein (1901), pp. 32–3, noted that the Imbangala marked children with a collar as a stigma but removed it when youths killed their first man; this made them *ngonso*, or initiated warriors. These details probably refer to aspects of the same initiation ceremonies not mentioned in Cavazzi's later description.

[26] Cavazzi (1965), i. 177–8. Battell noted, in Ravenstein (1901), p. 33, that Kalanda ka Imbe's attendants rubbed him with human fat. Although he did not specify the term for this ointment, it was almost certainly the *maji a samba* explained by Cavazzi. Joaquim John Monteiro (1875), ii. 155–7, found that mid-nineteenth-century Ovimbundu living in the interior behind Novo Redondo still anointed the bodies of their chiefs with human fat.

[27] Purchas, in Ravenstein (1901), pp. 84–5, seems to have interpolated this remark into Battell's account, arguing that the Imbangala literally killed their children in order that the infants would not encumber the military operations of the warriors. The rationale is obviously implausible. Cavazzi (1965), i. 227, cited individual cases of abandonment of children, but this did not constitute proof that the Imbangala killed *all* their children since abandonment was a normal means of ridding a community of deformed or 'bewitched' infants in many parts of Africa and Europe.

no Imbangala women at all in a technical sense, since no female could participate in the initiation ceremonies. This left all females accompanying the band with the status of non-Imbangala outsiders.[28]

The custom of 'killing' women who gave birth inside the *kilombo* probably meant in practice that most women lived in houses located outside the walls of the sacred ritual centre. They bore and raised infants there, but these children, even though biologically the sons and daughters of Imbangala males, had no social connection with the *kilombo* society until formally initiated. Open secular towns or camps built around a central sacred place accessible to only a few qualified initiates occurred commonly in Africa. Mbundu circumcision camps and hunters' retreats, although not located in the towns, conformed to the same sociological and physical model. The innermost quarters of chiefs' compounds provided another example of the phenomenon. All constituted secluded retreats where qualified initiates retired to conduct secret rituals.

The *kilombo* initiation endowed Imbangala kings with a monopoly of power and authority never attained by their Mbundu counterparts. The multicentric social structures of the Mbundu included many different types of independent specialized ritual leaders and political title-holders, each wielding limited authority over a defined sphere of activity. Some Mbundu officials had lineage titles responsible for an *ngola*, a *lunga*, or *pemba*, while others held non-lineage positions and ruled through other authority emblems. No single chief's authority comprehended all aspects of Mbundu life. But, since the monolithic Imbangala social structure contained no lineages, no independent officials competed with the kings for an individual's loyalties. All authority became centralized under a single title-holder, and this concentration of power distinguished them from their Mbundu predecessors.[29]

The Imbangala kings' dual competence in both the temporal and supernatural spheres further distinguished them from Mbundu kings like the *ngola a kiluanje* or the *vunga*-holders from Libolo. Mbundu political officials' relations with their subjects extended only to temporal matters and left relations with the supernatural to *yimbanda* diviners and the lineage officials. Imbangala kings, on the other hand,

---

[28] The modern Imbangala of Kasanje still claim that their women are all Songo, Mbondo, Pende, and so on, and that the only true Imbangala are males.

[29] Anonymous *relação* (*c.* 1619) (Cordeiro (1881), v. 10) implied that the unusually comprehensive authority of the Imbangala chiefs distinguished them from other African political authorities known to the author of the document.

assumed the supernatural functions which non-political officials performed for the Mbundu. Among the Imbangala, an absence of mediumistic symbols comparable to the wooden figurines which maintained artificial contact between Mbundu chiefs and their limited supernatural resources clearly distinguished their kings from those of the Mbundu.[30] European observers, who only partially comprehended the differences between the Imbangala kings and Mbundu holders of political titles (the *sobas*, as they were known), used precisely this aspect of their position to distinguish them, noting that the Imbangala chiefs resembled 'priests' more than 'political' officials in the usual sense. On the African side, a nineteenth-century Bihe tradition drew the same contrast quite explicitly by recalling that the Imbangala kings resembled 'priests' more than 'chiefs'.[31] Nearly all seventeenth-century sources implicitly recognized a strong distinction between *soba* and 'Jaga' as they referred to the Imbangala kings.

Lower-ranking Imbangala officials had no independent authority which might detract from the power concentrated in the position of the single titled king. Unlike the Mbundu, who had characteristically organized states through the use of semi-autonomous subordinate perpetual titles controlled by lineages, the Imbangala employed only political officials of the *mavunga* type.[32] They probably brought these positions, such as the *ilunda*, a *mani lombo*, the *ikota*, a *tandala*, and an *ngola a mbole*, from Libolo.[33] The *vunga* titles made all other officials dependent on the Imbangala kings since each ruler could appoint and dismiss incumbents at his own discretion without regard for the claims of other lineages or corporate groups. The *mavunga* represented another fortunate complementarity between the *kinguri*'s lineageless Lunda band and the *kilombo* of the *kulembe*. These titles thus contributed to the absolute discipline which the Imbangala kings imposed on their followers.

The tightly-knit social and political structure of the *kilombo* gave seventeenth-century Imbangala armies a crucial tactical advantage over their Mbundu enemies. Translated into military terms, the

---

[30] Battell in Ravenstein (1901), p. 86.

[31] Magyar (1859), pp. 315–16. The seventeenth-century equivalent of this attitude influenced Cavazzi's description of the Imbangala and led him to refer to them continually as a religious sect and to emphasize the religious aspects of their customs.

[32] See chapter IV for the Libolo *mavunga*.

[33] A full description of these officials and their functions appears in Miller (forthcoming (d)).

unified structure of the Imbangala band created a relatively well-integrated field organization capable of executing disciplined and co-ordinated manoeuvres during major battles. Most Mbundu armies, by contrast, consisted of a loose amalgam of small groups drawn from the lineages subject to whatever king had raised the military force. Each unit of such an army operated under the immediate control of its own hereditary leaders, tactical and ritual, who often had no particular military skills. These, in turn, had no experience in carrying out orders received from the king.[34] Most Mbundu armies, as a result, attained only a fragile over-all unity and achieved minimal co-ordination which left them vulnerable to any enemy who could execute well-planned attacks.

All Imbangala troops received substantial military training during their initiation into the *kilombo* and could respond to directives from the single Imbangala king with a degree of co-ordination unattainable under the conditions present in Mbundu armies. The Imbangala king and his *vunga*-holders, the most prominent of whom acted as war leaders (the *ngola a mbole*), divided Imbangala warriors into squadrons, each under the command of an appointed leader, the *musungo*.[35] These *misungo* held their positions by virtue of demonstrated tactical ability rather than by hereditary right and thus made effective field commanders. Their close association with the king enabled them to follow his directives quickly and accurately.

Perhaps the most important strategic advantage of the *kilombo* was its capacity to co-opt unlimited numbers of alien males without diminishing the cohesiveness of the Imbangala army. Any male, no matter what his ethnic origins or how he came to the Imbangala, became a fully qualified Imbangala warrior by demonstrating his personal ability to fight and by completing the *kilombo* initiation rites. Freed from the need to observe complex and restrictive kinship rules in recruiting new members, the Imbangala quickly built up armies large enough to overwhelm any opponent. Defeat and even capture rarely destroyed the *kilombo*'s ability to resist since its leaders could regenerate their forces by co-opting as many new warriors as they required.[36]

The contribution of training and discipline to Imbangala military superiority became most apparent on the battlefield. Long and

[34] Mattos (1963), p. 247, has an excellent description of such an army, *c.* 1800.

[35] Modern Mbangala retains *musungo*, a personalized form of the same root, meaning an appointed war leader; testimony of Apolo de Matos, 6 Oct. 1969.

[36] Cf. Cerveira Pereira's experiences near Benguela, chapter VII.

continual wars had taught the Imbangala how best to deploy the *misungo* and their squadrons, but the model Imbangala battle plan differed little from those of the Mbundu. One unit, a scouting party called the *pumbo*,[37] ranged ahead of the main army to seek initial contact with the enemy. It tried to locate him in time to allow the main body of Imbangala forces to ready itself for battle before the enemy discovered them. The main Imbangala army moved more slowly and with considerably less mobility than the *pumbo* since it included the women and children of the soldiers, as well as a great deal of non-military baggage. The main Imbangala force differed little from Mbundu armies in this respect. When the *pumbo* reported contact with the enemy, commanders hid the women, children, and baggage in a nearby woods. They then arrayed the warriors in a convenient elevated position and waited for their enemies to attack.[38] The basically defensive Imbangala manoeuvres did not differ significantly from tactics employed by non-Imbangala armies when they adopted a defensive stance.[39]

When the battle finally began, the two opposing hordes clashed in apparent confusion by European standards. Each Imbangala warrior, like his enemies, wore identifying insignia which distinguished friend from foe during the hand-to-hand fighting. The Imbangala in general used the same weapons as the Mbundu: bows and arrows, with or without poison, lances, stabbing spears, hatchets, knives, and so on.[40] Their armaments varied at different times and places, as one Imbangala group or another occasionally developed special techniques based on a particular weapon. Those who fought against the Portuguese in Kisama during the 1640s seem to have made especially effective use of a war hatchet.[41] Another group of Imbangala south of

[37] Miller (forthcoming (d)).

[38] For example, Cordeiro (1881), v. 11, 13.

[39] Few records describe autonomous Imbangala offensive formations other than as parts of a Portuguese army, and so no comparison can be made with the tactics of Mbundu or Kongo armies on the offensive (three assault waves). The records leave the impression that the Imbangala rarely initiated an attack but relied on defensive strategies.

[40] Cavazzi (1965), i. 154, listed all these weapons for the Imbangala and 'Mushikongo' alike, clearly implying that they were not distinguishable in this respect. Battell in Ravenstein (1901), p. 29, listed their weapons as 'bows, arrows, and darts'.

[41] Relação de Viagem de Socorro de Angola de Teixeira de Mendonça e Lopes Sequeira, B.N.M., MS. 8187, fols. 61–65ᵛ; published in Brásio (1952–71), ix. 332–45; Veigas (1923), pp. 13–18; *AA*, sér. II, i. nos. 3–4 (1943–4), 135–44. Compare the hatchet ('casengula') mentioned by Battell in Ravenstein (1901), pp. 32–3.

Kisama introduced a longbow so powerful that an archer had to plant one end on the ground and brace it against his feet in order to draw the bowstring. These Imbangala also employed an arrowhead uniquely shaped in the form of a halberd.[42]

The actual battle between an Imbangala army and its opponents rarely lasted very long,[43] since the superior discipline and execution of the *kilombo* quickly proved decisive. The fighting ended as soon as the first small unit on either side gave way and the mates of the defeated squadron abandoned their resistance and fled in disorder. It was at this point that Imbangala training gave their warriors a crucial advantage over their enemies, since their belief in their own invulnerability and faith in the *maji a samba* instilled a confidence that they could not lose. They tended to fight better than their opponents as a result, and the Mbundu, accepting superior Imbangala performance as proof of their invincibility, had little desire to resist what they regarded as inevitable defeat.

Although the end of the battle decided the direct clash between massed armies, it marked only the beginning of the damage inflicted on the losers. The defeated side lost relatively few soldiers during the hand-to-hand-fighting, but they sustained serious losses as the victorious army pursued the fleeing remnants for days, stealing supplies, kidnapping the women and children who accompanied the troops, killing, and taking as many prisoners as possible for sale as slaves.[44]

The brevity of the actual battle showed that both the Imbangala and their enemies both accepted it as an omen. They regarded the physical combat as only a small part of a much larger war strategy based on supernatural preparedness. During the days and weeks before a battle, the Mbundu conducted rituals which, they believed, could predetermine which army would prevail, arming themselves with the best magical charms available, waiting for omens to indicate the most propitious moment to attack, and cementing their good relations with spiritual forces which could turn the actual battle in their favour. The war leaders who performed these ceremonies thus had already executed their most important duties long before the actual fighting began. The emphasis on magic accounted in part for the lack of attention to more mundane matters such as battlefield discipline. Both sides entered the fray in hopes that their magical

[42] Cadornega (1940–2), ii. 104.
[43] Cavazzi (1965), i. 219.
[44] See descriptions of battles, ibid. i. 154–5, 185, 193, 217–19.

preparations had given them invulnerability or had disarmed their opponents' charms.

At the same time, they feared that they might have overlooked a potentially fatal detail and accepted the possibility that their enemies had discovered charms even more powerful than their own. These doubts explain why the Mbundu fled at the first sign of weakness on either side; they accepted it as a sign that their preparations had failed and that supernatural forces had doomed that army to defeat. The defeated unit's comrades, assuming that further resistance was futile, therefore fled from what they viewed as inevitable defeat. This attitude resembled their approach to divination ceremonies, since they regarded the actual battle as a decisive omen which revealed once and for all which army had justice on its side. Victory turned less on force of arms than on supernatural revelation of truth.

In the area of morale, the Imbangala had an overwhelming advantage which made the crucial difference in a situation where the failure of a single small unit could prove decisive. The *kilombo* rituals kept Imbangala warriors in a state of perpetual supernatural readiness through their strict observance of the *yijila* laws. This explains why they laid such extreme emphasis on constant and exact adherence to the *yijila*; they kept the Imbangala morally and supernaturally fit as well as in a state of disciplined physical prowess. Individual charms carried by each warrior gave additional supernatural assistance. Feathers, horns, bones, animal claws, bird beaks, and body paint, they believed, conferred the strength and invulnerability needed to win wars.[45]

The Mbundu, usually occupied with hunting, agriculture, and lineage affairs, could not keep themselves similarly ready for war. They instead had to perform lengthy and elaborate ceremonies on the occasion of each engagement to bring themselves to the proper degree of preparedness. These required many days of drumming and dancing which gave their opponents advance notice of an impending attack. The Imbangala, on the other hand, could fight Mbundu armies without warning and beat their opponents before they felt prepared to defend themselves. The cumulative effect of all these factors made the Imbangala certain victors in these literal wars of

---

[45] Ibid. i. 219; if this practice served to identify individual Imbangala soldiers in the manner of European armies' emblems and insignia, as Cavazzi supposed, it also was closely connected to the customs of *yibinda* professional hunters who used such charms for protection against supernatural animals.

nerves. Mbundu and Kongo fears of the Imbangala confirmed the importance of their strategic advantages since the mere rumour of their presence was enough to send large armies fleeing in complete disarray.[46]

The Imbangala warcamp itself had less direct military significance than most contemporary observers claimed. It was true that the *kilombo* often took the form of a fortified town surrounded by wooden palisades,[47] but the use of fortified towns probably did not distinguish the Imbangala from their neighbours. Africans everywhere built brush piles and stake palisades around their homesteads and villages as basic means of defence in unsettled times.[48]

These palisades only protected the Imbangala from enemy assaults or provided an offensive base under certain rather limited conditions. The *kilombo* provided an effective means of making war only against opponents too powerful to defeat by outright attack but weak enough not to beseige the *kilombo*. In such cases, the main Imbangala army remained inside the *kilombo* while small squadrons (the *pumbo*?) engaged the enemies in frequent skirmishes. They gradually weakened the opposing army to the point where the main Imbangala army could pierce his defences. When the proper time came, they executed this assault by sending out a diversionary force to attack the town just as if they intended to provoke another small-scale engagement. The main body of Imbangala troops remained hidden in the *kilombo* until their enemies came out into the open and then rushed out to win a quick and decisive victory.[49]

Since the Imbangala did not use the *kilombo* in this fashion against large massed armies of Portuguese or other opponents, the walled palisade was effective only against relatively weak chiefs whose limited resources might permit them to harass the outskirts of an unfortified village but would not allow them to storm a walled refuge. The function of the *kilombo* as a military redoubt, while real enough in some cases, does not alone explain the widespread successes which the Imbangala achieved against large Mbundu, Kongo, and Portuguese armies.

[46] Relação do Bispo do Congo (?) to el-Rei, 7 Sept. 1619; Brásio (1952–71), vi, 375–84; also Fernão de Sousa to el-Rei, 28 Sept. 1624; Brásio (1952–71), vii. 255.

[47] Battell in Ravenstein (1901), p. 20; Cavazzi (1965), i. 191, has a rather schematic drawing of a *kilombo*; the drawing has been reproduced in Kent (1965).

[48] The construction of fortified villages in unsettled regions was often noted by later travellers; it was obviously a very ancient response to danger.

[49] Battell in Ravenstein (1901), pp. 31–2.

Men and Non-Men

The Imbangala north of the Kwanza achieved their overwhelming victories at least in part as a result of their ability to terrify their opponents into submission, sometimes without having to face any serious opposition at all. Their fundamental technique involved the manipulation of symbols and rituals which identified them in the eyes of the Mbundu as supernatural beings, or at least as superhumans.[50] The Imbangala pretensions to non-humanity added to their apparent invincibility by placing them theoretically beyond the range of the material weapons at the disposal of their enemies. The means they used become intelligible through comparing the characteristics which the Mbundu used to classify beings as humans or non-humans[51] with known Imbangala customs.

The Mbundu defined humanity according to the attributes they themselves possessed: sedentary farmers grouped in lineages which collectively controlled specified parcels of land. The three complementary elements of land, lineages, and agriculture made civilized human life possible. Membership in a lineage endowed a living being with the qualities of humanity through the blood which he shared with his kinsmen, the individuals united to him through the females of his *ngundu*. Complex supernatural bonds united each kin group to its lands and integrated the people and territory into a single collectivity. The relationship between land and people meant, for example, that the spirits of deceased lineage members remained part of the living kin group and rested easily only when their bodies lay in the lineage's own lands.

The category of non-humans included all other beings: animals, the spiritual forces of a closely related but invisible supernatural world, and most other people unrelated to the Mbundu.[52] The Mbundu basically regarded non-humans with fear because they, as human beings, had no physical means of controlling the actions of non-humans. Weapons provided effective protection against normal animals and human enemies, but, the Mbundu believed, supernatural

---

[50] M. Crawford Young (1970), pp. 987–90, provides an excellent discussion of the effectiveness of magic as a tactic in the 1964 Congo rebellions. He stresses that 'magical' techniques can work only when the enemy believes in them.

[51] This discussion, like that dealing with Mbundu beliefs about circumcision, derives from Mbundu attitudes expressed in 1969. The same logic justifies its extension to their seventeenth-century ancestors.

[52] Cf. Middleton's discussion of similar attitudes (1965).

beings invulnerable to arrows and knives often disguised themselves in the bodies of men or beasts. Since no visible marks distinguished these supernatural beings, they presented special difficulties for the Mbundu who consequently took special precautions to protect themselves from unidentifiable but potentially dangerous strangers or supernatural beasts. These precautions took the form of rituals performed by such magical specialists as the *yibinda* master hunters or by lineage officials.

No human being could survive outside the protective shield which these rituals established around the Mbundu lineages. Kinsmen had to act, for example, with one eye constantly cocked towards the spirits of their deceased ancestors. Only charms and magic, and the mediation of diviners skilled in communication with non-human beings, enabled them to influence the capricious characters of the supernatural world. The duties of the *lemba dya ngundu* included rituals in which he represented the concerns of the living to the ancestors of the kin group. Each lineage had a *kibinda* master hunter who dealt with non-human beings which appeared in the form of large beasts. The diviners or *yimbanda* communicated with other types of spiritual beings.

Mbundu kings, by contrast, were relatively vulnerable to supernatural dangers since they dealt only with human spheres of activity and ruled primarily through straightforward coercion. Still, political chiefs ruled their primarily temporal domains in part through controlling supernatural forces associated with their titles. They often employed *yimbanda* to fabricate special wooden figures (*yiteka*, singular *kiteka*) which gave a limited ability to ward off the dangers which they saw in the non-human part of the cosmos. Few, however, possessed the skills of the *kibinda* which Lunda and Cokwe positions like the *munjumbo* and the *kulashingo* possessed.

The attention which the Mbundu evidently devoted to protection from the supernatural in all spheres of their lives suggests how susceptible they must have been to Imbangala tactics which deliberately portrayed the warriors of the *kilombo* as the opposites of human beings in as many ways as possible. The Imbangala invaders may have borne a superficial resemblance to normal humans in the eyes of the Mbundu, but Mbundu cosmology made ample allowance for the deceptiveness of physical appearances and, as a result, the Mbundu readily accepted the Imbangala as supernatural beings. Because they had no specialists or techniques to deal with non-humans like the Imbangala, they dreaded the Imbangala even more than they feared other such beings, such as large forest animals or ordinary spirits, which their established magical specialists, lineage officials, and *yibinda* could combat. The Imbangala image of non-humanity thus explains some of the fear with which the Mbundu (and some Europeans[53]) regarded the invaders. In conjunction with tactical superiority and Mbundu beliefs about the function of magic and charms in warfare, this accounts for the effectiveness of the Imbangala against Mbundu kings and their armies.

The Imbangala built their rituals and symbolism of non-humanity on ideas already present in the cultures of western Central Africa, in conformity with a pattern which has appeared at numerous other times and places. Most Central African political authorities made limited use of such imagery to set themselves apart from their subjects by commiting deeds strictly forbidden to normal humans. Ritual incest, murder, and other acts symbolically established a king as something more than human and thus qualified him to rule normal people.[54] They also separated the king from his kinsmen. These beliefs normally did no more than establish the ruler as a neutral arbiter believed to exercise impartial judgement in disputes involving his former lineage or clan, but in the case of the Imbangala they reinforced the absence of kin groups in the Imbangala *kilombo*. African history records a number of other groups who used the symbolism of non-humanity in similar ways to overawe their opposition and to forge tight bonds of unity in the face of hostility (e.g. Mau Mau, Majimaji, the Simba of the Congo in 1964, and so on, to name only recent and well-known examples).

Cannibalism, a favourite means of describing non-human outsiders in cultures all over the world, provided an underlying theme in many of the *yijila* rituals and customs of the *kilombo* which symbolically negated the humanity of the Imbangala. Their use of cannibalism drew on analogies which the Mbundu saw between cannibals and wild beasts or witches, all non-human beings which lived on human flesh. Lions and other large animals obviously attacked and ate humans from time to time. Witches, the Mbundu believed, nourished themselves on the flesh of their victims; they materialized on dark nights and danced slowly around the bodies of their human prey

[53] Mbundu attitudes towards the Imbangala penetrated even to Europeans who knew little of the specific symbolism used by the Imbangala to convey their non-human status to the Mbundu. European sources almost without exception compared the Imbangala to the Devil or to 'savages', the seventeenth-century European antitheses of civilized Christian humanity.

[54] Cf. the Mbukushu king mentioned in chapter VI above.

before devouring them slowly, piece by piece.[55] Cannibalistic rituals thus effectively portrayed the inhumanity of the Imbangala in terms which no Mbundu could fail to perceive.

Contrary to the rumours of Imbangala bloodthirstiness which circulated in seventeenth-century Angola, the warriors of the *kilombo* actually consumed human flesh in only a limited number of rituals, most of which fit familiar models of ceremonies found elsewhere in Africa but without the distinguishing element of cannibalism. The addition of cannibalism converted these ceremonies, performed elsewhere as expressions of humanity, into manifestations of the non-human status of the Imbangala participants. One such ritual, which took place in advance of all battles, tested the courage of Imbangala warriors and the effectiveness of their supernatural charms just before they would be needed. In this ceremony, the Imbangala king, as the foremost warrior in the *kilombo*, killed a youth within the confines of the *kilombo*; the kings' councillors then killed two adults inside the *kilombo* and two more outside the walls. They mixed the flesh of the five[56] human victims with meat from five cattle, five goats, and five dogs killed inside the *kilombo* and the flesh of five more of each species sacrificed outside. The assembled warriors, the king, and his advisers then ate the mixture, and each subordinate chief repeated the entire sequence of killings before leaving the *kilombo* to fight.[57] Successful completion of this series of sacrifices demonstrated the readiness of the chiefs and warriors to defeat their enemies.

A related ceremony, or another part of the same ritual cycle, apparently detected potential cowards before they could endanger their companions through faint-heartedness on the battlefield. Before all important military engagements, a *kimbanda* specialist who had charge of preparing the war charms, built five bonfires in and around the *kilombo*.[58] The *kimbanda* ran a long cord from the main bonfire, which burned in the large open space in front of the king's dwelling, into the surrounding cleared area. The Imbangala warriors then danced around the fire, taking care not to step on the rope which lay on the ground beneath their feet. If any soldier touched the cord, all

---

[55] Testimony of Apolo de Matos, 7 Oct. 1969; compare with Redinha (1958), p. 89.

[56] The number five is quite rare in Central African symbolic systems but reappears in modern Ovimbundu ceremonies accompanying chiefs' burials; Verly (1955), p. 683.

[57] Battell in Ravenstein (1901), p. 34.

[58] The use of the number five may link this ceremony (reported about 1650) with that reported about 1600; both were held immediately before wars.

the others present immediately killed him and ate his body on the spot.[59] The structure of this ceremony resembled divination rituals found elsewhere in central Africa; in this case, the rope represented a medium leading to the supernatural forces symbolized by the fire and theoretically singled out disloyal and faint-hearted warriors before they could betray their comrades on the field of battle.

From the Imbangala point of view, this and other rituals purged their band of any member who might violate the strict *yijila* laws of the *kilombo*. Several reported customs document the seriousness with which the Imbangala took these laws. Later in the seventeenth century, for example, Nzinga's relatively Mbundu-ized Imbangala still sacrificed and ate humans at annual harvest ceremonies adapted from Mbundu rituals, but they consumed only the bodies of persons who had offended the spirits of the *yijila*.[60] According to Imbangala belief, the *maji a samba* conferred invulnerability on the members of the *kilombo* only so long as they complied strictly with the *yijila*. Strict observance of these rules was the psychological key to the behaviour of Imbangala warriors who neither wavered on the battle-field nor, as they believed, died from wounds or disease. The Imbangala therefore assumed that cowards, fallen warriors, and even invalids and elderly people whose imperfect physical condition revealed symptoms of mortality and humanity had broken the *yijila* and forfeited the non-human status conferred by initiation into the *kilombo*. The Imbangala consequently ate their own fallen soldiers and shunned the elderly and the sick in order to purify their war camp.

Cannibalism also resolved several ideological difficulties which the homeless wandering of the Imbangala created for people whose background lay in sedentary agricultural communities. A widespread Central African belief held that the spirits of unburied kinsmen wandered the earth causing illness and death among the living.[61] Moreover, Mbundu standards of proper burial demanded much more than simply placing a body in the ground; the spirit did not rest easily unless it lay in the lands of its own lineage. There the dead person's kinsmen could assume responsibility for both the body and the spirit which lingered near it. Since possession of land occupied by kinsmen gave the only assurance of freedom from troubles caused by these spirits, the Imbangala exposed themselves to the malice of

[59] Cavazzi (1965), i. 200–1.

[60] Ibid. i. 89, 123.

[61] Ibid. i. 212 confirmed this belief for seventeenth-century Mbundu. The same idea appeared in the Cokwe narrative of Kinguri's crossing of the Kwango (van den Byvang (1937), pp. 433–4).

their own dead when they abolished their lineages and abandoned their homes. They could not bury the corpses of their comrades or their enemies and they therefore ate their bodies in the hope of destroying their potentially troublesome spirits.[62]

This hypothesis explains several Imbangala habits noted but misunderstood by contemporary Europeans. Imbangala warriors carefully retrieved the bodies of slain adversaries from the field of battle and brought them to the *kilombo* where they ate the corpses in a communal feast. Some attempted to wound their enemies in special ways to identify which soldier had done the killing. European observers noted that these markings enabled each warrior to claim the body later at the *kilombo*. They presented specified portions of the corpses, such as the heart and head, to their chiefs in recognition of their status as the 'head' or 'heart' of the *kilombo*.[63] The custom of maiming enemies in ways which identified the assailant did not derive from gluttonous desires for human flesh (as critics of the Imbangala charged), but came instead from each warrior's need to tame the spirits of all the opponents he had killed by claiming and eating their bodies. Without lands of their own, the Imbangala could protect themselves against retribution from the spirits of their unburied enemies only in this fashion.

A new Imbangala king and his councillors always sacrificed and ate a human being at his installation as ruler of the *kilombo*.[64] Human sacrifices during a king's initiation (without the consumption of the victim's body) did not distinguish the Imbangala from most other Central African peoples. Such ceremonies occurred widely to demonstrate the ruler's powers of life and death over his people and to set him above other title-holders in his realm. Kings usually took the life of their human sacrifice with a special sacred weapon which symbolized the supernatural forces entrusted to the ruler's hands.[65] Human sacrifices thus tested the chief's control over the spirits behind

[62] The failure to bury fallen comrades carried through the non-kinship ideology of the Imbangala; cf. Horton (1967), p. 68.

[63] Cavazzi (1965), i. 183, 217. Monteiro (1875), ii. 155–7, found the same practice east of Novo Redondo in the nineteenth century.

[64] No seventeenth-century observer recorded the installation of an Imbangala king, but evidence survives in the form of rituals conducted by the Imbangala of Kasanje in the nineteenth century. My field notes generally confirm the descriptions given by Rodrigues Neves (1854) and Salles Ferreira (1854–8). One may also compare the ceremonies described for Bihe by Magyar (1859), pp. 270–7, for the mid-nineteenth century.

[65] In the case of the Imbangala, perhaps the 'casengula' mentioned by Battell in Revanstein (1901), pp. 32–3. Cf. the *munjumbo's mwela* (p. 156 above).

his magical weapon. His victim's death demonstrated these spirits' capacity both to protect and to punish the king's subjects. The Imbangala king and his advisers merely extended this common ceremony to include consumption of a part of the body.

Cannibalism strengthened the discipline of the *kilombo*, since each warrior derived strong encouragement to respect the laws of the band and to resist the temptation to flee from their enemies from his knowledge that violation of the *yijila* meant instant death and the disgrace of being eaten. Even if a coward escaped detection in the preliminary dance around the bonfire, he might still be killed and eaten afterwards if he revealed his loss of courage during the battle. On the theoretical plane, cannibalism purified the *kilombo* by erasing all contaminating physical remains of unworthy comrades. Imbangala and non-Imbangala alike believed that spirits lingered near the bodies they had once inhabited. These spirits could return to plague the living unless the physical remains associated with the spirit were destroyed. Imbangala rituals therefore specified that they had to destroy the entire bodies of such offenders by eating them.[66]

Imbangala and Europeans alike exaggerated the extent of the cannibalism practiced in such ceremonies. Some observers claimed that the Imbangala ate only people and refused to touch the flesh of cattle or goats.[67] Others recorded that the Imbangala ravenously consumed the bodies of all their enemies to relieve their hunger and fed 'chiefly' on human flesh. Even though the list of Imbangala rituals involving the consumption of human flesh probably remains incomplete, the evidence does not support such extreme claims. The Imbangala may have eaten parts of relatively large numbers of human bodies in certain rituals, especially those conducted after large battles, but they habitually lingered in fertile areas (such as 'Calicamba' in Kisama) precisely because they found an abundance of cattle and grain there. They did not raise cattle themselves but they regularly stole from the herds of their neighbours, presumably for meat to eat since no record survives of Imbangala mounted on oxen.[68]

---

[66] Monteiro (1857), ii. 155–7, attributed this practice to unidentified groups living east of Novo Redondo in the nineteenth century (perhaps the Sele, who still possessed a reputation for cannibalism seventy years later; Hambly (1934), p. 120); they lived not far from the places where the *kilombo* originated.

[67] Purchas in Ravenstein (1901), p. 84. Cavazzi (1965), ii. 188, varied the idea by arguing that the Imbangala ate people solely for nourishment.

[68] Battell in Ravenstein (1901), pp. 25, 30. see *parecer* of Francisco Leitão, 4 Dec. 1643; A.G.S., secretarias provinçales, maço 2639; published in Brásio (1952–71), ix, 86–7; also Leite de Faria (1952), p. 240. Leitão stressed that the 'Jaga' (or Imbangala) ate meat other than human flesh, as if to rectify rumours

The Imbangala in fact ate only the bodies of enemies they killed and preferred to capture as many women, men, and children as possible alive to sell as slaves to Europeans or to augment their own numbers. Much of the exaggeration surrounding the extent of Imbangala cannibalism came from European misunderstandings of the idiom in which the Mbundu described the Imbangala. Africans commonly attributed cannibalistic practices to all their enemies, including Europeans, and this habit certainly contributed to the formation of fantastic beliefs about Imbangala cannibalism among those who did not know the situation first-hand. Further sources of confusion lay in the semantic field of the Kimbundu word which included the European meaning of 'to eat'. Unlike European words for 'eating', the corresponding Bantu term had much broader senses which could apply to capture or appropriation of another's possessions for one-self. Enemies thus 'ate' their captives by killing them, enslaving them, or actually consuming parts of their bodies. Chiefs 'ate' the tribute which they received from their people whether it consisted of food-stuffs or of palm cloths and ivory.

From the Mbundu point of view, the Imbangala 'ate' captives they stole from the lineages in the sense that they incorporated individuals into their bands through a ritual death and transformation into non-human beings. This meant that captured Mbundu abandoned their lineage affiliation forever and became lost permanently to their kin groups. In addition, some Africans undoubtedly played on the credulity of the Europeans when fighting against them. On at least one occasion, they brought out 'pots' (probably mortars used for grinding flour) and told the naïve Portuguese that they intended to put all prisoners taken alive into the pots and cook them in order to eat them.[69] Only rare perceptive observers saw how restricted their cannibalism was and pointed out that nearly all peoples in Angola practiced similar customs, though to a more limited degree. One such writer noted the use of cannibalism in Benguela early in the seventeenth century and emphasized that all the groups living there used it in ceremonies for communication with their 'ancestors'.[70]

[69] Brito, 'Rellação breve', in Albuquerque Felner (1931), pp. 17–18.
[70] Cordeiro (1881), v. 18; the author of the anonymous document stated the point as if to correct an erroneous but generally current impression to the contrary.

---

to the contrary then current in Europe. The argument that the Imbangala turned to the consumption of human flesh because their bands grew beyond the capacity of the land to support them will not hold; Battell in Ravenstein (1901), p. 30.

The Imbangala also set themselves apart from normal human beings with distinctive physical markings which supplemented cannibalism as indications of their supernatural status. Nearly all peoples of Angola used certain types of bodily mutilation, especially scarification and chipping or filing of the teeth to signify their humanness and to produce physical distinctions mirroring the cultural and social differences between them.[71] The Mbundu matrilineal kin groups, for example, achieved a sense of community and identity through such techniques. Lineage members, however, never pulled teeth or amputated parts of their own bodies, since they reserved such markings for non-humans (either superhuman, as chiefs, or subhuman, as criminals and slaves). These beliefs allowed the Imbangala symbolically to emphasize their non-humanity by extracting at least the upper two incisor teeth and perhaps the lower incisors as well.[72]

The Mbundu saw dental extraction in particular as significantly different from their own practices of filing or chipping teeth. They pulled teeth only from the jaws of deceased occupants of permanent titles and associated these teeth with access to strong supernatural forces. A dead chief's successors commonly preserved his teeth as a relic which helped them to communicate with his spirit; the exact tooth to be extracted varied from office to office, but in the case of the *kinguri* of Kasanje later Imbangala always removed an upper canine.[73] During the burial rituals of a *kibinda* master hunter, the surviving *yibinda* took an upper molar from their dead colleague's jaw and kept it in a shrine along with other possessions of the dead hunter.[74] Chiefs and *yibinda* both underwent special initiations which placed them outside the lineage structure of the society and gave them a semi-human status not unlike that claimed by the Imbangala. Tooth extraction in Mbundu thought symbolically ran directly counter to dental mutilation and effectively reinforced the image of the Imbangala as non-human beings. It cut across lineage lines, while

[71] Antonio de Almeida (1937).

[72] Battell in Ravenstein (1901), p. 34, noted that the Imbangala extracted four teeth. Cadornega (1940–2), iii. 225, specified the upper incisors and added that the lower incisors were removed only on certain (unspecified) occasions. Cavazzi (1965), ii. 240, mentioned only the upper incisor teeth; he also pointed out (i. 171) that Nzinga's Mbundu-ized Imbangala no longer extracted but merely filed the upper incisors by the middle of the seventeenth century.

[73] Testimony of Sousa Calunga; also R. Verly (1955), pp. 689, 690, for a record of the identical custom in Libolo.

[74] Testimony of Sousa Calunga.

mutilation reinforced them, and applied only to the dead in contrast to the symbolic functions of mutilation which was practised on the living.

Many recorded rituals of the *kilombo* society thus contributed to the Imbangala image of non-humanity by reversing the humanizing functions of normal Mbundu circumcision rites, converting Imbangala initiates from persons into non-human beings. The *maji a samba*, prepared from the bodies of children, symbolically covered the Imbangala warriors with death. Cannibalism equated the Imbangala with witches and supernatural beasts. Proscriptions against births in the *kilombo* denied the most basic biological functions of human beings. The absence of circumcision further underlined the differences between Imbangala and the circumcised Mbundu, and dental extraction completed their connection with the supernatural world. Even if the effects of these practices on the Mbundu cannot be documented directly, they must have contributed to the terror which the Imbangala caused in the ranks of Mbundu armies.

Disappearance of the Kilombo

Ironically, the same quality of alienness which enabled the Imbangala to sweep over most of the Mbundu during the early years of the seventeenth century also made it impossible for the Imbangala to build a permanent state on the basis of the *kilombo* rituals and laws. Thus, although the *kilombo* proved revolutionary in its ability to destroy existing Mbundu political structures, it had already proved to be an ephemeral method of political and social organization by 1650 and played only a small part in forming the permanent Imbangala states among the Mbundu.

The Imbangala kings, on the other hand, made a far more lasting impression, since many of them survived into the twentieth century as rulers of durable Mbundu states. Strict observance of the *yijila* declined rapidly and the Imbangala adopted customs practically indistinguishable from those of the people among whom they settled. Even the modern Imbangala of Kasanje, the most direct Mbundu heirs of Kulashingo and the Lunda *makota*, today retain almost none of the characteristics which distinguished their seventeenth-century forebears.

The assimilation of the Imbangala *kilombo* into the Mbundu lineages may be traced by comparing the unique features of each to show decreasing differences through the seventeenth century.

Increasing similarities between the two would have resulted from Imbangala borrowings from the dominant Mbundu culture and would reveal rapid change in the relatively short span of forty to seventy years. Although it is theoretically difficult to distinguish certain widespread Central African customs which the Imbangala may have brought to Angola and only coincidentally shared with the Mbundu from distinctive Mbundu habits which they borrowed directly from the local population after their arrival north of the Kwanza, some tentative conclusions still emerge from the available data. Several beliefs held by the Imbangala of the later seventeenth century, for example, have such intimate connections with uniquely Mbundu institutions that the Imbangala could only have obtained them after they settled north of the river.

The evidence in support of this point includes a number of words attributed to the Imbangala at different times after 1600. These show a progressively higher proportion of Kimbundu terms later in the century. The Imbangala probably had no distinctive language of their own when they first reached Angola, since the band at that time consisted of a mixture of different peoples co-opted all along the path of the advance of the *kinguri* to the west: perhaps a few remaining Lunda and Cokwe/Lwena, more Songo, many Ovimbundu, and undoubtedly others as well. The earliest recorded 'Imbangala' word-list came from the period before they had crossed the Kwanza river.[75] This limited and inaccurate vocabulary consisted mainly of words in use among the Portuguese sailors all along the western coast of Africa. It included no uniquely Kimbundu words but had one clearly Umbundu term (*imbangala*). Wordlists from the middle of the seventeenth century, some fifty years later, show a mixture of Kikongo-Portuguese terminology, Kimbundu words, and Umbundu. These reflected a stage in the evolution of the Imbangala vocabulary (and culture) after it had begun to evolve under the influence of contact with Europeans who spoke Kikongo and Portuguese and with African speakers of Kimbundu. By the end of the century, however, several terms noted earlier in other languages had shifted to their Kimbundu equivalents (*mani lumbu* to *mwene lumbu*, *ilunda* to *kahu*, and so on).[76] The basic vocabulary of the modern Imbangala represents the final phase of the modification of the dialect in the direction of Kimbundu and exhibits no significant differences from other eastern Kimbundu dialects except for a reported vague resem-

[75] Battell in Ravenstein (1901).
[76] Detailed analysis in Miller (forthcoming (d)).

blance to the Libolo dialect, which presumably shows some similarities to neighbouring Umbundu dialects.[77]

In contrast to the deliberately inverted customs of the original *kilombo*, many Imbangala beliefs reported by the middle of the seventeenth century differed little from those found among the local Mbundu lineages. Although some of these have also been reported in Central Africa generally, their emphasis on female fertility and child-bearing, for example, shows that the Imbangala had already abandoned their early laws prohibiting the birth of children to members of the *kilombo*. The Mbundu-ized Imbangala of the later period interpreted the birth of twins as an omen of misfortune and performed rituals after such a birth to purify the mother and her kinsmen.[78] If a child's upper teeth appeared before its lower ones, the Imbangala took this as a sign that the child was a witch.[79] The Imbangala of Nzinga celebrated the first menstruation of young girls as evidence that they were ready to bear children.[80] Since a woman's kinsmen placed this kind of importance on her fertility only in a unilineal society where the kin group's survival depended on her ability to bear children, these beliefs indicate a return to matrilineages and concomitant abandonment of the *kilombo*.[81]

Mid-seventeenth-century Imbangala veneration of deceased relatives also indicated that they had adopted lineages of the Mbundu type. Ceremonies identical to those described for the Imbangala during the 1650s occur today in Mbundu descent groups and may be assumed to have come from local roots before the arrival of the Imbangala in Angola.[82] Mbundu attitudes towards ancestors derived from the idea of positional succession, which placed strong emphasis on communication between the living incumbent in a name or title and the spirits of his predecessors.[83] Although one observer noted the

[77] Comparative 200-word vocabularies of Mbangala, Mbondo, Songo, Jinga, Ambakista, and related Kimbundu dialects; for the Libolo–Mbangala connection, Magalhães (1922), p. xxiii.

[78] Cavazzi (1965), i. 182.

[79] Ibid. i. 121, 181.

[80] Ibid. i. 183–4.

[81] The lineages tends to assume greater responsibility for female fertility in matrilineal societies where the descent group's survival depends on its own women; in many patrilineal systems, since the group propagates itself through its males, it is less concerned with their wives (who are members of other kin groups); Robin Fox (1967), pp. 119–20.

[82] Linguistic evidence supports this point; Miller (forthcoming (d)) under *mukwa a kushingilisa*. The connection of these rituals with the *pemba* and other very old lineage symbols confirms the argument.

[83] Although some present-day Luba have similar practices (Vansina (1966b),

practice of 'ancestor' veneration among the Imbangala before they made contact with the Mbundu, he specified that the ceremonies occurred in connection with political officials (probably Lunda titles), not lineage ancestors of the Mbundu type.[84] His description of the related rituals made no mention of spirit possession, and he probably mistakenly applied the name of 'ancestor worship' to ceremonies which maintained contact between the incumbents in Lunda positions and the previous occupants of their titles.

The distinctively Mbundu form of spirit possession operated exclusively within the context of lineage ceremonies and dealt only with the spirits of deceased kinsmen (*jinzumbi,* singular *nzumbi*). Since the *jinzumbi* harmed only their own relatives, an offending spirit always belonged to the same lineage as the person afflicted. Responsibility for the ceremonies designed to relieve his suffering therefore fell to lineage officials who conducted the rites before the assembled members of the kin group. Seventeenth-century Imbangala spirit possession rituals possessed all these features; the only Imbangala priests who used spirit mediums were the *nganga a nzumbi,* specialists in dealing with *jinzumbi* ancestor spirits described as 'deceased kinsmen' who bothered living Imbangala through dreams or by causing sickness or death.[85] The *nganga a nzumbi* first excavated the grave of the dead relative accused of causing trouble. He always found the grave easily accessible since it lay in lineage lands occupied by the living members of the *ngundu.* He then examined the body to see if it had begun to decompose. A decomposing corpse showed that the *nzumbi* had left the body to wander contentedly elsewhere in the supernatural world. But if the *nganga a nzumbi* found that the corpse had not decomposed as much as expected, he announced that he had detected the spirit responsible for sickness and death in the kin group, blaming the dead relative for having been an undiscovered witch while alive. The priest in this case performed rites to ensure that the spirit should not again visit the living.[86]

If trouble persisted even after the *nganga a nzumbi* had taken these steps, he arranged a spirit possession ceremony in which a medium attempted to communicate with the *nzumbi* to discover the cause of

[84] Battell in Ravenstein (1901), pp. 34–5.
[85] Cavazzi (1965), i. 203–4.
[86] Testimonies of Sousa Calunga; Apolo de Matos, 6, 7 Oct. 1969.

p. 423), the century and a half and the institutional changes that separated the Imbangala settled in Angola from the Luba make a historical connection between the two a less likely explanation than an origin in local customs.

his displeasure. The entire living membership of the afflicted person's lineage witnessed the rituals which attended this effort. Under the guidance of an *nganga a nzumbi* and the other officials of the lineage, the assemblage consumed intoxicants and performed dances and chants calculated to bring on the trancelike state necessary to contact the dead. Eventually, some member of the lineage (today, often a woman specializing in such matters) felt himself possessed by the spirit his kinsmen wished to reach. This individual was called a *mukwa a kushingilisa*.[87] The *mukwa a kushingilisa* transmitted questions from the living to the *nzumbi* and in turn interpreted the answers of the supernatural to his relatives.[88] The close association of the *mukwa a kushingilisa* with Mbundu lineage rituals indicated that the Imbangala had adopted Mbundu *jingundu* by the middle of the seventeenth century.

The spirits of the dead evidently communicated with living Imbangala in other typically Mbundu ways as well. Imbangala grave-keepers could feel the will of the spirit whose grave they guarded through their own emotions;[89] a period of moroseness, for example, might send a grave-keeper in search of a diviner to discover the cause of the spirit's displeasure. The Mbundu also believed that *jinzumbi* ancestor spirits appeared to the living in the form of animals possessed by spirits. An Imbangala *nganga a nzumbi*, summoned to relieve sufferings caused by such a spirit, often placed a snare near the house of the afflicted patient and baited it with special substances intended to attract the brothersome *nzumbi*. The *nganga a nzumbi* then presented any small animal which fell into the trap as proof that the spirit had returned to harass his victim but had fallen into the snare. He then destroyed the animal with special techniques believed to put an end to the spirit concealed in the animal's body.[90]

The other types of spirit mentioned by seventeenth-century sources as unique to the Imbangala in fact represented adaptations of Mbundu beliefs which had survived from much earlier periods. Most of these had some connection with earlier political systems which had become obsolescent by 1650 as a result of the changes brought by the Samba and the *ngola* during the preceding 100 years. The Imbangala living north and east of the upper Kwanza (the modern Songo and

---

[87] The word given by Cavazzi, *shingila*, to denote the spirit medium is today *mukwa a kushingilisa* (from the verb *kushingila*, indicating the act of being possessed by an *nzumbi*); testimony of Alexandre Vaz and Ngonga a Mbande.

[88] Cavazzi (1965), i. 128–9.

[89] Ibid. i. 203–4.   [90] Ibid.

probably the Mbondo and Pende), for example, believed that super-natural beings resided in the springs of rivers. In the seventeenth century, they explained that water flowing from these springs represented the tears of once great spirits who had become sorrowful because their human followers had abandoned them. The tears of the female spirits formed the lakes of the region and those of the males had become rivers.[91]

Widely held Central African beliefs about water spirits make exact identification of these beings uncertain, but they present obvious similarities to the *malunga* of the early Pende who had lived in the same region where these spirits occurred. Modern Mbundu have numerous equivalent water spirits; some, for example, claim to have seen white supernatural beings emerge from rivers in Kasanje. Other river spirits cause floods which destroy the crops and posses-sions of those who offend them.[92] The names of some of the spirits mentioned in the seventeenth century survive in the present as the names of the rivers and lakes where the spirits allegedly once lived.[93]

A second type of local spirit attracted the loyalties of Imbangala in areas formerly influenced by the state of Libolo. The observer who reported these beliefs called these spirits 'idols', implying that carved figurines of the type called *mukishi* in Kimbundu represented these supernatural beings in the real world. These 'idols' occurred in male-female pairs and, although they had no apparent connection with ancestors, some communicated with the living through the medium of a *mukwa a kushingilisa*. Each claimed adherents only in a specified geographical region. The people in Kisama obeyed the priests who spoke for idols called Navieza and Kasuma; Ibundo was the domin-ant spirit of this type in Libolo itself. Kasuto and Nkishi held the loyalty of people in the 'Ganguellas', roughly the Songo area east of Pungo Andongo.

Available data give only a vague idea of the nature of these spirits,

[91] Ibid. i. 215. 'Spirits' tears' seem to be a common cliché explaining the disappearance of no longer dominant belief systems, some probably associated with earlier political systems.

[92] Testimony of Sousa Calunga.

[93] Notably Sashia, which is a river and lake, and the Kwango (river); the 'Bala' may be any one of several rivers called Mbale. The Unga, Mwala, and Lamba remain unidentified, probably owing to subsequent changes in the names of the bodies of water where they were believed to live. The Mbundu told Cavazzi that these spirits had once resided elsewhere but had fled to take refuge in the waters at the time of the arrival of the Imbangala. This story probably meant that these spirits had once stood behind political authorities, such as the *lunga*-kings, who declined in importance when the Samba authority emblems entered northern Angola.

but several factors suggest that these 'idols' may have represented distant memories of former Libolo political officials. Mbundu *mukishi* figurines occurred mainly in association with political chiefs, and the localization of these 'idols' in specific areas formerly controlled by the *hango* recalls the positions of Libolo territorial governors. The occurrence of the idols in male–female pairs is reminiscent of the figures in the political genealogies united by symbolic marriages between political authorities and lineages. Each pair of idols, according to this hypothesis, represents a survival from earlier forms of political authority, probably Libolo overrule in these cases. Later conquests by the *ngola a kiluanje* and the Imbangala had reduced them to the status of priestly wielders of supernatural authority, who remained faithful to the spirits of their old positions but no longer commanded much temporal authority in relation to newer sets of titles and spirits.

The re-emergence of lineages among the Imbangala by the middle of the seventeenth century, Imbangala veneration of local spirits and their concomitant incorporation of older, non-Imbangala, political titles and symbols, their emphasis on female fertility and procreation and—most obviously—the fact that they had ceased to wander through the countryside and had settled as farmers among the Mbundu all show the extent to which the original Imbangala *kilombo* had yielded to the indigenous institutions and ideology of the Mbundu.

The *kilombo* had represented an effective response to the extremely unsettled conditions among the Mbundu at the end of the sixteenth century and the beginning of the seventeenth century, but it provided an inefficient means of establishing permanent control over restive Mbundu kinsmen. Disruptions accompanying the decline of the *kulembe* state system and the rise of the *ngola a kiluanje*, as well as the opening of the Atlantic slave trade and the development of the Portuguese territory of Angola, created a place for fast-moving armies which could rapidly assimilate people cast adrift by the instability of the times. But the Imbangala ideology of non-humanness and the rigorous conditions of life in the *kilombo* differed too dramatically from the backgrounds of the people they incorporated. Life as Imbangala placed too great a strain on individuals to endure for very long without alteration in the direction of more familiar institutions. The wandering style of Imbangala life contradicted the basic belief systems and material culture of recruits who had grown up in villages of sedantary farmers. As these recruits grew into positions of responsibility in the *kilombo*, they gradually replaced the *yijila* with normal Mbundu lineage structures and abandoned the artificial denials of human biology and psychology on which the *kilombo* depended.

The same ability to assimilate aliens, which had accounted for Imbangala military strength, ironically contributed to the disappearance of the *kilombo* in the longer run. Prohibitions against the birth of Imbangala infants meant that bands tended to sustain themselves by assimilating boys from surrounding non-Imbangala villages, and the continual infusion of Mbundu novices quickly diluted whatever alien cultural and linguistic characteristics the Imbangala brought to an area. The Imbangala also obtained most of their women from non-Imbangala living near them, so that most of the youths brought into the *kilombo*, whether born of Imbangala women or not, had been raised in homes where the culture and language were basically Mbundu. This continual replenishment of trained Imbangala by raw Mbundu recruits had produced its predictable effect by 1650 when, slightly more than a single generation after the first Imbangala had crossed the Kwanza river, many Mbundu words and customs had already replaced the Cokwe/Lwena, Lunda, and Ovimbundu institutions brought from beyond the river.

The demonstrated capacity of the Mbundu *jingundu* to absorb alien rulers without losing their own characteristic identities also contributed to the decline of the *kilombo*. The basic incompatibility between the appointive titles used by the Imbangala and the permanent positions of the Mbundu placed the invaders at a disadvantage among the Mbundu; their precarious position there contrasted with their security south of the river and explains why they readily accepted Portuguese support in the former case but regularly opposed European penetration in the latter.

Finally, fortuitous effects of Portuguese administrative policies indirectly strengthened Mbundu lineages at the expense of the *kilombo*. The Luanda authorities adopted the Mbundu *sobas*, usually either lineage headmen or holders of lineage-controlled political titles, as the official 'native authorities' in Angola. Portuguese officials preserved the positions of the *sobas* (though not, of course, the tenure of individual incumbents) by making them responsible for tribute and taxes payable to the European administration. Itinerant merchants supported those outside the sphere of direct Portuguese administration by accepting them as their main trading partners. Since these *sobas* represented lineages, their increasingly secure status tended to preserve the Mbundu *jingundu* at the expense of the Imbangala *kilombo*.

Nearly every factor which worked against survival of the *kilombo* had a counterpart which encouraged preservation of the titles of the Imbangala kings. Just as the *kilombo* disappeared in part because it embodied ideas and institutions alien to the Mbundu, the kings' titles rested on Lunda and Cokwe concepts of positional succession already familiar to the Mbundu. In particular, the Mbundu social and political system, like that of the Lunda and Cokwe, rested on the theory that the living occupant of a title ruled through his control of physical relics preserved from his predecessors.

The similarity between the Imbangala and the Mbundu titles appeared most clearly in their common association of bones with spirits. An Mbundu *kimbanda* (specialist in magic) who wished to dispose of a troublesome spirit, though not particularly that of a chief, did so by locating the bones of the body, digging them up, and burning them.[94] Rituals connected with the Imbangala kings made similar use of bones. They preserved the bones of dead chiefs in boxes called *misete* (singular, *musete*) which they treated with veneration in public ceremonies.[95] The bones enabled them to communicate with the spirits of these positions in a manner which the Mbundu recognized without difficulty. The Imbangala in particular used the bones to request the aid of deceased kings to bring military victories. Because their unsettled life style kept them from claiming lands of their own, they carried the bones in boxes rather than burying them as the Mbundu did.[96]

Much of the symbolism surrounding Imbangala kings was common to many Central African states beyond the Mbundu and Lunda systems of titles. One of the common Central African symbols involved the use of 'peacock' feathers in the head-dresses of Imbangala kings.[97] Kalanda ka Imbe wore 'peacock' feathers when first

[94] Testimony of Apolo de Matos, 6 Oct. 1969.

[95] Cavazzi (1965), i. 185, 208; Cadornega (1940–2), iii. 228.

[96] Preservation of chiefs' bones distinguished modern Ovimbundu from Mbundu; Verly (1955), p. 690. But R. de Sousa Martins (1973) reported very similar practices from the *ndembu* region of southern Kongo. Battell's description (in Ravenstein (1901), pp. 34–5) of Imbangala 'graves' and 'relatives' sacrificing to ancestral spirits is inconsistent with nearly all other data on Imbangala burial customs.

[97] The recurrent identification of the feathers in question as those of a 'peacock' does not specify which bird they might have come from, as the true peacock does not occur in Angola. The *koshi, ngwadi*, or *ngumbi* identified by Plancquaert (1971) in the lower Kwango region is properly a francolin; personal communication from Mr. Kenneth P. Enright.

encountered by Europeans south of the Kwanza.[98] 'Peacock' feathers have also been widely reported in association with chiefs elsewhere in Angola. An old woman tended fifty 'peacocks' called the 'njila mukiso' near the grave of the *shila a mbanza*, a non-Imbangala title-holder in Kisama.[99] In the sixteenth century, the *mani* Kongo and the *ngola a kiluanje* both used 'peacock' feathers as symbols of royalty.[100] Twentieth-century Yaka associate the same symbol with their Lunda chiefs, although it has no connection with chiefs of other origins.[101] A nineteenth-century Lunda chief, Kibwiko, who lived near the Kasai river, had a feather head-dress made from the plumes of the 'peacock'.[102]

The use of white feathers to symbolize peaceful intentions on formal occasions and 'red' ones to indicate war provided further common ground between seventeenth-century Imbangala kings, as well as the later *kinguri* of Kasanje,[103] and other Central African kings. It occurs today at least among the Lunda, Cokwe, Minungo, Yaka, Tyo, Ovimbundu, and Kuba, as well as among the Mbundu.[104] The 'red' feathers in these cases appeared 'purple' rather than 'red' in the Mbundu system of colour perception and came from the *ndua* bird, a type of plantain eater which had strong supernatural significance.[105] They believed that the *ndua* lived in the forests far from human habitation where its loud, hoarse, unbirdlike cry warned travellers of dangers, both natural and supernatural. It could frighten robbers, animals, and spirits waiting to molest unwary passers-by. The Mbundu interpreted its presence near civilization as a bad omen, and believed that misfortune always followed,

---

[98] Purchas in Ravenstein (1901), pp. 1, 86.

[99] Battell, ibid., pp. 26–7, 86. The name was obviously *njila a mukishi* ('the birds of the *mukishi* charm'), but his attribution of the practice to the Imbangala is doubtful owing to the description of suspiciously similar circumstances at the court of the Kisama *shila a mbanza*. The trait was not elsewhere ascribed to seventeenth-century Imbangala but is very common among modern Mbundu.

[100] Lopes in Bal (1965), p. 62; also Jean Barbot (1732), p. 520.

[101] Plancquaert (1971).

[102] Joaquim Rodriques Graça (1854–8), p. 125.

[103] Cavazzi (1965), i. 219.

[104] Redinha (1963), pp. 48–9; Capello and Ivens (1882), for the *mwata yamvo* in the 1870s; Hambly (1934), p. 135; testimonies of Alexandre Vaz, 31 July 1969; Apolo de Matos, 5 Oct. 1969; personal communication from Jan Vansina.

[105] Monteiro (1875), i. 74–9, correctly identified the species as *Corythaix Paulina*, adding that it was found in wooded areas all over Angola. Mr. Enright adds that the name applies in Lunda to two species of arboreal Louries or turacos (*Corythaix Schaloui* and *Musophaga Cossae*).

especially if the bird perched on the roof of a house and called out.[106]

The Mbundu associated the *ndua* with blood. Its wing feathers are blood-red in colour, and contain pigmentation which dissolves in water containing ammonia; it then runs like blood from a wound. The blood which trickles from the nose of a corpse was also called *ndua*. The same word designated various diseases believed to result from 'excess blood'.[107] The eighteenth-century Ambakista traders applied the term to poison oath ceremonies conducted in Kasanje.[108] The similarity between the Imbangala kings' connection of the *ndua* bird with blood and with the supernatural world and its significance in Mbundu cosmology showed a common level of symbolism which facilitated the settlement of Imbangala rulers north of the Kwanza by making them more acceptable to the descent groups they ruled.

Other customs associated with the Imbangala title-holders which occurred widely in Central Africa included court etiquette requiring persons assembled before the king to applaud and show great pleasure whenever their ruler sneezed or showed any other involuntary reflex.[109] The modern Imbangala explain that a sneeze indicates contact between the living chief and the supernatural powers behind his position. Since the most important functions of an incumbent in a perpetual title concerned his communication with the spirit world, a sneeze indicated that he was actively performing his duties. This news deserved the applause of the people.

Imbangala kings preserved only two recorded distinctive traits possibly indicative of their Lunda origins. The incumbent *kalanda ka imbe* had extensive tattooing all over his body in 1601.[110] Scarification associated him with the east, since it was relatively rare among the Mbundu and Ovimbundu but highly developed in eastern Angola among the Cokwe and Lunda.[111] The Imbangala also painted the

[106] Monteiro, ibid. The later incumbents in the *kulashingo* position in Kasanje kept the carved figure of an *ndua* on the peak of their compound roof.

[107] Assis Jr. (n.d.), p. 32.

[108] These oath ceremonies, for which Kasanje was renowned throughout western Angola, probably evolved from the *ibundu* or *kanu* 'drink' noted in the seventeenth century (Cadornega (1940–2), ii. 402–3; Cavazzi (1965), i. 190); also Dias de Carvalho (1890a), p. 69. The name probably stemmed from a belief that the gall bladder of the *ndua* was extremely poisonous; Alfredo de Albuquerque Felner (1940), ii. 14.

[109] Cavazzi (1965), i. 193.

[110] Battell in Ravenstein (1901), p. 33.

[111] Almeida (1937), p. 79.

kalanda ka imbe's body with a white powder;[112] this was probably the *pemba*, a white clay associated with chieftainship, as opposed to lineages, primarily among the Lunda, Luba, Kuba and in the forest kingdoms of Zaïre. Among the Mbundu, however, *pemba* belonged only to lineage officials. This marked the origin of its use by the Imbangala kings as somewhere to the north-east and probably in Lunda.

Two other customs noted in the documents connected Imbangala kings with the Ovimbundu antecedents of the *kilombo*. Seventeenth-century Imbangala allowed only their noble title-holders to lie on cattle skins.[113] In Angola, only the kingdoms south of the Kwanza associated cattle with nobility; there mourners wrapped the body of their dead chief in the skin of an ox before transporting his corpse to its burial place.[114] The Imbangala sometimes hung their human sacrifices upside down during the seventeenth century, probably in order to facilitate the drainage of blood from the body. They collected this blood in vessels and drank it in certain unspecified ceremonies.[115] This custom has been reported elsewhere only in Kakonda, one of the southern Ovimbundu kingdoms descended from Imbangala founders.[116]

The consonance of ideology and ritual associated with the Imbangala kings' titles and the existing Mbundu political systems helped the rulers to survive despite the failure of the *kilombo* to replace the lineages. The simultaneous success of the kings and failure of the *kilombo* thus reflected the different origins of the two major components of the Imbangala bands, Lunda titles and an Ovimbundu warrior initiation society. The *kulashingo* had therefore made a portentous decision when he discarded the *kilombo* rules in favour of the Lunda title of the *kinguri* in order to join the Portuguese. The later growth of the Kasanje state, based on the Lunda position, may have been a partial result of his choice. Elements drawn from two such disparate systems could remain together only as long as adversity forced them to unite. The relative tranquillity which followed each time the Imbangala settled inevitably allowed them to drift apart, as it did soon after the *makota* and the *kulashingo* settled among the Mbundu.

[112] Battell in Ravenstein (1901), pp. 33–4.
[113] Cavazzi (1965), i. 190.
[114] Testimony of Sousa Calunga, 10 Sept. 1969, for Libolo. Magyar (1859), p. 316, for Bihe. Alberto Ferreira Marques (1949), p. 14, for Kakonda.
[115] Cavazzi (1965), i. 187.
[116] Ferreira Marques (1949), p. 14.

The Imbangala title-holders found themselves unable to establish rapport with their Mbundu subjects by means of the *kilombo* and turned for support to the Portuguese who, for reasons of their own, welcomed Imbangala settlements on the periphery of their own territories. Acceptance by the Europeans contributed to their survival since their status as intruders ironically gave them certain rights under Portuguese law not conceded to the Mbundu *sobas*.[117] Governors of Angola, for example, rarely demanded labour or ' supplies from Imbangala kings without a formal treaty specifying the terms and conditions of co-operation. They in turn made it clear that they regarded the kings as dependent on Portuguese approbation for their positions. The slave trade, carefully controlled in the mutual interest of these rulers and their European commercial partners, provided economic underpinnings for the role defined by formal diplomacy.

Seen from the perspective of Mbundu history, finally, the Imbangala invasion continued the pattern of repeated but unsuccessful attempts by outsiders to impose centralized authority on the Mbundu lineages. Just as the *jingundu* had survived previous challenges by the *vunga*-kings, by Libolo, and by the *ngola a kiluanje*, they resisted incorporation into the *kilombo*. The lineages had either taken control of earlier overlords' titles for themselves, as they had done with the Libolo *mavunga* and most positions derived from the *ngola a kiluanje* or adopted new forms of political organization to counteract the centralizing tendencies of their current rulers, as they had done with the original form of the *ngola*. In the case of the Imbangala, the inherent weaknesses of the *kilombo* made it especially vulnerable to Mbundu opposition.

The ability of the *jingundu* to dilute the power of their kings paradoxically left them open to further invasion by limiting their capacity to offer unified resistance. The lineages had gradually taken control

---

[117] The stereotyped contrast between friendly, peaceful *sobas* and the warlike intrusive 'Jaga' ran consistently through Portuguese sources from the sixteenth to the nineteenth century. Examples: Fernão Martins (1591); B.N.L., Coleção Pombalina, códice 644, fol. 334; published in Brásio (1952–71), iii. 433–4, and Fernão Guerreiro (1930–42), ii. 191. Also Cadornega (1940–2), *passim*, for the seventeenth century, Thomas Bowdich (1824), p. 25, from the eighteenth century, and Duarte (1859–61), p. 134, for the nineteenth. It was this vague sense of the word 'Jaga' to denote any warlike invader that led to confusion of the Imbangala with other unrelated marauders in Mbundu and even Kongo areas; for the latter, see Oliver de Bouveignes and J. Cuvelier (1951), pp. 63, 71–2, where at least two distinct unidentified enemies of the Kongo *mani* Mazinga were called 'Jagas'.

of the titles subordinate to the *ngola a kiluanje* even as the central kings spread their authority more and more widely during the sixteenth century. The increasing autonomy of the *jingundu* rendered the kingdom incapable of mounting solid resistance to either the Portuguese or the Imbangala. When the two invaders combined their forces in pursuit of slaves, they doomed the older Mbundu kings to defeat.

Although the Mbundu lineages had emerged victorious over the *kilombo*, they could not similarly banish the Imbangala kings. Many headed the Mbundu-ized Imbangala kingdoms which prospered as the primary suppliers of slaves sent to European traders throughout the eighteenth and part of the nineteenth century. Holo, Jinga, Kasanje, Mbondo, Kalandula, Kabuku ka Ndonga, as well as various southern kingdoms such as Bihe, Kakonda, and Wambo, all thrived under holders of Imbangala titles settled on the fringes of Portuguese-controlled territory. These states, formed by the combination of Imbangala kings and Mbundu kinsmen, dominated the political and economic history of Angola for the next two centuries, until the ending of the slave trade during the 1850s once again shifted the balance of power in favour of the lineages and sent even the Imbangala kings into a decline from which they have never recovered.

CHAPTER IX

Conclusions

BECAUSE THE several examples of state-formation found in the early history of the Mbundu all occurred in a relatively unvarying social and ideological background, they may be usefully compared to elicit some tentative generalizations about ways in which kingdoms may emerge in an environment featuring strong descent groups and, in particular, where people think in terms of perpetual kinship and positional succession. Although the constant social and ideological context of these cases simplifies the historian's task in one way, by reducing the number of variables he must consider, at the same time it complicates his job by limiting the applicability of his conclusions to cases where demonstrably similar circumstances obtain. The patterns which emerge from the history of the Pende *lunga*-kings, the *kulembe*, Libolo and its *vunga* appointive chiefs, the *ngola a kiluanje*, Lunda perpetual titles, the Imbangala *kilombo*, and the contacts between them should therefore be applied elsewhere only to the extent that the relevant aspects of Mbundu culture are also present. My present feeling—though not yet fully documented—is that roughly similar conditions existed throughout most of the matrilineal area of the southern African savannas.

This disclaimer requires explicit emphasis at the outset since, whatever the broader applicability of some of the points drawn from the experience of the Mbundu, the historian should always phrase his conclusions with an eye to the precise conditions under which they hold. If a wider comparative dimension emerges from these cases, it probably lies in the opposition which the Mbundu saw between their kings, or other forms of political structure, and their kinsmen, the members of the strongly corporate Mbundu unilineal descent groups. The value of examining several cases from a single society lies in the capacity of this methodology to illuminate the variety of ways in which states emerged from a background of unilineal descent groups and the strength these unilineal descent groups showed in their responses to the growth of states in their midst.

Defining a 'State'

The fundamental question of what constituted a 'state' in the context of Mbundu society has been deferred to the conclusion in order to develop a definition based on Mbundu theory and practice rather than on categories derived from Western experience. It is clear that the Mbundu had no conceptual category equivalent to that of 'state' in European terms but instead made a dichotomous distinction between their descent groups (and the related titles, etc.) and a residual category which included all other forms of what I have termed 'cross-cutting institutions'. Accepting the Mbundu categorization of their social institutions as a starting-point, a two-stage definition of 'state' follows. We may initially term all the hunting societies, circumcision camps, curing cults, and other organizations which related people to one another beyond the bonds of kinship as the Mbundu recognized it as 'political' in the sense that they existed outside the realm of purely 'social' relations as defined by the descent group structure.[1] The Mbundu typically expressed these relationships in terms of networks of permanent named positions, usually thought of as 'descendants' of single 'founders', which tied the lineages (and the people in them) to one another.

But the category of 'political', thus phrased, is a negative one, defined as *not* involving the descent groups, and is broader than anything which could usefully be termed a 'state' since it includes a great many small-scale and ephemeral phenomena. Some degree of duration seems necessary to distinguish the 'states' which appear in Mbundu political history, as well as size superior to the other institutions present in the society. Both the characteristics of size and duration, which separate Mbundu 'kingdoms' or 'states' from other non-kin-based institutions, are relative and ultimately subject to the historian's judgement. No clear line divides those 'states' which were large enough and sufficiently long-lasting to merit the designation from other structures relegated to the conceptual limbo of transitory and minute cross-cutting institutions. Precisely this difficulty marred the discussion of the incipient states which appeared from time to time in the history of the Songo, for example. 'States' thus occupy one corner of a two-dimensional plane defined in terms of size and duration and are not qualitatively distinguishable from other non-lineage, i.e. 'political', institutions.

[1] Although I arrived at this definition of 'political' on empirical grounds, my subsequent reading in political anthropology has shown me that it is a common theoretical concept; e.g. Lucy Mair (1962), p. 24.

The vagueness of the lines distinguishing 'states' from other 'political' structures, which might be called by a variety of terms ('statelike institutions', pre-states, or even proto-states occur as possibilities but show the fruitlessness of a quest for a single useful one), can be seen in the development of the *kilombo* from its origins as one cross-cutting institution, a circumcision camp, in a context of many, into a dominant instrument of state-building in the hands of the Imbangala kings. Having attained the status of 'state', the *kilombo* then metamorphosed into no more than a single relatively minor aspect of the court rituals of Imbangala kings who built enduring states on the basis of other political techniques. Similarly, some of the political *mavunga* originally associated with the state of Libolo lost their function as elements of the large kingdom and became the focus of local religious veneration among the Songo, still 'political' in the sense that they attracted unrelated disciples from many lineages but hardly describable as 'states' in an environment where the *ngola a kiluanje* and the Imbangala had become the dominant forms of state organization.

Not all characteristics of the Mbundu states defined in this way coincided with the categories which have customarily been used to define 'states' in Africa.[2] Mbundu states, for example, had no necessary territorial organization of the sort most writers have sought to discern in African kingdoms. Some Mbundu states, especially those based on the *lunga* and—to some extent—the Libolo *mavunga*, defined the authority spheres of political title-holders in terms of geography rather than in terms of people. But such indisputable kingdoms as the *ngola a kiluanje* and the *kilombo* at its mobile height defined themselves in terms of people rather than land. The notion of 'marriages' between title-holders sanctioned by the king and descent groups, expressed most clearly in the idiom of the genealogical traditions, made this point quite explicit. In fact, Mbundu cosmology reserved control of land and certain forms of authority over the people who lived on defined parcels of it to the lineages rather than to non-descent group political authorities. Each *lemba dya ngundu*, if he headed a landowning lineage, determined the rights of both kin and non-kin to till the soil, hunt in its forests and woodlands, fish in its streams, and harvest the fruits of its trees. The reliance of the early theorists on a 'territorial' definition of state authority probably represented their first approximation to what, at least in the case of the Mbundu, closer examination has suggested may

[2] Based on Fortes and Evans-Pritchard (1942), p. 5, and Vansina (1962a)

have been a definition of authority over persons other than one's kinsmen.

Centralization, another frequently cited defining characteristic of African states, varied greatly among Mbundu kingdoms, ranging from the barely incipient concentration of authority found among the Pende *lunga*-kings through intermediate degrees of central control in the *ngola a kiluanje* and Libolo states to near-total centralization in the Imbangala *kilombo*. Despite the evident trend towards greater centralization through time, all these structures were equally 'states' according to Mbundu standards. Nor was there a positive correlation between the degree of centralization in a kingdom and its durability, as the history of the *kilombo* demonstrated, since the Mbundu lineages clearly preferred less centralized political institutions to states with all power concentrated in a single theoretically omnipotent king. The degree of centralization also varied from time to time in the history of each state depending on the talent and resources available to its king relative to the peripheral title-holders in the provinces. Thus Libolo, theoretically among the more centralized of the early Mbundu states, owing to its development of the appointive *mavunga* titles, at times failed to retain control over outlying title-holders like the *ndala kisua* of Mbondo.

Monopoly over the legitimate use of force has ranked as another of the distinguishing aspects of states. Yet among the Mbundu this criterion failed to differentiate states from other sorts of institutions, both social and political. The Mbundu expanded the conventional Western sense of the term 'force' to include the magical coercive techniques which backed the authority of nearly all their political and social titles in addition to the simply physical means of coercion usually denoted by the term. But neither the magical forms of coercion nor the use of armed men were the monopoly of kings. The men at the heads of Mbundu states had constantly to strive for and assert their *de facto* superiority in charms and arms, since other sorts of title legitimately gave access to independent forms of coercion and the holders of these titles exercised them whenever they could. From this perspective, one important theme in the history of Mbundu states was constant competition between holders of different sorts of title in a pluralistic universe of forces. The assumption that a 'state' had exclusive access to coercive techniques would leave the historian at a loss to explain the rise of subordinate positions to ascendancy, the avidity with which the Mbundu searched continually for new forms of authority, and the multiple powers claimed by the most successful

Mbundu chiefs. Moreover, relatively few Mbundu states regarded themselves as dependent on the use of violence or even as specialists in its exercise, since only the Imbangala *kilombo* maintained a standing army and was prepared to conduct warfare on anything approaching a permanent basis. It may be accurate to speak of individual title-holders seeking to consolidate their positions through abrogating the use of force to themselves, but the concept has little meaning at the larger level of the state.

In some ways the most striking aspects of the Mbundu states before 1650 were the plurality and diversity of the institutions found within them. In addition to the set of titles which served to define the kingdom, all these states also included lineage titles, positions derived from earlier forms of political authority which had spread in the area, *ad hoc* officials such as war leaders and emissaries appointed in response to specific circumstances, as well as prophets, diviners, and other (nominally) religious specialists whose claims on the supernatural constantly threatened to detract from the equally mysterious powers of more explicitly political officials.

The kingdom of the *ngola a kiluanje* has left the best evidence in support of this point. The *ngola a kiluanje* state, narrowly defined, consisted of a network of titles based on *jingola* authority emblems, but the kingdom actually worked in terms of the corporate lineages which controlled the *jingola*. These lineages had predated the expansion of the *ngola a kiluanje* and continued to exist through the state's history. At times, judging from the evidence available, lineage officials used their control over the state-titles based on the *ngola* to play an important role in the politics of the kingdom. Simultaneously, non-lineage positions based on such earlier forms of authority as the *malunga* and the Libolo *mavunga* received important commissions from the central kings and/or provided centres of localism opposed to the tendencies towards increased centralization represented by the central kings. War leaders, appointed by the *ngola a kiluanje* for the conduct of a single campaign, must have represented another potent element in the balance of power in the state, even though the record of their influence has not survived in the available evidence. We may assume, from comparison with other times and places, that unrecorded prophets also arose from time to time and had to be taken account of by those who presumed to control the state.

The emphasis on plurality and diversity of authority leads to several related general points. For the historian, who is less interested in typologies of state-structures than in examining the processes by which states come into being and change through time, the tension created by the simultaneous presence of a variety of competing forms of authority has significant heuristic value. A major theme of Mbundu political history, for example, concerned the constant tension between the particularism of the descent groups and expansions in political scale promoted by the kingdoms. In such areas as Songo, particularism seems to have won out most often, while farther west among the Libolo, Ndongo, Lenge, and others, kingdoms occasionally managed to suppress lineage loyalties in favour of a wider political perspective. The growth of the usual sort of Mbundu kingdom from a single local position to a widespread network of related titles may also be interpreted as a different type of confrontation between authority emblems in a pluralistic universe. The rise of the *ngola a kiluanje* must have appeared locally as a contest between the holders of the *ngola* and those with *mavunga*, *malunga*, and whatever other emblems may have commanded the loyalties of Mbundu on the eve of its expansion.

The process of forming Mbundu states necessarily produced this diversity of authority since expanding kings tended to incorporate rather than eliminate earlier titles. Later states therefore grew progressively more complex as each one introduced one more (temporarily dominant) element to the universe of title-holders in any given area. Later kings incorporated and reused, as it were, older titles because of the loyalty that these positions commanded from local peoples, who presumably accepted new authority forms more readily when they came cloaked in familiar garb. This prototypical version of what the British later enshrined as 'indirect rule' may have been necessary to incorporate successfully new areas into an expanding state. Non-literate peoples, like the Mbundu, seem to dread abrupt and total changes in their thought and society,[3] and this sort of state mitigated the appearance of change in the theoretically static world of positional succession and perpetual kinship.

How and Why Mbundu States Were Formed

The history of the Mbundu provides a number of explanations for the formation of states in a so-called 'stateless' environment which presume no outside stimulus or inspiration from Hamites or anyone else. In fact, the degree to which local social and ideological conditions affected the structures of almost all Mbundu states precluded the possibility that simple contact with alien ideas or institutions

[3] Horton (1967).

would have significant results for Mbundu politics. Nearly all Mbundu states can be accounted for in terms of older, perhaps 'political' but still non-state institutions found in the society, as the *kilombo* grew from Ovimbundu circumcision ceremonies and the *ngola a kiluanje* developed out of an earlier form of the *ngola*. The assumption which lies beneath all the explanations I have offered is that people tended to create institutions in response to felt needs, specifically that the desirability of contact between unrelated members of different lineages forced the Mbundu to find ways of structuring relationships between non-kinsmen. These relations, by definition, were political, and the variety of state institutions already noted emerged in response to this need.

The assumption of a functional need[4] to relate people without blood ties explains why political institutions emerge, but it does not account for why some but not others emerge as dominant. That is, it does not explain why 'states' in the narrower sense of the term appeared. Mbundu history shows that, whatever the structural tendencies prompting people to create political structures, non-structural historical circumstances determined which of the myriad cross-cutting institutions grew to sufficient size and lasted long enough to be termed 'states'. No doubt, more than one factor promoted the growth of any single kingdom, but for purposes of summarizing the experience of the Mbundu it may be useful to classify the sorts of historical circumstances which were important, illustrating each type with examples drawn from Mbundu history.

(1) control over a scarce but valuable resource—the relevant Mbundu examples include the authority which some of the Pende *lunga*-kings exercised over the salt pans of the Baixa de Cassanje, as well as the iron-ore deposits in the Nzongeji river valley controlled by the *ngola a kiluanje*. The *ngola a kiluanje* kings seem also to have moved toward control of the Baixa de Cassanje salt deposits as they expanded their kingdom and to have claimed other salt sources located south of the Kwanza in Kisama. The economic value of these natural resources stimulated just the sort of social circumstances in which political institutions might appear and led to the eventual emergence of states. A rare but necessary resource such as iron or salt presumably attracted unrelated persons from a large area in

---

[4] My use of these 'functionalist' insights does not imply acceptance of the early functionalist tendency to emphasize the static and harmoniously integrated aspects of a society. Cf. the uses made of tension by Max Gluckman or the dialectical opposition of elements in African societies in Coquery-Vidrovitch (1969).

search of the desired commodity. As these unrelated individuals congregated about the salt pans or iron diggings, the etiquette provided by purely kinship links would not have sufficed to regulate their contacts with one another which, we may assume, would not always have been friendly.

As disorders increased among strangers flocking to the site of salt or iron supplies, a number of solutions might theoretically have been possible, including the establishment of a market-place authority like that associated with the 'port of trade' defined by Karl Polanyi.[5] In such a case, a local authority might originally have regulated contacts between strangers present at the resource without claiming any authority over them after they left to return to their own descent groups. The crucial shift from limited and local 'port of trade' market regulation of this sort to a kingdom would have occurred when the market authorities had accrued wealth and prestige enough to allow talented or ambitious local governors to convert their economic capital into political authority, forming a state claiming jurisdiction over adjacent and even distant lineages as well as over the natural resource itself.[6] These incipient kings could then have awarded titles derived from their own position to formalize *de facto* links between outlying lineages and themselves, in effect licensing their trading partners to share in the political wealth. If force was involved in this process, as it undoubtedly was, the ability of Mbundu kings to convert their economic resources (i.e. wealth derived from possession of the resource) into human capital by purchasing slave retainers provided aspiring rulers with a means of acquiring the manpower they would need to convince dissidents of the legitimacy of their authority.[7]

(2) military or strategic position—at least one Mbundu example, that of the Mbondo, suggests that occupation of a strong defensive position may have led to the creation of a kingdom centred on a site such as that of the Katanya escarpment above the Baixa de Cassanje. The circumstances promoting the adoption of a state form of political organization in this case would have been the same as those found at the type of economic resource described in category (1)—the

[5] Karl Polanyi, C. M. Arensberg, H. W. Pearson (1957), and Karl Polanyi (1963). The relevant aspect of the concept that I emphasize is the independent market-policing authority in its political function, rather than the economic (price-administering) functions to which Polanyi devoted most attention.

[6] A conversion analogous to the distinction drawn between subsistence-oriented and market trade in David Birmingham (1971).

[7] On slaves and kings, Miller (forthcoming (b)), and Terray (1974).

presence of a variety of strangers, in this case refugees from lineages gathered together for self-defence, who needed to find a basis for co-operation where kinship ties did not extend.

Once states existed, whatever the causes which first brought strangers together, a variety of new factors encouraged the formation of new states at defensible sites, especially if they lay in the interstices between large neighbouring kingdoms. In point of historical fact, the Mbondo *ndala kisua* emerged under the latter circumstance, since its location atop the mountains of Katanya placed it on the frontier where Libolo influence confronted the Pende *lunga*-kings of the lower Baixa de Cassanje.

(3) institutional innovations capable of attracting manpower—the case of the Imbangala *kilombo* shows the potential for state-formation in the ability to recruit large numbers of men and to co-ordinate their activities. The amassing of manpower played an especially critical role in the particularistic and divisive atmosphere created by the strong Mbundu descent groups. The *kilombo*, which was able to suppress nearly all potentially fragmenting claims from lineage or other types of authority, represented the fullest development of this technique in known Mbundu history. But the same element of institutional innovation was present in nearly all examples of Mbundu state-formation, since the institution of slavery equally represented a means of divorcing people from their old (in this case, lineage) ties and attaching them to new structures (usually the king, in the instance of Mbundu kingdoms). Slaves were therefore closely associated with kings throughout Mbundu history.

(4) ideological innovation—the power of an idea should not be underestimated in the history of state-formation among the Mbundu, since an essential component of every title-holder's political authority was his ability to convince people that he not only had a right to rule but also possessed supernatural methods of implementing the powers he claimed. In this sort of environment, the rise and fall of kingdoms depended in a very real way on the elaboration of ideas to which people responded with loyalty. The history of the *kilombo*, where the Imbangala ideology of non-humanness at first terrified their opponents into submission but then failed to retain their loyalties because of its extreme break with prevailing Mbundu cosmology, provided the most dramatic example of both success and failure in this regard.

It was the Mbundu kings' political use of ideology which obscured the conventional Western distinction between 'force' and 'magic', since magical components bulked large in a king's panoply of forces. The idiom of the political traditions, which described wars exclusively in terms of charms and magic, showed this clearly, as did the more tangible concern of Mbundu war-leaders for lengthy magical preparation when they confronted the always ready Imbangala warriors with their shield of invulnerability provided by the *maji a samba*. Correlative to this point, and also to the importance of organization and mobilization as political techniques, it may be added that superior physical weaponry seems *not* to have played a significant role in state formation among the Mbundu. Ideological superiority, on the other hand, may have been an important means of attracting manpower and thus closely related to the factors discussed under (3).

(5) outside allies—the importance of an outside ally in the formation of Mbundu states appears in several cases. From the point of view of an Mbundu lineage, a local political title-holder's authority over his kinsmen depended on the support of outsider kings who had granted the position. Conversely, the power of distant Libolo kings provided a local *vunga*-holder's only guarantee of superiority over the lineages. The history of the Mbondo again provides an example, since the lineages of Lambo claimed the *ndala kisua* and other Libolo *vunga*-positions when the expansion of the *ngola a kiluanje* cut them off from their sponsors south of the Kwanza. In a somewhat different sense, alliances between local kings and outsiders may have been important in the early history of the Lunda, where reactions to and utilization of the neighbouring Luba provided a continuing theme in the evolution of the *lueji*'s kingdom, the growth of the *mwata yamvo*, and the expulsion of the *kinguri*. The best-documented example of state-formation by alliance with an outside power occurred when the Imbangala and Portuguese made contact in a situation where neither could have succeeded without the aid of the other. This principle worked on numerous occasions in the history of Portuguese–Imbangala relations: *kulashingo*'s use of the Portuguese to gain ascendancy over the holders of the Lunda *makota* positions, the Portuguese alliance with the *kulashingo* in beginning their territorial conquests between 1610 and 1620, and later the dependence of such Imbangala kings as the *kabuku ka ndonga* and the *kalandula* on the Portuguese as the *kilombo* withered away.

(6) commercial monopolies—the ability to control the movement of commodities (analytically distinguishable from control of the economic resource itself) lay at the basis of the slave-trading states built by later Imbangala rulers in Matamba and Kasanje. The

Portuguese state of Angola thrived on control of another stage in the same commerce in slaves. Although these cases superficially resembled states based on control of a natural resource in that both were 'economic' in nature, they were historically different since simple control of a resource was capable of generating a state in an environment devoid of large-scale political institutions. The trading state, on the other hand, appeared only later when other states already existed capable of buying or selling sufficient quantities of a commodity to support this type of parasite kingdom. A trading state like Angola usually lay between two older states (Kasanje, Matamba, etc., on one side, and Portugal and Brazil on the other), one in control of production and the other in charge of distribution or consumption. It was thus historically derivative in ways that a king in control of a valuable resource was not.

(7) agricultural surplus—no sedentary state could appear without agricultural techniques capable of producing a surplus to support the agriculturally non-productive specialists in magic, war, and arbitration who ran the state machinery. The absence of an agricultural surplus does not seem to have limited the opportunity to develop states in the recoverable history of the Mbundu, yet neither does the simple abundance of food in itself seem to have prompted the formation of a state. Production in excess of local populations' need for food may in any case be treated as a special subcase of the category (1) of possession of a valuable natural resource, since the historical relationship between agricultural plenty and the formation of states depended on creating kings to regulate access by strangers to the surplus. That is, extra food would not have been produced, whatever the potential of the combination of land, climate, and cultigens, unless farmers had the opportunity to trade it to outsiders who either had less suitable lands or had specialized in other economic activities such as trade, crafts, and so on. This category is worth mentioning separately only because the Imbangala represented the opposite limiting case. They theoretically grew no food of their own and lived entirely by preying on the production of others. The history of the Imbangala showed only that states may exist without any agricultural base whatsoever if they move continually, seeking new areas to plunder as they devastate the regions where they have passed.

(8) technological superiority—technological superiority, construed in the narrow but conventional sense of possession of superior weapons, may have led to the creation of Mbundu states when the *ngola* arrived if the Samba in fact introduced the Mbundu to

techniques of forging iron into broad-bladed weapons. The evidence on this point, however, is less than clear, and technological superiority generally seems to have been less important than the ideological and organizational techniques mentioned under categories (3) and (4). In particular, Portuguese firearms seem to have made little difference in the ability of the Europeans to form a state before they combined these weapons with conventional African weapons in the hands of their Imbangala allies.

(9) individual genius—the nature of the data, both oral and written, makes it impossible to assess the role of 'great men and women' in the history of the Mbundu. But all of the eight categories mentioned above implicitly allow for the role of individual human genius in the formation of Mbundu states. Clearly, it took an exceptional person to convert an early 'port of trade' into a full-fledged kingdom, just as only human inventiveness could devise a successful new symbol of authority, convert a circumcision camp into a *kilombo*, or bring two potentially hostile mercenary camps into a mutually beneficial alliance. The checkered record of the Portuguese–Imbangala alliance, as it passed through the hands of governors and Imbangala kings of varying talents, shows how great a difference the identity and genius of the partners made. The influence of 'great men and women' is implicit in all Mbundu political history, but the sources highlight it only in exceptional cases.[8]

The historical process of state-formation may be categorized in a variety of other ways, of which I shall mention two. First, three logically exhaustive categories constructed in terms of a new state's relation to its predecessors comprehend all the cases of state-formation known among the Mbundu.[9] (a) Primary states may arise through the conversion of a purely local political institution, as happened in the case of the *kilombo* and the *ngola* and probably in the rise of the early *lunga*-kings in control of salt pans in the Baixa de Cassanje. These states are distinguished by the extent to which they were based on local ideas and practices, and they may be uncommonly stable and enduring for that reason. (b) Some secondary states, such as the *ndala kisua* of the Mbondo, originated as breakaways from older states. These states had to adapt their original

[8] The major exception is, of course, queen Nzinga of Matamba; Miller (1975).

[9] This is basically the distinction between 'primary' and various types of 'secondary' states favoured by cultural evolutionists; e.g. Morton H. Fried (1960), and Lewis (1966) for an extension of this sort of typology to African examples.

alien institutions to local circumstances if they were to survive. The history of the Imbangala *kilombo* north of the Kwanza provided abundant evidence both of the process of disintegration, as the holders of the *makota* titles fled the *kulashingo* after 1619, and of their subsequent tendency to embrace Mbundu ideas and institutions. (c) Other states appeared independently of outside control but in imitation of institutions present nearby. This process, known to anthropologists as stimulus diffusion, accounted (possibly) for part of the history of the successive *kinguri*-states east of the Kwango and probably for some of the Imbangala bands which appeared farther west during the late sixteenth and early seventeenth centuries. Given the deficiencies in the historical record, it may be difficult to distinguish stimulus diffusion from the extension of an existing state structure through the award of political titles by one Mbundu lineage to another. Title-holders may have fabricated false links with neighbouring titles, indistinguishable in the genealogies from real ones, when historically they merely copied the idea without the formal award of a title.

The second alternative method of describing Mbundu state-formation develops conceptual themes which seem to have recurred in several cases. I choose to deal with three of these: the concept of the 'outsider', the importance of manpower, and the function of the king as arbiter. The history of the Mbundu leaves little doubt that states resulted in most cases from the presence of people defined according to local standards as 'outsiders'.[10] For the Mbundu, only kinsmen qualified as 'insiders', while all non-relatives had the status of 'outsiders' with regard to the underlying lineage structure of the society and the fundamentally kin-oriented cosmological system. Mbundu political structures, by definition, were organizations which structured relationships between 'outsiders', or non-kin. Mbundu kings were themselves outsiders, removed from their descent groups and kinsmen through initiation ceremonies which placed them in a non-lineage limbo where they acted as theoretically neutral arbiters in disputes which divided competing groups of kinsmen.

Kings mediated relations between 'outsiders', whether they acted as market authority over traders congregated at a salt pan, as judges between unrelated lineages in their kingdom, or as war leaders against warriors from an alien neighbouring people. Kings could justify their monopoly of trade in commercial states since theirs was the responsibility for regulating contact between the subjects of the kingdom (the

[10] Here my debt is to Lucas (1971) and Igor Kopytoff (1971).

insiders) and traders who came from the outside. This definition of a king's power accounts for the limitations on their powers since their authority extended only to relationships between people who regarded one another as 'outsiders'. They could not interfere in the internal functioning of the constituent institutions of their states, notably the descent groups in the case of the Mbundu. Hence the plural nature of authority in Mbundu kingdoms. Political history among the Mbundu was to a large extent the history of 'outsiders', the kings, in their attempts to extend their authority over the relations between strangers. And the Mbundu traditions' unanimous attribution of state-founding to such 'outsider' hunters and conquerors as Ngola Inene and Cibinda Ilunga provides metaphorical confirmation that the Mbundu themselves saw things in this way.

The second major theme, that of manpower, derives its importance from the fact that Mbundu society was non-literate and hence non-technological. Europeans later built states and expanded their range of political hegemony by applying administrative and military technology simply not attainable under the conditions of the oral Mbundu society. Thus, Mbundu kings could not create institutions of ideological penetration in the absence of pervasive communication technology, nor instruments of physical coercion without the ability to train, equip, and provision large armed forces, nor firm administrative control without bureaucratic structures based on written records and instructions. Mbundu kings could erect states only on the basis of sheer manpower, their ability to co-ordinate the raw labour of relatively large numbers of people in pursuit of ends they defined.

The critical importance of absolute members of people in state-formation gave slaves their important position at the heart of many Mbundu kingdoms. The unusual successes of the Imbangala depended on recruitment and organizational techniques which gave them literally incredible (in the context of Mbundu ideas) advantages. The numbers of people surrounding a powerful king at his populous capital were the visible manifestation of this principle and were the only sources of strength which distinguished him from the impoverished and lonely priest or holder of an obsolescent position, whose ancient and grandiose title theoretically ranked him above the successful king except for the fact that he had no followers. The portrait of the proud but ragged African 'king' recurs often in the accounts of later travellers who met these individuals, and such ancient Mbundu 'kings' as the *lunga*-holding Butatu persisted in this form long after abandonment by their followers had caused them to lose effective power. The legend of the *kinguri*'s death provided an explicit Mbundu acknowledgement of the importance of manpower.

Third, the emphasis on the pluralistic structure of Mbundu states identifies the essential role of the king as arbitrator between the competing groups in the kingdom. As the chief judicial official, he weighed the conflicting claims of lineages to find peaceable settlements and enforced his decisions through whatever sanctions he could muster. The important implication of the king's arbitration function is that it emphasizes the initiative of the local population in creating a kingdom and accepting the king, in deliberately introducing stratification of a kind which did not exist where there were no states. It consequently removes the need to develop 'conquest' hypotheses to explain why people would assume a position subordinate to a monarch. The neutrality imparted by the king's status as 'outsider' supported his reputation as an arbiter capable of rendering impartial judgement.

Conclusions about Mbundu History

In addition to conclusions about the general process of state-formation, as represented by the Mbundu, some fresh insights into the course of Mbundu history emerge from the story of these kingdoms. In so far as the Mbundu may be said to have existed as a group separate from their neighbours, it seems useful to view the formation of Mbundu states in terms of the interaction of three adjacent ethno-cultural complexes, Kongo, Ovimbundu, and the Lunda/Cokwe/Lwena area of strong segmentary lineages, each with certain distinguishing characteristics above and beyond the elements of language, economy, and thought which they shared. The *lunga* was a nearly indigenous form of Mbundu political organization, whose origins may be traced back to ideas either so old or so basic to Mbundu culture that external sources of influence cannot be identified. Most later Mbundu political history, however, consisted of successive waves of influence emanating from the neighbouring areas: the *ngola* came from Kongo, the *mavunga* and later the *kilombo* from the Ovimbundu, and political titles connected with the Imbangala came to the Mbundu from the Lunda and Cokwe.

It should be emphasized that this model is a relative one, ultimately derived from the arbitrary focus on the Mbundu as the subjects of the study. Presumably a parallel model of a central area with some indigenous state forms and a number of influences from neighbouring regions would also have emerged had I chosen the Kongo, the

Ovimbundu, or the Cokwe/Lwena as protagonists. Some indication of how an alternative focus would have yielded a parallel analysis may be seen in the brief review of Luba influences on the Lunda in Chapter V. It may also be pointed out that the study as it stands presents only one side of what was in fact a two-way process, since Mbundu political structures presumably were influencing their neighbours as much as their neighbours influenced the Mbundu. The only glimpse of the complementary process was seen in the spread of titles based on the *ngola* far south of the Kwanza into Ovimbundu areas.

From what we have seen of state-formation among the Mbundu, it would seem futile to identify, as many studies claim to have done, the ultimate 'origins' of states anywhere in Africa. The 'earliest' Mbundu states are no longer visible in the surviving evidence, and processes of state-formation which characterized the Mbundu suggest that political (if not 'state') institutions have existed, almost by definition, since the remote coalescence of the economic and social bases of Mbundu society as it existed by the sixteenth century. 'States', too, were therefore very old, and the keys to the most ancient phases of Mbundu political development await archaeological investigation rather than the conventional search for documents and oral traditions. The available evidence paints only a selective picture of the conversion of some (not all) very old political institutions to larger-scale kingdoms but does not reveal the 'origins' of states for the Mbundu. In a certain sense, there was very little 'new' in Mbundu political history, since most of the story consisted of adaptations of existing ideas and institutions to new purposes.

Neither simple migration nor diffusion hypotheses make much sense of state-formation in the case of the Mbundu. The *ngola*, the *kinguri*, and the *vunga* show how institutions spread without a corresponding movement of people, particularly not the large-scale, rapid mass migrations which lay behind such theories as the 'Hamitic hypothesis' and its derivatives. In addition, the relative insignificance of weaponry makes so-called 'conquest' theories seem unlikely in the light of the Mbundu experience; arms may account for victories on the battlefield, but they are insufficient to explain the much more complex process of forming a state. The tendency of the Mbundu traditions to personalize abstract ideas accounts for the appearance of 'migrating conquerors' in the oral histories, and the role of the king as an 'outsider' explains why he was said to have come from far away. In actual fact, the appropriation by local ambitious and clever men of someone else's good idea seems a far more likely explanation of most early Mbundu states. It was thus the idea or the institution which travelled in most cases, while the basic population of the Mbundu region has remained relatively stable for a very long time. Otherwise, it would be difficult to account for the obvious antiquity of most of the lineages in the region.

Diffusion hypotheses, while closer to historical fact in some ways, must be applied very carefully, since the experience of the Mbundu shows that the simple availability of an idea diffused from the outside did not guarantee its implementation or long-term success. The Mbundu transformed both the *mavunga* and the *kilombo*, for example, after they adopted them as methods of political organization. In the case of the *kilombo*, the transformation was so dramatic that it lost its distinctive characteristics and became assimilated to the prevailing local type of political title. Thus diffusion did not explain state-formation but merely provided the opportunity for local innovators to change an outside idea into a form which they could use to create new states. State-formation occurred in the adaptation and modification processes rather than in the spread of the idea. The key lay in the institutionalization rather than in the innovation, since new ideas and institutions appeared constantly, both from within and from without, but few left a permanent mark on Mbundu political history.

Mbundu state-formation never took place as an 'event' in the sense of introducing fully-developed state structures into an area and simply implanting them in a form which remained largely unaltered until picked up much later by written sources and modern ethnographers. This false impression of state-formation is, of course, a logical corollary of the old and discredited assumption that little changed before the coming of Europeans disturbed the static equilibrium of African state forms and caused them to evolve for the first time. The notion of states as composed of multiple historical layers is useful because it forces us to recognize that Mbundu state structures resulted from lengthy historical development, as successive waves of political innovation altered the organizational components of Mbundu society. Each stage differed from its predecessor in the addition of one or several new elements and in the changed roles of the older titles and symbols. Only a hypothesis which takes specific account of time and sequence can explain the often bewildering complexity of mature Mbundu and other African states. The often noted multiplicity of officials, internal contradictions, and reduplication of functions resulted from the nature of a multi-layered state in which much was added but relatively little was dropped.

The history of the Mbundu adds another nail to the coffin which already encases simplistic evolutionary hypotheses which posit such unidirectional movements as development from simple to complex forms, from small-to larger-scale institutions, from primitive communalism to feudal states, or whatever else. Mbundu political history moved in no single direction but consisted of an irregular alternation between the triumph of institutions based on the loyalties of kinship and those articulating the demands of kings. Kings repeatedly rose to claim the services of Mbundu kinsmen, who persistently saw themselves first as members of their lineages and only secondarily, and usually under duress, as obedient to outside authority. Many of the kings fell foul of the lineages in the long run. Ancient and powerful *lunga*-kings' titles, for example, survive today as minor descent group positions in remote corners of the area their holders had once ruled. The *ngola a kiluanje* kingdom foundered in part on the particularistic rivalries of lineages within its domain. The *kilombo*, most notably, disappeared because it implied too extreme a restructuring of the underlying Mbundu kinship structure. The lineages were constantly in the background of Mbundu political history, and the long record of state-formation and disintegration which has formed the subject of this study has as yet done little to woo Mbundu kinsmen away from their descent groups.

It is not really ironic to conclude a study ostensibly concerned with states with the remark that the real history of Mbundu political institutions lies in the non-political milieu in which they existed. The differences in the history of the *kilombo* among the strongly segmentary lineages of the eastern Mbundu, among the western Mbundu under the sway of the *ngola a kiluanje*, and among the non-Mbundu south of the Kwanza demonstrate more clearly than any other case the importance of the societal background in understanding state-formation. As the antiquity of states among the Mbundu, and the elusiveness of the distinction between non-state, statelike, and state political structures demonstrate, the potential for states was inherent in the milieu, and the conditions which stimulated and guided the emergence of mature states likewise were found in the social and economic surroundings. If any single lesson emerges from the history of the Mbundu, it is that a fascination with the customary but false opposition between 'states' and 'stateless societies' has lured historians away from the local bases of most states in a futile search for Hamitic and other equally chimerical exotic bringers of civilization.

Bibliography

I. LIST OF ORAL TESTAMONIES CITED[1]

Bango Bwila
Imbangala Group
Kabari ka Kajinga
Kasanje ka Kanga
Kasanje ka Nzaje
Kijinda ka Nokena
Kiluanje kya Ngonga
Kilundula
Kimbwete
Kingwanga kya Mbashi
Kisua kya Njinje, Kambo ka
  Kikasa, Sousa Calunga
Kitubiko
Kulashingo
Luciano, Wencislau
Mahashi
Matamba, Luis
Matos, Apolo de—18, 19, 20 June;
  7, 8 July; 4, 5, 6, 7 October 1969
Mbande a Ngongo
Mbondo Group
Mbumba a Kasambi
Mushiko a Kingwangwa

Mwa Ndonje
Mwanya a Muhimba
Mwanya a Shiba—14, 15 June 1969
ndala kandumbu—see Sousa
  Calunga
Ngandu a Kungu
Ngonga a Mbande—26 June 1969
  (see also Kasanje ka Kanga)
Ngunza a Kasanje
Nzaje
Sokola
Sousa Calunga—16 June; 9, 21,
  22, 24, 26, 28 July; 21, 22, 23
  August; 10, 11, 29, 30 Septem-
  ber; 1, 2, 10 October 1969
Sousa Calunga, Kambo ka Kikasa
Vaz, Alexandre—30, 31 July 1969
Vaz, Alexandre, and Domingos
  Vaz
Vaz, Alexandre, Ngonga a
  Mbande
Vaz, Domingos
Vaz, Domingos, Alexandre Vaz,
  Ngonga a Mbande
Vaz, Manuel

II. LIST OF PUBLISHED WORKS CITED

ABREU E BRITO, DOMINGOS de. See Brito.

ABSHIRE, DAVID M., and MICHAEL A. SAMUELS, eds. 1969. *Portuguese Africa: A Handbook*. New York.

[1] The designations refer to an index of tapes and notes in the possession of the author. In general, the name of the major informant(s) identifies the interview; however, in cases where more than one interview was held with the same individual, dates indicate the second and all following sessions.

AIRY SHAW, E. K. 1947. 'The Vegetation of Angola'. *Journal of Ecology*, XXXV, 23–48.

AJAYI, J. F. ADE and MICHAEL CROWDER, eds. 1971–3. *History of West Africa*. 2 vols. London.

AKINJOGBIN, I. A. 1971. 'The Expansion of Oyo and the Rise of Dahomey, 1000–1800'. In Ajayi and Crowder, eds., *History of West Africa*, I, 309–43.

ALAGOA, E. J. 1970. 'Long-distance Trade and States in the Niger Delta'. JAH, XI.3, 319–30.

—————. 1971a. 'The Development of Institutions in the States of the Eastern Niger Delta'. *JAH*, XII.2, 269–78.

—————. 1971b. 'The Eastern Delta City States and their Neighbors, 1600–1800'. In Ajayi and Crowder, eds., *History of West Africa*, I, 269–303.

ALBUQUERQUE FELNER, ALFREDO de. 1933. *Angola; Apontamentos sôbre a ocupação e início do estabelecimento dos Portugueses no Congo, Angola e Benguela, estraídos de documentos históricos.* Coimbra.

—————. 1940. *Angola; Apontamentos sôbre a colonização dos planaltos e litoral do sul de Angola.* 3 vols. Lisboa.

ALMEIDA, ANTONIO de. 1937. *Sôbre mutilições étnicas dos aborígenes de Angola.* Lisboa.

ALVES, PE ALBINO. 1951. *Dicionário etimológico Bundo-Português.* 2 vols. Lisboa.

ANGOLA. Serviços Meteorológicos. 1955. *O clima de Angola.* Luanda.

ARMSTRONG, R. G. 1960. 'The Development of Kingdoms in Negro Africa'. *JHSN*, II.1, 27–39.

ASSIS JUNIOR, ANTONIO de. n.d. *Dicionário Kimbundu-Portugues.* Luanda.

ATKINS, GUY. 1954. 'An Outline of Hungu Grammar'. *Garcia de Orta*, II.2, 145–64.

—————. 1955. 'A Demographic Survey of the Kimbundu-Kongo Language Border in Angola'. BSGL, LXXIII. 7–9, 325–47.

BAL, WILLY, ed. 1965. *Description du Royaume de Congo et des Contrées Environnantes (par Filippo Pigafetta et Duarte Lopes–1591).* Louvain et Paris.

BALANDIER, GEORGES. 1968. *Daily Life in the Kingdom of the Kongo.* Trans. Helen Weaver. New York.

—————. 1970. *Political Anthropology.* Trans. A. M. Sheridan Smith. New York.

BARBOT, JEAN. 1732. *A Description of the Coasts of North and South-Guinea, and of Ethiopia inferior, vulgarly Angola . . .* London.

BASEHEART, HARRY W. 1972. 'Traditional History and Political Change among the Matengo of Tanzania'. *Africa*, XLII.2, 87–97.

BASTIAN, A. 1874–75. *Die Deutsche Expedition an der Loango-küste.* 2 vols. Iena.

BATTELL, ANDREW. See Ravenstein, ed.

BAUMANN, HERMANN. 1935. *Lunda: Bei Bauern und Jägern in Inner-Angola*. Berlin.

—————. 1936. *Schöpfung und Urzeit des Menschen in Mythes des Afrikanischen Völker*. Berlin.

BAUMANN, HERMANN, and D. WESTERMANN. 1962. *Les Peuples et civilisations de l'Afrique*. Trans. L. Homburger. Paris. (Originally *Völkerkunde von Afrika*, Essen, 1940)

BEATTIE, JOHN. 1964. *Other Cultures*. London.

BEIDELMAN, T. O. 1970. 'Myth, Legend, and Oral History: A Kaguru Traditional Text'. *Anthropos*, LXV.1, 74–97.

BIEBUYCK, DANIEL. 1957. 'Fondements de l'organisation politique des Lunda du Mwaanta Yaav en territoire de Kapanga.' *Zaïre*, XI. 8, 787–813.

BIRMINGHAM, DAVID. B. 1965. 'The Date and Significance of the Imbangala Invasion of Angola'. *JAH*, VI. 2, 143–52.

—————. 1966. *Trade and Conflict in Angola*. Oxford.

—————. 1970. 'Angola and its Hinterland'. In Gray and Birmingham, eds., *Pre-Colonial African Trade*, pp. 163–73.

BOHANNAN. PAUL. 1953. 'Concepts of Time Among the Tiv of Nigeria'. *SWJA*, IX. 3, 251–62.

BOHANNON, PAUL, and LAURA. 1953. *The Tiv of Central Nigeria*. London.

BONTINCK, FR, ed. 1970. *Diaire Congolais (1690–1701)*. Louvain et Paris.

BOSTON, J. S. 1964. 'The Hunter in Igala Traditions of Origin'. *Africa*, XXXIV.2, 116–25.

—————. 1969. 'Oral Tradition and the History of the Igala'. *JAH*, X.1, 29–44.

BOUVEIGNES, OLIVER, de and J. CUVELIER. 1951. *Jérôme de Montesarchio*. Namur.

BOVILL, E. W. 1968. *Golden Trade of the Moors*. 2nd rev. ed. London. (Originally *Caravans of the Old Sahara*, London, 1933.)

BOWDICH, THOMAS. 1824. *An Account of the Discoveries of the Portuguese in the Interior of Angola and Mozambique*. London.

BOXER, CHARLES R. 1952. *Salvador de Sá and the Struggle for Brazil and Angola, 1602–1686*. London.

BRANDÃO, PAES. 1904. 'Diário da marcha do chefe do Conselho do Libollo, Tenente Paes Brandão, à região da Quibala'. *PA*, XI. 22–5, 76–9, 137–40, 223–37, 288–91, 349–55, 406–12, 481–5.

BRÁSIO, ANTÓNIO. 1952–71. *Monumenta Missionária Africana–Africa Ocidental* (Sér. I). 11 vols. Lisboa.

BRITO, DOMINGOS de ABREU E. 1931. *Um inquérito à vida administrativa de Angola e do Brazil*. Ed. Alfredo de Albuquerque Felner. Coimbra.

BUCHNER, MAX. 1883. 'Das Reich des Mwata Yamvo und seine Nachbarländer'. *Deutsche Geographische Blätter*, VI, 56–67.

CADORNEGA, ANTÓNIO de OLIVEIRA de. 1940–2. *História Geral das*

Guerras Angolanas, 1680. Eds. José Matias Delgado and M. Alves da Cunha. Lisboa.

CALTANISETTA, FRA LUCA da. See BONTINCK.

CANNECATTIM, BERNARDO MARIA DE. 1804. *Diccionario da lingua bunda ou angolense, explicada na lingua portugeza e latina.* Lisboa.

————. 1854. *Collecção de observações grammaticaes sobre a lingua Bunda ou Angolense e Diccionario da lingua Conguenza.* 2nd ed. Lisboa.

CAPELLO, H., and R. IVENS. 1882. *From Benguella to the Territory of Yacca.* Trans. A. Elwes. 2 vols. London.

CARDOSO, FONSECA. 1919. *Em terras do Moxico: Apontamentos de ethnographia angolense.* Porto.

CARNEIRO, JOÃO VIEIRA. 1859–61. 'Observações feitas em 1848 relativas a diversos objectos que lhe pareceram não exactos no 3° volume dos Ensaios sobre a Estatistica das Possessões Portuguezas da Africa Occidental pelo Conselheiro José Joaquim Lopes de Lima'. *ACU*, II, 174–9.

CARNEIRO, ROBERT L. 1968. 'Slash-and-burn Cultivation among the Kuikuru and its Implications of Cultural Developments in the Amazon Basin'. In Yehudi A. Cohen, ed., *Man in Adaptation, The Cultural Present,* Chicago, pp. 131–45. (Reprinted from *Antropologica* (Caracas), Supp. No. 2 (1961).)

CARVALHO, HENRIQUE AUGUSTO DIAS de. See DIAS de CARVALHO.

'CATALOGO DOS GOVERNADORES DO REINO DE ANGOLA'. See MONTEIRO DE MORAIS(?).

CAVAZZI DE MONTECUCCOLO, PE JOÃO ANTÓNIO. 1965. *Descrição histórica dos Três reinos do Congo, Matamba e Angola.* Trans. and ed. Pe Graciano Maria de Luguzzano. 2 vols. Lisboa.

CHATELAIN, HÉLI. 1888–89. *Grammatica elementar do Kimbundu ou lingua de Angola.* Genebra.

————. 1894. 'Folk-Tales of Angola'. *Memoirs of the American Folk Lore Society,* I, 1–315.

CHILDS, GLADWYN M. 1949. *Umbundu Kinship and Character.* London.

————. 1964. 'The Kingdom of Wambu (Huambo), A Tentative Chronology'. *JAH*, V. 3, 367–79.

————. 1970. 'The Chronology of the Ovimbundu Kingdoms.' *JAH*, XI. 2, 241–8.

CHINYANTA NANKULA, MWATA KAZEMBE XIV. 1961. *Historical Traditions of the Eastern Lunda.* Trans. Ian Cunnison. Lusaka. (Rhodes-Livingstone Cummunication no. 23.)

COHEN, DAVID W. 1972. *The Historical Tradition of the Busoga: Mukama and Kintu.* Oxford.

COIMBRA, DR. CARLOS DIAS de. 1953. *Livro de Patentes do Tempo de Salvador Correia de Sá e Benevides.* Luanda.

BIBLIOGRAPHY   287

COQUERY-VIDROVITCH, CATHERINE. 1969. 'Recherches sur un mode de production africain'. *La Pensée*, no. 144, 61–78. Trans. Susan Sherwin, in Martin A. Klein and G. Wesley Johnson, eds., *Perspectives on the African Past*, Boston, 1972, pp. 33–51.

CORDEIRO, LUCIANO, ed. 1881. *Viagens, explorações e conquistas dos Portugueses: Colleção de documentos.* 6 vols. Lisboa.

CORDEIRO da MATTA. J. D. 1893. *Ensaio de diccionario kimbundu-portuguez.* Lisboa.

CORREA, ANTONIO da SILVA. See SILVA CORREA.

CRINE, FERNAND. 1963. 'Aspects politico-sociaux du système de tenure des terres des Luunda septentrionaux'. In Daniel Biebuyck, ed., *African Agrarian Systems* (International African Seminar), London, pp. 157–72.

CRINE-MAVAR, BRUNO. 1963. 'Un Aspect du symbolisme Luunda: l'association funéraire des Acudyaang'. *Miscellanea Ethnographica* (*MRAC*, no. 46), Tervuren, pp. 79–108.

————. 1968. 'A propos de la sterilité artistique des Lunda'. *Études congolaises*, XI. 2, 59–67.

————. 1973. 'Histoire traditionnelle du Shaba'. *Cultures au Zaïre et en Afrique*, I, 5–108.

CUNHA MATTOS, R. J. da. See MATTOS.

CUNNISON, IAN. 1956. 'Perpetual Kinship: A Political Institution of the Luapula Peoples'. *RLJ*, no. 20, 28–48.

CURTIN, PHILIP D. 1968a. 'Epidemiology and the Slave Trade'. *Political Science Quarterly,* LXXXIII. 2, 190–216.

————. 1968b. 'Field Techniques for Collecting and Processing Oral Data'. JAH, IX. 3, 367–86.

————. 1969. *The Atlantic Slave Trade: A Census.* Madison.

DAVIDSON, BASIL. 1959. *Lost Cities of Africa.* Boston.

————. 1961. *The African Slave Trade.* Boston.

DECKER, H. C. de. 1939. 'Die Jagazüge und das Königtum im mittleren Bantugebiet'. *Zeitschrift für Ethnologie*, LXXI. 4–6, 229–93.

DELAFOSSE, MAURICE. 1912. *Haut-Sénégal-Niger.* 3 vols. Paris.

————. 1931. *Negroes of Africa.* Washington.

DELGADO, RALPH. 1948–55. *História de Angola.* 4 vols. Lobito.

'DESCOBERTA DE ANGOLA E CONGO: RELAÇÕES DE ANGOLA, TIRADAS DO CARTORIO DO COLLEGIO DOS PADRES DA COMPANHIA'. 1883. *BSGL*, IV. 6, 300-4; 7, 338–52; 8, 364–86.

DIAS de CARVALHO, HENRIQUE AUGUSTO. 1885-6. 'Expedição ao Muata Yanvo (Cartas à Sociedade de Geographia)'. *BSGL*, V. 8, 476–92; VI. 3, 133–62.

————. 1890a. *Ethnographia e história tradicional dos povos da Lunda.* Lisboa.

————. 1890b. *Methodo pratico para fallar a lingua da Lunda contendo narrações historicas dos diversos povos.* Lisboa.

——————. 1898. *O Jagado de Cassange na Provincia de Angola, Memoria*. Lisboa.

DINIZ, JOSÉ de OLIVEIRA FERREIRA. See OLIVEIRA FERREIRA DINIZ.

DRAKE, ST. CLAIR. 1959. 'The Responsibility of Men of Culture for Destroying the 'Hamitic Myth'.' *Présence Africaine*, special issue. Paris.

DUARTE, VICENTE JOSÉ. 1859–61. 'Noticias de alguns dos districtos de que se compõe esta província (Angola)–Districto do Duque de Braganca'. *ACU*, II, 123–8, 129–35, 141–4, 145.

DUYSTERS, LÉON. 1958. 'Histoire des Aluunda'. *Problèmes de l'Afrique Centrale*, XII. 40, 75–98.

EDWARDS, ADRIAN C. 1962. *The Ovimbundu under Two Sovereignties*. London.

EHRET, CHRISTOPHER. 1971. *Southern Nilotic History*. Evanston.

ESTERMANN, CARLOS. 1956. *Etnografia do sudoeste de Angola*. 2 vols. Lisboa.

EVANS-PRITCHARD, E. E. 1939. 'Nuer Time-Reckoning'. *Africa*, XII. 2, 189–216.

——————. 1940. *The Political System of the Anuak of the Anglo-Egyptian Sudan*. London.

——————. 1949. *The Sanussi of Cyrenaica*. Oxford.

'EXPLORAÇÕES DOS PORTUGUEZES NO INTERIOR D'AFRICA MERIDIONAL'. 1843. *AMC*, III. 5, 162–90; 6, 223–40; 7, 278–97; 9, 423–39; 10, 493–506; 11, 538–52.

'EXPLORAÇÕES DOS PORTUGUEZES NO SERTÃO D'AFRICA MERIDIONAL'. 1844–45. *AMC*, IV. 7, 286–300; 8, 303–14; 9, 334–43; 10, 377–81; 11, 397–408; V. 1, 19–26; 2, 63–77; 3, 108–120; 4, 149–64; 5, 199–208; 7, 264–78; 9, 321–37; 10, 364–72; 11, 428–37; 12, 468–81.

FAGAN, BRIAN M. 1969. 'Early Trade and Raw Materials in South Central Africa'. *JAH*, X. 1, 1–14.

FAGE, JOHN D. 1961. *An Introduction to the History of West Africa*. London.

——————. 1965. 'History. In Robert Lystad, ed., *The African World*, New York, pp. 40–56.

——————. 1974. *States and Subjects in Sub-Saharan African History*. Johannesburg.

FALLERS, LLOYD A., ed. 1964. *The King's Men; Leadership and Status in Buganda on the Eve of Independence*. New York.

——————. 1965. *Bantu Bureuucracy: A Century of Political Evolution among the Basoga of Uganda*. 2nd ed. Chicago. (Original edition, Cambridge, 1956).

FARIA, PE FRANCISCO LEITE de. 1952. 'A Situação de Angola e Congo apreciada em Madrid em 1643'. *PA*, IX. 52, 235–48.

FEIERMAN, STEVEN. 1974. *The Shambaa Kingdom, A History*. Madison.

FELNER, ALFREDO de ALBUQUERQUE. See ALBUQUERQUE FELNER.

FEO CARDOSO de CASTELLO BRANCO E TORRES, JOÃO CARLOS. 1825. *Memórias contendo a biographia do vice almirnate Luis da Motta Feo e Torres, A história dos governadores e capitaens generaes de Angola desde 1575 até 1825, e A Descripcão geographica e politica dos reinos de Angola e de Benguella.* Pariz.

FERREIRA, FRANCISCO de SALLES. See SALLES FERREIRA.

FERREIRA DINIZ, JOSÉ DE OLIVEIRA. See OLIVEIRA FERREIRA DINIZ.

FERREIRA MARQUES, ALBERTO. 1949. 'Contribuição para o estudo da etnografia dos povos da Lunda'. *MA*, 26–27, 77–85; 28, 13–20.

FICALHO, CONDE de. 1947. *Plantas Úteis da África portugueza.* 2nd ed. Lisboa.

FINLEY, M. I. 1965. 'Myth, Memory, and History'. *History and Theory*, IV. 3, 281–302.

FORDE, DARYLL. 1967. 'Anthropology and the Development of African Studies.' *Africa*, XXXVIII. 4, 389–406.

FORDE, DARYLL and P. M. KABERRY, eds. 1967. *West African Kingdoms in the Nineteenth Century.* London.

FORTES, MEYER. 1969. *Kinship and the Social Order: The Legacy of L. H. Morgan.* Cambridge.

FORTES, MEYER, and E. E. EVANS-PRITCHARD, eds. 1940. *African Political Systems.* London.

FOX, ROBIN. 1967. *Kinship and Marriage.* Baltimore.

FRANÇOIS, CURT VON. 1888. 'Geschichtliches bei den Bangala, Lunda und Kioko'. *Globus*, LIII, 273–6.

FRIED, MORTON H. 1960. 'On the Evolution of Social Stratification and the State'. In S. Diamond, ed., *Culture in History*, New York, pp. 713–31.

GALEY, JEAN-CLAUDE. 1973. 'L'Etat et le lignage'. *L'Homme*, XIII. 1–2, 71–82.

GOODY, JACK. 1968. 'The Myth of a State'. *Journal of Modern African Studies*, VI. 4, 461–74.

——————. 1971. 'The Impact of Islamic Writing on the Oral Cultures of West Africa'. *CEA*, XI. 3 (no. 43), 455–66.

GOODY, JACK and IAN WATT. 1963. 'The Consequences of Literacy'. *CSSH*, V. 3, 304–45.

GOSSEWEILER, JOHN. 1939. *Carta fitageografica de Angola.* Lisboa.

GOUVEIA, DOMINGOS H. G. 1956. *Reconhecimento da Baixa de Cassanje.* Lisboa.

GRAÇA, JOAQUIM RODRIQUES. 1854–58. 'Viagem feita de Loanda com destino às cabeceiras do Rio Sena, ou aonde for mais conveniente pelo interior do continente, de que as tribus são senhores, principada em 24 de Abril de 1845'. *ACU*, I, 101–14, 117–29, 133–46. (Republished as 'Expedição ao Muatayanvua'. *BSGL*, IX. 8–9 (1890), 365–468; excerpted in *Boletim Oficial de Angola* (1855) and in *AA*, sér. II, II. 9–10 (1945), 225–39.)

GRAY, RICHARD, and DAVID BIRMINGHAM, eds. 1970. *Pre-Colonial African Trade*. London.

GREENBERG, J. 1949. 'The Negro Kingdoms of the Sudan'. *Transactions of the New York Academy of Sciences*, ser. II, XI. 4, 126–35.

————, 1972. 'Linguistic Evidence Regarding Bantu Origins'. *JAH*, XIII. 2, 189–216.

GREVISSE, F. 1946–7. 'Les Traditions historiques des Basanga et de leurs voisins'. *Bulletin du centre d'étude des problèmes sociaux indigènes*, II, 50–84.

GUEBELS, LÉON. See de BOUVEIGNES.

GUERREIRO, FERNÃO. 1930–42. *Relação anual das cousas que fizeram os padres da Companhia de Jesus nas partes da India Oriental das cartas dos mesmos padres que de la vierão*. 2nd ed. 3 vols. Coimbra. (First ed., Lisboa, 1605.)

GUTHRIE, MALCOLM. 1967. *The Classification of the Bantu Languages*. London.

————. 1967–72. *Comparative Bantu: An Introduction to the Comparative Linguistics and Prehistory of the Bantu Languages*. 4 vols. Farnborough.

HAMBLY, W. D. 1934. *The Ovimbundu of Angola*. Chicago. (Field Museum of Natural History Publication No. 329: Anthropological Series, XXI. 2.)

HAUENSTEIN, ALFRED. 1960. 'Le Serpent dans les croyances de certains tribus de l'est et du Sud de l'Angola'. *Estudos Etnográficos*, I, 217–34.

————. 1964. 'Les Voyages en caravane des Tjiaka.' *Anthropos*, LIX, 926–32.

————. 1967a. 'Considerations sur le vase sacré ombia yohasa de la residence royale de Civonga de la tribu des Hanya.' *Anthropos*, LXII, 907–36.

————. 1967b. *Les Hanya*. Wiesbaden.

HAVEAUX, G. L. 1954. *La Tradition historique des Bapende orientaux*. (*IRCB*, XXXVII. 1.) Bruxelles.

HEINTZE, BEATRIX. 1970. 'Beiträge zur Geschichte und Kultur der Kisama (Angola)'. *Paideuma*, XVI, 159–86.

HENIGE, DAVID P. 1971. 'Oral Tradition and Chronology'. *JAH*, XII. 3, 371–90.

————. 1974. *The Chronology of Oral Tradition*. Oxford.

HEUSCH, LUC de. 1972. *Le Roi ivre ou l'origine de l'état: mythes et rites bantous*. Paris.

HOMBURGER, LILIAS. 1925. 'Le Group sud-ouest des langues bantoues'. *Mission Rohan-Chabot (Angola et Rhodesie) 1912–1914*, III.1. Paris.

HONORÉ-NABER, S. P. 1'. 1933. 'Nota van Pieter Mortamer over het gewest Angola, 1643'. *Bijdragen en Mededeelingen van het historisch Genootschap gevestigd te Utrecht*, LIV, 1–42.

HORTON, ROBIN. 1967. 'African Traditional Thought and Western Science'. *Africa*, XXXVII. 1, 50–71; 2, 155–87.

——————. 1969. 'From Village to City-State'. In M. Douglas and P. Kaberry, eds., *Man in Africa*. Garden City, N. Y., pp. 38–60.

——————. 1971. 'Stateless Societies in the History of West Africa'. In Ajayi and Crowder, eds., *History of West Africa*, I, 78–119.

HUFFMAN, T. N. 1972. 'The Rise and Fall of Zimbabwe'. *JAH*, XIII.3, 353–67.

HYMES, D. H. 1960. 'Lexicostatistics so far'. *CA*, I. 1, 3–44.

INTERNATIONAL INSTITUTE OF AFRICAN LANGUAGE AND CULTURES. 1930. *A Practical Orthography of African Languages*. London.

JADIN, L. and J. CUVELIER. 1954. *L'ancien Congo d'après les archives Romaines (1518–1640)*. (*IRCB*, XXXVI. 2.) Bruxelles.

JONES, G. I. 1963. 'European and African Tradition on the Rio Real'. *JAH*, IV. 3, 391–402.

JORDÃO, LEVY MARIA. See PAIVA MANSO.

KABERRY, PHYLLIS. 1957. 'Primitive States'. *British Journal of Sociology*, VII. 3, 224–34.

'KARTE ZUR ÜBERSICHT DER REISE JOAQUIM RODRIGUES GRACA'S'. 1856. *Petermanns Geographische Mittheilungen*, II, Tafel 17.

KATOKE, ISRAEL K. 1971. 'The History of Pre-colonial States of North-western Tanzania, An Introduction'. *Journal of World History*, XIII. 3–4, 512–14.

KENT, R. K. 1965. 'Palmares: An African State in Brazil'. *JAH*, VI. 2, 161–76.

KIWANUKA, M. S. M. 1969. 'The Evolution of Chieftainship in Buganda, ca. 1400–1600'. *University of East Africa Social Sciences Council Conference (1968/1969), History Papers*, vol. III. Kampala.

KOPYTOFF, IGOR. 1971. 'Ancestors as Elders in Africa'. *Africa*, XLI. 2, 129–42.

KOTTAK, CONRAD P. 1972. 'Ecological Variables in the Origin and Evolution of African States: The Bugunda Example'. *CSSH*, XIV. 3, 351–80.

LADEIRO MONTEIRO, RAMIRO. See MONTEIRO.

LANGWORTHY, HARRY W. 1971. 'Conflict among Rulers in the History of Undi's Chewa Kingdom.' *Transafrican Journal of History*, I. 1. 1–23.

LARSON, THOMAS J. 1971. 'The Hambukushu Migrations to Ngamiland'. *African Social Research*, XI, 27–49.

LEITÃO, MANOEL CORREIA. See SOUSA DIAS, GASTÃO.

LEITE de FARIA, pe FRANCISCO. See FARIA.

LEITE de MAGALHÃES, ANTÓNIO. 1924. *Distrito do Cuanza-Sul: Geographia Historica, Fiscia, Política e Economica do Distrito; Relatório do Governador (do Cuanza-Sul)*. Lisboa.

LÉVI-STRAUSS, CLAUDE. 1966. *The Savage Mind*. Chicago.

LEWIS, HERBERT. 1966. 'The Origins of African Kingdoms'. *CEA*, VI. 3 (no. 23), 402–7.

LIMA, MESQUITELA. 1971. *Fonctions sociologiques des figurines de culte Hamba dans la société et dans la culture Tshokwé (Angola)*. Luanda.

LLOYD, PETER C. 1954. 'The Traditional Political System of the Yoruba'. *SWJA*, X. 4, 366–84.

——————. 1965. 'Political Structure of African Kingdoms: An Exploratory Model'. In Michael Banton, ed., *Political Systems and Distribution of Power*. (ASA Monographs No. 2.) London.

——————. 1968. 'The Political Development of West African Kingdoms'. *JAH*, IX. 2, 319–29.

LOPES, DUARTE. See BAL.

LOPES de LIMA, JOSÉ JOAQUIM. 1846. *Ensaios sôbre a statistica das possessões portuguezes na Africa Occidental e Oriental*, vol. III: *Angola e Benguela*. Lisboa.

LUX, ANTON E. 1880. *Von Loanda nach Kimbundu. Ergebnisse der Forschungsreise in äquatorialen West-Africa (1875–1876)*. Wien.

MCCULLOCH, MERRAN. 1951. *The Southern Lunda and Related Peoples*. (Ethnographic Survey of Africa: West Central Africa, Pt. 1.) London.

——————. 1952. *The Ovimbundu of Angola*. (Ethnographic Survey of Africa: West Central Africa, Pt. 2.) London.

MCCALL, DANIEL F. 1964. *Africa in Time Perspective*. Boston.

MCGAFFEY, WYATT. 1970. *Custom and Government in the Lower Congo*. Berkeley.

MAGALHÃES, AFONSO ALEXANDRE de. 1948. 'Origem dos Basongos'. *MA*, 8, 33–8.

MAGALHÃES, ANTONIO MIRANDA. 1922. *Manual de linguas indígenas de Angola*. Loanda.

——————. 1934. 'Os Ambundos de Angola e o percurso provável da sua migração para aquela hoje nossa colónia.' *Trabalhos do I° Congresso Nacional de Antropologia Colonial, Porto – Setembro de 1934.* 2 vols. Porto, II, 537–57.

MAGYAR, LÁSZLÓ. 1859. *Reisen in Süd-Afrika in den Jahren 1849 bis 1857.* Vol. I. Pest und Leipzig.

MAIA, ANTONIO da SILVA. n.d.a. *Dicionário Elementar Português-Omumbuim-Mussele*. Cucujães.

——————. n.d.b. *Dicionário Rudimentar Português-Kimbundo*. Cucujães.

MAIR, LUCY. 1962. *Primitive Government*. Baltimore.

MANUEL, FRANK E., and FRITZIE P. 1972. 'Sketch for a Natural History of Paradise'. *Daedalus,* XI. 1, 83–128.

MARTINS, R. de Sousa. 1973. 'Etno-história da Quibaxe-Dembos-Angola: occupações antigas'. *Trabalho* (Luanda), no. 43, 93–178.

MARWICK, M. G. 1963. 'History and Tradition in East Central Africa through the Eyes of the Northern Rhodesian Cewa'. *JAH*, IV. 3, 375–90.

MATTENKLODT (ed. H. BAUMANN). 1944. 'Die Kisama.' *Koloniale Völkerkunde* (Wiener Beiträge zur Kulturgeschichte und Linguistik), VI, 71–108.

MATTOS, R. J. da CUNHA. 1963. *Compéndio Historico das Possessões Portuguezas na Africa*. Rio de Janeiro.

MELO, FRANCISCO de. See FICALHO.

MIDDLETON, JOHN. 1965. *The Lugbara of Uganda*. New York.

MILLER, JOSEPH C. 1970. 'Cokwe Trade and Conquest'. In Gray and Birmingham, eds., *Pre-Colonial African Trade*, pp. 175–201.

—————. 1972a. 'The Imbangala and the Chronology of Early Central African History'. *JAH*, XIII. 4, 549–74.

—————. 1972b. 'A Note on Kasanze and the Portuguese'. *Canadian Journal of African Studies*, VI. 1, 43–56.

—————. 1973a. 'Requiem for the "Jaga".' *CEA*, XIII. 1 (no. 49), 121–49.

—————. 1973b. 'Slaves, Slavers, and Social Change in Nineteenth Century Kasanje'. In Franz-Wilhelm Heimer, ed., *Social Change in Angola*, Munich, pp. 9–29.

—————. 1975. 'Nzinga of Matamba in a New Perspective'. *JAH*, XVI. 2, 201–16.

—————. Forthcoming (a). 'Cavazzi's History of the "Jaga". *History in Africa*.

—————. Forthcoming (b). 'Imbangala Lineage Slavery'. In Igor Kopytoff and Suzanne Miers, eds., *Slavery, Wardship and Serfdom in Africa* (provisional title).

—————. Forthcoming (c). 'Kasanje Kinglists—Theory and Facts: Miscalculating African History?' In David P. Henige, ed., *Essays on Oral Tradition and Chronology* (provisional title).

—————. Forthcoming (d). 'Words, History and the Imbangala'.

MIRANDA MAGALHÃES, ANTONIO. See MAGALHÃES.

MONTEIRO, JOACHIM JOHN. 1875. *Angola and the River Congo*. 2 vols. London.

MONTEIRO, RAMIRO LADEIRO. 1973. *A família nos musseques de Luanda*. Luanda.

MONTEIRO de MORAIS, JOÃO.(?) 'Catalogo dos governadores do Reino de Angola, com uma nota previa noticia do principio da sua conquista e do que nelle obrarão os governadores dignos de memória.' In Feo Cardoso de Castello Branco e Torres, *Memórias*; also Academia Real das Sciencias (Lisboa), *Colecção de Noticias para a História e Geografia das Nações Ultramarinas*, III. 1 (1826) and reprinted in *AA*, sér I, I. 1 (1937).

MOTA, AVELINO TEIXEIRA da. 1964. *A Cartografia antiga da Africa Central e a travessia entre Angola e Moçambique, 1500–1860*. Lourenço Marques.

294 BIBLIOGRAPHY

Mouta, F., and H. O'Donnell. 1933. *Notícia Explicativa do Esboço geológico de Angola*. Lisboa.

Murdock. George P. 1959. *Africa: Its Peoples and their Culture History*, New York.

Neves, Antonio Rodrigues. See Rodrigues Neves.

'Noticias do paiz de Quissama e do Exercito que foi a castigar os gentios daquella provincia . . .' 1844. AMC, sér. VI. 4, 119–27.

O'Fahey, Rex S. 1970. *States and State Formation in the Eastern Sudan*. (African Studies Seminar Paper No. 9.) Khartoum.

Ogot, B. A. 1964. 'Kingship and Statelessness among the Nilotes'. In Vansina, Mauny, and Thomas, eds., *Historian in Tropical Africa*, pp. 284–304.

Oliveira Ferreira Diniz, José de. 1918. *Populações indígenas de Angola*. Coimbra.

Oliver, Roland. 1968. 'Western Historiography and its Relevance to Africa.' In Ranger, ed., *Emerging Themes* pp. 53–60.

Oliver, Roland, and J. D. Fage. 1962. *A Short History of Africa*. Harmondsworth.

Paes Brandão. See Brandão.

Paiva Manso, Levy Maria Jordão, Visconde de. 1877. *Historia do Congo (Documentos), 1492–1772*. Lisboa.

Pereira do Nascimento, J. 1903. *Diccionario Portuguez-Kimbundu*. Huilla.

Pigafetta, Felippo. See Bal.

Pinheiro de Lacerda, J. 1845. 'Noticia da Cidade de Benguella, e dos costumes dos gentios habitantes daquella Sertão'. *ACU*, V, 486–8.

Plancquaert, M. 1971. *Les Yaka: Essai d'histoire. (MRAC*, no. 71.) Bruxelles.

Pocock, D. F. 1964. 'The Anthropology of Time Reckoning'. *Contributions to Indian Sociology*, VII, 18–29. Reprinted in John Middleton, ed., *Myth and Cosmos*, Garden City, N.Y., 1967, pp. 303–14.

Polanyi, Karl. 1963. 'Ports of Trade in Early Societies'. *The Journal of Economic History*, XXIII, 30–45.

Polanyi, Karl, C. M. Arenberg, and H. W. Pearson, eds. 1957. *Trade and Market in the Early Empires*. Glencoe, Ill.

Ranger, Terence, O., ed. 1968. *Emerging Themes of African History*. Dar-es-Salaam.

Ravenstein, E. G., ed. 1901. *The Strange Adventures of Andrew Battell of Leigh in Angola and Adjoining Regions*. London.

Rebello de Aragão, Balthasar. See Cordeiro, vol. III.

Redinha, José. 1958. *Etnossociologia do Nordeste de Angola*. Lisboa.

——————. 1961. 'Distribuição étnica de Angola'. *MA*, 107–12, 3–22. Reprinted as *Distribuição étnica de Angola: introduçao, registo étnico, mapa*. Luanda.

—————. 1962. 'Quem são os Ambundos?' *MA*, 183–5, 37–48.

—————. 1963. 'Insignias e simbologias do mando dos chefes nativos de Angola'. MA, 22–3, 37–46.

—————. 1968. 'Subsídio para a história e cultura da mandioca entre ospovos do nordeste de Angola'. *BIICA*, V. 1, 95–108.

RIBEIRO da CRUZ, JOSÉ. 1940. *Notas de Etnografia Angolana*. Lisboa.

RICHARDS, AUDREY. 1940. 'The Political System of the Bemba Tribe— North-Eastern Rhodesia.' In Fortes and Evans-Pritchard, eds., *African Political Systems*, pp. 83–120.

ROBERTS, ANDREW. 1974. *A History of the Bemba*. London.

RODRIGUES, A. V. 1968. 'Construções bantas de Pedra em Angola'. *BIICA*, V. 2, 169–89, photos, maps.

RODRIGUES, PE FRANCISCO. 1936. 'História Inédita de Angola (Manuscrito do Século XVI)'. *Arquivo Histórico de Portugal*, II. Reprinted in *AA*, sér. II, XVII. 67–70 (1960), 189–216, and Brasio, *Monumenta*, IV, 546–81.

RODRIGUES NEVES, ANTONIO. 1854. *Memoria da Expedição a Cassange*. Lisboa.

ROTBERG, ROBERT I. 1965. *A Political History of Tropical Africa*. New York.

ROWE, JOHN. 1970. 'Major Themes in African History'. In John N. Paden and Edward W. Soja, eds., *The African Experience*. (3 vols.), Evanston, I, 154–76.

SAHLINS, MARSHALL D. 1961. 'The Segmentary Lineage: An Organization of Predatory Expansion.' *American Anthropologist*, LXIII. 2, 322–45.

SALLES FERREIRA, FRANCISCO de. 'Memória'. 1854–8. *ACU*, I, 26–8. *Republished in Boletim Oficial de Angola*, No. 696 (20 April 1853), as 'Memoria sobre o sertão de Cassange'.

SALVADORINI, V. 1969. 'Biblioteche e archivi d'Angola'. *Bolletino della Associazione degli Africanisti Italiani*, II. 3–4, 16–29.

SANDERS, EDITH. 1969. 'The Hamitic Hypothesis: Its Origin and Functions in Time Perspective'. *JAH*, X. 4, 521–32.

SCHEUB, HAROLD. 1975. *Xhosa Ntsomi*. Oxford.

SCHÜTT, OTTO. 1881. *Reisen in Südwestlichen Becken des Congo*. Berlin.

SELIGMAN, CHARLES G. 1957. *Races of Africa*. 3rd ed. London. Originally published 1930.

SILVA CORREA, ELIAS ALEXANDRE da. 1937. *História de Angola*. 2 vols. Lisboa.

SILVA MAIA, ANTONIO da. See MAIA.

SMITH, ABDULLAHI. 1970. 'Some Considerations Relating to the Formation of States in Hausaland'. *JHSN*, V. 3, 329–46.

—————. 1971. 'The Early States of the Central Sudan'. In Ajayi and Crowder, eds., *History of West Africa*, I, 158–201.

SMITH, M. G. 1960. *Government in Zazzau*. London.

296 BIBLIOGRAPHY

SOUSA DIAS GASTÃO. 1934. *Relações de Angola: Primórdios da occupação portuguesa pertencentes ao cartório do Colégio dos Padres da Companhia, de Luanda, e transcritas do códice existente na Biblioteca Nacional de Paris*. Coimbra.

——. 1938. 'Uma viagem à Cassange nos meados do seculo XVIII'. *BSGL*, LVI. 1–2, 3–30.

——. 1942. *A Batalha de Ambuíla*. Lisboa.

SOUTHALL, A. W. 1953. *Alur Society*. Cambridge.

SOUTHWOLD, MARTIN. 1961. *Bureaucracy and Chiefship in Buganda; The Development of Appointive Office in the History of Buganda*. (East African Studies, no. 14.) Kampala.

STATHAM, JOHN CHARLES BARON. 1922. *Through Angola–A Coming Colony*. London.

STEVENSON, ROBERT F. 1968. *Population and Political Systems in Tropical Africa*. New York.

SURET-CANALE, JEAN. 1964. 'Les Sociétés traditionnelles en Afrique noire et le concept du mode de production asiatique'. *La Pensée*, no. 117, 19–42.

TARDITS, CLAUDE. 1973. 'Parenté et pouvoir politique chez les Bamoum (Cameroun)'. *L'Homme*, XIII. 1–2, 37–49.

TEIXEIRA da MOTA, AVELINO. See MOTA.

TERRAY, EMMANUEL. 1974. 'Long-Distance Exchange and the Formation of the State: The Case of the Abron Kingdom of Gyaman'. *Economy and Society*, III. 3, 315–45.

THOMAS, E. V. and D. SAPIR. 1967. 'Le Diola et les temps: Recherches anthropologiques sur la notion de durée en Basse-Casamance'. *Bulletin de l'Institut Fondemental de l'Afrique Noire*, sér. B. XXIX, 321–424.

TORRE do VALLE, EUGENIO and JOSÉ VELLESO de CASTRO. 1913. *O Cuanza desde Quibinda a Cumanga*. Lisboa.

TORRES, JOÃO CARLOS FEO CARDOSO de CASTELLO BRANCO E. See FEO CARDOSO.

TRAVASSOS VALDEZ, FRANCISCO. 1861. *Six Years of a Traveller's Life in Western Africa*. 2 vols. London.

TURNER, VICTOR W. 1955. 'A Lunda Love-story and its Consequences'. *RLJ*, no. 19, 1–26.

——. 1967. *The Forest of Symbols; Aspects of Ndembu Ritual*. Ithaca, N. Y.

——. 1968. *The Drums of Affliction*. Oxford.

VALDEZ, FRANCISCO TRAVASSOS. See TRAVASSOS VALDEZ.

VAN DEN BYVANG, M. 1937. 'Notice historique sur les Balunda'. *Congo*, I. 4, 426–38; 5, 548–62; II. 2, 193–208.

VAN GEEL, JORIS. See VAN WING.

VANSINA, JAN. 1962a. 'A Comparison of African Kingdoms'. *Africa*, XXXII. 4, 324–35.

——————. 1962b. *L'Évolution du royaume rwanda des origines à 1900* (ARSOM, XXVI. 2.) Bruxelles.

——————. 1962c. 'Long-distance Trade Routes in Central Africa'. *JAH*, III. 2, 375–90.

——————. 1963a. 'The Foundation of the Kingdom of Kasanje'. *JAH*, IV. 3, 355–74.

——————. 1963. *Geschiedenis van de Kuba.* (MRAC, no. 44.) Tervuren.

——————. 1964a. *Le Royaume kuba.* (MRAC, no. 49.) Tervuren.

——————. 1964b. 'Process Models in African History'. In Vansina, Mauny, and Thomas, eds., *Historian in Tropical Africa*, pp. 375–89.

——————. 1965. *Oral Tradition.* Trans. H. M. Wright. Chicago.

——————. 1966a. *Kingdoms of the Savanna.* Madison.

——————. 1966b. 'More on the Invasions of Kongo and Angola by the Jaga and the Lunda'. *JAH*, VII. 3, 421–9.

——————. 1968. 'The Use of Ethnographic Data as Sources for History'. In Ranger ed., *Emerging Themes*, pp. 97–124.

——————. 1969. 'The Kingdom of the Great Makoko.' In Daniel F. McCall, Norman R. Bennett, and Jeffery Butler, eds., *Western African History* (Boston University Papers on Africa, IV.), New York, pp. 20–44.

——————. 1970. 'Cultures through Time'. In Raoul Naroll and Ronald Cohen, eds., *A Handbook of Method in Cultural Anthropology.* Garden City, N. Y., pp. 165–79.

——————. 1971a. 'Les Mouvements religieux kuba (Kasai) à l'époque coloniale'. *EHA*, II, 155–87.

——————. 1971b. 'Once upon a Time: Oral Traditions as History in Africa'. *Daedalus*, C. 2, 442–68.

——————. 1973. *The Tio Kingdom of the Middle Congo, 1880–1892.* London.

——————. 1974. 'Comment: Traditions of Genesis'. *JAH*, XIV. 2, 317–22

VANSINA, JAN, R. MAUNY, and L. V. THOMAS, eds. 1964. *The Historian in Tropical Africa.* (International African Seminar.) London.

VAN WING, J. and C. PENDERS. 1928. *La Plus Ancien Dictionnaire Bantu.* Louvain.

VEIGAS, ARTUR. 1923. 'Duas tentativas da reconquista de Angola em 1645'. *Revista de Historia*, XII. 45–48, 75–45, 5–23.

VELLUT, JEAN-LUC. 1972. 'Notes sur le Lunda et la frontière Luso-Africaine (1700–1900)'. *EHA*, III, 61–166.

VERHULPEN, E. 1936. *Baluba et Balubaïsés du Katanga.* Antwerp.

VERLY, R. 1955. 'Le 'Roi divin' chez les Ovimbundu et Kimbundu de l'Angola'. *Zaïre*, IX. 7, 675–703.

WALTER, E. V. 1969. *Terror and Resistance: A Study of Political Violence.* New York.

WEECKX, G. 1937. 'La Peuplade des Ambundu (District du Kwango)'. *Congo*, I. 4, 353–73; II. 1, 13–35; 2, 150–66.

WHEELER, DOUGLAS and RENÉ PÉLISSIER. 1971. *Angola*. London.

WHITTLESLEY, D. S. 1924. 'Geographic Provinces of Angola: An Outline based on Recent Sources'. *Geographical Review*, XIV, 113–26.

YOUNG, M. CRAWFORD. 1970. 'Rebellion and the Congo'. In Robert I. Rotberg and Ali A. Mazrui, eds., *Protest and Power in Black Africa*, Oxford, pp. 968–1011.

III. LIST OF UNPUBLISHED WORKS CITED

BASTIN, MARIE-LOUISE. 1966. 'Tschibinda Ilunga: Heros Civilisateur'. Diss. Université Libre de Bruxelles.

BIRMINGHAM, DAVID. 1971. 'The Origins and Consequences of Market-Oriented Trade in Africa'. Paper read to the East Africa Social Research Conference, Dar-es-Salaam.

COHEN, DAVID W. 1971. 'Emergence and Crisis: The States of Busoga in the Eighteenth and Nineteenth Century'. Makerere University, Kampala.

HEWSON, GLYN CHARLES. 1970. 'Shaka's Kingship and the Rise of the Zulu State, 1795–1828'. MA Thesis, University of Wisconsin.

LUCAS, STEPHEN ANDREW. 1971. 'The Outsider and the Origin of the State in Katanga'. Paper presented to the Annual Meeting of the African Studies Association, Denver.

MILLER, JOSEPH C. 1971. 'The Dual Slave Trade in Angola'. Paper presented to the Annual Meeting of the African Studies Association, Denver.

—————. 1972. 'Kings and Kinsmen: The Imbangala Impact on the Mbundu of Angola'. Diss. University of Wisconsin.

MISSÃO DE INQUÉRITOS AGRICOLAS DE ANGOLA. (Reports on farming techniques.) Luanda.

N'DUA, EDOUARD. 1971. 'L'Installation des Tutschokwe dans l'empire Lunda, 1850–1903'. Mémoire, Grade de Licencié en Philosophie et Lettres: Groupe Histoire, Université Lovanium de Kinhasa.

PIRES, ALBERTO AUGUSTO. 1952. 'História dos Sobados do Posto de Cinco de Outubro'. Xá-Muteba.

REQUIER. 1930. 'Rapport d'enquête sur la chefferie de Kasongo-Lunda'. Manuscript in Fonds ethnographiques, M.R.A.C.

RONSMANS (?) n.d. 'Remarques relatives à l'histoire des Bayaka (Notes sur l'étude de Dequenne et les remarques de Roelandts)'. Manuscript in Fonds Ethnographiques, M.R.A.C.

SALAZAR, SIGURD VON WILLER. n.d. (*c.* 1965?) 'Bondos e Bângalas: Subsídios etnográficos sobre as duas tribos, recolhidos na área da Circunscrição do Bondo e Bángala, do Distrito de Malanje—Angola'. Dissertação para o acto de licenciatura pelo I.S.C.S.P.U. 2 vols.

VAZ, MANUEL. 1970. 'História dos Bângalas'. Manuscript in possession of author.

WAUTERS(?). n.d. 'Notes sur les populations du district du Kwango'. Manuscript in Fonds Ethnographiques, M.R.A.C.

XAVIER MARTINS, FERNANDO BARROS. 1963. 'Origem dos Povos Lunda: Lenda e História'. Manuscript taken from 'Relatório da inspecção Circumscrição Administrativa do Cassai-Sul, em 1963 pelo Inspector Adm.ᵒʳ Xavier Martins'. Lunda. (In possession of Vitor António dos Santos, then secretário do Posto do Quela, Distrito de Malanje.)

IV. LIST OF ARCHIVES CONSULTED

Lisbon, Portugal	Arquivo Histórico Ultramarino (A.H.U.)
	Arquivo Nacional da Torre do Tombo (A.N.T.T.)
	Biblioteca da Ajuda (Ajuda)
	Biblioteca da Sociedade de Geografia de Lisboa (B.S.G.L.)
London, England.	British Museum (B.M.).
Luanda, Angola.	Arquivo Histórico da Câmara Municipal de Lunda (A.H.C.M.L.)
	Arquivo Histórico de Angola (A.H.A.)
	Arquivo da Câmara Episcopal (A.C.E.)
	Arquivo do Quartel Geral (A.Q.G.)
Tervuren, Belgium.	Section Ethnographique, Musée Royal de l'Afrique Centrale (M.R.A.C.)

Glossary

(African Language Terms Used in the Text)*

baka a musendo	plural of *muku a musendo*
jingola	plural of *ngola*
jingundu	plural of *ngundu*
jinzumbi	plural of *nzumbi*
jisabu	plural of *sabu*
kabungu	Lunda title, the most ancient known, of the type of the *kinguri*, the *lueji*, and others
kibinda	professional hunter, an Mbundu initiated status entailing possession of supernatural powers to deal with large wild animals.
kota	Mbundu title, the elders of a lineage entrusted with guarding lineage positions; in the context of a kingdom, court officials attending the king, often the electors of the occupants of the royal position
kumbu	Imbangala praise name
kijila	in general, a prohibition of any kind; with specific reference to the Imbangala *kilombo*, one of the laws which all members had to respect scrupulously
kilamba	title of Pende kings who ruled the Baixa de Cassanje before the arrival of the Imbangala
kilombo	the warrior initiation society of the Imbangala; also the sacred enclosure into which only members might enter; also the Imbangala war camp
kimbanda	an Imbangala magical specialist; there were various types of *kimbanda* depending on the type of spirit which they treated and the means they employed
lemba	an Mbundu lineage official, 'uncle' of the matri-lineage (or the *ngola*)
lukano	the Lunda bracelet, symbol of royal authority
lunda	Mbundu tale, narrative in form, of which some deal with the names in the formal genealogies

* Terms occurring only once or in the footnotes have not been included in this glossary.

lunga	ancient Mbundu authority symbol, associated with the Pende in particular; believed to come from the sea and have close connections with bodies of water.
maji a samba	the magical ointment believed to confer invulnerability on Imbangala warriors
makota	plural of *kota*
malemba	plural of *lemba*
malunda	plural of *lunda*
malunga	plural of *lunga*
maluvo	fermented palm wine, any intoxicant
mavunga	plural of *vunga*
milemba	plural of *mulemba*
misete	plural of *musete*
misungo	plural of *musungo*
mpat	Lunda term for the territories of the ancient Lunda lineages
mukishi	a figurine representing supernatural forces attributed to some types of Mbundu political titles
muku a musendo	professional Imbangala historian
mukwa a kushingilisa	Mbundu lineage spirit medium (usually female)
mukwale	knife in Kimbundu; also a special knife attributed to some kings
mulemba	tree closely associated with Mbundu lineages and lineage headmen
musendo	Imbangala formal genealogy
musete	Mbundu reliquary
musungo	appointed warleader
muyombo	tree believed to be the residence of lineage spirits
ndua	a plantain eater of complex symbolic significance in many parts of West-Central Africa
nganga	magical specialist, of various types
ngola	a piece of iron held by most Mbundu lineages as an important authority emblem; associated with the Samba people
ngundu	Mbundu matrilineage
nzumbi	Mbundu lineage ancestor spirit; by extension, the spirits of deceased occupants of permanent positions
nzungu	a magical weapon believed to belong to Kinguri
pemba	the white clay powder distributed by the Mbundu lineage headmen to their nieces (female members of their lineages)

pokwe	a fighting knife, especially associated with the nineteenth-century Lunda
sabu	Mbundu proverb
soba	Portuguese-appointed chief (plural, *sobas*)
takula	red powder which lineage headmen distribute to the males of their lineages
tubungu	plural of *kabungu*
vunga	an appointive title introduced from Libolo among the Mbundu, distinct from the hereditary perpetual positions
yibinda	plural of *kibinda*
yijila	plural of *kijila*
yilamba	plural of *kilamba*
yimbanda	plural of *kimbanda*

Index